Britain's Part-time Soldiers

Britain's Part-time Soldiers

The Amateur Military Tradition 1558–1945

Ian F. W. Beckett

Pen & Sword
MILITARY

For Andrea and Mark

First published in Great Britain as
The Amateur Military Tradition 1558–1945
by Manchester University Press in 1991

This edition published in 2011 by
Pen & Sword Military
an imprint of
Pen & Sword Books Ltd
47 Church Street
Barnsley
South Yorkshire
S70 2AS

Printed and bound in the UK by CPI

Pen & Sword Books Ltd incorporates the Imprints of Pen & Sword Aviation, Pen & Sword Maritime, Pen & Sword Military, Wharncliffe Local History, Pen and Sword Select, Pen and Sword Military Classics, Leo Cooper, Remember When, Seaforth Publishing and Frontline Publishing.
.
For a complete list of Pen & Sword titles please contact
PEN & SWORD BOOKS LIMITED
47 Church Street, Barnsley, South Yorkshire, S70 2AS, England
E-mail: enquiries@pen-and-sword.co.uk
Website: www.pen-and-sword.co.uk

Contents

List of illustrations

Preface and acknowledgements

It is now over twenty-five years since I was first encouraged to study the auxiliary forces of my home county of Buckinghamshire by my history master at Aylesbury Grammar School, the Rev. Arthur Taylor. Neither of us perhaps envisaged that what I like to call the amateur military tradition would become such an obsession but I am extremely grateful for that initial push into historical research. In time, and at the suggestion of Professor John Gooch of the University of Lancaster, this led to postgraduate study of the rifle volunteer movement under the supervision of Professor Brian Bond of King's College, University of London. It was always my intention to go on to produce a monograph on the development of the auxiliary forces as a whole but, for various reasons, it kept slipping further down the list of priorities and I am very grateful to Manchester University Press for finally forcing me to put pen to paper by accepting this volume as one of the 'Manchester History of the British Army' series. Even then, I fear that I put considerable strain on my editors at the Press, Ray Offord and his successor, Jane Carpenter, by further delays.

My only defence is that this book could not have been written at the time that I originally conceived it because few components of the auxiliary forces had attracted scholarly attention and the scattered nature of archival remains spread throughout the country's county record offices and other local depositories would have made primary research impossibly time-consuming. Fortunately, that situation has been increasingly remedied by the work undertaken by scholars over the past few years and, as a synthesis, this book draws upon the expertise of many historians. Accordingly, I am most grateful to the many who have so generously given of their knowledge in one way or another in the course of the preparation of this book including Dr Duncan Anderson, Dr Stephen Badsey, Matthew Bennett, Dr Michael Blanch, Professor Brian Bond, Dr John Childs, Professor Peter Dennis, Professor Clive Emsley, Professor John Gooch, Dr Paul Harris, Dr Tony Hayter, Nicholas Hooper, Clive Hughes, Dr Keith Jeffery, R. A. Johnson, John Keegan, Dr Andrew Lambert, Sir Mervyn Medlycott, Major P. J. R. Mileham, Boris Mollo, Dr Patricia Morris, Dr John Pimlott, Colonel John Sainsbury, Gary Sheffield, Peter Simkins, Keith Simpson, Dr Edward Spiers, Dr Glenn Steppler, Dr Hew Strachan and Colonel Wallace Earl Walker. Naturally, none of the foregoing are responsible for any mistaken interpretation on my part.

Nor could the book have been written without the assistance of the staffs of many archive depositories and I am grateful not only to Hugh Hanley and my old friends in the Buckinghamshire Record Office but also the county archivists and their staffs in Bedfordshire, Berkshire, Cheshire, Clwyd, Devon, Dorset, Essex, Gloucestershire, Greater London (Middlesex), Hampshire, Herefordshire and Worcester, Hertfordshire, Humberside, Lancashire, Northumberland, Oxfordshire, Somerset, Staffordshire and Wiltshire. Similar thanks are due to Dr Alan Guy, Dr Peter Boyden and the Department of Records at the National Army Museum; Colonel Pip Newton and his successor, Colonel Peter Walton, and the staff of the Army Museum's Ogilby Trust; the Bodleian Library; the British Library; the Duke of York's Headquarters; the Ministry of Defence Library; the Guildhall Library; the Huntington Library; Rod Suddaby and the Department of Documents at the Imperial War Museum; the City of Manchester Leisure Services and Manchester Central Library; the Public Record Office; the University of Nottingham Library; the University of Southampton Library; and John Hunt and his successor, Andrew Orgill, and the staff of the library at the Royal Military Academy, Sandhurst. I am grateful to all the foregoing for permission to consult and to quote from archives in their possession and, in addition, I am similarly grateful to the Marquess of Salisbury, the Earl of Radnor, the trustees of the Croome Estate, Mrs P. Gordon-Duff-Pennington, the late Major L. M. Yearsley, Captain P. J. B. Drury-Lowe, Nigel Arnold-Forster Esq, and C. C. Goodwyn Esq while quotation from Crown Copyright material in the Public Record Office, the Greater London Record Office (Middlesex) and the Wellington Papers at the University of Southampton is by permission of Her Majesty's Stationery Office.

Due to the pressures on space, it has been decided that the volumes in this series will endeavour to minimise the use of footnotes. Consequently, it has been my practice to footnote only those primary sources, theses and secondary authorities directly quoted in the text, sources for statistical information and arguments specifically attributable to a particular historian. This is not intended to disguise the debt I owe to so many authors whose work is acknowledged only in the bibliography.

Dates prior to 1752 are rendered in Old Style but with the new year deemed to commence on 1 January rather than 25 March. All monetary values and measurements used are traditional English and Imperial.

IFWB
RMAS

December 1990

Introduction to second edition

The year 2008 marked the centenary of the creation of the Territorial Army, for which an official history was produced by myself, though an official publication is perhaps a better description since it was primarily intended for serving and former Territorials and the general reader. Since it was the period since 1945 that was least familiar from my previous research, most of the new material was concentrated in the second half of the book. Nonetheless, since the short opening chapter was a survey of the amateur military tradition prior to 1908, it was an opportunity to revisit work on the auxiliary forces since the original publication of *The Amateur Military Tradition* in 1991. It was a chance to assess whether those themes of continuity then identified remained relevant to those who had since worked in the field and/or whether new research imperatives had emerged to reshape the story fundamentally.

The intention back in 1991, apart from establishing the reality of an amateur military tradition, was to provide a thematic framework for the continuities detected, particularly in respect of the purposes served by the auxiliary forces and of the relationship between the auxiliaries forces and society as reflected through the county and local community. There were seemingly five purposes or functions for the auxiliaries. First, and most obviously, they were a defence against invasion. Secondly, however, one could not lose sight of the idea that the auxiliaries also safeguarded against internal disorder. Thirdly, and not too far distant from preserving the status quo, there was what might be termed social control deriving from perceived military virtues and habits of discipline and orderliness. Fourthly, the auxiliary forces existed as a supplement to and an alternative to regular standing armies, the former function being increasingly more significant than the latter. Fifth, the existence of the auxiliary forces had also meant effectively that the army could not be enlisted by conscription.

In terms of the relationship between the auxiliaries and society and community, there were fairly obvious continuities in terms of the social composition of particular components of the auxiliary forces but, in addition, there seemed to be seven essential components of the relationship. Firstly, the auxiliary forces were always far more visible to society as a whole than the regular army, which was literally mostly out of sight and out of mind in that it was small, and mostly serving overseas. By contrast, the auxiliaries were ever present in terms of the administration of auxiliary forces at county, hundred and parish level, and through the high degree of visibility of their various activities. Secondly, while being far more visible than regulars, the auxiliaries also bore the brunt of popular anti-militarism expressed in a variety of ways from outright hostility to subtle or not so subtle satire. Yet, thirdly, there was also a sense in that the prestige of the community itself could become closely bound up with that of the auxiliaries for good or ill, not least when bad behaviour was evident. Fourth, moreover, despite the possibility of bad behaviour, auxiliaries were welcome within the community in that their presence was bound to increase trade from the routine provision of uniform, equipment and supplies. Business was also generated by military spectacle from annual camps to the great field days and reviews. Spending money locally began to suggest interdependence between auxiliaries and society, and a fifth factor was that there was also dependence in terms of the relationship of the auxiliary to his employment. They were civilians temporarily in uniform and the ability to fulfil training commitments rested on the state of a man's employment, be it as casual agricultural labourer, artisan, tradesman, or factory worker. Sixth, there was the inevitable political link between auxiliaries and society, auxiliaries not only being on occasions a major issue in national politics but frequently an issue within local politics and patronage. Lastly, they provided opportunities of various kinds. At one level this might only be the opportunity of experiencing something different or of enjoying recreational facilities or comradeship that might not otherwise be attainable. On a different level, it could be a conscious commitment to the status quo, a demonstration of loyalty to country or perhaps to landlord or employer. It might be, too, a means of upwards-social mobility, of becoming respectable: it seemed that the yeomanry in particular was a major entrée to local society.

Putting all these elements together in terms of continuities, it was my contention that the auxiliaries rather than the regular army provided the real link between army and society in Britain. Few of those who joined the auxiliary forces would have come into contact with the army in any other way. In the process, therefore, they absorbed and, in turn, transmitted military values to society as whole, both favourable and unfavourable. Above all, they were ever present in local society at least until the second half of the twentieth century, being part of the very fabric of this country at the county and local community level. The framework appeared applicable to the whole period between 1558 and 1945.

Since 1991, what was originally a concern largely with the dating of the 'military revolution' between the mid-sixteenth and the late eighteenth century has been substantially extended well beyond tactical, technological and organisational issues into one of growing sophistication concerning the complexity of the relationship between warfare, the rise and formation of the state, and the instruments of state power. Roger Manning, Steven Gunn, David Grummitt, Hans Cool, James Scott Wheeler and Michael Braddick have all raised these issues specifically in terms of the early modern British state. Inevitably, the status of the militia impinges upon the debate. In passing, Manning stresses the contrast between civic militia traditions and military professionalism between 1585 and 1702. Gunn, Grummitt and Cool also make useful, albeit brief, comparisons of the English militia with that of the Netherlands for the period between 1477 and 1559. Victor Stater's important study of the Stuart lieutenancy between 1625 and 1688, published in 1994, characterises the development and politicisation of the lieutenancy as that of 'machine bosses', but also views the lieutenancy as a focus for loyalism in the post-1660 period. Loyalism, however, is interpreted as a defence of monarchy and church even against the monarch himself, since 'Tory' lords lieutenant helped overthrow James II. Other than Stater, however, there have been no specific studies on auxiliary forces for the early modern period since 1991, though John McGurk's largely administrative study of Elizabethan campaigns in Ireland deals in passing with the burden on counties in providing levies and the relationship to the militia and trained bands. Useful articles have also appeared from time to time such as that of John Nolan on the muster of 1588, H Langelüddecke on the militia in the 1630s, and P R Seddon on the Restoration Militia in Nottinghamshire.

By 1991, both Linda Colley and J E Cookson had begun to examine the volunteer movement of the Revolutionary and Napoleonic Wars in the light of an emerging interest in the formation of national identity. The articles by Colley and Cookson upon which I was able to draw were the forerunners of their major studies, published respectively in 1992 and 1997, though Cookson also contributed another article in 1993. Another significant contribution was Austin Gee's study of the volunteer movement between 1794 and 1814, published in 2003. Gee's original Oxford doctorate covering the period up to 1807 had actually been completed in 1989, but the thesis was embargoed and, therefore, could not be used in the preparation of my own work in 1991.

Colley's focus is only partly on the volunteer movement and her general emphasis was upon the fashioning of national identity. In so far as she considers the auxiliary forces, she concludes that they showed that patriotism transcended social divisions, although she also recognises some of the wider complexities of motivation. Back in 1986, she had suggested that the expansion of militia and volunteers had 'democratic implications'. Rather than Colley's identification of emerging centralisation, Cookson's major study emphasises the extent of self-mobilisation and self-organisation upon which the British state depended, but also displays the wide regional differences in the nature of the response to the threat of invasion, and distinguishes between loyalism and patriotism, loyalism being marked as an active anti-radical and anti-democratic political force. His conclusion is that patriotism was less significant than working class pragmatism and what he characterises as the 'town-making' interests of the emerging urban elite. As he puts it, patriotism was 'opportunistic, interested, and conditional'. Cookson is also concerned to integrate Scotland and Ireland into the overall picture. His view is that there were few long-term repercussions of wartime mobilisation, which stemmed from what he regards as an *ancien regime* structure of public life. Cookson does conclude, however, that there had been new opportunities for 'lesser men' to enter public leadership and service with concomitant implications for political representation, a theme which Anderson had explored in terms of the militia debate in the 1830s and 1840s.

Though not only relevant to the auxiliary forces, by emphasising the weakness of the centre even in national defence, Cookson also explicitly challenges John Brewer's thesis that a strong 'fiscal-military state' underpinned Britain's emergence as a great power. Similarly, Gee, whose examples extended to the yeomanry as well as the volunteers, views the volunteer movement as one rooted in local communities, which further stimulated localism, and afforded new opportunities for the respectable elements of the urban population though not as great as those represented by volunteering in the Victorian period. Despite the considerable autonomy granted volunteer corps, the growth of the movement was accomplished, however, without increasing political partisanship and, indeed, reinforced constitutionalism. Mobilisation was thus achieved without concessions to popular reform and in ways designed to increase central control. Clearly, in suggesting that the volunteer movement's lack of political activity was more significant than their loyalism, Gee's analysis does not bear out the apparent establishment fears identified by Smith as the primary reason for replacing the force with the local militia, for the fear of disaffection was exaggerated. Volunteers after 1803, indeed, were less socially exclusive but also more reliable. Subsequently in 2003, Cookson considered regular army, militia and the volunteers in both the American War of Independence and the French Revolutionary Wars, concluding that the militia soon adopted the 'apolitical' habits of the regular army while the emergence of the external threat from France 'levered volunteering away from local interests and loyalties', neutralising any potential internal political threat from the movement.

Cookson's inclusion of Ireland is a significant one in that he devoted attention not only to the militia, revived in 1793, but also to the Irish yeomanry, raised in 1796 and which continued to exist until 1834. Ireland had not been one of my principal concerns in 1991, hence its inclusion only as an appendix and, on reflection, it should have been far more integrated into the overall analysis. The bicentenary of the Irish rebellion of 1798 saw a number of works touching upon the performance of the militia, including the impressive catalogue of the major exhibition at the Ulster Museum by W A Maguire, which includes a section on militia, volunteers and yeomanry. Arguably the most significant work, however, is Allan Blackstock's substantial monograph on the Irish yeomanry, which was followed by his relatively short study of the Belfast volunteers and yeomanry. In many respects, the Irish yeomanry is so specifically located in the Ulster Protestant tradition that it has few applications to the mainland, beyond perhaps a very particular legacy that equates to a certain extent to the persistence of the amateur military tradition on the mainland. Thomas Bartlett has also strikingly argued that volunteers and yeomanry in Ireland were 'the military expressions of two rival nations'. There has also been a partial updating of McAnally's work in Ivan Nelson's study of the militia between 1793 and 1801. Nelson, on balance, provides a convincing analysis of the militia's foundation, raising, social composition and operations during this period. It modifies Bartlett's argument as to the militia riots in 1793, as well as providing new evidence as to the religious affiliations of the militia: more were Protestant than is usually suggested. The force also emerges as recruiting well, and performing reasonably in the '98 despite the lack of clear direction from its political masters. Nelson, however, does not always engage with the full scope of the literature available on the auxiliaries and there is little mention of the emergence of the yeomanry as a rival to the militia.

Local studies generally have also continued to appear both in terms of articles and doctoral theses including, for example, John Beckett's two articles on responses to war in Nottinghamshire between 1793 and 1815, both published in 1997, and that by Kevin Linch on the West Riding, which appeared in 2001. Specialised regimental histories can also be of value and have continued to appear, such as Glenn Steppler's analysis of Leicestershire and Rutland, and John Sainsbury's continuing examinations of units in Hertfordshire, which extend over the whole period of the amateur military tradition.

If much of the work since 1991 has been on the Revolutionary and Napoleonic Wars, one should also acknowledge the work of Stephen Conway on the mid eighteenth century since this has certainly touched upon the militia and the first stirrings of the volunteer movement in the American War of Independence. Articles appeared in 1997, 1999 and 2001, but there were major works on Britain during the American War of Independence in 2000, and upon Britain in the mid-eighteenth century in 2006. In *The British Isles and the War of American Independence*, Conway stresses the now familiar theme that wartime mobilisation strengthened localism to the extent that it represented a 'negation' of national force since government was forced to respect its strength. Yet if this suggests he is leaning towards a similar stance to Cookson's view of local forces and a similar critique of Brewer, there is also recognition of the state's war-making capacity. As it happens, there is also a distinct nod towards Colley in the suggestion that invasion fears 'engendered a sense of beleaguered Britishness' for all that the war was in itself politically divisive. Conway's *War, State and Society*, covering the period 1739 to 1763, returns to the issues of centrality and locality. It suggests the partnership of government and private interests was itself fundamental to success in the Seven Years War, a conflict in which he also sees more evidence supporting Colley albeit that 'Britishness' took a different form from that in the late eighteenth century.

It has to be said that Conway's discussion of the volunteers and even the militia is rather limited in *War, State and Society*, with only brief reference to militia reform. One piece, however, that just escaped my deadline in 1991 was Eliga Gould's article on militia reform in the 1750s, which suggests that those advocating a new militia wished to integrate English landed society more fully into armed service in support of the Hanoverian dynasty and emerging national unity. In a sense, of course, this falls into the general trend since 1991 to view the auxiliary forces through the lens of issues of nationalism and of localism. Consequently, the recent work of Matthew McCormack, in situating the question of the establishment of the new militia in terms of the debate on masculinities and gender issues is strikingly different. McCormack argues that the debate on militia reform was 'fundamentally gendered' as part of a wider cultural crisis aimed at national regeneration after the early setbacks in the Seven Years War. Indeed, in this context, a 'new' militia might prove a 'comprehensive cure' for Britain's perceived military, political and moral failures. A new approach to the Irish Volunteers from the perspective of concepts of 'manliness', reflecting the current interest in military masculinity is also now promised in Padhraig Higgins's *A Nation of Politicians: the Volunteers, Gender and Patriotism in late Eighteenth Century Ireland*, to be published shortly by the University of Wisconsin Press.

A new theme, such as masculinity, raises the issue of where the study of the auxiliary forces might go in the future. In some ways, it is still something of a Cinderella area compared to studies of other aspects of the relationship between war and society, and the impact of war upon states, institutions and individuals. This is true generally for the whole period between 1558 and 1945 though, in recent years, there has been some welcome new interest in the Territorials, the Volunteer Training Corps of the Great War, and the Home Guard. Thus Bill Mitchinson has contributed recently two significant monographs on the Territorial Force between 1908 and 1914, and on the National Reserve, Volunteer Training Corps and other home defence formations between 1914 and 1918, as well as an earlier battalion history. Mitchinson's detailed study of the Territorial Force, focuses on the work of the County Territorial Associations, and fills an important gap in the understanding of the difficulties and heavy administrative workload of the associations in such areas as recruiting, training, equipment, finance and mobilisation amid the general indifference of the War Office. Individual battalion studies by Jill Knight and Helen McCartney also give further information on Territorial wartime experience and performance. McCartney in particular usefully provides a corrective to my text in demonstrating that Lancashire, Cumberland and Westmoreland within Western Command were able to retain a degree of pre-war identity longer than most others through the influence of the Earl of Derby. Mitchinson's study of the wartime home defence formations places the VTC in particular into the wider context of both an evolving manpower policy that made most home defence formations transient bodies and also of continuing official hostility to another unwanted spontaneous popular response to invasion fears. It lends additional emphasis to the manner in which I portrayed the VTC as a forerunner of the Home Guard.

The Home Guard itself was the subject of a full-length study by Paul Mackenzie in 1995, primarily concentrated on military and political aspects, which followed an article in 1991. He judiciously balances the element of truth in the popular image of the force against the seriousness with which the threat of invasion was taken by the Home Guard. Indeed, what is notable from his work is the way in which the Home Guard's parliamentary and other influential representatives wielded far more political muscle than any previous auxiliaries. An illustration is the defeat of the proposal in 1943 to reduce the number of clothing coupons granted by way of compensation for the free issue of uniform. Mackenzie also deals briefly with the unsuccessful revival of the Home Guard in cadre form between 1952 and 1957, the story of which is amplified in another of John Sainsbury's invaluable books on Hertfordshire: Sainsbury also separately covers the VTC in Hertfordshire. Mackenzie neglects the social context of the Home Guard, which would have added to his discussion of the ideal on the political left of the force as a people's militia and an instrument of social and democratic reconstruction. Just prior to the appearance of Mackenzie's book, an article by David Yelton had also contrasted image and military reality while the cultural legacy of the Home Guard is a particular theme of Penny Summerfield and Corinna Penniston-Bird in the context of the popular television series, *Dad's Army*. They also raise the question of the contrast between official rhetoric and left-wing opinion, while exploring the contribution of women to the Home Guard in terms of collective memory and gendered representation of the past.

A number of areas for future examination suggest themselves. Gender and masculinity was certainly not an issue of general examination in 1991 and clearly there is a great deal of scope for extending this beyond the 'new' militia debates of the 1750s and the Home Guard. There is also scope for some work on the cultural legacy of the auxiliary forces, and their place in popular culture and memory generally, something that has really only been done thus far for the Home Guard. Certainly, the literary, pictorial and musical references are considerable, not least for the period between 1750 and 1850. An indication, indeed, of the wealth of material is the catalogue of an exhibition, 'Napoleon and the Invasion of England', held at the Bodleian Library in 2003 tracing the reaction to the French invasion scares of 1798 and 1803–05 through prints and cartoons. Similar material was also displayed in the National Maritime Museum's 'Nelson and Napoleon' exhibition in 2005. A start has been made, however, in the collection of essays edited by Mark Philp in 2006, which was significantly part of a wider research project embracing the exhibition at the Bodleian. In addition, the collection also addresses issues of loyalism in the sea fencibles, the Manchester and Liverpool Volunteers, and the London volunteers.

One crying gap in the historiography that remains is certainly the British yeomanry. There is a Birmingham doctoral thesis dating from 2005. To date only two articles have appeared and, unfortunately, they strike one as a little antiquarian, one being a listing of previously unremarked yeomanry troops, and the other a somewhat potted listing of aristocrats in yeomanry regiments. There is another thesis on the yeomanry, however, under way at the University of Kent that seems to promise more. Further local studies can only assist in the wider understanding of the operation of the auxiliaries within local communities. Indeed, in terms of my own priorities in 1991, while acknowledging the significance of the centralism-localism debate, there are considerable possibilities for the further examination of such issues as links to trade, employment, and patronage and, particularly social mobility at the local level, but also nationally. Local record or historical societies have been active in publishing militia lists and rolls, such as editions of Bedfordshire muster rolls between 1539 and 1831 and Hertfordshire muster books between 1580 and 1605, but the motivation is primarily genealogical and the editorial content often lacking in depth. Fortunately, some editors are aware of wider issues, such as Paul Morgan in his study of the surviving rolls of the Warwickshire Yeomanry and B W Quinnell's edition of the Maynard lieutenancy book from Essex covering the period from 1606 to 1639.

It is noticeable that so much attention has been devoted to the auxiliary forces in Ireland in the light of the significant political and religious issues involved in their raising, as well as the 1798 rebellion. In addition to those works already cited, Irish military history generally has been well served with a general history by Thomas Bartlett and Keith Jeffery, in which David Miller and Bartlett himself deal with the auxiliary forces for the period in question. As suggested earlier, Conway makes strenuous efforts to incorporate the Scottish experience (as well as Ireland) in his work on both the mid-eighteenth century and the American War of Independence. Gee also makes reference to Scotland, and Cookson devotes a chapter to Scotland, as well as to Ireland. Nonetheless, auxiliary forces in Scotland deserve a more specifically centred study, most existing work relating to regular regiments. Andrew Mackillop, however, does highlight the important differences between the mid-eighteenth century militia debates in England and Scotland where the militia was seen as a means by which Scotland might 'reclaim its traditional martial ethos'. As Hew Strachan has pointed out, Scotland provided 36.4 per cent of the British volunteer force in 1797 and the proportion of its male population in the auxiliaries generally between 1793 and 1798 was twice that of England. For the time being, there is at least Bruce Lenman's article on militia and fencibles generally between 1660 and 1797. For Wales, there is not even a single article, and relatively few references in the major monographs.

My own work for the centenary study of the Territorials suggests that, in the context of the period between 1908 and 2008, most of my themes are still relevant but that in itself could and perhaps should be tested, especially as nothing else is really available for the post-1945 period. Indeed, not having looked seriously at the period since 1945 before, I was struck for the first time by the tensions between what might be termed the militia tradition and the volunteer tradition. In effect, Haldane tried to fuse these two traditions in 1908 by creating a force that would both supplement and expand the regular army in time of war as had the militia, but also build strong links between army and society as had the volunteers and yeomanry. What he actually got was largely the latter but, since 1945, and, especially since new legislation in 1996, the Territorials have ended up rather more of a militia than a volunteer force with particular implications for the relationship between army and society and for what might be termed the military footprint within communities. It is just one more illustration of the fundamental part played by the auxiliary forces in the relationship between army and society in this country. But then, of course, the whole construct of an 'amateur military tradition' and its function in representing the real link between army and society in Britain may yet be challenged.

IFWB, November 2010

Bibliography for second edition

Thomas Bartlett and Keith Jeffery, eds., *A Military History of Ireland* (Cambridge: Cambridge University Press, 1996).

Ian F W Beckett, *Territorials: A Century of Service* (Plymouth: DRA Publishing for TA100, 2008).

J V Beckett, 'Responses to War: Nottingham in the French Revolutionary and Napoleonic Wars, 1793–1815', *Midland History* 22, 1997, pp. 71–84.

J V Beckett, 'Recruitment into the Armed Forces in Nottinghamshire, 1793–1815', *Transactions of the Thoroton Society of Nottinghamshire* 101, 1997, pp. 145–55.

Allan Blackstock, *An Ascendancy Army: The Irish Yeomanry, 1796–1834* (Dublin: Four Courts Press, 1998).

Allan Blackstock, *Double Traitors? The Belfast Volunteers and Yeomen, 1778–1828* (Belfast: Belfast Society and Ulster Historical Foundation, 2000).

Michael Braddick, 'An English Military Revolution?' *Historical Journal* 36, 1993, pp. 965–75.

Michael Braddick, *State Formation in Early Modern England, c. 1550–1700* (Cambridge: Cambridge University Press, 2000).

John Brewer, *The Sinews of Power: War, Money and the English State, 1688–1783* (London: Routledge, 1989).

Linda Colley, *Britons: Forging the Nation, 1707–1837* (New Haven, CT: Yale University Press, 1992).

Stephen Conway, 'The Politics of British Military and Naval Mobilisation, 1775–83', *English Historical Review* 112, 1997, pp. 1179–1201.

Stephen Conway, 'British Mobilisation in the War of American Independence', *Historical Research* 72, 1999, pp. 58–76.

Stephen Conway, 'War and National Identity in the Mid-Eighteenth Century British Isles', *English Historical Review* 116, 2001, pp. 863–93.

Stephen Conway, *The British Isles and the War of American Independence*, (Oxford: Oxford University Press, 2000).

Stephen Conway, *War, State, and Society in Mid-Eighteenth Century Britain and Ireland* (Oxford: Oxford University Press, 2006).

J E Cookson, *The British Armed Nation, 1793–1815* (Oxford: Clarendon Press, 1997).

J E Cookson, 'Patriotism and Social Structure: The Ely Volunteers, 1798–1808', *Journal of the Society for Army Historical Research* 71, 1993, pp. 160–79.

J E Cookson, 'Service without Politics? Army, Militia and Volunteers in Britain during the American and French Revolutionary Wars', *War in History* 10, 2003, pp. 381–97.

Alexandra Franklin and Mark Philp, *Napoleon and the Invasion of Britain* (Oxford: Bodleian Library, 2003).

Austin Gee, *The British Volunteer Movement, 1794–1814* (Oxford: Clarendon Press, 2003).

Andrew Gilks, 'A History of Britain's Volunteer Cavalry, 1776–1908', Unpub. Ph.D., Birmingham, 2005.

Andrew Gilks, 'Britain's Unknown Cavalrymen', *Journal of the Society for Army Historical Research* 85, 2007, pp. 237–46.

Andrew Gilks, 'Aristocratic Participation in the Volunteer Cavalry', *Journal of the Society for Army Historical Research*, 86, 2008, pp. 204–15.

Eliga Gould, 'To Strengthen the King's Hands: Dynasty, Legitimacy, Militia Reform, and Ideas of National Unity in England, 1745–60', *Historical Journal* 34, 1991, pp. 329–48.

Steven Gunn, David Grummitt and Hans Cool, eds., *War, State, and Society in England and the Netherlands, 1477–1559* (Oxford: Oxford University Press, 2007).

Ann King, ed., *Muster Books for North and East Hertfordshire, 1580–1605* (Hertfordshire Record Society, 1996).

Jill Knight, *The Civil Service Rifles in the Great War* (Barnsley: Pen & Sword, 2004).

H Langelüddecke, '"The Chiefest Strength and Glory of the Kingdom": Arming and Training the "Perfect Militia" in the 1630s', *English Historical Review* 118, 2003, pp. 1264–1303.

Bruce Lenman, 'Militia, Fencibles, and Home Defence, 1660–1797', in Norman MacDougall, ed., *Scotland and War, AD79 –1918* (Edinburgh: John Donald, 1991), pp. 170–92.

Kevin Linch, 'A Geography of Loyalism? The Local Military Forces of the West Riding, 1794–1814', *War and Society* 19, 2001, pp. 1–22.

Margarette Lincoln, ed., *Nelson and Napoleon* (Greenwich: National Maritime Museum, 2005).

Nigel Lutt, ed., *Bedfordshire Muster Rolls, 1539–1831* (Bedford: Bedfordshire Historical Record Society, 1992).

Andrew Mackillop, *More Fruitful than the Soil: Army, Empire and the Scottish Highlands, 1715–1815* (East Linton: Tuckwell Press, 2000).

Paul Mackenzie, 'Citizens in Arms: The Home Guard and the Internal Security of the United Kingdom, 1940–41', *Intelligence and National Security* 6, 1991, pp. 548–72.

S P Mackenzie, *The Home Guard: A Military and Political History* (Oxford: Oxford University Press, 1995).

Paul Mackenzie, 'The Real Dad's Army: The British Home Guard, 1940–44', in Paul Addison and Angus Calder, eds., Time to Kill (London: Pimlico, 1997), pp. 50–59.

W A Maguire, ed., *The 1798 Rebellion in Ireland: A Bicentenary Exhibition* (Belfast: Ulster Museum, 1998).

Helen McCartney, *Citizen Soldiers: The Liverpool Territorials in the Great War* (Cambridge: Cambridge University Press, 2005).

Matthew McCormack, 'The New Militia: War, Politics and Gender in 1750s Britain', *Gender and History* 19, 2007, pp. 483–500.

Matthew McCormack, 'Citizenship, Nationhood and Masculinity in the Affair of the Hanoverian Soldier, 1756', *Historical Journal* 49, 2006, pp. 971–93.

John McGurk, *The Elizabethan Conquest of Ireland: The Burdens of the 1590s Crisis* (Manchester: Manchester University Press, 1997, reprinted 2009).

Eve McLaughlin, ed., *The Muster Roll of the Bucks Militia, February 1798* (Aylesbury: Bucks Genealogical Society, 2007).

Roger Manning, *An Apprenticeship in Arms: The Origins of the British Army, 1585–1702* (Oxford: Oxford University Press, 2006).

K W Mitchinson, *Gentlemen and Officers: The Impact and Experience of War on a Territorial Regiment* (London: Imperial War Museum, 1995).

K W Mitchinson, *Defending Albion: Britain's Home Army, 1908–19* (Basingstoke: Palgrave, 2005).

K W Mitchinson, *England's Last Hope: The Territorial Force, 1908–14* (Basingstoke: Palgrave, 2008).

Paul Morgan, ed., *The Warwickshire Yeomanry in the Nineteenth Century: Some Fresh Aspects* (Stratford-upon-Avon: The Dugdale Society, 1994).

Ivan Nelson, *The Irish Militia, 1793–1802: Ireland's Forgotten Army* (Dublin: Four Courts Press, 2007).

Ivan Nelson, 'The First Chapter: Restoring a Military Perspective to the Irish Militia Riots of 1793', *Irish Historical Studies* 33, 2003, pp. 369–86.

John Nolan, 'The Muster of 1588', *Albion* 23, 1991, pp. 387–407.

Mark Philp, ed., *Resisting Napoleon: The British Response to the Threat of Invasion, 1797–1815* (Aldershot: Ashgate, 2006).

B W Quinnell, ed., *The Maynard Lieutenancy Book, 1608–39* (Chelmsford: Essex Record Office, 1993).

John Sainsbury, *The Hertfordshire Yeomanry* (Welwyn: Hart Books, 1994).

John Sainsbury, *Herts VR* (Welwyn: Hart Books, 2005).

John Sainsbury, *The Home Guard in Hertfordshire, 1952–57* (Welwyn: Hart Books, 2008).

P R Seddon, 'A Restoration Militia and the Defence of the Shire: The Nottinghamshire Militia, 1660–70', *The Historian* 47, 1995, pp. 23–25.

Victor Stater, *Noble Government: The Stuart Lord Lieutenancy and the Transformation of English Politics* (Athens, GA: University of Georgia Press, 1994).

Glenn Steppler, *Britain to Arms: The Story of the British Volunteer Soldier and the Volunteer Tradition in Leicestershire and Rutland* (Stroud: Alan Sutton, 1992).

Hew Strachan, 'Scotland's Military Identity', *Scottish Historical Review* 85, 2006, pp. 311–32.

Penny Summerfield and Corinna Peniston-Bird, *Contesting Home Defence: Men, Women and the Home Guard in the Second World War* (Manchester: Manchester University Press, 2007.

James Scott Wheeler, *The Making of a World Power: War and the Military Revolution in Seventeenth Century England* (Stroud, 1999).

David Yelton, 'British Public Opinion, the Home Guard and the Defence of Great Britain, 1940–44', *Journal of Military History* 58, 1994, pp. 461–80.

Introduction

Traditionally, Britain has relied upon command of the sea as the main line of defence against invasion, itself a constant theme in English and British history. In consequence, the existence of a large standing army has been distrusted on the grounds that such a regular force was both unnecessary and dangerous in that it might promote military despotism, a lingering fear that actually predated the creation of a standing army. Thus, there has been a preference for amateur and temporary soldiers – the auxiliary forces – brought into existence as needs dictated both for defence against invasion and disorder and as a wider means of social control and assimilation through participation and example. The military obligations imposed upon the English and British peoples from earliest times and the more systematic organisation of local auxiliary forces from the mid sixteenth century have therefore continuously reflected and transmitted traditional attitudes towards military participation in Britain. Indeed, in the absence of a large standing army prior to 1660 (technically, prior to 1689) and in the absence of regular troops permanently visible to society as a whole thereafter, it is the ever present auxiliaries who have more often provided the essential point of contact between society and army in Britain.

This amateur military tradition has taken varying forms. Despite the wilder claims of Victorian historians, the origins of auxiliary forces are undoutedly rooted in the military obligations of the Anglo-Saxons transmitted through mediaeval legislation to be enshrined in what might properly be termed the first militia statutes of 1558. Thereafter, the militia had a formal statutory existence until 1604, from 1648 to 1735, from 1757 to 1831 and from 1852 until 1908. Even the absence of such enabling legislation did not necessarily imply that the militia had ceased to function and technically at least the authority to raise the militia did not cease until 1953.

As an institution of state the militia always implied a distinct element of compulsion for at least a section of society although the basis of that obligation varied from time to time as indicated by the addition of epithets such as 'Exact', 'Select', 'Supplementary' or 'New' militia. Essentially, the obligation was one imposed upon property until 1757 and then as a tax upon manpower through compulsory ballot until 1831, the militia being the only component of the state's armed forces implying such compulsion until the introduction of conscription for the army in 1916. However, a voluntary system of enlistment was applied to the militia between 1852 and 1908.

In contrast to the militia, supposedly self-sufficient volunteer forces existed at other times or simultaneously with the militia. Such volunteer forces were raised in the 1650s, 1660s, in 1715 and 1745 and between 1778 and 1782 when the first specific volunteer legislation was enacted. Volunteers are principally associated, however, with the French Revolutionary and Napoleonic wars, being raised both as volunteer infantry and artillery and as mounted yeomanry. Many infantry units transferred to the so-called local militia in 1808 but this was suspended in 1816 although the legislation remained on the statute book long after. Other volunteers survived the Napoleonic wars but virtually all had disappeared by the 1840s, only for the volunteer movement to be revived in 1859. Volunteers raised in 1859 were initially governed by provisions dating from 1804 until new volunteer legislation in 1863 while the yeomanry, which had survived post-1815 reduction largely intact, continued to be governed by 1804 statute until 1901 when it was renamed imperial yeomanry.

In fact, the imperial yeomanry was short-lived in title for in 1908, a major consolidation of auxiliary forces resulted in the effective abolition of the militia and the merging of volunteers and imperial yeomanry in the territorial force. Yet, the territorial legislation did not remove that of 1863 from the statute book and volunteer training corps (later the volunter force) were raised under its provisions in the First World War. The territorials were reconstituted in 1920 as the territorial army and have continued to the present time. On occasions they have been encouraged to join ad hoc volunteer bodies such as the defence force in 1921 and the civil constabulary reserve in 1926. In addition, volunteering was again revived during the Second World War when the local defence volunteers, later the home guard, were raised under defence regulations bearing a striking similarity to older volunteer legislation.

It will thus be apparent that there is indeed what can justifiably be termed an amateur military tradition with a remarkable continuity from the mid sixteenth century if not before. Figures are not always reliable for earlier periods but, at any one time, a significant proportion of the country's male population was either serving in the auxiliary forces or had so served. In 1806, for example, perhaps 3.5 per cent of the population as a whole were serving in auxiliary forces. In 1877 some 6.36 per cent of the male population aged between 15 and 35 were serving in auxiliary forces, representing 3.6 per cent of the population as a whole. If such figures appear superficially small, they must be put into perspective. Thus, over 818,000 men passed through the volunteers between 1859 and 1877 with the force rarely below a quarter of a million strong after 1885. A total of 953,000 men passed through the militia between 1882 and 1904. Figures should also be compared with the experience of mass mobilisation during the First World War when the 5.7 million men passing through the army, including the territorial force, still represented only 22.1 per cent of the male population of the United Kingdom and only 10.73 per cent of the population as a whole.[1]

Such a degree of participation alone might have been expected to lead to detailed study of the relationship between auxiliaries and society in Britain over the past five hundred years. Yet, despite its importance, the amateur military tradition has been woefully neglected by historians. Fortunately, individual components of the auxiliary forces – with the notable exception of the yeomanry – have received sufficient modern attention to make this book possible but rarely do these studies or the auxiliaries as a whole rate more than an isolated passing reference in standard accounts of British social, economic, political, cultural and even military history. The Tudor and Stuart militia is usually mentioned in standard sixteenth- and seventeenth-century histories, the latter because of its crucial role in the crisis leading to the outbreak of the civil war. Eighteenth-, nineteenth- and twentieth-century manifestations of the tradition are virtually never mentioned.

Even when some allusion is made to the auxiliary forces, the historical analogies employed are invariably inappropriate and, at best, confused. A case in point, which may serve as illustration of the problem as a whole, is the treatment of the home guard. During the Second World War itself, for example, the under-secretary of state for war, Sir Edward Grigg, likened the home guard to the yeomanry of the Napoleonic wars while what amounted to a semi-official history penned by Charles Graves in 1943 referred both to the 'levee en masse' of 1803 and, rather vaguely, to a miscellany of dates – 1545, 1588, 1642, 1667, 1719, 1759, 1794, 1803, 1859 and 1914 – of which some were more relevant than others. A ministry of information pamphlet in the same year evoked the example of an even more mysterious 'volunteer militia when Napoleon threatened invasion' in apparent ignorance of the fact that the ballot had been suspended only rarely between 1792 and 1815 if, indeed, ministry officials were even aware that compulsion had theoretically applied to the militia for over seventy years.[2]

Later historians betrayed a similar unfamiliarity with suitable historical example, the official historian of civil defence raising the doubtful analogy of the abortive Shelburne circular of 1782 as a precedent for the air raid precautions service and one social history of Britain at war referring to the home guard in the context of militia musters in 1545, which have no significance for the overall development of British auxiliary forces. The most relevant parallel – that of the volunteer training corps in the Great War – was generally ignored. Moreover, the most recent historian of the home guard has made much of the force's uniqueness based inter alia upon the so-called 'housemaids clause' enabling personnel to resign on 14 days' notice until February 1942.[3] In reality, the right applied not only to the volunteer training corps but to Victorian and earlier volunteers since it was first enshrined in the Volunteer Consolidation Act of 1804.

It will be the task of this book, therefore, to set the auxiliary forces in their proper historical context and to trace continuities both of role and of impact. The emphasis will be upon the period from 1558 to 1945 but it is necessary to trace the general development of the precursors of the organised militia prior to 1558 and some brief mention is also made of developments since 1945. In terms of the purposes for which auxiliaries have existed, it will examine the response to the threat of invasion at differing periods as well as the constabulary role fulfilled by auxiliaries, both issues which inevitably raise the question of the relationship between auxiliaries and the standing army. Yet, not too distant from the role in aid of the civil power is what might be loosely termed the concept of social control and this, too, will be examined. That, in turn, raises the wider relationship between auxiliaries and society, not least the social composition of the auxiliary forces and their precise function within society and state. Indeed, something of the differing levels of relationship and the effective inter-dependence of auxiliaries and society will become apparent and will assist in explaining the paradoxical attitude of British society towards military affairs. It should become clear that nothing which consumed so much time and effort for succeeding generations could really fail to be of considerable significance in both local and national affairs and it is to be hoped that historians will be encouraged to devote more attention to auxiliary forces in the future than has been the case in the past.

In many respects, the study of auxiliary forces is still in its infancy and this book provides one suggested framework of analysis based upon the author's interpretation of the research so far carried out by historians. Such an analysis may or may not prove acceptable but, if it only arouses greater interest in the amateur military tradition in Britain, it will be sufficient.

Notes

1 *Volunteer Service Gazette* 8 Nov 1884, pp. 16–17; *British Parliamentary Papers* (hereafter *BPP*) (1904) XXXI, Cd. 2064, Appendix XXXIII; I. F. W. Beckett, *Riflemen Form* (Ogilby Trusts, Aldershot, 1982), p. 85; G. J. Hay, *An Epitomised History of the Militia* (United Service Gazette, London, 1905), p. 167; *Statistics of the Military Effort of the British Empire during the Great War* (HMSO, London, 1922), pp. 30, 156–9, 363–4.

2 C. Graves, *The Home Guard of Britain* (Hutchinson, London, 1943), pp. 19, 114–20; Ministry of Information, *The Home Guard of Britain* (HMSO, London, 1943), p. 7.

3 T. H. O'Brien, *Civil Defence* (HMSO, London, 1955), p. 60; A. Calder, *The People's War* (2nd edit., Panther, London, 1971), p. 140; N. Longmate, *The Real Dad's Army* (Arrow Books, London, 1974), p. 22.

1

The evolution of a
national militia (to 1601)

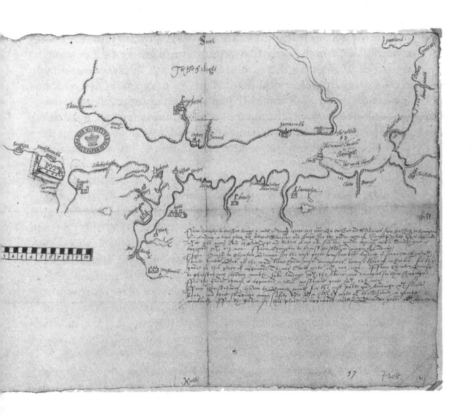

The continuities of the amateur military tradition in Britain are such that they have been remarked upon even by commentators in the distant past. In the reign of Elizabeth I, for example, Sir Roger Twysden prepared a short history of the warning beacons in maritime counties, concluding that they dated from at least the reign of Edward III. The majority of surviving documentary references do indeed date from the early fourteenth century, the earliest being to the Isle of Wight in 1324. Yet these documents themselves invariably record a much greater antiquity. Thus, in instructions issued for beacons between 1338 and 1340 phrases used included 'as was wont to be done' or 'as is customary' while those defensive measures undertaken on the Isle of Wight were prefaced with 'as was wont to be done in the time of our forefathers during the disturbances of war'.[1]

Similarly, many Victorian and Edwardian historians of the auxiliary forces were aware of the theme of continuity although this was manifested largely in the form of speculative excursions which substituted regimental tradition for known fact, G. J. Hay's *An Epitomised History of the Militia* even bearing the subtitle, 'The Military Lifebuoy, 54 BC to AD 1905' and claiming the origins of the militia in the army gathered by Cassivelaunus to oppose Caesar's second invasion of Britain. Nevertheless, most of these older works did correctly sense the link between the Anglo-Saxons and the system of military obligation which became enshrined in the first militia statutes of 1558, even if they misrepresented the Anglo-Saxon system in certain respects.

While it was always recognised that household or mercenary troops of one kind or another were widely employed by the Crown in

Anglo-Saxon England, Victorian historians maintained that all able-bodied freemen were liable under the *trimoda necessitas* (or threefold obligation) to build and repair fortifications, repair bridges and undertake military service in the fyrd. In reality the phrase *trimoda necessitas* appears only in a forged tenth-century charter but there is no doubt that there were 'common burdens' in Kent by the end of the seventh century and in Mercia by the mid eighth century as a consequence of the Crown granting some immunities to the church but simultaneously reserving its right to claim military service. The significance of the imposition of the burdens on the church was that 'bookland tenure' granted clerics in perpetuity would otherwise have deprived the Crown of manpower since, normally, the King granted 'loan land tenure', which was not hereditary and obliged successive generations to perform personal service. As bookland tenure extended beyond the church so did the application of the burdens and all three elements were certainly obligatory in Mercia by 796 at latest. The pressure for codification in Mercia appears to have coincided with Mercia's 'imperial years' in the eighth century but it was the threat from the Norsemen that probably led to similar developments in Kent and Sussex in the late eighth and early ninth centuries. The association of the three obligations was also paralleled in the Frankish kingdoms but seemingly came more belatedly to Wessex in the reign of Aethelbald (855–60). The basic obligation to serve in defence of the community pre-dated the association with bridges and fortifications, the fyrd itself evolving over three centuries of the Norse threat.

It was previously suggested that military service in the fyrd, which was no more than the Old English word for army, might be either in a general levy or 'great fyrd', usually called out only in times of particular urgency, or in the 'select fyrd', which was a more suitable local response in countering the mobility of Norse raiders. More recent research has cast doubt on this theory and the general Victorian notion of an Anglo-Saxon 'nation in arms' in the light of the fragmentary sources actually available.[2] By contrast it is now suggested that there was in effect only a 'select fyrd' – invariably mounted in Wessex – representing individuals who owed personal service to the Crown and their military tenants in turn.

According to Domesday Book evidence, in some areas at least a man served for a period of approximately 60 days and almost universally on behalf of a unit of land assessment. The precise unit varied from region to region – sulungs (double hides) and juga in Kent, six carucates in the Danelaw and East Anglia but in Berkshire, Wiltshire and Devon it was one of five hides. The latter was a fiscal and military unit based on land valuation rather than actual area and on the ground the hide might vary from 60 to 100 acres. In effect, therefore, the real obligation was on the landholder and not the land itself. An individual might be assessed on all five hides himself or only a part (or none), in which case he might possibly be supported financially by his fellow owners. Among the West Saxons from the seventh century onwards, failure to serve would result in a fine or fyrdwite – usually set at 40s – but larger landowners, favoured by the King with privileged tenure or seigneurial rights, who failed to find sufficient manpower, risked forfeiture of their estates. Towns were similarly assessed on a hideage and it is also likely that fyrd service could have been fulfilled simply by providing supplies for the fyrd.

No distinction was apparently made between land and sea service and the obligation to provide ships was also a general liability by the tenth and eleventh centuries: it is possible that the ship obligation was assessed on a 300 hide unit and that the internal organisation of some counties such as Cambridgeshire and Warwickshire into groups of three hundreds may represent ship sokes. In any case, particular divisions of areas such as tithings and hundreds emerged in the late tenth century both for the maintenance of law and order and, in the case of the hundred, as a probable unit of the fyrd. To some extent developments in England reflected earlier developments in Carolingian Europe but it must be emphasised just how sophisticated a system had evolved in Anglo-Saxon England. Indeed, the celebrated document known as the Burghal Hidage dating from about 911 to 919 indicates that, in theory, over 27,000 men could have been raised for immediate defence of 30 West Saxon boroughs. If not exaggerated, the document also implies an extraordinary potential mobilisation of one in five of the estimated able-bodied manpower available – comparable to that achieved in Britain during the French Revolutionary and Napoleonic wars or the two world wars of the twentieth century.

The nature of the fyrd suggests that the Norman Conquest did not newly introduce the concept of feudal quotas to England as has sometimes been assumed even if these were now to be calculated on an honorial rather than a hideage basis. Moreover, Norman feudal obligation was slow in its introduction after 1066 and did not lead to the eradication of the older fyrd obligation. Thus the bearing of arms remained a distinct characteristic of the freeman and there is evidence of the continued existence of the fyrd until at least the beginning of the twelfth century whilst the principle of the common burdens was preserved in the Ten Articles of the Conqueror's reign, the Assize of Arms of 1181, the Statute of Westminster of 1285 and beyond. Much of the evidence for the existence of the fyrd prior to the Conquest derives from Domesday Book in 1086 whilst there are references to it in other documents of the late eleventh and early twelfth centuries and evidence from thirteenth-century Cheshire.

The fyrd appears to have been employed against both external agressors, such as Danes who landed in Suffolk in 1069, Scots in 1072 and the Welsh who attacked Cheshire in 1098. It was similarly utilised against English rebels such as Harold's illegitimate sons in 1068 and Hereward the Wake in 1071. If anything, the fyrd was a more reliable military instrument in its loyalty to the Crown than feudal hosts in the rebellions of 1075, 1088 and 1101 and it even appears to have served in Maine in 1073. In many respects, it could also be argued that the fyrd actually outlived classic feudalism, which was already declining by the twelfth century – the feudal array last appeared in an English army in the reign of Richard II – while the Assize of Arms of 1181 represented a fusion of the older English and newer feudal obligations by dividing the free population into four categories with prescribed weapons according to wealth. The first category was equivalent to the feudal host, the second and third (worth 16 and 10 marks respectively) to the fyrd and the fourth to a more general levy. The main differences between the second and third categories and the fyrd of old was that assessment was now firmly based on rents and chattels, which were more easily calculated than a notional hideage. Subsequent revisions in 1223, 1230, 1242 and 1253 together with the Statute of Westminster and its revisions merely adjusted the categories and took account of modern developments in warfare such as the introduction of archers and light horsemen.

The Statute of Westminster in 1285 increased non-feudal categories from three to five including the non-free in a general obligation of all able-bodied males between the ages of 15 and 60 to bear arms. In a sense, however, the statute had more relevance to internal policing than to war, stressing that the equipment was 'for keeping the peace according to the ancient assize',[3] and the real revolution in thirteenth-century military organisation was Edward I's introduction of the commission of array as a means of raising levies in the shires. At the same time, counties also became responsible for supplies to the army in the field. Commissioners of array replaced the sheriff as the official responsible for summoning men for service but the latter did retain the power of calling out the *posse comitatus* or civil power of the county both for the arrest of felons and for local defence.

In practice, the burden of military service applied by the commissioners did not fall equally across the shires since it was customary to levy the northern counties against the Scots, midland counties against the Welsh and southern counties against the French. This had nearly always been so with, for example, shire levies from East Anglia alone alerted during the invasion scare of 1264 and levies called to Kenilworth during de Montfort's rebellion in the following year only from adjacent counties. Thus, when Edward's regent, the Earl of Cornwall, requested a contingent from Chester in 1287 for service in southern rather than northern Wales as was usual it was stressed that this would not be regarded as a future precedent. Some 1,400 men were levied from southern shires for Edward's stillborn Gascony expedition in 1295 but the greater prevalence of raid and counter-raid along the Scottish border ensured that the north bore the real brunt of war although any destructive impact upon localities was invariably offset by economic benefits derived from the militarisation of the frontier. At the same time the impact of military service as a whole was circumscribed by the limited duration of contingents' appearance in the field. Few appear to have served longer than a month although a picked body of 100 archers from Macclesfield was paid special rates to remain out longer than customary in 1277.

Nevertheless, despite the relatively limited burden, Edward was still compelled to concede many royal powers in order to raise his armies, notably tolerating the continuation of the mid-thirteenth-century practice whereby the Crown assumed payment of levies once they crossed the county boundary. Edward II attempted unsuccessfully to claw back some of the ground lost by his father, trying in both 1324 and 1325 to postpone the moment at which the Crown assumed responsibility for paying the levies. It proved equally difficult for the Crown to impose any general obligation embracing all classes of society and one reason for the continuation of feudal military obligation in the fourteenth century was the political advantage conferred by its now traditional and relatively uncontroversial nature as a basis for demanding military service. In order to raise his armies, Edward III was forced to enhance local political power as the price for securing co-operation from magnates and shires alike. None the less, disputes continued over the Crown's apparent stretching of the bounds of perceived legality. Parliament had asserted that military contingents could not of right be demanded from boroughs although assistance might be requested as a matter of grace. In 1327, therefore, when troops were being raised for the Scottish campaign several boroughs including Newbury and Lincoln refused to co-operate. At Bristol the burgesses taxed the city to cover the cost of levying 100 men but promptly pocketed the money so that none of the troops ever reached the army. In 1344 Edward agreed to concede formally that levies leaving the county to proceed overseas would pass on to the Crown's wages at port of embarkation, the men receiving no pay whilst in the county and county pay en route between county boundary and port.

Despite the difficulties, Edward's reign was marked by increasingly successful demands on the resources of the shires although even the greater costs of equipping what were still comparatively small numbers of levies can hardly have seriously disrupted communities or deprived the land of its labour force. For the campaign against the Scots between June and September 1335 only 5,621 men were levied from the shires and a high proportion of such levies appear to have returned home after such expeditions. From 1343 it was also possible to escape service altogether through payment of a fine varying according to means although the practice did not reach the height of abuse associated with later militia forces. In addition, while shire levies were used almost exclusively for some campaigns such as those in Scotland in 1346 and 1355, other campaigns such as that in 1337 were conducted by armies overwhelmingly drawn from lordly retinues raised by indenture (contracts) as the two systems continued to function side by side with armies led by the King in person raised by array and those led by nobles raised by indenture. Where levies were especially appropriate, however, was in defence of maritime counties against the increasing risks of French raids and attempted invasion.

Perception of the danger had seen beacons being put into order in Somerset, Devon and Dorset in September 1337 with further instructions issued from April 1338 for maritime counties from Devon to

Lincolnshire. In November 1338 some maritime counties were also ordered to sound church bells as warning of attack. This *garde de la mer* was entrusted to 'keepers of the maritime lands' (replaced by arrayers in 1369) while inland counties were also deputed to come to the assistance of those on the coast. Thus, in 1364 Rutland and Leicestershire forces were to be prepared to reinforce Lincolnshire while men from Oxfordshire, Berkshire and Wiltshire were to assist Hampshire. That such precautions were necessary was proved by a number of French raids on the south between 1338 and 1340. Another spate of raids commenced in 1360 and threats continued throughout the Hundred Years War. Gravesend, Rye and Hastings were all raided in 1377 and special precautions were again put in hand in 1385, 1386, 1404, and 1415 and 1416. Mayors of Sandwich still traditionally wear a black gown in commemoration of a predecessor killed in the French raid of August 1457.

The concern with invasion was also reflected in the number of towns either constructing or repairing defences since, by the late fourteenth century, nobility and gentry were increasingly evading their defence responsibilities. Grants to maintain walls increased steadily through the latter half of the fourteenth century and the French threat also goes some way to explaining the reversion of levies to the auxiliary local role they had fulfilled prior to the late thirteenth century. In June 1385, for example, the men of Orford in Suffolk successfully petitioned Richard II to allow them to remain in their own town rather than serve even in another part of the county in the event of French or Flemish raids. The concessions wrested by the House of Commons, notably the statute of 1352 by which no one was bound to find soldiers except by parliamentary common consent, were jealously guarded. Consequently, a 'model' commission of array issued by Henry IV in 1402 reaffirmed the right of levies not to leave their own counties unless in dire emergency. On the other hand, the Crown did achieve recognition of incursions by the Scots and Welsh as acts of invasion permitting the use of levies outside their shire boundaries. In the reign of Henry VI commissions of array were also used during internal revolts such as that of Jack Cade in 1450 while the Wars of the Roses saw a confusing variety of methods employed in raising troops ranging from letters under the privy seal or signet to commissions of array and the tried and trusty recourse to indenture.

In fact, the forces raised for the incipient warfare between 1455 and 1485 were relatively small and probably far less than the 20,000 men despatched into Scotland in 1482. Indeed, it has been estimated that those armies which were raised only fought for a total of 61 weeks in just ten out of the 30 years over which the conflict endured.[4] Among the noble and indentured retinues, upon which the real burden fell, levies are only rarely glimpsed such as the 'naked' men in the royal army before Ludlow in 1459, the 'new men of war' routed by the northern army at Dunstable in 1461 or the Essex forces contemptuously dismissed by London chroniclers ten years later. There is also a sighting of the posse in the Lancastrian summonses recorded in the Paston correspondence in 1460 and among forces raised by Yorkists in 1462 and by the Nevilles in the Marches in June 1463.

Most surviving evidence of forces raised derives from towns rather than the countryside, reflecting the fact that the former had remained generally well armed despite the overall decline in the amount of military equipment maintained across the country as a whole – the ratio of archers to men at arms had increased from 3:1 in 1415 to 7:1 by 1475. Moreover, it was in the towns that a prototype permanent military organisation already existed in the form of the mediaeval watches. The 'marching watch' in the City of London had existed since the reign of Henry III and continued at least until that of Edward VI. Although mainly used only in emergencies, watches organised by guilds and crafts were periodically paraded in a festive spirit on suitable occasions in the religious calendar. Generally, St Peter's Eve and Midsummer's Eve were the favoured occasions in London while torch-lit processions of the watch were held on St Peter's Eve and St John's Eve in Coventry, on Midsummer's Eve at Exeter and on Lamnas Eve in Faversham. Such parades were highly popular and persisted into the Elizabethan period, one being held at Bristol as late as 1571.

While there was a temporary if limited revival in the impressment of levies for wider service during the period between 1455 and 1485, Henry VII relied upon indenture as the traditional way of raising forces for overseas expeditions such as that to Brittany in 1495 and there was also some use of foreign mercenaries or auxiliaries borrowed from continental allies. However, levies were still useful against overmighty subjects or other rebels. In 1486 Henry mustered the Lincolnshire levies without weapons to ensure that no one else could use them and levies were also arrayed during Perkin Warbeck's rebellion in 1497 as well as in anticipation of foreign invasion. However, it was the reign of the second Tudor that marked a distinct change in the traditional emphasis upon duality and the emergence of the real beginnings of a single unified national militia system. This transition was by no means immediate and the Crown's preference for quasi-feudal forces endured at least until the mid 1540s while the doubtful loyalty of both local gentry and shire levies in many areas during the risings of 1549 led to the extensive employment of Italian, Spanish, German and other mercenaries. Nor indeed could Henry have mounted his limited campaigns abroad without the assistance of substantial numbers of mercenaries and auxiliaries. Similarly, while shire levies were generally regarded as sufficient to contain the Scots, Henry substantially bolstered his local forces in the north with foreign mercenaries in 1545.

In terms of the quasi-feudal system, Henry abandoned indenture after 1512 and reverted to the not especially successful earlier practice of issuing summonses to leading gentry under the privy signet. It is clear that the Crown had very little actual information upon which to base its demands. The great proscription or survey of the country's military and financial resources undertaken by Cardinal Wolsey in March 1522 in the likely event of England joining Emperor Charles V in war against France and the Scots was somewhat deficient in this respect since its primary purpose appears to have been to yield financial information for Wolsey's subsequent forced loans in 1522 and 1523. Some returns certainly suggest that county commissioners grasped this reality and were more conscientious in obtaining financial than military intelligence although the returns generally listed the numbers of able-bodied men in each county and the quantity of weapons and equipment retained.

None the less, not only was the Crown often working on sheer guesswork but the burden fell unequally anyway. In Buckinghamshire, for example, when 44 individuals were directed to muster tenants and retainers prior to renewed war with France in March 1543, one man summoned had been dead for two years, 11 had no land holdings and one neither lands nor retainers. At least four of the county's 23 justices were not summoned at all and only 13 individuals were actually required to find contingents for the Boulogne expedition in 1544 together with two who had not been summoned at all in the previous year: the choice of several among them simply defies rational explanation.[5] Similarly, Sir Adrian

Fortescue of Berkshire was compelled to find nine separate contingents over 25 years while the burden imposed on the temporal lords and religious houses was especially heavy. In 1536 some 18 out of 21 English and Welsh bishops were summoned to find contingents and 23 out of 27 in 1543; 21 heads of religious houses had been summoned in 1521.

In fact, the Boulogne expedition proved the apotheosis of the quasi-feudal system and when further reinforcements were required later that year they could only be found from a national levy. The quasi-feudal system occasionally re-appeared as in 1569, 1588 and 1599 but only as a supplement to the shire forces, who now provided the majority of the Crown's field armies. Several factors contributed to the final demise of the last vestiges of feudal military obligation, not least its inability to provide the required numbers of men. Some great families had disappeared by the 1540s as well as the monasteries; gentry households were being reduced in size; costs of military equipment were rising sharply and tenants were increasingly denying that they owed any military service to their landlords.

At the same time, the theories of classical authors such as Vegetius on the conduct of war were being more widely disseminated throughout western Europe in new vernacular editions and were encouraging not only the concept of communal defence as a civic virtue but also the belief that the wider bearing of arms was a measure of the confidence placed by the state in its own political stability. Thus, earlier attempts at creating national military institutions which had foundered, such as the French *francs-archers* of 1448, were newly revived. Tuscany attempted to reorganise its militia in 1505/6, Venice in 1507 and 1528, Urbino in 1533 and France itself in 1534. In England, despite the still relative insecurity of the Tudor dynasty and the innate conservatism that militated against more permanent military institutions, some form of national system built on local levies clearly offered greater scope for finding the desired manpower for expeditions and home defence. But here, too, there were enormous difficulties.

On 5 July 1511 Henry had ordered that the Statute of Westminster be more rigorously applied and in the following year an archery statute attempted to enforce provision of butts at local level and the practice of archery on holy days required since 1363. In 1515 masters and employers were further directed to arm their servants and employees with bows and to erect butts for their use. The Statute of Westminster had previously been enforced through the sheriff and the justices while archery obligations had fallen within the jurisdiction of manorial courts. Without actually overriding the responsibilities of these older offices, Henry entrusted the new effort to enforce the statutes to commissioners of muster generally chosen from existing justices. The 1522 survey served to demonstrate just how far Englishmen had neglected their theoretical obligations to retain arms and practise their use and how far parishes had failed to maintain communal harness or armour for parochial use, a liability dating from at least the reign of Edward II: surviving returns for 1522 indicate that there were 128,250 able-bodied men in 28 counties but only a third were archers – the strongest and most capable men. In Rutlandshire only a third possesssed any weapons at all.

In view of the appalling deficiencies revealed, strenuous attempts were made to remedy defects and from 1535 commissioners of muster held inspections of arms and equipment at three-yearly intervals. How far all the deficiencies were corrected is impossible to judge and by the 1540s there was growing concern at the way in which popular pastimes such as bowls and dice were allegedly undermining the manly virtues of Englishmen. Indeed, in 1514 the butts at Islington, Hoxton and Shoreditch had been enclosed and the inhabitants had forcibly seized and destroyed the bows of those attempting to practise there although Londoners subsequently levelled the hedges and ditches which encroached on the archery grounds. However, the growing popularity of martial pursuits in the City, which also saw the establishment by charter of incorporation of the Guild of St George (later the Artillery Company) in August 1537 to maintain 'the science and feate of shootinge'[6] with bows or handguns, may have been exceptional. Between 1522 and 1557 the proportion of those designated nationally as archers declined from a third to a quarter and added to this was the loss of manpower through the effects of depopulating enclosure and outbreaks of plague. By 1557–8 all counties were reporting fewer able-bodied men available than in 1545: to give but one example, the numbers of the able-bodied in Sussex fell from 6,037 in 1539 to 5,889 by 1557. Overall, there were just 87 firearms and 482 pikes recorded in 25 English counties.

Nevertheless, the increasing tensions in Europe necessitated the raising of larger numbers of men. Between 1536 and 1558 there were four major revolts, two serious invasion scares and, under Mary Stuart, the loss of Calais. The summoning of levies prior to 1544 was comparatively rare such as those called from Berkshire and Wiltshire to reinforce the army in Scotland in September 1513. After 1544 it became far more common although, in keeping with mediaeval tradition, counties were usually summoned according to their proximity to the potential threat. In effect there was a division of the country into two military provinces roughly corresponding to the ecclesiastical sees of Canterbury and York. When the French landed on the Isle of Wight on 21 July 1545, therefore, it was defended by 1,500 of its own levies plus some 2,700 from Hampshire and 900 from Wiltshire. When the French retired from the Wight and subsequently landed at Seaford in Sussex on 25 July the inhabitants had to rely upon Kent forces as their own were with the King's army at Southsea. Similarly, while counties such as Durham, Northumberland, Westmorland and Yorkshire were mustered only against the Scots in 1545 and 1558, only Lancashire, Cheshire, Gloucestershire, Somerset and Devon were levied for service in Ireland.

At best Henrician military organisation was highly uneven in its application not only over the country as a whole but within individual counties. Nor was it uncommon to find the quasi-feudal and national systems coming into conflict when both made simultaneous demands upon the same individuals. But as the Crown grew more confident and strong enough to overcome former traditional limitations on the liability of levies to serve outside their counties – at least 4,000 shire levies reinforced Boulogne in July 1544 – so the national system prevailed over the quasi-feudal. By the end of Henry's reign, the dominating force in English military organisation was moving rapidly from one end of the social scale to the other.[7]

The troubled reign of Edward VI and the respective ambitions of the dukes of Somerset and Northumberland also led to another development which would have lasting consequences for local military organisation. This was the appearance of the lord lieutenant, the prefix 'Lord' originally deriving from the rank of those who filled the office and becoming a matter of custom. Indeed, technically, there was no such office as lord lieutenant until the local government changes of April 1974: prior to 1974 there was officially only His or Her Majesty's Lieutenant for a particular county. In fact, Henry VIII had issued commissions to some individual nobles to assume command in more than one county: in 1545 England had been effectively divided in this way between the dukes of Norfolk and Suffolk and Lord Russell. Somerset appears to have placed lieutenants above sheriffs and commissioners in some areas in 1547, the first being the Earl of Shrewsbury to oversee Yorkshire, Lancashire, Chester, Derby, Shropshire and Nottinghamshire. Wide-ranging commissions were also issued two years later. In November 1549 Parliament recognised the appointments of lieutenants in times of crisis and Mary, after reverting temporarily to reliance upon sheriffs and commissioners, appointed lieutenants on the renewal of war with France in 1557. They were not appointed for all counties and most terminated at the Queen's death but lords lieutenant continued to make sporadic appearances under Elizabeth with individuals increasingly being named for single counties. Ultimately, the system would be extended to Scotland in 1794 and to Ireland in 1831.

If the interval between Henry's death and Elizabeth's accession marked the beginnings of the lieutenancy, it also brought about the coalescence of the quasi-feudal and national system in the form of two statutes which collectively became known as the 1558 Militia Act. The more important of the two (4 & 5 Philip and Mary, c 2) was that for the maintenance of armour and horses, repealing all arms and armour classes in previous legislation and finally displacing the Statute of Westminster as the basis for military obligation after 273 years. In its place, the new statutes created ten classes based on income but, in a sense, merely reasserted the older obligations and redefined responsibilities: they have been characterised as both 'old wine in new bottles' and as a 'compromise of old and new'.[8] However, by including all with the exception of larger boroughs (who none the less fell under the jurisdiction of lords lieutenant) in a national system the statutes effectively terminated the dualism implicit in English military organisation since the Conquest. In fact, the Crown had already anticipated the statutes for, in January 1558, commissioners of muster had been ordered not to spare tenants from the general levy designed to find troops for the defence of Calais.

The essential difference between earlier systems and that which pertained after 1558 was the Crown's growing determination to enforce obligations upon the citizen and, in many cases, to go beyond them. There was closer scrutiny by the privy council of the certificates of muster which purported to record the results of the general musters of the able-bodied. The musters, usually followed by some kind of military exercise, now took place approximately every three years at some convenient time, usually Easter, Whitsun or Michaelmas. After the initial inspection there was an interval in which those defaulting on their obligations had an opportunity to remedy the defects in their own or dependants' equipment. Invariably delays occurred, while a particular source of difficulty was the liability of wealthier groups – those with land worth 100 marks or more for light horse, or £200 or more for demilances (medium-heavy cavalry) – to provide mounted men. In the case of Northamptonshire, the local commissioners simply refused for seven years to accept the horse assessments made in 1580 and consistently evaded the demands with impunity.

Part of the problem lay in the means by which the militia rating system was calculated for the purposes of the 1558 statutes. These had not actually specified how the value of land and goods was to be assessed with the result that the commissioners usually based their estimates on the parish subsidy books. As the subsidy books themselves were far from accurate and seldom took account of an individual's land holdings elsewhere, larger landowners frequently escaped contributing their full share: in Devon in 1580 the lord lieutenant, the Earl of Bedford, specifically attempted to assess those of 'secret wealth and never charged with service as gentlemen be'.[9] There was an understandable sense of grievance in many areas and refusals to meet obligations became commonplace as costs of equipment escalated. Further grievance arose from the exclusion of retainers from the statutes and the lack of pressure placed on them except in grave emergencies such as that in 1588. The clergy, although similarly exempted, were subjected to fairly continuous demands through a separate rating system emanating from primates and bishops and independent of lords lieutenant. The larger boroughs were also theoretically exempt but, in practice, were seldom able to avoid the jurisdiction of the lieutenancy.

The problem of the rating system was compounded by the failure of the privy council to decide whether or not it wished to rely solely upon the subsidy assessment or whether commissioners should be urged to 'persuade' those rated to co-operate willingly in raising numbers beyond those implied by the assessment. Certainly, a policy of persuasion brought greater numbers in 1569 but persuasion alone could not solve the difficulty and, having briefly contemplated stricter enforcement of the subsidy, the council eventually resolved in

1580 to specify the numbers it expected from each county. Inevitably, some counties such as Essex ignored the council but, although there was a deficiency of 26,143 men, some counties such as Dorset did raise more men and some like Somerset even reached their target, resulting in a net increase of 11,068 men over 1577.

If the rating system was one difficulty that often promoted inefficiency, another was the fact that the information forwarded to the privy council varied according to the standards applied locally. The certificates differed enormously in listing the numbers of able-bodied irrespective of likely changes in population structure. In the case of Essex, the 1573 and 1577 certificates indicated that the foot had declined by a total of 1,398 men in the intervening period and light horse and demilances by 24 men. Upon further enquiry on the part of the council, the figures were adjusted by the county commissioners to show an increase of 1,254 foot and 124 horse. More convincingly, Buckinghamshire explained a decrease in 1577 over 1573 as the result of a more careful selection of men, and the effects of a decay in the local clothing industry and the fear of plague leading to the cancellation of musters.[10] Nevertheless, it must again be said that the council should bear a share of the blame for failing to issue a model certificate until 1577 and only issuing a printed form in 1580.

The real value of the certificates lies in their relative indication of the progress of modernisation within the militia. Modernisation itself was impelled by such factors as the poor showing of militia levies in the bungled Scottish campaign of 1560 and the belief of Sir William Cecil and others that England's insularity and inexperience in modern war necessitated urgent remedy. Henry Barrett's 1562 manual, *The Captain's Handbook*, appears to have been a direct consequence of the latter feeling but, in any case, there was a growing consciousness of developments in Europe. Continental military manuals were increasingly being translated into English and from the 1570s onwards were supplemented by those of indigenous theorists such as Thomas Digges, Barnabe Rich, Sir John Smthye and Thomas Styward. Cosimo de Medici's instalment as Duke of Tuscany in 1569 after a series of victories by his citizen forces was a further stimulus.

In particular, the council was anxious to see the introduction of modern firearms such as the harquebus or caliver. These were far more expensive than bows – though cheaper than the heavier musket – but the council also saw a role for the bow because of its supposed moral value in wooing the population from pernicious pastimes such as dice and bowls. Yet, in 1577, the council ascribed the decline in the popularity of archery to the advent of the very firearms they were trying to promote and made even greater efforts to persuade counties to enforce the use of the bow. A number including Buckinghamshire, Warwickshire, Wiltshire and Derbyshire responded favourably by agreeing to suppress unlawful games or to enforce archery on public holidays. But the counties prepared to assist in this way remained limited and the appearance of the so-called trained bands from 1573 onwards was an indication that the council had failed to implement wider reform and modernisation and had fallen back upon making a smaller proportion of the militia efficient.

Characteristically, the council failed to capitalise on the relative lack of opposition to selective training by not actually ordering any until 1577 though some counties do seem to have at least selected men in the intervening years. When the orders were issued in 1577 it was too late in the year to organise the first training at Easter and the trained bands only became a reality in 1578. In some ways the trained bands resembled a select militia system proposed by Sir Thomas Wyatt in 1549 but never implemented. They also followed a scheme considered both in 1567 and 1569 for training a force of harquebusiers in selected towns but which had foundered on the fears in counties such as Essex, Wiltshire and Suffolk as well as the City that frequent training of apprentices was a threat to internal order. After 1573 it became customary to muster only trained men, the work of choosing and training these individuals falling upon the commissioners and upon deputy lieutenants who increasingly assumed the role of the former. In 1575, for example, a total of 183,000 able men were recorded of whom 12,000 were selected for training, a further 63,000 equipped but not trained, some 3,000 told off for horse, and the remainder reserved for use as unarmed labourers or 'pioneers' in emergencies.

From 1577 training was normally carried out by experienced professional soldiers appointed as muster-masters – an appointment dating from 1560 – on a total of ten days spread throughout the year. Some four days would be utilised after Easter Monday, a further four days after Whit Monday and the remaining two days at Michaelmas or after harvest. Some counties attempted to do less training since all men were to be paid at a rate of 8d per day and the cost of both powder and shot was also high, Buckinghamshire calculating the total training cost for ten days as 13s 0d per man. Thus, Wiltshire applied to limit training to three or four days on the grounds of cost but this was firmly refused. The amount of work that could be achieved was also restricted by the inclusion within the statutory days of time spent travelling to the musters, which were held at traditional locations such as Mile End in London, Bowcombe Down and St George's Down on the Isle of Wight, Muster Oak at Codsheath in Kent and Muster Green in the Buttinghill hundred of Sussex. In 1578 the training days were reduced to two at Whit and two between Bartholomewtide and Michaelmas.

By 1580, therefore, the council had gone some way to resolving earlier inconsistencies and in that year the Spanish ambassador reported that a total of 25,000 men could be assembled at any point on the English coast within 12 hours of the firing of beacons. Moreover, an altogether greater urgency prevailed after 1583 at least from the point of view of the council as the threat from Spain increased. The country was divided into six classes of county for training purposes with intensified training ordered for the most vulnerable maritime shires in early 1587, the assumption being that the greatest danger was posed to Dorset, Hampshire and the Wight. Over a thousand veterans were recalled from the campaign in Flanders at the end of the year and the militia was warned to be on alert from April 1588 and placed on an hour's notice from mid-June. Inevitably some counties were more advanced than others while some were simply wary of allowing their militia to be drawn out of the county in the event of possible invasion – Dorset and Surrey had evinced some fears on this score in the 1570s and it was claimed that Warwickshire refused to send its forces beyond the county boundaries in 1588.

Actual defence plans were similar to those proposed since 1559 and envisaged four groups of forces: the northern forces of some 12,000 foot watching the Tyne and the Scots; 27,000 foot and 2,500 horse from the southern maritime counties shadowing the Armada as it sailed up the Channel; an army of 28,900 militia and 45,000 others to protect the Queen's person; and a field army of 17,000 foot and horse placed under the command of the Earl of Leicester. Arrangements were also made for mutual assistance between the maritime counties while able-bodied but untrained men were pushed into the major coastal ports. In the case of the Queen's army, the 45,000 were raised by the clergy and from the personal retainers of the nobility and gentry. A single county might therefore contribute men to several different groups. In Kent 2,000 foot were designated to join the Queen's army, 4,000 foot and 725 horse joined the standing maritime forces, and a further 4,824 foot remained in county defence reserves at Canterbury and Maidstone.[11]

The militia was mobilised on 23 July 1588 having been alerted some days previously: there had been no need to fire the beacons since mobilisation was effected by an efficient system of postal couriers. However, on 3 August counties were instructed to hold back the foot, partly because the county forces would have passed on to government expense once at Tilbury. With the end of the immediate threat, too, Leicester's army was disbanded between 5 and 10 August although the noble contingents remained for another fortnight to indulge in some spectacular military reviews about the capital. Many more gentry contributed to a 'voluntary loan' to clear debts incurred in meeting the emergency but there was also a number of refusals, which suggested the growing disenchantment with the constant demands being made upon the country as a whole.

It remains a matter of speculation, of course, how effective the militia forces might have proved against the 17,000 veterans of the Spanish army of Flanders – excluding the 19,000 regular infantry on board the Armada itself – intended to be landed in Kent. Parma's army had been engaged in almost continuous warfare since 1572. By contrast, the Kent militia was still being mustered in the threatened area as the Armada passed the Wight on 24 July and its preparations were far from complete as the Spaniards passed Dungeness three days later. Moreover, of the 10,880 foot fielded by Kent only 2,958 were both armed and trained and 2,000 of these had been sent to the Queen's army. Of the remainder, some 4,166 were armed but untrained and all the others only partially armed or told off as pioneers though it can be noted that such pioneers were armed in Dorset. Thanet and the area around Margate where the invading force was to have come ashore was undefended to all intents and purposes and England as a whole lacked sufficient modern fortifications. As has been pointed out, even a limited occupation of Kent by the Spaniards would have reaped enormous advantages[12] and there would have been little to prevent this in respect of any English ground forces available.

The fortunate defeat of the Armada did not end the threat of invasion and there were renewed scares in the 1590s. Beacons were manned in Kent in May 1591 when the Spanish fleet was sighted off

Brittany and were manned again in Kent, Hampshire and Sussex in 1592. Three years later the Kent forces were mustered and those of Essex, Sussex and Surrey prepared to reinforce the county in the event of a landing. An even more serious scare arose in 1596 when preparations were made for a possible landing in October or November and, yet again, in the following year. There were further scares in 1599 and, from time to time, actual raids such as that on Merionethshire in 1595 and the occasion in the same year when four galleys raided Mousehole in Cornwall to be met only by 200 or so unarmed men – the helmet of a former publican and the cannon ball alleged to have beheaded him are still displayed in a Mousehole public house.

Even more pressing, however, than the need to meet possible invasion were the demands for overseas expeditionary forces. Men were levied regularly for campaigns in Brittany, Normandy, the Low Countries and the running sore of Ireland. Frequently, the commissioners in counties such as Kent, Derbyshire or Northamptonshire, which was notorious for underestimating its military manpower in muster returns, ensured that trained men were retained within the county and that county armouries were not depleted. Thus, those levied for foreign service were the more undesirable elements of the county's population but, increasingly, the council violated the accepted exemption for the trained bands and in 1589 and 1590 resorted to the unprecedented conscription of whole companies from the trained bands for service in the Channel Islands. Similarly, at least a thousand men from the trained bands were despatched to Brittany in 1591, men from the Essex and Kent trained bands found themselves outside Rouen in 1592 and others in Normandy in the same year. The Cheshire trained bands were raided in 1594, 1596 and 1599.

Resistance manifested itself in evasion, delay or default in meeting the council's requests for returns or payments connected with the levies, the especially heavy scale of recruitment in 1586, 1591 and 1599 being far more disturbing to the normal pattern of county life than the small numbers levied in earlier centuries, not least in terms of its regularity. In all, some 105,820 men – possibly between 14 and 18 per cent of able-bodied males – were levied in England and Wales for overseas service between 1585 and 1602.[13] Less notice was taken of proximity to the campaign than hitherto in the sense that populous areas like London and Yorkshire were levied for both

Ireland and the continent. However, in the case of the Rouen campaign of 1590, the southern shires were not levied due to invasion fears and, overall, six English western maritime counties provided 25 per cent of Irish levies and London and south-eastern counties 45 per cent of those for Europe: Wales provided proportionally more men for Ireland than England. Nor did these men return in any significant numbers compared to the past: out of some 3,400 levied for Normandy in 1591 only an estimated 800 ever returned to England.[14]

The willingness to utilise the militia and trained bands in particular for such overseas campaigns was partly due to lessening demand for home defence – training dropped to only two days for the entire year in 1601 – and partly a recognition of the military value of the militia's training, those drafted from the trained bands to Europe often releasing veterans for service in Ireland. At the same time, however, it may also have reflected the fact that the council had largely failed to promote what has been called a 'bourgeois militia'.[15] The council's preference for householders, farmers, yeomen and the sons of such worthy citizens to fill the ranks of the militia reflected not only the belief that such men could afford better weapons than their poorer neighbours but also that they were more politically reliable. Nevertheless, what evidence is available points to a force of rather less social eminence than the council might have wished. The Isle of Wight forces were apparently mostly prosperous farmers and householders but in 1569 the Cornish forces were said to include husbandmen, tinners and fishermen while both the Northamptonshire and Cambridgeshire trained bands were composed of non-taxpayers and poor labourers and artisans respectively in the 1580s. One Hampshire company was principally composed of husbandmen and day labourers some years later while, in 1605, Salisbury's forces were 'mechanicals' or tradesmen. Indeed, it is clear that there was both limited substitution from 1573 onwards and considerable bribery on the part of the wealthier to avoid service.

In many ways the attempt to avoid service was merely traditional since the military obligations placed on the English had always met resistance. While the Crown still depended upon largely amateur forces for defence against both external aggression and internal rebellion that opposition was bound to persist: it was after all only in the reign of Henry VIII that royal bodyguards and paid regular forces in key garrisons such as Berwick and Carlisle took on a more permanent aspect. But, whereas obligations had been applied loosely in the past, by the close of Elizabeth's reign the militia system had become firmly entrenched in the life of every Englishman and Welshman with the lieutenancy – once merely an instrument of military expediency – increasingly translated into administrative necessity as the Crown's demands grew. So much so, indeed, that a sense of grievance and resentment against the rigid imposition of traditional obligations was far more apparent. Thus, the way was prepared for the militia to become one more issue in the growing confrontation between Crown and parliament although it had also proved so in the past. In short, English resentment of military service was not merely a product of the Stuart age but a tradition cultivated assiduously if unsuspectingly by the Tudors.

Notes

1   H. J. Hewitt, *The Organisation of War under Edward III* (Manchester University Press, 1966), p. 9, n. 4.

2   R. Abels, *Lordship and Military Obligation in Anglo-Saxon England* (University of California Press, Berkeley, 1988), pp. 1–9.

3   H. Rothwell (ed), *English Historical Documents: III 1189–1327* (Eyre & Spottiswoode, London, 1975), pp. 460–2.

4   A. Goodman, *The Wars of the Roses* (Routledge & Kegan Paul, London, 1981), p. 214.

5   J. J. Goring, 'The Military Obligations of the English People, 1511–1558' Unpub. Ph.D., London, 1955, pp. 113–117, 304–7.

6   G. Goold-Walker, *The Honourable Artillery Company, 1537–1926* (The Bodley Head, London, 1926), pp. 10–11.

7   C. G. Cruickshank, *Army Royal: Henry VIII's Invasion of France, 1513* (Oxford University Press, 1969), p. 204.

8   L. Boynton, *The Elizabethan Militia, 1558–1638* (2nd edit., David & Charles, Newton Abbot, 1971), pp. 9–10; A. Hassell-Smith, 'Militia Rates and Militia Statutes, 1558–1663' in P. Clark et al. (eds), *The English Commonwealth: Essays presented to Joel Hurstfield* (Leicester University Press, 1979), pp. 93–110.

9   Joyce Youings, 'Bowmen, Billmen and Hackbutters: The Elizabethan Militia in the South West' in R. Higham (ed), *Security and Defence in South-west England before 1800* (University of Exeter Studies in History No. 19, 1987), pp. 51–68.

10   Boynton, *Elizabethan Militia*, p. 43; R. V. Bonavita, 'The English Militia, 1558–1580: A Study in the Relations between the Crown and the Commissioners of Musters', Unpub. M.A., Manchester, 1972, p. 91.

11   J. J. N. McGurk, 'Armada Preparations in Kent and Arrangements made after the Defeat', *Archaeologia Cantiana* LXXXV, 1970, pp. 71–93.

12   G. Parker, 'If the Armada had landed?', *History* 61, 1976, pp.

358–368.

13   J. J. N. McGurk, 'The Recruitment and Transportation of Elizabethan Troops and their Service in Ireland, 1594–1603', Unpub. Ph.D., Liverpool, 1982, p. 109.

14   G. Scott Thomson, *Lords Lieutenant in the Sixteenth Century* (Longmans, London, 1923), pp. 111–12.

15   Boynton, *Elizabethan Militia*, pp. 107–13.

358–368.
   13   J. J. N. McGurk, 'The Recruitment and Transportation of Elizabethan Troops and their Service in Ireland, 1594–1603', Unpub. Ph.D.,
Liverpool, 1982, p. 109.
   14   G. Scott Thomson, *Lords Lieutenant in the Sixteenth Century*
(Longmans, London, 1923), pp. 111–12.
   15   Boynton, *Elizabethan Militia*, pp. 107–13.

2

The emergence of a constitutional force (1601–1745)

To the Right Honorable,

The Lords and Commons assembled in Parliament:

THE

HVMBLE PETITION

OF

The Captains, Officers, and Souldiers

of the Trained Bands, and Voluntiers of the County of
BUCKINGHAM, assembled at Alebury, June 17. 1642.

Humbly sheweth,

Hat they give you thanks from the depth of their hearts, for the great and main benefit they have already received, from Your no lesse chargeable then Indefatigable pains; And in particular, for your necessary Ordinance of the Militia, of which, as we conceive, (under God) our safety doth depend; unto which we most cheerfully submit, as is manifest by this dayes appearance; not onely of the Trained Bands, but of well neere 1000. Voluntiers, that made all demonstration of obedience, aswell to this, as to all other Commands that shall come from Your Honorable Houses, in opposition to the Popish or Malignant partie at home, or any other power from abroad; Notwithstanding the main visible discouragements from ill-affected persons, that made it their businesse, to blemish the validity of your Authority ; as also, by the Lord Lieutenants absence, contrary to the Trust reposed in him.

Therefore we humbly implore the continuance of your care for our safety, and to appoint such a Lord Lieutenant in whom we may confide, as surely as you may in us, who are resolved to lay our Lives and Fortunes at your feet, in defence of the King and Parliament.

And we shall pray, &c.

14 JUNII.

ORdered that the Lords be moved to joyn with this House, in nominating the Lord Wharton to be Lord Lieutenant of the County of Buckingham, in stead of the Lord Paget: And that this Petition shall be forthwith printed.

H: Elsynge, Cler: Parl: D: Com:

London, Printed by L.N. and J.F. for Edward Husbands and John Francis. June 25. 1642.

One of the most distinctive features of the first three decades of the seventeenth century was the growing distaste for the application of central government policies in the counties through the agency of the lieutenancy. While generally sympathetic to issues of national defence and local law and order, local gentry placed the preservation of local harmony first among their priorities. This was especially applicable in the case of the lieutenancy when a considerable amount of work fell upon a handful of deputy lieutenants whose ability to function rested almost entirely on the degree of co-operation they were able to foster. Moreover, that spirit of co-operation had to reach the lowest levels of administration in the form of the parish constables. Thus, the pace of government was set according to local taste and will and the essential problem of the early Stuart period was that the Crown failed to recognise that reality. It is not surprising, therefore, that the lieutenancy and the militia became such pressing issues. Along with billeting and martial law they figured in the Petition of Right in 1628; the Commons would investigate complaints against the lieutenancy in December 1640 and condemn the militia assessment system in the Grand Remonstrance of November 1641. And, of course, the struggle for the control of the militia would become a major factor in the outbreak of civil war and the repercussions of that struggle would dominate the militia system for over a hundred years.

One reason for the disatisfaction with the lieutenancy arose, paradoxically, from the fact that, having performed its last task in Elizabeth's reign of safeguarding the succession with armed camps around the capital, the militia all but ceased to exist. The new reign brought greatly reduced perceptions of European tensions and, as a result, only inspections were directed for the trained bands without training. A more complete muster was ordered for both militia and general populace in 1608 but only Gloucestershire appears to have gone beyond a cursory inspection in producing a detailed survey of males of military age. The lack of urgency was further demonstrated by the repeal of the Marian militia statutes in 1604 leading to considerable confusion, not least in terms of the basis for militia assessments since some maintained that even older statutes had been reinstated by default. In part, repeal reflected the dislike for increasing and unequal burdens in the previous reign. The parish rating system introduced by the Relief of the Poor Act in 1597 offered some solution but militia assessments invariably became a matter of discretion for the deputy lieutenants. However, such assessments now rested not on parliamentary statute but on the Crown's prerogative. Conceivably, it had been anticipated that repeal would allow the lieutenancy more flexibility to increase demands without the population having recourse to previously recognised statutory limits but it was largely a matter of bluff on the part of the deputies and the Crown was deprived of accepted coercive powers over defaulters other than recourse to common law.

Attempts to replace the lost statutes with new legislation failed in 1604, 1621, 1624, 1626 and 1628. Consequently, Charles I's claim in 1642 that the 1558 statutes were still in full force was somewhat hollow and it was possible for a persistent defaulter such as John Bishe of Brighton to justify evasion in 1620 on the grounds that 'there was no law to enforce him'.[1] Evasion was particularly noticeable in the case of assessments for horse where absentee landlords could claim exemption through liability elsewhere. By 1617 with counties such as Hertfordshire, Gloucestershire and Huntingdonshire complaining bitterly about the numbers of gentry escaping assessment in this way, the privy council prohibited exemption on such grounds. Unfortunately, this effectively 'repudiated the formerly accepted doctrine that a man was only liable once'[2] and disputes continued unabated. Nor was the attempt to incorporate the clergy into the national system after 1608 any more successful. In theory the clergy would now be assessed by the lieutenancy and mustered with the trained bands but in practice this was ignored. Even a compromise in 1611 to enable bishops to assess their own clergy proved ineffective. In Northamptonshire the clergy were still refusing to pay the rate levied for county training in 1614; the

Norfolk clergy were still in default in 1617 and the Essex clergy still mustering separately from the trained bands in 1624.

As the years of peace continued – with the exception perhaps of the danger posed to the south-west by Barbary pirates – the neglect of the militia increased. In Somerset it had become customary to delay the second inspection to discover if equipment deficiencies had been remedied until the following year while the borrowing of equipment to pass such inspections was sufficiently common for the lord lieutenant, the Earl of Hertford, to condemn 'the inconstant dealing of the vulgar'.[3] However, it is equally clear that, in turn, Hertford deliberately misled the council as to the true state of his county's militia. In 1611 the muster was cancelled while that in neighbouring Wiltshire was postponed indefinitely. Indeed, when the presence of Spinola's Spanish army in the Low Countries renewed invasion fears in 1613 and stirred the council into action there was not always great enthusiasm for the revival. Nevertheless, activity was markedly increased. Cheshire appears to have had its forces fully re-activated by 1616 and Buckinghamshire two years later when the outbreak of the Thirty Years War in Europe further heightened tension. The drawback was that greater endeavour on the part of the lieutenancy gave fuller scope to the fundamental opposition of the gentry to the burdens being applied.

The horse assessment continued to provoke anger in many counties but, frequently, the focus for opposition became the appointment of a professional muster-master responsible for training the foot. There had been one long-running dispute in Wiltshire between 1602 and 1606 over the muster-master's salary and objections were now registered in counties such as Sussex, Hampshire, Herefordshire, Somerset, Leicestershire and Suffolk. Partly, it arose from an appointment in the gift of the lieutenancy being considered venal but, more especially, the rates charged for the muster-master's services were regarded as being without legal basis. The issue was contentious enough for grand juries in Hertfordshire and Shropshire to raise it in 1629 and 1635 respectively as a constitutional grievance contrary to the Petition of Right. Of course, the muster-master was also in a good position to judge whether or not the deputies were actually complying with council instructions and the fact that he was often a stranger to the county did not help – one compaint in Wiltshire in 1604 was that the muster-master had not removed his hat in the presence of the deputies.

Despite these shortcomings there were signs of improvement in the militia as a whole. Weapons were progressively modernised with the musket replacing the caliver: in Essex the number of muskets increased from 917 in 1608 to 1,994 in 1623. More men were also being trained, the numbers in Northamptonshire being expanded from 600 in 1612 to 1,286 by 1629 and in Norfolk from 3,000 in 1612 to 4,744 in 1628. The social quality of the trained bands was generally held to have improved in several counties following the council's re-iteration in 1613 of the perennial Elizabethan desire for ranks filled with freeholders, farmers, landholders and householders. Evidence suggests such a transformation had taken place in Middlesex by 1615 and in Wiltshire by 1617 but it is possible that the 'better sort' were confined elsewhere by their own choice to the 'general' or untrained bands periodically mustered as a reserve for the trained bands proper. Significantly, the untrained bands in Lancashire in the late 1630s were referred to as 'freehold bands', freeholders generally being exempted and jealous of their independence from the trained bands.

One significant remaining problem was the difficulty in obtaining suitable officers for the trained bands, and a number of counties including Derbyshire, Devon, Nottinghamshire and Staffordshire were compelled to introduce local incentives such as pay. Yet, ironically, there was no shortage of young gentlemen willing to undertake military service overseas and there was a ready market for military manuals in England itself. Moreover, the now fashionable interest in military affairs was illustrated by the growth of artillery gardens and grounds in many towns. In addition to the 'Artillery Company' in Bishopsgate, which was revived in 1610 or 1611, a 'Military Garden' was established in St Martin's Fields in 1610, a 'Military Yard' in Westminster in 1635 and a 'Martial Yard' in Southwark. Many had strong Puritan connections, the frequency with which militaristic sermons were delivered to their members on ceremonial occasions reflecting the martial enthusiasm of many Puritan divines. Outside the capital similar military facilities and institutions were established in the 1620s in Colchester, Bury St Edmunds, Norwich, Bristol, Gloucester, Great Yarmouth, Derby, Coventry and Ipswich. Even the new world boasted a 'Military Company of Massachusetts' from 1637, indicating the exportation of martial (as well as anti-militarist) ideals to the American colonies, all of which with the exception of

Pennsylvania established militias on the English model during the seventeenth century.

Unfortunately, an acceptance of military activities in principle did not imply a readiness on the part of the gentry to share the military priorities of the Crown, which were increasingly influenced by the experience of the very continental campaigns in which so many Englishmen were willingly participating. Professional soldiers in particular were determined to modernise and improve the militia further in the light of European practice, and this found expression in the enhanced training orders issued in 1623, which heralded the energetic pursuit by the new monarch of the concept of the 'exact militia'. During the first few years of Charles's reign, however, the attention of the lieutenancy was drawn more to the the prosecution of his wars against the Spanish and French and the raising of forces for expeditions to Flushing, Cadiz, Rhé and La Rochelle. Sustaining a war effort was the greatest strain for the inherently weak financial state structures of early modern Europe and though, in this case, only some 50,000 men or approximately only one per cent of the total population were levied,[4] the demands were made over a comparatively short period of time at roughly double the annual rate of compulsory enlistment experienced during Elizabeth's reign.

At least the levy had the effect in Somerset of drawing new men into the trained bands, which were nominally exempt from the press, but the conduct of the troops levied left much to be desired. Often resorting to martial law to restrain the levies, who were billeted over much of southern England, hapless deputy lieutenants came under general attack in the Commons during the 1628 session, Sir Robert Phelips of Somerset claiming that deputies were 'the most insupportable burdens that, at this present, afflict our poor country, and the most cruel oppression that ever yet the Kingdom of England endured'[5] and the office was roundly condemned in the Petition of Right. Yet, ironically, Phelips shortly accepted office as a deputy himself and he and some other opponents of the lieutenancy appear to have been motivated primarily by their exclusion from office due to local political factionalism. Indeed, it is arguable that the abortive attempt to pass a new militia bill in 1628 failed due to a general satisfaction with the status quo. However, hostility was undoubtedly engendered by the preparation of overseas expeditions and made the deputies' attempts to establish the exact militia more difficult, particularly in counties such as those in East Anglia where the burden of the levy had been keenly felt.

The Crown's determination to create an improved militia was assisted to a certain extent by a renewed invasion scare in 1626 although the treatment of both this episode and a similar scare in 1635 leads to the suspicion that the government found it convenient to stress a danger that appeared slight. Thus, in Essex much good will had been lost in the autumn of 1625 when the trained bands were called out for a month in defence of Harwich at a time of poor harvest, plague and other severe local economic difficulties without the expected remuneration. Nevertheless, there was some risk. French ships had seized shipping off Shoreham in 1628 and foreign seamen landed on the Sussex coast on ten occasions between 1625 and 1630 for plunder or as a result of shipwreck. But, even if the likelihood of invasion was small, it was still necessary to adopt more modern military practises.

Efforts at modernisation took three forms – the establishment of county magazines with modern weapons, the employment of experienced soldiers brought home from the Low Countries as instructors and the improvement in the efficiency of the horse through regional rather than shire musters. In all some 84 sergeants were recalled from the continent initially for three months' duty but, in many cases, they were retained far longer. Some boroughs such as Manchester and Great Yarmouth also hired foreign professionals to carry out the same task. In the case of the horse, the cost of holding musters at Cardiff, Denbigh, Leicester, Shaftesbury and York and on Hounslow Heath raised so much opposition when coinciding with preparations for the Rhé expedition that they were almost immediately cancelled. Another reform attempted was the imposition of uniform weapon standards, a proclamation in 1628 requiring the marking of individual weapons to prevent the abuse of passing them from man to man at musters.

Many counties claimed that they had taken the concept of the exact militia seriously but there were undeniable difficulties in translating aspiration into results. One problem was the uneven and unequal application of assessment tolerated by the council in some areas but arbitrarily punished in others and a great strain could be placed upon deputies even if they sought to avert the implications of Crown policy. Small wonder that the Norfolk deputies wished to be relieved of the burden of office in 1626 or that those in Essex complained in February 1628 that they had been deserted by many 'of our neighbours with whom wee were able to persuade much by love, and our tenents whom wee used to command'.[6] In Somerset the deputies became so unpopular that their local administration had broken down completely by 1640 and, significantly, when the Crown turned to ship money as a possible source of income its collection was entrusted not to deputies but to sheriffs, who as individuals could be more readily controlled from the centre.

Thus, despite the general regularity of musters of foot in most counties between 1625 and 1629; evidence of continued militia activity even after 1629 in counties such as Cheshire, Lancashire, Sussex and Norfolk; and the enthusiasm of some lords lieutenant such as the Earl of Exeter in Northamptonshire and the Earl of Rutland in Lincolnshire, there is contrary evidence of failure. Four counties were censured by the council in 1630 for neglecting to pay the muster-master's salary and, four years later, there were 21 counties that had not sent certificates of muster to the council for three years. Even where deputies did furnish information, it was not necessarily reliable. Thus, in Lancashire, either horse or foot were mustered for 14 out of the 16 years to 1640, missing only 1631 through plague and 1640 itself through demobilisation at the close of the Second Bishops War. Habitual defaulters on horse assessments represented only 13 per cent of those charged between 1625 and 1633 and opposition to the deputies came primarily from freeholders resisting the training of the 'freehold bands'. Yet, in 1639 an independent observer sent by the council reported deficiencies which had been effectively concealed.[7] Similarly, many contemporaries thought little of the trained bands' efficiency in 1639. The military theorist, Colonel Robert Ward dismissed militia musters as 'matters of disport and things of no moment' while the contemporary historian of Gloucester, John Corbet, equally described the trained bands as 'effeminate in courage and incapable of discipline, because their whole course of life was alienated from warlike employment'.[8]

However, it may be that there has been too ready an acceptance of the universal failure of the exact militia and it would appear that the 99,000 or so men in the trained bands in 1639 were in relatively good order in many counties including even strongly Puritan shires such as Northamptonshire. Moreover, the lieutenancy functioned sufficiently well to find the 20,000 levies demanded for the First Bishops

War. The real difficulty arose with the demobilisation of these levies with all the attendant problems of resettlement being followed so swiftly by orders the next spring to begin the process again for the Second Bishops War. With a parliament in the offing which might become an instrument of retribution, deputies were distinctly reluctant to make the same efforts as in the previous years to renew the press. There was also considerable opposition to the requisition of trained bands' weapons and to the possibility that the trained bands themselves might be ordered out of the county, a bill being apparently introduced into the short parliament on 27 April addressing this very issue: it was lost when Parliament was dissolved on 5 May. Simply too great a strain was placed on the stability of local communities and the operation of the lieutenancy became virtually paralysed, the accumulated grievances against the institution finding expression in the Grand Remonstrance of November 1641.

The underlying hostility towards the Crown's policy on the militia and its enforcement by the lieutenancy, as well as the continuing belief that the Crown's discretionary powers in military matters required statutory definition, was also apparent in the growing controversy over a guard for parliament, which developed into a struggle for control of the militia in the spring and early summer of 1641. While this has been exhaustively examined elsewhere,[9] it will be necessary to recount some of the detail. The trained bands of the City and its suburbs of Westminster, Southwark and the Tower Hamlets had a unique significance for the security of the capital and were frequently called upon to keep order during the riots that often occurred in association with traditional holidays such as Shrove Tuesday and May Day. Rumours of royal plots, the presence of disbanded soldiery, the Scottish 'Incident' and the outbreak of rebellion in Ireland necessitating the attempt to raise yet another army had all contributed to a sense of unease at Westminster in the autumn of 1641. Indeed, the City trained bands had already been out for 55 days and ten nights during Strafford's trial earlier in the year.[10] In October 1641, therefore, parliament arranged for a guard from the City, Middlesex and Surrey trained bands under the command of the Earl of Essex.

Upon his return from Scotland on 26 November Charles, who was generally suspicious of the trained bands as a whole, dismissed the guard and appointed his own from the Westminster trained bands under the command of the Earl of Dorset, the significance lying not so much in the choice of militia but in that of the commander. After a clash between the guards and demonstrators Charles agreed to dismiss the guard only for John Pym to move immediately for parliament to substitute another of its own. At the same time the Lords' rejection of a Commons attempt to amend the impressment bill – designed to raise an army for the suppression of the Irish rebellion – to prevent levies being taken out of counties except in the case of invasion prompted a new militia bill sponsored by Sir Arthur Haselrig, which proposed the substitution of a lord general nominated by parliament for the authority of the King over the militia.

In fact, the parliamentary leadership seemed ready to allow the matter to rest but the issue was then forced by Charles ordering a new guard on 9 December and the Commons despatching the Middlesex justice who had signed the warrant to the Tower two days later. The militia bill was given a first reading on 21 December and a second reading on 24 December. Charles's response was to refuse to allow parliament control of the guards at Westminster, and the Commons, in turn, reacted by ordering the 8,000 men of the City trained bands to mount guards throughout the capital. On the following day Charles's attempt to seize the 'five members' justified the Commons' worst fears of the King's future conduct and on 8 January 1642 they requested the City to raise a force for parliament's defence.

The climate of opinion in the Commons was changed by Charles's introduction of troops within the precincts of the House and considerable pressure was exerted on the Lords to gain support for wresting control of the militia from the Crown. The King refused to surrender his sovereignty and on 1 February the Lords agreed to join the Commons in the revolutionary step of assuming control of the militia through an ordinance of both houses. By the militia ordinance, which came into force on 5 March, parliament assumed the right to administer the militia through its own nominees as lords lieutenant. Having left his capital, Charles indicated on 7 February that he might be prepared to accept parliament's nominations as militia commanders subject to his veto. He repeated the offer later in the month but on 2 March both houses voted to place the kingdom in a 'posture of defence'.

That the militia ordinance was illegal without the King's consent was a point of some concern to both sides, the Commons establishing a committee to justify its actions and the ensuing pamphlet campaign generating more tracts than any other issue in either 1642 or early 1643. Subsequently, the eagerness displayed by many members in seizing on a new militia bill forwarded by Charles, which suggested vesting control of the militia in parliament's hands for a year, indicated a desire to work within the context of a familiar legal framework rather than the uncertainties of the ordinance. The King's bill was therefore passed on 22 April but with the crucial amendment of extending its provision to two years and other changes which moved the King to reject it six days later. Charles claimed that he had 'never denied the thing, only the way'[11] but he was now well on his journey to the north and the muster of the City trained bands on 2 May signalled the efforts by parliament to apply its ordinance. A bill sponsored by Sir John Holland sought to achieve some kind of compromise but none was possible over an issue of intrinsic sovereignty and on 12 June the King responded to the challenge by issuing his own commissions of array to summon the militia.

In a sense the enactment of a permissive militia ordinance had begun as a propaganda exercise to involve local communities in practical defiance of the Crown. Its actual effect was to bring hostilities closer, the calculated reference to the dangers of Irish papist intervention in England serving to convince many who executed it that it was necessary to choose sides. However, in winning de facto recognition in those areas where it was implemented, the acceptance of the ordinance did not necessarily imply a willingness to fight the King and it may be that many simply felt more secure as a result of undertaking some measures for local defence in an increasingly threatening situation. At least the ordinance bore some relation to accepted practices in that it was to be administered through the lieutenancy whereas, by comparison, the use of the mandatory commission of array was unfortunate in its appeal to moribund legislation. In theory the array took its authority from the model array of Henry IV but parliament claimed that this had ceased to operate with the passing of the Marian statutes, itself an ironic argument in view of the previous claim by the Crown's opponents that the Marian statutes had been lost upon repeal in 1604.

In part the array enabled Charles to sidestep the disputed control of the militia and the need to work through lords lieutenant of doubtful loyalty and offered some flexibility in the raising of a 'marching army' since forces summoned under array were not subject to the same restriction of county service as the militia. But the unfamiliarity of the array and the fact that its basic text was in Latin added to the difficulties of the King's commissioners. On 20 June, for example, four MPs were successful in disrupting Lord Strange's attempt to implement the array at Preston Moor in Lancashire and it met similar opposition in Worcestershire, Gloucestershire, Devon and Somerset. But parliament was not entirely free of such problems and the ordinance was never effectively completed in either Lancashire or Cheshire due to opposition. Elsewhere some county communities resisted both array and ordinance as in the case of Derbyshire, County Durham, Northumberland, Cumberland, Westmorland and all of Wales except Monmouthshire or enacted both as in Cornwall, where the two sides were deadlocked until the arrival of the King's forces to sway the balance in his favour in late September. In all, the ordinance had been enacted in 23 counties and the array in 14 counties by October 1642.

Just how far the trained bands were a prize for either side clearly depended partly upon the extent to which the exact militia reforms had been implemented in a particular county. Thus, the adherence of the trained bands of Anglesey or Caernarvonshire was unlikely to confer any great military advantage. That of Essex and Lincolnshire conferred little advantage but that of Cheshire rather greater advantage and so on. However, the relative efficiency or otherwise of a county's militia was not as significant as the practical legal difficulty to be overcome in persuading the trained bands to venture beyond the county boundary. Charles met considerable reluctance to such a course in Yorkshire, Lincolnshire, County Durham and Leicestershire and preferred to raise a 'marching army' of volunteers who were not subject to any such parochialism. In consequence, few trained band regiments were incorporated wholly into the royalist field armies. Neither the main 'Oxford army' nor the army of the North Midland Association appear to have contained any at all but the 18 units of the 'Western army' did include one from Cornwall and a regiment and another company from Devon. The Earl of Newcastle did attempt to raise the foot of his northern army from the trained bands and this initially contained the six Yorkshire trained band regiments and a regiment from the Northumberland trained bands. However, the latter and two of the Yorkshire regiments never actually marched with Newcastle's army and Lord

Darcy's regiment was unusual in marching south with the Queen to join the Oxford army in July 1643.[12]

The same difficulty continued to recur during the war itself. Sir Ralph Hopton was unable to persuade the Cornish trained bands to cross the Tamar in January 1643 although they did attend the siege of Lyme Regis in Dorset in the following year. The Radnor trained bands declined to leave their county in February 1643 unless led in person by the Marquess of Hertford and they had to be excluded from a planned operation to reduce Brampton Bryan Castle. Similarly, in May 1643 Arthur, Lord Capel replaced the Shropshire militiamen in his forces as 'soldiers of place' unfit for service.[13] In Dorset one militia officer was reputedly murdered by soldiers refusing to leave the county and in February 1643 those Devon trained bands loyal to parliament refused to invade Cornwall. Even the much vaunted City trained bands, which together with the forces in the suburbs and auxiliaries numbered over 18,000 men in 1643, were far from immune to such failings. In November of that year contingents serving with Sir William Waller's parliamentary army – principally those of the Westminster trained bands – mutinied before Basing House and deserted with cries of 'Home! Home!'. The City regiments also clamoured to return home in April 1644 and one of the Southwark regiments deserted en masse after the battle at Cropredy Bridge in June 1644.

Apart from the legal complications, another factor to be borne in mind is that the militia was just as subject to political fragmentation as other social groups. In such circumstances, it was often the case that the county armouries were more valuable than the regiments themselves. Thus, Charles or his adherents disarmed the trained bands in Derbyshire, Leicestershire, Nottinghamshire, Lincolnshire, Denbighshire and Flintshire and even the well regarded Cheshire trained bands. The arms obtained were utilised to arm volunteers although, on occasion, these would also include those who had been directly recruited from the trained bands such as those from the Glamorgan trained bands who joined the King's forces besieging Gloucester in August 1643.

A third limitation to the employment of the trained bands was the possibility that the personnel had also improved sufficiently in social quality as to render them unwilling or unable to serve for protracted periods in the field. While the political unreliability of the Cheshire trained bands had been the major factor in the decision to disarm them in September 1642, it had also been necessary to gather the harvest. When the Essex and Hertfordshire trained bands with Waller's army mutinied in July 1644 and Waller dismissed them as 'only fit for a gallows here and a hell hereafter', the Committee of Both Kingdoms recognised the Essex men as those in 'trade and employment' who 'cannot well be absent from their occasions' and 'men of that quality and course of life as cannot well bear the difficulties of a soldier's life'.[14] By contrast, the disciplinary problems among the City trained bands may reflect the undermining of social cohesion through rapid wartime expansion in which substitution was permitted and service was no longer restricted to householders.

For all these reasons the trained bands often failed the test of war. Two regiments from the Yorkshire trained bands virtually disintegrated when deployed before Hull in the autumn of 1642, the trained bands of Somerset melted away before Hopton's army in May and June 1643 and those of Cumberland and Westmorland fled without resistance before the invading Scots army in September 1644. The Cornish trained bands also failed to perform well once the King's army in the west began to fall apart in late 1645 and early 1646. However, they had proved valuable in blockading Plymouth earlier in the war and, when deployed purely on local defence, the trained bands generally could be a valuable adjunct to the main armies simply by releasing professional soldiers from more mundane duties. In a sense, of course, it was also a matter of local defence when the City trained bands contributed so greatly to the mobilisation at Turnham Green in November 1642 which, by denying the King access to the capital following his advance after Edgehill, had a decisive impact on the eventual outcome of the war.

If the military record was occasionally unimpressive, the political significance of the militia remained of considerable importance at both national and local level. Both the Uxbridge negotiations in February 1645 and the Newcastle Propositions of July 1646 saw parliament's continued demands for control of the militia for seven years and 20 years respectively. The new model army's heads of the proposals of July 1647 similarly specified a period for parliamentary control of the militia set at ten years. As part of his concessionary policy Charles yielded to the latter demand during the course of 1648. During the war itself the control of most local forces in parliamentary areas had passed into the hands of the county committees. In the same way that many of those committees progressively fell under the influence of elements other than those of the older county elites so, too, was the same process to be observed in many militia forces.

In Cornwall the militia continued to be controlled even after the war by a militia committee which was still composed over-whelmingly of gentry as late as 1659 and in counties such as Suffolk and Sussex where traditional elites also remained in control, it can perhaps be assumed that this also applied to the militia. In Somerset, however, militia officers became of much lower social eminence than hitherto. By 1650 commissions were held by a South Petherton innkeeper, a Crewkerne postman and an illiterate yeoman. In Buckinghamshire, where only one member of the pre-war elite remained in the county to command local forces by the end of 1643, militia command devolved upon two minor farmers, a paper manufacturer and Thomas Shelborne, whose rise is a classic illustration of the social mobility created by a war in which fewer candidates were available for a multiplicity of new appointmemnts. *Mercurius Aulicus* described Shelborne as John Hampden's former shepherd 'better able to conduct sheepe then Dragoones' and, while some allowance must be granted for the journal's royalist bias, even the parliamentary commander at Newport Pagnell, Sir Samuel Luke, referred to Shelborne as a pasture keeper 'and one of the meaner rank of men'.[15] It was not surprising, therefore, if one proposal in 1648 was for a reorganised national militia which would take local control out of the hands of committees and return it to the gentry. More important, however, was the relationship of the militia forces to the new model army after 1645.

Charles's total regular forces had amounted to no more than a thousand men before 1642 but, at the height of the war, there were perhaps 110,000 men under arms in England and in January 1645 parliament created a standing army of some 22,000 men exclusive of supernumeraries and other provincial forces. Many surplus troops were subsequently reduced but the new model, which through the self-denying ordinance had become an army open to 'talents' and a radical political instrument, declined to be reduced in 1647 unless its arrears were met. The growing militancy of the new model brought about the effective collapse of a parliament torn between the demands of the army and those of the City, one aspect of the dispute again revolving around the issue of the control of the militia.

The City trained bands had been a prey to party strife since the end of the war. Thus, when parliament returned control to the corporation in May 1647 the City's presbyterian faction purged those officers of the independent faction sympathetic towards the army. Three new regiments were raised by the lord mayor who mustered the trained bands as a whole upon pain of death to defend the City in June 1647. However, the majority of the men chose to remain at home rather than follow their Presbyterian officers. Parliament resolved on 21 July to take back control of the City trained bands but was forced to relinquish this just five days later when invaded by a mob. The army itself then marched into the capital on 6 August to take effective control. At that point, if not before, a situation was initiated in which the militia as a whole could either be regarded as a supplement to a standing army or as an alternative. In this regard a tract of August 1648, *The Peaceable Militia or the Cause and Cure of the late and present War*, was significant in being the first to synthesise popular arguments against the existence of a standing army which threatened political liberties and to advocate placing trust in the militia instead.

The ability of the militia to replace the standing army was being tested even as the pamphlet was published by the abortive royalist risings that marked the second civil war in 1648. In Kent the trained bands failed to detect let alone prevent the raising of royalist forces but, by contrast, 5,600 men from the Suffolk and Essex trained bands performed creditably in support of the army at the siege of Colchester. Nevertheless, interest in the constitutional issue had been effectively revived and, having voted to revive the old militia powers in May, parliament passed a new militia ordinance on 2 December 1648 vesting control firmly in the hands of the Presbyterians and of parliament. Two earlier ordinances in July 1644 had placed the responsibility for raising the militia on property owners with lands or goods worth £100 or more, these new rates being the first formally set since the repeal of the Marian statutes in 1604. The new ordinance now carefully set down the powers relating to the militia and replaced deputy lieutenants with new militia commissioners. However, four days later, Pride's Purge created a 'rump' sympathetic to the army which immediately repealed the new ordinance though it remained a model for the future and the role of commissioners was retained. After much debate, the rump's own militia bill on 11 July 1650 vested control of the militia in hands more inclined to regard it as a supplement rather than a counterweight to the army under the jurisdiction of the council of state. Again, local control was in the hands of commissioners, who now received statutory powers to undertake measures such as disarming or detaining suspected dissidents, administering oaths, patrolling the shires and administering funds. The militia would now be supported by assessment on all those with an income of over £100 per annum or £200 worth of property. Having been due to expire in January 1651 the rump's measures were extended until May 1651 and then revived on 12 August following the Scots' invasion of England. But the forces thus raised were allowed to lapse at the end of the Worcester campaign and the legislation itself once more expired in December 1651. Ironically, the militia had performed far better with troops primarily drawn from the Essex, Norfolk and Suffolk trained bands comprising a third of the field army in what has been described as the interregnum militia's 'crowning achievement'.[16] Other county forces garrisoned vital centres such as Ludlow, Hereford and Bristol and mobile forces in the northern shires such as Yorkshire responded remarkably well to the threat of invasion, albeit primarily due to their hatred of the Scots. Moreover, 3,000 horse and dragoons were also raised from the militia for six months' service with the army from 1 May 1651.

With the crisis safely past, the first parliament of the protectorate returned to the attack on the army urging its reduction from its current strength of 50,000 men and attempting to wrest back control of the militia. It was dissolved in January 1655 without having passed any bills while the militia itself was again briefly revived amid rumours of fresh royalist conspiracy. However, with the appointment of the major-generals in October 1655, the revival took the form of a 'select' militia reduced in size to barely 6,200 horse and 200 foot and resembling experimentation with volunteer forces in June 1651. The reduction helped to lessen the tax burden on at least those gentry who had not fought against parliament, since the new militia were all volunteers paid £8 per annum and maintained by a decimation tax on 'malignants'. In practice, the force, which amounted to little more than one troop per county, was a kind of mounted gendarmerie capable of being utilised anywhere in the country as a whole and the very antithesis of traditional militia. When parliament reassembled in September 1656, therefore, there was considerable criticism of the select militia as well as of the major-generals and, especially, of the decimation tax. Moreover, the concept of the citizen militia as the only acceptable instrument of military power capable of guaranteeing individual liberty was materially advanced through James Harrington's contemporary tract, *The Commonwealth of Oceania*.

The major difficulty with the select militia was that not only was the decimation tax of dubious legality but it broke the established link between those who bore the burden of maintaining the militia and those who did service on their behalf. In fact, due to the uneven distribution of the disaffected the select militia often had to be subsidised from other funds including those vested in the militia commissioners for the support of the general militia. Thus, in Hampshire only 50 per cent of the funds needed to maintain even a reduced establishment could be found from the decimation tax alone and the select militia soon ceased to function. The force as a whole was effectively removed altogether through the failure of a bill to renew the decimation tax in 1657 although there was some attempt to call it out both during an invasion scare in February of that year and on Cromwell's death in September 1658. The rump re-embodied the select militia between May and June 1659 but it was finally disbanded in September 1659.

Nevertheless, in many other counties besides Hampshire it also seems likely that the select militia had only a paper existence after 1656 and, in fact, the same was true of the general militia. In Norfolk the militia appears to have had no existence at all between 1651 and 1659 while there was no apparent activity in Essex between 1651 and 1655 and no revival in that county as there was in some others in 1659.[17] Local militia commissions did largely remain in existence as in Suffolk and they were regarded as sufficiently important for there to be official concern in July 1659 at the number of radicals, sectaries and Quakers serving on them despite the fact that army officers were also increasingly appointed as members through the 1650s as in Lincolnshire and Hampshire. In 1659 the restored rump again tried to revive parliamentary control with new bills in July while Booth's rebellion saw a temporary cessation of hostilities between army and parliament and the hasty expansion of both militia and volunteer forces. But parliament was dissolved once the crisis was over and both volunteers and militia disbanded in September 1659. In any case, financial difficulties had arisen through the perceived delay on the part of the authorities since 1651 to reimburse the month's pay which could be demanded in advance of embodiment from those liable to raise militiamen. The resentment greatly hindered the calling out of militia forces in Cornwall and Devon in 1659 while militia commissioners were actually kidnapped in both Staffordshire and Suffolk as a security for the men's pay.

In December 1659 the rump ordered the dissolution of all forces it had not expresssly authorised but when secluded members of parliament were readmitted in February 1660 they, in turn, passed a new militia bill disbanding all local levies raised by the rump and appointing new militia commissions. Monck approved the bill despite army opposition and thus parliament and, with it, the gentry finally reasserted control over the militia to guarantee its survival as a counter to the standing army.

Within four months of Charles II's return to England in May 1660 the Commons was considering a systematic programme for disbanding the new model and, with the exception of some regiments retained at Dunkirk for another two years, it was all but completed by December. The absence of any enabling legislation meant that those regular forces that could be raised by the Crown would remain limited by its financial difficulties while the very real dangers posed by republican conspiracies such as Venner's plot in January 1661 could only be met by recourse to the militia or those large numbers of volunteers who had appeared in many counties pending the reorganisation of the militia. To a large extent the three militia bills passed between 1661 and 1663 (13 Car II c 6, 13–14 Car II c 3 and 15 Car II c 4) were an indemnification for measures already put into effect, the privy council having reissued the 1558 statutes in December 1660 as a temporary expedient. The militia acts were also firmly rooted in the recent past, the interregnum arrangements being especially important in establishing a financial framework for the future.

Following the drift of the tracts that had appeared in the closing years of the protectorate, parliament appeared to surrender command of the militia to the Crown through the royal prerogative, the very right denied Charles I in 1642. In reality, Charles II appeared too impoverished and indolent to realise any of the few military ambitions to which he might aspire and effective control devolved upon the lords lieutenant, who were restored in July 1660 as the principal channel of influence and patronage within the county communities. Through the lieutenancy, control was also restored to the gentry, who were now rather more prepared to make the system work than had been the case before the war through their recognition of the militia as the main bulwark against disorder and a guarantee of the political settlement.[18] However, a commitment to the militia was not necessarily universal and in Lancashire at least the actual arrangements for the militia were far more loosely organised than other aspects of local administration. It could also be argued that the relatively ready co-operation for raising a militia in 1651 compared to say 1640 had already marked a considerable change in attitudes towards the militia and a gradual reinstatement of its perceived position as a principal component of the nation's defences given the reduction of the standing army.

The basis of service remained the possession of property, echoing the ancient precedents of the Statute of Westminster and before, but with a system of rating owing more to the monthly assessments of the civil war and the decimation tax. However, it was now generally recognised that those of wealth would not serve personally and that the basic manpower would consist of hirelings and substitutes. Thus, those with an income of over £50 per annum or an estate worth £600 per annum would be liable to provide horse. Property owners worth less than the stipulated minimum levels could be joined in groups to find horse or foot under the 1662 act and the 1663 act enabled petty constables to raise foot from parishes in respect of estates liable to find less than one man. In effect, the numbers raised in each county would depend upon the value of property as a whole and the ratio of horse to foot upon the actual distribution of that property between larger and smaller estates. In addition, those property owners liable to find men – 'finders' – would also contribute to the provision of ammunition and other expenses through a rate based on a quarter of monthly assessment and known generally as 'trophy money'. Finders also had to pay men under training at 1s 0d a day for foot and 2s 0d (2s 6d from 1663) for horse, regiments being expected to muster for four days' training annually and companies for two days up to four times each year. If the militia was ordered out for longer periods, finders were liable to provide a month's pay in advance which would be fully reimbursed subsequently by the Crown before another month's pay could be charged.

At first the Crown was authorised additionally to raise a sum equal to the county monthly quota based on the 1661 assessment for each of three years in order to maintain the militia in service during the period of greatest threat and this was utilised from 1662 to 1664 when it lapsed. The ability to create a standing militia in this way naturally meant less need for a standing army and the restoration militia was thus tailored very much to parliamentary rather than royal perceptions despite the command being placed unequivocally in the hands of the King. Charles would have preferred a militia not unlike that of 1655 and there were attempts to create a more specialised force but this was anathema to the gentry and, in accordance with the balance of opinion against specialised forces, the 1663 act also abolished the trained bands with the exception of those of the City. These technically continued in existence until 1794 and by a curious anomaly, the City lieutenancy is still able to levy 'trophy money' under the 1662 legislation.

Although the burden upon the gentry might at first appear onerous, only very small amounts were actually charged and the numbers liable to be charged had been greatly increased. Moreover, since the gentry were still under no statutory obligation to declare actual income the militia assessments were only rough calculations on the part of the assessors and worked frequently to the advantage of those assessed. In Herefordshire, for example, the assessors were refused admission to Gatley Park in 1666 so 'tooke the advantage of a foote path through the middle of the parke from one side to the other' as well as what gossip they could glean from the locals in order to assess the acreage.[19] There was also frequent slackness in the collection of assessments but despite the discrimination with which smaller estates often bore a proportionally greater charge than larger estates, the adaptation of monthly assessments to militia rating had eliminated most of the older inequalities. All estates in a county were now charged – even non-residents – and no estate was charged with finding both horse and foot.

A difficulty arising from the assessment system, however, was that a militia distribution based entirely on the geographical distribution of property did not make much actual military sense. This was especially so when there were so many tasks for a military force to perform immediately after the restoration. The Norfolk militia was engaged in disarming 'phanaticks' as early as April 1660 and similar action by militia and volunteers had necessitated indemnification as a matter of urgency. Through the application of the special sums raised for the militia the Crown was able subsequently to maintain a standing guard of one twentieth of the militia for fourteen-day periods at a time from 1663 to 1666 although in smaller counties such as Cumberland and Westmorland a troop or company would perform the duty in rotation.

A regular task was seizure of arms, and the militia was also responsible for the active harassment of potential troublemakers. This invariably implied dissenters against whom were arraigned a variety of punitive legislative measures. Not all counties pursued dissenters to the same extent since Crown policy was at best ambiguous and, as in the case of the militia's efficiency, much depended upon the attitude of the lord lieutenant. In Norfolk, where moderates controlled the lieutenancy, little was done and in Hampshire, 'having no mind to meddle', the militia allowed the Quaker George Fox to escape from Ringwood in May 1663.[20] By contrast, the militia was used extensively against dissenters in Durham, Lancashire, Hertfordshire and Buckinghamshire. In Wiltshire militiamen went so far as to wreck a Quaker burial ground.

Other duties included the dismantling of town fortifications while, in the capital, the trained bands were a key factor in maintaining order. Their performance during Venner's rising when barely twenty rebels had held off both City trained bands and the King's guards for half an hour had not been impressive but, thereafter, they were more successful. Certainly, the established custom of City trained band officers and NCOs being trained by the Artillery Company, which received the additional title of 'Honourable' in 1685, assisted in promoting greater professionalism as did membership of other military clubs such as that in Cripplegate. In the autumn of 1662 they patrolled London streets against fifth monarchist plots, enforced the conventicles in 1670 and, above all, patrolled the City by night and day from October 1678 following the murder of Justice Godfrey until December 1681 to ensure the Crown's control of the capital during the exclusion crisis. Initially, a full regiment with anything from 1,252 to 1,660 men did duty each day but the number required was then progressively reduced in March and July 1679 and May 1680 although temporarily reinstated to two-company strength between September 1680 and the end of the crisis. Such deployment on the streets not only served to prevent 'popish' conspiracies but, at the same time, the manipulation by the Crown of the numbers called out also prevented Whig exploitation of popular fears by making the overall danger appear much less threatening.[21]

The militia appears to have been reasonably adept in curtailing political opposition to the restored monarchy although it should be noted that the evidence of activity in counties such as Hampshire, Norfolk and Lancashire needs to be balanced by that of far less commitment in the western counties of Dorset, Somerset and Wiltshire where major deficiencies remained and the militia itself appeared to be far less popular.[22] The militia was also generally less well regarded by contemporaries for its role in defence of the country against external aggressors. The Second Dutch War between February 1665 and August 1667 brought two relatively brief direct crises, the first from June to July 1666 and the second from May to July 1667. The first saw beacons watched, patrols mounted in maritime shires and a partial mobilisation of the horse but the danger passed rapidly. But in 1667 the militia of 14 maritime counties was ordered out in May and a concentration organised in June when the Dutch appeared off the Thames. On 10 June the Dutch destroyed ships anchored off Chatham and effected a landing against which the defenders, including detachments from the Essex and Kent militia, proved powerless. When the Dutch landed at Landguard Fort near Harwich on 2 July the defence, which comprised almost only Suffolk militia, did successfully drive them off but largely because the attackers believed that the fort was too strongly held.

In the circumstances, the militia had performed reasonably well but it simply could not be drawn out for longer periods than the month or so it had been kept out in 1666 and 1667. In response, the Crown attempted reforms but these were frustrated by its fraudulent appropriation of funds raised for the militia to other purposes. Some funds were intended to be spent on a new 'select militia' of three regiments of horse, a regiment of foot and 17 independent troops, views having been expressed in some quarters as to the greater economy, proficiency and social order that might result from a smaller and more carefully selected force under more closely centralised royal control. However, the force was dismissed almost at once in September 1666 though temporarily re-embodied in 1667. The controversy over illegal diversion of militia funds thus effectively destroyed any possibility of co-operative reform between Crown and the counties and the militia declined gradually in effectiveness.

While some county forces such as those of Hampshire or Lancashire and the West Riding of Yorkshire readily mustered as required in the late 1670s – though merely mustering was no guarantee of efficiency – and there is evidence of activity in both Oxfordshire and the Blackburn hundred of Lancashire in 1681, many others were allowed to lapse. There is little evidence of regular musters in western counties while, in the North Riding, the militia had not met for two, three or four years at a time. The militia of Cumberland did not assemble at all between 1676 and 1679. However, despite the absence of comparable traditional institutions of local county government north of the border, the 20,000 foot and 2,000 horse of the Scottish militia raised under the 1663 act was noticeably more efficient than that in England. Indeed, there were some fears that a 1669 act pertaining to the Scottish militia might enable the King to bring it into England.

The evidence of increasing difficulties in England and Wales ironically coincided with regular ritual employment of the militia as the symbol of the health of the body politic in the rhetoric of the continuing controversy over a standing army. The 'country' party in the Commons kept demanding a reorganisation of the militia, tracts still equated the force with political liberty and large numbers of MPs were content to identify themselves as militia officers. A bill was brought forward in November 1678 to replace the standing army totally with the militia but nothing was actually done to effect reform, a situation persisting well into the eighteenth century. Partly, of course, this reflected the fact that the militia was merely a convenient tactical lever to be used against the 'court' and it also fell increasingly foul of the turbulent nature of party politics.

Even before the acession of James II the militia had been prey to political factionalism. Danby had purged several lords lieutenant in 1675–6 and individual county forces had also witnessed factional disputes as in Kent between 1660 and 1669, in Norfolk between 1666 and 1683 and in Cumberland between 1678 and 1683. But these were relatively minor compared to the experiences of James's reign. The crucial turning point was probably the militia's alleged inept performance in face of Monmouth's rising in June and July 1685 although it is likely that James would have neglected the force anyway. Not unexpectedly in view of its previous failings, the militia in the western counties proved especially fragile. The Dorset militia failed to prevent Monmouth's landing and holed up in Bridport while the Devon militia disintegrated before his advance on Axminster and some joined the rebels. Of two regiments of Somerset militia, half fled and at least two companies went over to Monmouth while the royal commander-in-chief, Lord Feversham, sent two regiments of Hampshire militia away rather than trust it and kept the three regiments of Wiltshire militia he retained – some 3,000 men – well out of the battle of Sedgemoor until Monmouth's ragged army was broken and the pursuit had begun. Monmouth's men had equally boasted that 'three valiant rebels may beat three score of them'.[23]

Nevertheless, the militia had performed usefully outside the west in maintaining order, releasing regulars for the field army, intercepting recruits heading westwards, and preventing Monmouth permanently occupying areas through which his forces had passed. In fact Monmouth himself was apprehended by a patrol of the Sussex militia when he was attempting to reach a boat at Poole. But the militia was too costly and too inflexible an instrument for the kind of policing force that the King had in mind and James and his supporters were quick to criticise the force in the first parliamentary session of the reign in the autumn of 1685. A bill to reform the militia failed when the session was dissolved and the King turned to the army as a more suitable agent of central government, expanding it from 8,800 men in 1685 to a paper establishment of 34,000 by 1688 and spreading troops throughout the country to exert government control. The army was also used as a ready source of loyal supporters to replace those purged from lieutenancies, magistracies and militia commands in 1686 and 1687.

By 1688 Roman Catholics had been appointed as lords lieutenant in 16 counties and at least a third of all deputy lieutenants were also Catholics. In the process the militia itself was ignored. In May 1687 the forces of Cornwall, Devon, Dorset and Somerset were ordered not to muster again until further notice. By 1688 there was virtually no militia in Staffordshire, that of Lincolnshire had mustered only once and that of Essex was greatly disorganised. Only the City trained bands had been maintained with any enthusiasm, presumably through James's recognition of the importance of securing the loyalty of the capital although co-operation was also encouraged through the judicious threat of introducing regulars into London. Thus, when James was faced with the expected invasion by William of Orange and turned to the militia it was far too late to repair the damage of the previous three years.

There was distinct hostility among the gentry of Yorkshire, Warwickshire, Kent and Essex to James's attempt to entice them back into the militia to serve under inexperienced Catholics. The militias of Norfolk, Dorset and Gloucestershire proved reasonably efficient and the latter intercepted Lord Lovelace and 70 followers en route to join William, but the Isle of Wight militia was badly disaffected and during December 1688 all or part of the forces of Oxfordshire, Buckinghamshire, Northamptonshire, Leicestershire and Nottinghamshire declared for William. In Norfolk, too, the lieutenancy eventually declared for a free parliament and the militia turned to disarming Catholics while the forces in the west once more failed to prevent invasion.

After 1688 there were still frequent emergencies in which the assistance of the militia was required. In June 1690, for example, the force was called out for over a month following the naval battle off Beachy Head which briefly exposed Britain to French and Jacobite invasion. Even the *posse comitatus* was summoned at Torbay but the French landed and sacked only Teignmouth. In May 1692 some militia units were also called out and the customary arms searches undertaken when the French again threatened to land James back on English soil. An invasion threat recurred in 1696–7 and there were internal security duties to perform in the wake of the assassination plot in May 1696. Yet another French and Jacobite threat emerged with Scotland as the likely target in 1708–9 and, of course, there were Jacobite invasions in 1715 and 1745. There were also threats from the Spanish in 1718–9 and 1726–7 and, in May 1744, a serious surprise French naval concentration upon their entry into the war between Britain and Spain. On other occasions purely localised dangers presented themselves as when the Norfolk militia was mustered against privateers in both 1694 and 1697.

Yet, despite such threats, the militia still deteriorated. One factor was the lack of interest in the Commons and the legislative confusion that resulted. Comprehensive reforms were advocated by pamphleteers such as Andrew Fletcher of Saltoun and John Toland. But such theoretical military constructions as those advanced by Fletcher, who envisaged a Scottish militia as a means of institutionalising his country's autonomy within a new federal British system, or other anti-army ideologists such as John Trenchard and Walter Moyle bordered on fantasy amid continuing invasion threats in which reliance on defence by the militia alone was hardly practicable. In any case, the various bills actually proposed were invariably lost when sessions ended and those passed were but temporary expedients.

In 1690, for example, an act enabled the Crown to call out the militia for a year without the necessity of reimbursing the month's pay advanced by finders before the commencement of the subsequent month's duty as required under the 1663 legislation. The need to reimburse the first month's pay was again suspended by an act of 1715 but this lapsed in 1720, was renewed for seven years in 1722 and renewed again for a year in 1734. Once more the measure lapsed with the result that after 1735 the militia could not theoretically be mustered again until pay advanced by counties in the past had been repaid by the Crown. When the crisis arose in 1745 the problem was accentuated by the prorogation of parliament, which could not meet until the King's return from Hanover, and a bill had to be passed through all its stages in a single day in November 1745 since those lords lieutenant who had summoned the militia had done so illegally. Even where the militia was called out enormous difficulties presented themselves. In 1715 the small militias of Cumberland and Westmorland had prevented total occupation by the Jacobite army. Similarly, the Lancashire militia, which had not received any training since the end of William's reign, fought well beside the army at Preston although an attempt to summon the posse to Penrith failed through the general population's lack of and of familiarity with weapons. In 1745, however, there was almost universal failure.

The lord lieutenant of Cumberland and Westmorland held out no great hopes that his forces would prove effective and there was confusion as to whether or not the force should be employed as a single entity or split between the two counties. At Carlisle militiamen deserted en masse and surrendered the city on being allowed to disperse by the Jacobites on a promise of not serving in the field again for a year and a day. In Cheshire the militia rolls had been lost and no arms could be found while the county force in Lancashire was also ill equipped and had not been mustered since its relative success thirty years previously. The lord lieutenant considered it both unfit for service and unwilling to stomach a fight in November 1745 and withdrew it to Liverpool to put those arms it did possess on ships in the port to prevent capture. Small wonder that a captured Jacobite code gave 'small beer' as the word for the militia.[24] Militiamen did become bolder once the Jacobites began to retreat in December 1745 and a useful role was found in delaying the Scots by breaking roads and felling trees. Effective pursuit was ended by the fear of French intervention which also led to militia being called out in the southern maritime counties: there was even one false report that the French had landed at Pevensey.

Given the legal and other problems, it proved easier to raise ad hoc bodies of volunteers in counties such as the East Riding, Lancashire, Durham, Cumberland, Northumberland and Kent where between 4,000 and 5,000 men gathered on Barham Down in December 1745. Thirteen regiments were raised for temporary service with the army by various noblemen acting under the royal warrant and it was also utilised for local units in Yorkshire. At Carlisle a unit was raised through the agency of the lieutenancy but others were raised entirely outside the lieutenancy structure by the royal sign manual with associations being formed at Bristol, Exeter, Kensington and Spitalfields as well as by the Bishop of Durham. One allegedly comprised 1,000 Sussex smugglers while that of 530 men raised in Northamptonshire in April 1744 consisted of substantial freeholders and yeomen and their sons. At Exeter wealthier tradesmen declined the 9*d* a day pay being offered as worthy only of 'mercenaries' while requiring 'common men' to take an oath undertaking not to sell the uniforms with which they had been provided.[25] Elsewhere, the lieutenancy also resorted to the *posse comitatus* as at Newcastle in September 1745 and in Kent in January 1746 or summoned men through 'special commission' as in Sussex.

Rather similarly, the Scottish Militia Act of 1663 had been allowed to lapse without provision for renewal being made in the Act of Union in 1707. Queen Anne had vetoed a bill – the last use of a royal veto – to remedy the deficiency in 1708 presumably through fear of Jacobite influence since the magistracy had been widely infiltrated by Jacobites when extended to Scotland. The abolition of the privy council in Scotland had also left no authority capable of naming lords lieutenant to vacancies and there was thus comparatively little that could be done to meet the invasion in 1745. Only the Edinburgh militia appears to have been called out and the Duke of Argyll resorted to raising a regiment of 'fencibles' outside the lieutenancy system.

In reality, little could have been expected from a military force whose members received only twelve days' training annually in the best of circumstances and which, in most cases, had not actually mustered seriously in a generation. The militia could still be employed in attacks upon the standing army such as that mounted in 1697 and, in turn, ritually assaulted by supporters of the Crown. But while serving to give the impression of a proper concern for defence on the part of the politicians, this process did not lead them to abandon a primary concern with cutting costs. Thus, the Commons contrived to prevent the development of an efficient militia whilst simultaneously contesting the expansion of the army. The militia was left ineffectual and the butt of popular ridicule although the celebrated barbs of Dryden's *Cymon and Iphigenia* or Fielding's *Tom Jones* fell within a tradition that had endured at least since Beaumont and Fletcher had satirised the City trained bands in their *The Knight of the Burning Pestle* in 1610–11.

Nevertheless, the failures of 1745 and the French invasion threat of the previous year did begin a new agitation for a reformed militia as an adequate and more cost-effective means of home defence. Since the country as a whole still set its face against a large standing army the only viable alternative to an efficient militia would have been the importation of foreign mercenaries at times of crisis but that was equally undesirable. The agitation was to reach a climax with the loss of Minorca in 1756, an operation which the French had originally intended as a diversion for invasion itself. There was to be a far more ambitious French plan in 1759 but by this time the militia had finally been reformed and an entirely new kind of force created which, through conscription, was to break with the past and to affect society in ways which the militia of old could never have done.

Notes

1   A. Fletcher, *A County Community in Peace and War: Sussex, 1600–1660* (Longman, London, 1975), p. 187.

2   Boynton, *Elizabethan Militia*, p. 234.

3   W. P. D. Murphy (ed), *The Earl of Hertford's Lieutenancy Papers, 1603–1612* (Wilts Record Society, 1969), p. 155.

4   S. J. Stearns, 'Conscription and English Society in the 1620s', *Journal of British Studies* XI, 2, 1972, pp. 1–23.

5   *CSPD*, 1627–8, p. 488 quoted in L. G. Schwoerer, *No Standing Armies* (Johns Hopkins University Press, Baltimore, 1974), p. 26.

6   Bodleian Library, Ms Firth c.4, fos 442–3.

7   D. P. Carter, 'The Exact Militia in Lancashire, 1625–40', *Northern*

History 11, 1975, pp. 87–106.

8   Robert Ward, *Animadversions of Warre* (London, 1639), p. 30; John Corbet, *A True and Importientt History of the Military Government of the Citie of Gloucester* (London, 1647), p. 11.

9   L. G. Schwoerer, 'The Fittest Subject for a King's Quarrel: An Essay on the Militia Controversy, 1641–42', *Journal of British Studies* X, 1971, pp. 45–76; L. C. Nagel, 'The Militia of London, 1641–49', Unpub. Ph.D., London, 1982, pp. 26–41.

10   K. J. Lindley, 'Riot Prevention and Control in Early Stuart London', *Transactions of the Royal Historical Society* 33, 1983, pp. 109–26.

11   R. Ashton, *The English Civil War: Conservatism and Revolution, 1603–1649* (Weidenfeld & Nicolson, London, 1978), p. 164.

12   Calculated from M. Bennett, 'The Royalist War Effort in the North Midlands, 1642–46', Unpub. Ph.D., Loughborough, 1986; P. R. Newman, 'The Royalist Army in Northern England, 1642–45', Unpub. Ph.D., York, 1978; I. Roy, 'The Royalist Army in the First Civil War', Unpub. D.Phil, Oxford, 1963; and M. D. G. Wanklyn, 'The King's Armies in the West of England, 1642–46', Unpub. M.A., Manchester, 1966.

13   R. Hutton, *The Royalist War Effort, 1642–1646* (Longman, London, 1982), p. 61.

14   Nagel, 'Militia of London', p. 198; J. P. Kenyon, *The Civil Wars of England* (Weidenfeld, London, 1988), p. 124.

15   *Mercurius Aulicus* 17 Feb 1644; H. G. Tibbutt (ed), *The Letter Books of Sir Samuel Luke, 1644–5* (HMSO, London, 1963), p. 291.

16   J. G. A. Ive, 'The Local Dimensions of Defence: The Standing Army and the Militia in Norfolk, Suffolk and Essex, 1649–1660', Unpub. Ph.D., Cambridge, 1986, p. 341.

17   Ive, 'Local Dimensions', pp. 228–36; A. M. Coleby, *Central Government and the Localities: Hampshire, 1649–89* (Cambridge University Press, 1987), p. 37. Ive is the best source for interregnum militia arrangements but see also H. M. Reese, 'The Military Presence in England, 1649–60', Unpub. D.Phil., Oxford, 1981.

18   A. Fletcher, *Reform in the Provinces: The Government of Stuart England* (Yale University Press, New Haven, 1986), pp. 319–31.

19   M. A. Faraday (ed), *Herefordshire Militia Assessments of 1663* (Royal Historical Society, 1972), p. 9.

20   Coleby, *Central Government*, p. 140.

21   D. Allen, 'The Role of the London Trained Bands in the Exclusion Crisis, 1678–81', *English Historical Review* 87, 1972, pp. 287–303.

22   P. J. Norrey, 'The Restoration Regime in Action: The Relationship between Central and Local Government in Dorset, Somerset and Wiltshire, 1660–78', *Historical Journal* 31, 4, 1988, pp. 789–812.

23   J. Childs, *The Army, James II and the Glorious Revolution* (Manchester University Press, 1980), p. 8.

24   R. C. Jarvis (ed), *Collected Papers on the Jacobite Risings* (Manchester University Press, 1971), II, p. 98.

25   Cecil Sebag Montefiore, *A History of the Volunteer Force: From the Earliest Times to 1860* (Archibald Constable, London, 1908), pp. 78–80.

3

Compulsion and its alternatives (1745–1802)

Apart from a number of temporary impressment acts for debtors, vagrants and other marginal members of society during the eighteenth century, the regular army was not recruited by conscription until 1916. Paradoxically, compulsion in one form or another was a feature of military obligation for home defence from earliest times and no more so than between 1757 and 1831 when the so-called 'new militia' was liable to be raised through a compulsory ballot of the able-bodied male population. Although falling short of true conscription, the experience was to colour British attitudes towards military service well into the twentieth century, not least in the popular preference for raising bodies of volunteers rather than militia.

Major invasion scares always have a tendency to concentrate minds and 1745 was no exception especially when the issue of militia reform also offered the chance of political advantage. There was now relatively little mileage to be had from fears of a standing army when its existence was so demonstrably necessary for defence but such an army still provided too many opportunities for Crown patronage to be safely ignored. Thus, the opposition masked underlying motive with military arguments concerning the cheapness of a militia as compared to any further expansion of the army. Simultaneously, the intellectual debate had also largely ceased to focus on constitutional issues and Scottish militia enthusiasts such as Alexander Carlyle and David Hume now stressed the benefits of partnership between army and militia. In particular, proponents of the militia such as George Townshend argued that it could release more regulars for service overseas and obviate the need to import foreign mercenaries for home defence.

A bill to reform the militia was therefore brought forward as early as February 1746 but this and later efforts in 1752 and 1753 foundered. Agitation was revived at the beginning of the Seven Years War when only 30,000 regular troops were available for home defence and there was the usual recourse to mercenaries. Townshend's new bill was defeated in the Lords but the loss of Minorca in June 1756 enabled him to exert additional pressure with a stream of orchestrated petitions and when Pitt entered office in the autumn a new bill was a foregone conclusion. Pitt's temporary ejection from office delayed matters but a bill finally passed the hurdle of the Lords in May 1757. The new legislation (30 Geo II c 25) was not quite the scheme originally intended, a clarifying act being required in June 1758 and a further act to extend the provisions for seven years in March 1762. Thus, the 'new' militia was not finally made permanent until April 1769.

The tortured progress of the new militia owed much to the nature of Townshend's creation. Britain was alone among leading European states in lacking a fully organised citizen reserve for the army and Townshend was undoubtedly influenced by the example of continental states such as Brandenburg-Prussia, Piedmont and Spain where the militia was subject to a ballot. However, he compromised the military advantages of compulsion for home defence with the desire of the gentry to shift the burden of military obligation firmly down the social scale. The act that finally emerged envisaged a ballot of able-bodied males to produce a force of 32,000 men serving a three-year term and training on some 20 days annually between May and October. However, there were numerous exemptions including deputy lieutenants, parish officials administering the scheme, clergy and teachers and, in addition, substitution was permitted and exemption by a £10 fine. Effectively, the new militia introduced a tax on manpower rather than genuine conscription.

The burden now lodged on the poorer members of society was widely recognised and as the lieutenancies proceeded to implement the act widespread disturbances occurred. In all, 13 counties experienced riots in late August and early September 1757 with Lincolnshire and the North and East Ridings the most badly affected. The underlying cause of resentment was occasionally manifest as in Lincolnshire where the Duke of Ancaster was told that the rioters complained of poor men being kept alive merely to fight for the landed. Similarly, an anonymous letter addressed to two of the county's justices enquiring, 'if a Ticket be drawn and to fall To a Poor Man's lot to go that has a large family which of you Buntin Ars'd Coated fellows will maintain his family …', has been described as a 'middle class manifesto'.[1]

Certainly farmers appeared to be encouraging opposition through a disinclination to incur the burden of the upkeep of militiamen's families. However, there were other contributory factors such as misunderstanding of legislation, which was rarely explained adequately. The absence of any mention of pay – it was intended to incorporate this in separate legislation – aroused suspicion and there was a fear that enlistment implied overseas service. Purely local influences including opposition to mill machinery in Yorkshire and high grain prices in Lincolnshire were also in evidence.

The riots usually followed the announcement that ballot lists would be drawn up. Indeed, in Nottinghamshire the listing itself was equated with David's sin of numbering the people and lists were destroyed, officials abused and threatened. Although mostly spontaneous there were also cases where disturbance spread through example and, in face of the cumulative threat to order, lords lieutenant capitulated and suspended proceedings in the East Riding, Lincolnshire and Bedfordshire. Elsewhere there was more resolute action but all the disturbances subsided quickly once the initial demonstration had been made. Nevertheless, the riots had been serious enough to warrant concessions and the 1758 act sought specifically to allay grievances. Deputy lieutenants and parish officials lost their exemption while volunteers were to be accepted to spare parishes from the ballot. Allowances would also be paid from local rates to the families of militiamen on service. Subsequently, a further concession in 1762 eased the burden on the parish rates by exempting those with three or more children under the age of 10 born in wedlock – from 1786 to 1796 those with children under the age of 10 were exempted, and after 1806 all with those children under 14.

Above all, the 1758 act also sought to prevent lieutenancies from defaulting on their obligations by laying down a timetable for establishing the militia in each county. Some progress was made in counties where supporters of the militia were strong but by the summer of 1759 the militia could still muster barely half its proposed establishment. Fortunately, the revival of invasion fears – the French planned a diversion in Ireland and extended raids on Scotland and Essex – invested the militia with a suitably patriotic image. Opponents of the militia, now almost exclusively identified with older Whig politicians, did manage to prevent the extension of the force to Scotland in 1760. Agitation there had been revived by the appearance of the French privateer, Thurot, off the coast but, despite Scottish militia supporters stressing that lowlanders rather than highlanders would be those armed, the proposals were defeated on the grounds that arms would pass into the hands of Jacobites.

In the same year the gentry also counter-attacked on the provision of allowances by successfully restricting them only to the families of militiamen serving in person – substitutes and even volunteers were not granted the allowances until 1778. But those opposed to the militia were unable to prevent the 1762 act prolonging the life of the force or introducing fines to compel those English and Welsh counties still refusing to participate to do so. The war ended before this could have much effect and six counties persisted in their non-compliance. Two – Worcestershire and Derbyshire – surrendered in the face of more severe fines imposed in 1769 but the remaining four counties – Staffordshire, Sussex, Oxfordshire and Nottinghamshire – only complied with the further threat of a Franco–Spanish invasion during the American war. None the less, for all intents and purposes, the system was established in the great majority of English and Welsh counties by 1762.

Under the legislation each county was required to submit an annual return to the Privy Council of those men aged between 18 and 50 (45 from 1762) eligible to serve. A county quota would then be fixed so that each county theoretically contributed the same proportion of its able-bodied manpower. In reality, those quotas fixed in 1757 were left unchanged until 1796 irrespective of intervening variations in population. A general lieutenancy meeting would order chief constables to produce hundredal lists, a task effected by parish constables, and would then proportionally fix hundredal quotas. A series of subdivision meetings in the hundreds would hear appeals against inclusion and, having notified the results to a further general meeting, would apportion parochial quotas and ballot to fill them. After the ballot would follow a further opportunity to claim exemption and to make up deficiencies thus caused. Although clerks were permitted from 1758 it could prove both cumbersome and expensive and also involved localities in a virtual annual census of the able-bodied which, from 1758, not only encompassed all males whether eligible or not but demanded more and more information.

It was within the means of large numbers to avoid service either through payment of the statutory £10 fine or by providing a substitute willing to serve. The advantage of substitution lay in the three-year exemption (two years for those aged over 35) then granted while payment of the fine (until 1782) resulted in a man being automatically appointed to serve the following year. A balloted man might also escape through the somewhat haphazard determination of what constituted physical disability. In some cases parishes might (from 1758) find volunteers to serve for a bounty while poorer men (from 1762) could claim up to £5 from the parish rates in order to try and meet the price of a substitute. As a last resort, a man might join an insurance club in which subscriptions were either used to hire substitutes for members drawn or returned if none was required. From 1762 onwards such clubs were only permitted within individual parishes but, although technically illegal, there were several instances of commercial enterprises operating schemes on a wider scale and, when prohibition lapsed altogether in 1786, a plethora of these firms entered the field. The proportion of men balloted who actually served in person – 'principals' – was thus likely to be small with no man forced to do so unless he was willing for some individual economic or domestic reason or unable to afford one of the common means of evasion.

Consequently, most principals and substitutes were manual workers and invariably young, single and illiterate. To take the example of Buckinghamshire, 93 per cent of all farmers drawn in the ballot in 1759 found the means to avoid service. This was equally true for 86 per cent of tradesmen, 74 per cent of artisans and craftsmen and even 58 per cent of labourers and 41 per cent of farm servants. Out of 238 men known to have served that year – the quota was 560 – only 50 were principals and but four were volunteers. Some 107 were labourers and 66 farm servants with 41 artisans or craftsmen, 23 tradesmen and a solitary farmer. The reliance upon manual workers of one kind or another did not materially change. In February 1797 only seven out of 113 men serving for the three hundreds of Newport in Buckinghamshire were principals and 68 of the 97 with known occupations were labourers. The 131 militiamen recruited to fill vacancies in the county force as a whole between December 1798 and February 1799 included 97 labourers. In September 1807 the Newport hundreds had only nine principals serving alongside 51 substitutes, of whom 31 were labourers.[2]

Although a proportion of substitutes invariably came from counties other than that for which they served, the militia remained primarily a territorial force compared to the army, which tended to concentrate recruiting activities in larger towns. However, there is some evidence to suggest that in many counties militiamen were more likely to be manual workers from an urban rather than a rural environment. In 1780 nine tenths of the Warwickshire militia was from either Birmingham or Coventry and these towns also provided a large number of substitutes for neighbouring counties. Similarly, in November 1792 the West Riding militia was said to be filled with 'manufacturers and Sheffield men' while the Westminster militia comprised 'the very refuse of London'.[3]

Certainly the militia never seriously aspired to the kind of respectable propertied force that many enthusiasts had envisaged in 1757. Nor were large numbers of gentlemen always forthcoming to command their county forces. Thus, the property qualifications on first appointment – ranging from possession of land worth £50 per annum for ensigns to land worth £400 or an inheritance worth £800 per annum for colonels – were progressively reduced or even ignored. Edward Gibbon, who served in the South Hampshire militia from 1759 to 1770, has left a particularly vivid image of the militia and its officers in his journals. In December 1762, for example, he described his peers as 'a set of fellows all whose behaviour was low and most of whose characters were despicable'.[4] In particular, there was a shortage of subalterns although their qualifications were halved in 1769 and the turnover was high as many younger officers contrived to transfer to the army without purchase. In turn, unemployed regulars were encouraged to take commissions in the militia, especially after 1778, but they tended to be either those who had retired to manage an estate with relatively little spare time or those too poor or too old to achieve high army rank.

Even ignoring the low quality of its officers, the militia laboured under conditions of some difficulty in terms of its likely efficiency. Beyond the machinery for filling vacancies militia regiments had little existence in peacetime other than the annual training. Although improved after 1762 in the form of a continuous 28-day period in summer the training was still unlikely to yield more than a passing acquaintance with musketry and drill. None the less, some commanding officers were unusually vigorous and the West Norfolk militia produced its own drill manual. However, this much vaunted regiment only achieved its enviably high standard during wartime embodiment.

Such embodied service, of course, was precisely what the militia had been revived to perform. During the Seven Years War some battalions were embodied as early as June 1759 and, in all, 43 English and Welsh counties had their units called out before the close of hostilities. All were embodied again in March 1778 together with the remaining 17 counties which had raised their militias for the first time in the intervening years. Upon embodiment, militia received full army pay and allowances and were subject to the same nomadic existence as regulars, serving only occasionally in their own counties. The most valuable periods were undoutedly those spent in the large wartime training camps such as at Warley and Coxheath but even embodied service was not necessarily continuous. Many battalions were allowed home in winter months and it was far from unusual to allow large numbers of furloughs at harvest time. Nor was it unusual to allow men to work for themselves in spare moments and the government itself employed militiamen as labourers on public works.

The latter was emblematic of the mundane tasks to which the militia was often assigned. One of the most common duties was guarding prisoners of war while some were involved in coastal watching or the control of smuggling. More important were the few occasions upon which militiamen were called upon to repulse actual or expected attack or, indeed, to assist the civil power in maintaining order. Of the former, the West Norfolk's exchange of shots with a French privateer off the Lincolnshire coast in June 1781 affords one example while nine militia battalions were employed in the suppression of the Gordon riots in the capital in June 1780.

Yet, while serving to stimulate the militia's establishment, the Seven Years War had not been a serious test of home defences since British naval victories had forestalled French plans. The outbreak of hostilities in the American colonies in 1775 was to pose far greater dangers. A bill was introduced in that year to enable militia to be embodied to replace regulars needed in the colonies but, while passed in the face of considerable opposition, it was never enacted. A further attempt was also made to extend the militia to Scotland where privateers such as John Paul Jones had provoked new fears. However, the government preferred Scots in the army rather than a militia and the bill was lost, four regiments of 'fencibles' or regulars enlisted for home defence being raised instead. In England the subsequent shock of Saratoga brought offers from both noblemen and towns to raise new regular regiments but the entry of France into the war in February 1778 at a time when only 25,000 regulars were available in Britain required still further measures.

One local solution was the raising of volunteers in Whitehaven after a raid by John Paul Jones in April 1778 but the government preferred to trust in the militia, which had been embodied a month earlier. A new bill was then passed in September enabling volunteers to be attached to the militia. Ironically, it was now the government that had become the greatest advocate of the militia and it was the opposition, which feared the extension of patronage through such measures, that now pressed for voluntary rather than compulsory augmentation. When Spain also entered the war in April 1779, therefore, the government bill proposing a doubling of the size of the militia met much hostility. A Commons amendment recommended the addition of separate volunteer companies and this was the only clause to survive passage through the Lords. There had been fears of labour shortages at harvest should the bill pass unamended and also fear of renewed anti-militia riots since disturbances had occurred again in 1769 when the militia became permanent and in some counties upon embodiment in 1778 and 1779. The emasculated legislation was initially only to last for 18 months but it was then extended until December 1782. In fact, it never amounted to much and only 14 companies had been added to the militia by March 1780. As the government clearly had no intention of enforcing the ballot, society as a whole found the prospect of serving in entirely independent volunteer corps under localised terms rather more attractive than volunteer companies under militia regulations.

The precise plans of the French and Spanish were unknown as their combined fleet entered the Channel in August 1779 – they actually intended to seize Portsmouth and the Isle of Wight – but the threat was obvious. A crucial public meeting was that of the Middlesex lieutenancy on 16 July 1779 which endorsed the official desire for augmenting army and militia but also proposed establishing 24 independent volunteer companies to defend the capital. The attempt to raise volunteers met with a mixed reception – the churchwardens of Edgware, for example, claimed in response to an appeal for funds that 'the great number of taxes which are already raised for our defences were such a burden that they could not afford anything for this particular purpose'. Nevertheless, companies were formed by the Swiss community in Grafton Street, American Loyalists, the employees of Sheridan's and Harris's theatres, artificers employed by the Board of Works and gentlemen of the Temple. City bankers and merchants formed a 50-strong corps of Light Horse Volunteers. Elsewhere some counties such as Staffordshire subscribed funds for augmentation but the response more often took the form of volunteer units: six in Dover, 17 in Sussex, 24 in Devon and so on. The character was varied as indicated by the composition of Middlesex units. The mounted Norfolk Rangers, who appear to have survived at least until 1784 if not longer, were similarly described as 'a very respectable body of gentlemen, farmers and tradesmen'. At the very least, therefore, these corps were above the social level normally recruited into the ranks of the militia and army.[5]

The volunteer movement as a whole did not long flourish once delays and bad weather had sent the Franco–Spanish fleet back into port by September 1779. The Middlesex and Westminster Volunteers stopped drilling as early as May 1780 and disbanded altogether four months later. Coming to power in March 1782 the opposition revived the volunteer ideal temporarily, Lord Shelburne passing a bill in May to encourage and legalise corps coming forward in defence of towns and coastal areas. A number of new units appeared as a result but a plan circulated to lords lieutenant and mayors at the same time, which suggested volunteer battalions in principal towns including 45 Scottish burghs, was poorly received. There was concern at weapons falling into untrustworthy hands with the recent precedents of the Irish Volunteers and the Gordon riots. Only 16 counties expressed any degree of support and, while 20 boroughs submitted plans, 22 more rejected Shelburne's scheme completely. In any event, the war ended in November 1782 and virtually all corps were disbanded. The most lingering legacy of Shelburne's scheme was in Scotland where it had served to revive agitation for a militia. Militia enthusiasts such as Adam Ferguson and Alexander Carlyle put forward ambitious schemes for what amounted to national training but Scots themselves were not sufficiently united for the agitation to succeed and many apparent supporters of a Scottish militia may even have subscribed to the view that agitation alone was enough to satisfy the national rejeuvenation they sought without actually risking possible economic disruption of the labour force.[6]

Amid the general demobilisation, the desire for further economies brought crucial changes in a militia consolidation bill in 1786. Substitutes were now made liable to serve for the duration of any war for which the militia was embodied, avoiding the problem experienced, for example, by the Worcestershire militia in August 1779 when the terms of service of so many men had expired that it had to be withdrawn from the coast at the height of the invasion threat. However, the extension of service generally from three to five years was also an economy measure since fewer men would now be required annually. The bill as it eventually emerged in June 1786 also restricted peacetime training to only two-thirds of the strength of each regiment annually. Not unexpectedly, therefore, the most pressing problem when Britain found itself at war once more in January 1793 was the need to repair the deficiencies resulting from the demobilisation ten years previously.

The militia was embodied on 1 December 1792 primarily as a precautionary and preventative measure amid government fears of insurrectionary subversion although, in practise, not all regiments were immediately called out. However, with most regulars required overseas, the militia immediately became the main defence against the raids expected to be launched by the new revolutionary government in France which entertained plans for landings in peripheral areas such as Cornwall and Wales with the intention of stirring domestic unrest and had offered assistance to all seeking to overthrow their monarchs.

The revolutionary potential in Britain is a matter of some controversy[7] but there was undoubtedly a revolutionary fringe and the authorities were understandably nervous of the possibility of insurrection. Certainly, there was soon apparent evidence of the attempted subversion of the militia upon which so much depended. It had frequently been said since 1757 that service in the militia ruined a man for civil employment – a theme elegantly expressed by William Cowper in *The Task* – but the other side to militia service was that the force was not segregated from the population as a whole in the same way as the army. Militiamen thus remained politically vital since they took into military life their civilian interests and opinions, this link with civilian society remaining strong at least in the initial period of a man's embodied service before habits of discipline prevailed. Thus, it was not unexpected that signs of unrest should be detected in a force composed predominantly of manual workers.

In November 1792 it was reported that 'little books' were circulating among militiamen from northern and industrial areas and six regiments – those of Cumberland, Derbyshire, Nottinghamshire, Warwickshire, Westminster and Yorkshire – were suspected of disaffection.[8] In one celebrated case a noted radical, Major John Cartwright, whose tracts were among literature in the possession of his own Nottinghamshire regiment, was dismissed from the militia. One result of such fears was a barrack building programme while another was the practice of stationing militia regiments as far away as possible from their own counties: in 1793 the authorities in Durham and Northumberland actually requested that their own militias be sent away. But such measures did not necessarily isolate the militia and soldiers or militiamen figured in 16 of the food and grain riots duirng the course of 1795.

Much was due to the poor discipline of the militia and the frequent absence of officers but, more importantly, the militia was as vulnerable to price rises as the rest of the population. The militia's food allowance was just 5d a day and they required to purchase flour for dressing regulation pigtails but there was also often a determination to identify with local grievances. Men of the Gloucestershire militia forced butchers to lower prices in Portsmouth, South Hampshire militiamen were involved at disturbances at Canterbury, Northamptonshire militiamen at Plymouth and Herefordshire militiamen at Chichester. The most serious occurrence was at Seaford involving as many as 400 Oxfordshire militiamen who broke ranks on 16 April 1795 with the intention of forcing local butchers to lower prices and, on the following morning, marched into Seaford and seized and sold meat while others visited farms and mills. Fencibles, cavalry and artillery were all summoned and 200 men arrested of whom 18 were subsequently tried and five executed.

Concessions forthcoming included bread at fixed prices, increased pay and the abolition of the pigtail but, thereafter, there was an understandable tendency to distrust the militia at least in its own areas. In 1802 it was alleged that discharged militiamen were among those leading opposition to mill machinery in Yorkshire while the later machine breaking disturbances in the north in 1812 also brought renewed suggestions that it was inadvisable to employ northern militia. Such fears appear to have been unfounded after

1795. In 1797 when seditious handbills were being widely distributed in barracks they invariably invoked strong protestations of loyalty from those militia regiments that received them. The widespread food riots of 1800 saw no repetition of militia indiscipline and in 1812 there was but one occasion on which a militiaman declined to fire upon rioters. But, even if the militia had proved unreliable during the food riots, there were still other newly raised forces upon which the authorities would have been able to call with confidence, principally the volunteer cavalry or 'yeomanry' raised in 1794.

With some reason to fear the consequences of a successful French landing the government had considered additional means of defence. Wary of unpopular ballots it suggested on 14 March 1794 that citizens could assist in raising new forces by voluntary financial contributions which could provide bounties for an augmentation of the militia, new fencible units or independent volunteer corps. The opposition claimed this was levying men and money without parliamentary sanction and at one of the first public meetings held in Surrey on 27 March there was a pointed resolution 'to refuse any countenance to private subscriptions, at the request of the Ministers for any public purposes'. Similar protests elsewhere led the government to resort to hasty legislation allowing both augmentation of the militia by voluntary means (34 Geo III c 31) and for accepting voluntary offers (34 Geo III c 16). Consequently, a second Surrey meeting in April reacted favourably and within a week the county had raised £4,934 for defence.[9] Over the country as a whole an additional 5,000 militia and 6,000 fencibles were brought in by the legislation. Substantial sums were contributed amounting to at least £93,000 from 17 counties and six major urban centres between April and May and some even went to coastal defences as in the East Riding and Devon but, more often than not, the amount given over to militia augmentation or other causes represented only the surplus after provision for volunteers and yeomanry.

Some offers for volunteer corps had been accepted (primarily in maritime counties) in 1793, of which some appear an extension of that loyalist upsurge evident in the widespread association movement of the previous year. A few of the associations had been semi-military in character such as those at Bolton and Manchester and in eastern Kent where coastal patrols were initiated by loyalists in May 1793. There was certainly continuity between associations and volunteers in Ipswich, Macclesfield, Lancaster, Bradford, Gateshead, Leominster, Rochdale and Birmingham. However, most associations had dissolved as the growth of national unity and the introduction of legislation for which they had striven rendered them less necessary. One or two corps may have survived from earlier times and the Norfolk Rangers were certainly back in existence by September 1792. But what precisely motivated the revival of the volunteer movement in 1794 is something of a controversy.

It has been argued that the formation of the volunteers and yeomanry played a crucial role in the establishment of a party of 'order' with the fear of insurrection being the most dominant factor in their creation given the increased radical activity in early 1794. More recently, the fear of invasion has been stressed as the more important with the volunteers themselves not necessarily viewing their own role in the same light as the government, who did regard them as a predominantly anti-revolutionary movement. Yet a third interpretation has also emerged which places the volunteers within the context of the growth of national consciousness and self-assertion among the urban middle classes with distinct implications for their relationship with traditional elites.[10] The third interpretation will be addressed later and, for the moment, attention given to the arguments advanced as to the relative significance of the fear of insurrection and the fear of invasion. Both have some validity but both tend to regard the volunteers and yeomanry as a whole between 1794 and 1802 rather than in terms of the two distinct periods of formative activity, namely from 1794 to 1795 and from 1797 to 1798. It can be argued that many corps – probably well over half – formed in 1794 or 1795 were concerned primarily with coastal defence but this is not the whole story as the examples of Devon and Yorkshire will illustrate.

In Devon, the initial meeting took place at Exeter on 22 April 1794 with the first meeting of a county defence committee that same day. At a second meeting on 16 May the committee approved offers of volunteers from Exmouth, Beer and Seaton but deferred one from Cullompton to await a decision on whether to accept inland corps. On 10 June it was resolved 'not to encourage any offers of raising such Corps, unless from places not exceeding six miles from the Coast'. Another offer from Torrington was similarly declined later in June but by October the committee had accepted corps at both Cullompton and Torrington as well as at Honiton. It had also been stressed as early as 16 May that volunteers should be 'Householders who have an interest in the Defence of their Property', the imputation being that those without property had little to gain from volunteering. The actual terms of service also tended to indicate a wider concern than that of invasion. At Axminster the corps would not only serve against invaders but 'in cases of riots and tumults'; that at Exeter would go up to 20 miles 'upon the requisition of the Lord Lieutenant or Sheriff' as well as being prepared to face invasion 'by order of His Majesty'.[11]

In the North Riding it could equally be said that the first corps were formed on the coast in 1794 but the county's first four troops of yeomanry were envisaged both 'to strengthen the Means of National Defence against any Attempt of Foreign Invasion, and to assist and support the legal constituted Authorities of the Kingdom, in suppressing any Riots or Tumults which may be excited by seditious and designing Men . . .'. Significantly, Richmond initially declined to raise men not due to its inland position but because 'being not a manufacturing town, we have no idle unemployed wanderers, every man employed with high wages and not a discontented man appears'. By contrast it was noted that Leeds and 'such places have laudably and as a self defence against disappointed workmen embodied the respectable inhabitants'. The Leeds volunteers were indeed enlisted for 'the express purpose of Internal Defence of this Borough against insurrection or any sudden commotions'.[12]

In the case of the yeomanry, of which 32 corps were in existence by the end of 1794, there is no especial preponderance of coastal counties although it is fair to state that all but one southern maritime county did raise yeomanry that year. But the almost universal terms of yeomanry service equally stressed insurrection and invasion. In the North Riding one fifth would always remain at the disposal of magistrates even in event of invasion while yeomen in Somerset refused to serve out of their county under any circumstances. Lord Somerville of the West Somerset corps was quite explicit in June 1794 in stating that not only would he exercise his yeomen 'only as will not interfere with the Harvest of Hay and Corn' but also that the intention in so safeguarding the 'Private interests' of his men was 'for the purpose of protecting Private property, not of injuring it'.[13]

Somerville's reference to the convenience of yeomen draws attention to another aspect of the argument as to whether the volunteer movement as a whole constituted a party of order in embryo, namely that this could not be so when the volunteers generally were of relatively low social status. While this may apply to the infantry volunteers, it hardly applies to the yeomanry. The very term 'yeomanry' defined the membership to a great extent. Thus, when the Isle of Wight belatedly raised a corps in 1798, one officer's election was resented by the farming community, 'a body from whom it was expected the principal part of our Yeomanry would be drawn – and who, in part, are the Class of People chiefly composing the discription [sic] of Yeomen'. In Devon the Pynes troop near Exeter was to consist of 'Gentlemen, Yeomen and other respectable Persons'. Of course, the ability to provide and ride a horse was essential although several units were prepared to accept substitutes of good character. As it was anticipated that only arms and accoutrements would be received from government, the need to provide all other requirements also tended to restrict likely membership. Figures available for five troops in Buckinghamshire and Derbyshire at various dates between 1798 and 1804 show a large preponderance of farmers and their sons ranging from 19 to 69 per cent but also a substantial secondary intake of professional men and tradesmen ranging from 16 to 39 per cent and, perhaps surprisingly, a steady 10 to 16 per cent proportion of skilled craftsmen. In any event, they would be those unlikely to serve in the militia or army.[14]

The reliance upon the farming community also explains the frequent allusion to the unchanging nature of the agricultural year of which Somerville's notice is but one example. Most yeomanry units thus discontinued exercises at the approach of harvest or other demanding tasks such as shearing. Apart from such occasional exercises, the most frequent call upon a yeoman's time was what might be termed spectacle. Over 20,000 people attended the presentation of colours to the Wiltshire Yeomanry by Lady Bruce on Beckhampton Down in June 1798 and there were countless similar field days and extravagances in other counties. Given such a character, it was hardly surprising that yeomanry should also prove trustworthy if not always efficient police. The London and Westminster Light Horse Volunteers were called out by the lord mayor in anticipation of a riot in August 1794 just three months after their revival and they were constantly on duty during the London Corresponding Society trials of the autumn. Similarly, the food disturbances of 1795 saw frequent use of yeomanry.

None the less, it was the threat of invasion rather than insurrection that was to grow appreciably after 1795 as each of Britain's allies in the First Coalition fell to or made accommodation with the French. Invasion fears and large casualties incurred by the army overseas brought yet further suggestions for new defensive measures in November 1796 including a corps of sharpshooters recruited from gamekeepers, a corps of guides, a provisional cavalry and a supplementary militia. The latter two suggestions were enacted, the provisional cavalry reverting to a pre-1757 concept of an obligation imposed on property since one man and one horse would be levied for every ten horses retained for riding or carriage drawing. Like the restoration horse troops, the provisional cavalry's strength would depend on a county's wealth and not military considerations but the immediate impact was to swell the yeomanry as it was believed that the bill would be suspended if sufficient volunteers came forward. Only six regiments of provisional cavalry were actually embodied, that of Worcestershire alone serving in Ireland. But the army required no more cavalry and those units not embodied were absorbed into county yeomanries where their lower social status led to frequent ostracism. By March 1800 all trace of the provisional cavalry had disappeared with the disbanding of remaining embodied regiments.

The supplementary militia legislation (37 Geo III c 3, 22) was more durable with an intention to raise 60,000 men by ballot or, in effect, trebling county quotas. However, the force would not be embodied at once but would be trained for 20-day periods in contingents of one-twentieth of total strength. It was hoped that lack of initial commitment would avoid undue opposition and even attract men of property who had so far shunned militia service. Warnings had been given that any ballot would provoke hostility and some counties offered to try and raise additional numbers by voluntary means but this was refused. Almost immediately there was another wave of anti-militia riots which affected 10-counties. As in 1757 the worst disturbances were again in Lincolnshire. Little official explanation of the legislation had been forthcoming to allay fears of overseas service and there was wide concern that the price of substitutes would prove too high. Nor was it clear what family allowances might be payable and, although there is evidence of radical attempts to exploit the situation, the disturbances were largely spontaneous. The response of local authorities was far more vigorous than 40 years previously and the legislation was not thereafter disputed although some regiments did not complete their quotas until the autumn of 1798.

Through expansion the supplementary militia touched far more individuals than the old militia but the actual membership was not significantly different, although substitutes were now confined to the county concerned. There were familiar problems in finding principals prepared to serve despite the exemption fine being raised to £15 and there were also deficiencies in the numbers of officers with the result that commissions were opened to regular subalterns on half pay and an attempt was even made to admit Catholics. Nor could the supplementary militia solve the manpower problem in face of mounting dangers. Only bad weather averted a French descent on Ireland in December 1796 and weather and mutiny similarly frustrated an expedition to Newcastle although William Tate's Legion Noire blown off course while en route to Bristol did manage a landing at Fishguard in Pembrokeshire on 22 February 1797.

Tate's force – 1,400 strong but undisciplined – was compelled to surrender after two days but there had been initial confusion among the local auxiliaries, who eventually mustered some 599 officers and men drawn from the Fishguard fencibles, Pembrokeshire militia and Castlemartin Yeomanry supplemented by upwards of 750 assorted civilian volunteers. Nevertheless, the auxiliaries performed well enough despite their lack of equipment and training and the Castlemartin Yeomanry earned a unique battle honour for action in Britain. Fishguard also fostered the myth of the French surrendering by mistaking the red capes of local women for approaching regulars: at Ilfracombe, off which the French ships had also been sighted, a slightly different version had them frightened off by one Betsy Gannon's red bloomers! Local traditions notwithstanding, the raid had caused considerable panic in government circles resulting not only in considerable military movements but also in the Bank of England suspending payments in specie to prevent a run on the banks, a suspension enduring 21 years. Another response was extending the militia laws to the Tower Hamlets and (in 1798) to the Stanneries while another attempt was made to raise a Scottish militia.

An earlier proposal in 1793 had been rejected but the unreliability of fencibles was such that legislation finally passed Westminster on 19 July 1797. The first riot occured in Berwickshire eight days later with over 40 others in August and September. By way of intended concession the government had restricted service to those aged between 18 and 23 but had failed to recognise the economic importance of this age group in Scotland. There was also resentment at the absence of provision for volunteers in lieu of ballot and the same failure as in England and Wales to explain legislation. Other more local grievances were also apparent, the disturbances generally more violent than in England and suppression by predominantly English fencibles particularly vigorous. In fact, at Tranent in east Lothian, Pembrokeshire and Cinque Ports fencibles fired on a crowd of over 5,000 on 29 August killing at least 12 people, a higher death toll than that at the 'Peterloo' incident in 1819.

In many respects 1797 was a crisis year with the naval mutinies at the Nore and Spithead and the French Directory's establishment of an Army of England. However, money was so short that the government was forced to suspend recruitment of fencibles while the raising of the supplementary militia had not only made it more difficult to find recruits for the army but resulted in prices of substitutes soaring. Consequently, in January 1798 the government tried to obtain up to 10,000 men for the army from the supplementary militia but lords lieutenant were strongly opposed to any part of the militia becoming merely a draft-finding body for the army and feared the drain on the agricultural labour force. They also opposed any attempt to extract the grenadier and light companies from the 'regular' militia regiments in April 1798. Subsequently, the Marquess of Buckingham did suggest enabling the militia to serve in Ireland, where rebellion had erupted, and legislation was passed in June which enabled 14,000 militiamen – Buckingham's own regiment was the first – to be despatched there.

Offers to serve in Ireland declined noticeably after 1798 as the difficulties of military life there became apparent. In June 1799, however, further legislation reduced the size of the militia to 66,000 to allow up to a quarter of the new county quotas to be enlisted in the army. In July army commissions were opened to militia officers where at least 60 men transferred and in October the establishment was again reduced to induce the surplus to enlist. By such means over 26,000 militiamen joined the army in 1799, effectively permitting the Dutch campaign to proceed. In fact, despite their inexperience and indiscipline – over 800 of the 1,414 casualties before Bergen in September 1799 were militiamen – they proved good military material. Abercrombie proclaimed them 'a superior race of men, and a great acquisition to the army' and it has been argued that their arrival regenerated the army Abercrombie was later to lead to victory in Egypt even if the restriction of their service to the European theatre necessitated major reorganisation.[15]

As far as home defence was concerned, the supplementary militia was progressively embodied in February and April 1798 although it led to immediate labour shortages in some areas. Sea fencibles were raised in some maritime counties and an even more ambitious scheme of mobilisation in the form of a *levee en masse* of the civilian population was suggested in Dorset. The high sheriff, William Clavell, proposed utilising common law to raise the *posse comitatus* and in May 1797 ordered the listing of all able-bodied males between 15 and 60, vehicles and draught animals. Clavell's initiative was emulated in both Buckinghamshire and Northumberland in early 1798 as well as being actively considered in Lancashire. Moreover, the secretary of war, Henry Dundas, singled out Clavell for praise and on 27 April 1798 new legislation (38 Geo III c 27) inspired by the Dorset example passed on to the statute book. Generally known as the 'Defence of the Realm Act', it authorised raising of 'armed associations' and permitted the government to seek details of the resources of every county through returns of men, horses and other livestock, vehicles, mills, boats and barges. A further circular on 26 April reviving the idea of corps of gamekeepers inspired little support – only five men came forward in Essex – but the call for armed associations stimulated a massive expansion of volunteering.

So many offers were received that as early as 6 May Dundas attempted to encourage only those from 'respectable householders' who resided in 'great and populous towns'.[16] Thus, offers from inland towns with less than a thousand inhabitants were rejected unless special local needs were certified by lords lieutenant. Similarly, when Pitt had expressed public support for voluntary associations in March 1797 the Duke of Portland had rejected any offers not emanating from ports, coastal towns or major manufacturing towns with the exception of yeomanry. This might suggest that the government still regarded volunteers as police and to some extent this also appears the view of volunteers themselves even when invasion seemingly provided a more immediate stimulus. Some of the units formed in 1797 and 1798 were concerned by invasion – in Berkshire two Reading companies were prepared to go to the coast and the Wiveliscombe Volunteers in Somerset were ready to serve anywhere in the south-west. However, in most cases patriotism had a decidedly local flavour even in the event of actual invasion. The Frampton Volunteers in Gloucestershire would serve only up to 8 miles distant, the Marlborough Association only up to 5 miles and the Hitchin Association but three miles.

The stated aims of such corps also displayed more concern for insurrection than invasion. The Lancashire lieutenancy expressed grave concern at Dundas's attempt to get volunteers to extend services beyond parishes as this might strip the 'great commercial towns' of protection while the Loyal Oxford Volunteers undertook to prosecute rioters privately and the Wednesbury Loyal Volunteers in Staffordshire stood plainly for 'strengthening the hands of Government, the security of private property, and the preservation of good order . . .'.[17] Very similar sentiments can be detected in units such as the Westminster Volunteer Cavalry, Cornhill Military Association, East India Company Volunteers and the Candlewick Ward Association and, beyond the metropolis, the Bywell Volunteer Cavalry in Northumberland, infantry units raised in Buckinghamshire to support the yeomanry and other units as far apart as Ashburton in Devon and Glasgow.

None the less, it is appropriate at this point to consider the most recent interpretation of the purpose and dynamic of what was rapidly becoming 'the greatest popular movement in Georgian Britain'.[18] It has been argued, it will be recalled, that the volunteers fit into a pattern of activity approximating to the growth of a national consciousness. Traditional county elites displayed a certain ambiguity towards the promotion of a national identity which might imply greater citizenship and, hence, greater democratisation. By contrast, the assertion of a national consciousness by the British urban middle classes served not only to help establish a distinctive civic culture but also to claim for them a parity with traditional elites in an ostensibly national cause. Indeed, the ceremonial potential of volunteer units as displayed, for example, in the military funeral accorded Robert Burns by his erstwhile fellows in the Royal Dumfries Volunteers in July 1796, was better suited than the activities of the increasing number of other voluntary societies in which urban elites invested their energy in contributing to the growing taste for civic spectacle as a visible expression of civic pride and status.

The very nature of the rules and regulations by which volunteers

governed themselves demonstrated the degree of assertive independence from traditional elites. Outside the yeomanry, volunteer units
were rarely organised on a county basis – as late as 1803 only five
counties had county-wide volunteer battalions. The role of the lieutenancy was therefore limited to all intents and purposes to the
granting of commissions and lords lieutenant only rarely intervened
to overturn local choices. Nor was there much external control by
the military authorities. The 1794 legislation had stipulated that
volunteers would pass under military discipline only in the event of
invasion and no terms of service were defined by the state other than
the provision of pay for drill on two days a week at a rate of 1s 0d for
a three-hour drill. The circular of March 1797 had encouraged
associations serving under local terms without pay or military
discipline and the new legislation of April 1798 again lacked precise
definition of appropriate terms of service beyond providing pay for
one day's drill per week and clothing allowances if a corps was
prepared to serve throughout the relevant military district. Those
corps receiving two days' pay under the older legislation continued
to do so until similarly restricted to one day's pay a week in
September 1798.

To some extent, the promotion of associations by the government
reflected a new official interest in realising the military potential of
volunteer corps and persuading them to extend their services to the
military district marked the first attempt to purge the volunteers of
their purely amateur status and to fashion a volunteer army rather
than a volunteer movement. However, this would not be achieved
easily given their independent nature, and the tension between the
authorities and the volunteers would increase noticeably after the
renewal of war in 1803.

Those mainly envisaged by such local rules and regulations as
being likely members of associations and corps were the more
respectable elements of society since the urban elite was as intent
upon establishing its own authority over the urban poor as it was on
escaping that of the traditional rural elites. At Marlborough members had to be either 'housekeepers' or recommended by housekeepers while at Oxford prospective members were scrutinised by
both the committee and local magistrates. There were ballots for
entry and annual subscriptions. At Hitchin members could be dismissed by majority vote while all took it in turns to act as non-
commissioned officers in the Westminster Cavalry. Discipline was

usually left to fines and at Oxford it was even possible to appeal against unreasonable orders although persistent offenders were also liable to have their names published in the *Oxford Mail*.[19] The emphasis upon equality amongst those of the same social status was also commonly displayed through election of officers and frequent rotation of committee members. Characterised by an MP as miniature armed parliaments, the committees were an effective manifestation of independence approximating to the pattern of 'subscriber democracy' observed of other urban voluntary organisations such as literary, philosophical and temperance societies and organisations for the relief of the poor.[20]

However, it must be recognised that corps and associations formed in 1797 and 1798 frequently included those of a lesser social status. In some cases employers almost certainly pressured employees to join as in Liverpool and in the East India Company, which threatened to dismiss those not undertaking training in its London battalions. Even where there was no direct pressure it may well have been difficult for an employee to avoid joining an employer's unit and the same could be said of tenants. In Scotland the Earl of Bradalbane compelled tenant service, and other corps with large numbers of tenants included the Frampton Volunteers, those at Forcett and Larkin in the North Riding and that on the Delaval estate in Northumberland. On occasions, however, the reverse could apply, the Duke of Newcastle believing strongly that his tenants should reserve themselves for any call he chose to make on them, not only opposing their enlistment in the Alnwick Association in February 1797 but also blacklisting tradesmen who supplied it. Undoubtedly, there was an element of what might be termed social control in compelling participation as emphasised by several lords lieutenant in Scotland. The good moral effect of habits of discipline and subordination was also stressed by elements as varied as Samuel Wilberforce and the Chiswick Armed Association, which maintained that volunteering 'induced the heedless to reflect fairly upon the advantage they actually enjoy and the doubtful issue of innovation . . .'.[21]

Other factors also led to the recruitment of volunteers of lower social status. The pay afforded corps, although many either refused it or were not entitled to it, could act as a kind of unemployment insurance – the commanding officer of one Manchester corps openly admitted the attraction of paid service for his men in 1800 – and some units such as the Knaresborough Volunteers or the Renfrew Yeomanry had more than a hint of the friendly society. The social and recreational activities offered by corps were also of account as apparently in the Warrington and Bury corps. For others there might be the expectation of reward in some form such as profiteering on supplying clothing. In Berwick in July 1796 the mayor had even attempted to turn the volunteers to electoral account since, as commanding officer, he refused to dismiss from a parade outside the town those likely to vote for his opponent. Political partisanship is also apparent in the composition of some corps in Liverpool and Manchester. But patriotism might also be tinged with self-interest in terms of the exemption it afforded from the militia ballot.

Exemption was first granted in 1794 provided a volunteer could produce a certificate of attendance at drill during the six weeks preceding the hearing of appeals against ballot selection. Those associations formed in 1797 were not exempt from the militia and, indeed, no volunteers enlisted after October 1796 were exempt from the ballot for the supplementary militia until the legislation was revised in 1799 but the legislation of April 1798 did then exempt corps from militia ballots provided they extended their service to the military district. Although possibly not as great a motive as it was to become after 1803, exemption was a powerful attraction and there is evidence to show that it was used consciously to recruit. Another advantage available for mounted units was exemption from the horse duty from 1795 onwards. There are a few examples of corps declining to avail themselves of the exemption from the ballot including the St James Volunteers in London and the Bath Volunteer Light Horse but such denial of self-interest was not widespread.

The actual social composition of the volunteer movement was thus rather more cosmopolitan than might have been intended. Privates in the Manchester and Salford Volunteers were 'chiefly labouring men' and surviving muster rolls indicate that many volunteers were dependent upon their fellows for assistance in providing basic equipment. At Hitchin only 13 could find all the necessary equipment, 32 men could find only part and 35 none at all; at Marlborough only 29 out of 89 volunteers could provide weapons and 36 had been recommended by householders rather than being householders themselves. Elected officers were similarly varied in terms of occupation despite a tendency to look first to leading urban professionals or, occasionally, to members of the aristocracy. Those at Poole included a number of ship owners in the Newfoundland fisheries trade as well as several attornies. At Oxford there were a gentleman and three bankers but also two apothecaries, two booksellers and a tailor. At Marlborough two gentlemen were joined by a grocer while a tanner was elected at Chesham and a butcher at Cullompton.[22]

Detailed work on the composition of the volunteers in Devon reveals a force drawn predominantly from the lower strata of society. Gentlemen, farmers and professional men together represented no more than 28 per cent at Sidmouth in 1794, less at Sidbury in 1796 and 1797 and barely 12 per cent in Exeter between 1794 and 1800. The majority were artisans or skilled manual workers representing 48 per cent at Brixham in 1800, 67 per cent at Exeter, between 48 and 67 per cent at Northam between 1794 and 1800 and between 49 and 59 per cent at Sidbury between 1796 and 1801. Mariners provided between 14 and 22 per cent at Northam, Sidmouth and Brixham between 1794 and 1800 while totally unskilled labourers contributed just over 8 per cent at Exeter, just over 12 per cent at Sidmouth, between 10 and 24 per cent at Sidbury and as many as 34 per cent at Bideford in 1800.[23]

Such findings can be supplemented by figures available for the corps at Marlborough, Frampton and Bicester in 1798 and those at Exeter and Bicester in 1803. In the case of the three former corps, tradesmen comprised 47, 29 and 40 per cent respectively while craftsmen and skilled manual workers comprised 39, 13 and 24 per cent respectively. At Frampton alone there was a substantial proportion (44 per cent) of farmers but one corps at Cayton in Yorkshire in 1803 not only drew 29 per cent of its strength from farmers and their sons but a further 39 per cent from farm servants and unskilled labourers. The latter trend is similar to that observed in Ely where only 4 per cent of the corps of 81 men had been labourers or servants in 1799 but 42 per cent out of the 262 members were so classed six years later.[24] More rurally based units did appear after the renewal of war in 1803 but there is some evidence that the movement as a whole, which still had an overall urban bias, lost much of its previous social exclusiveness placing many ordinary volunteers not only beyond the control of the traditional elite but also of the urban elite.

In fact, the more representative nature of the volunteers was reflected in the unreliability of some units in the face of the second wave of food disturbances which affected the country in 1800 and

1801. Volunteers in Coventry and Leicester had threatened to march on rural areas in July 1795 but this had not been generally true of these earlier disturbances and volunteers had often been utilised successfully. Indeed, in January 1795 a bandsman from the Newcastle Volunteers had been murdered by pitmen because he was 'one of the volunteers raised to prevent our lowering the price of corn'.[25]

Many units were still perfectly reliable in 1800 such as the Seaton Delaval Volunteers who helped restore order among pitmen in April and May 1800 and those volunteers called out at Sunderland, Durham and Unsworth in anticipation of a colliers' strike. However, in Sheffield, where the volunteers were mainly 'journeymen manufacturers', there were many misgivings should men be ordered to disperse any 'assemblage of people composed probably of their particular friends and messmates, perhaps even of their own wives and children calling out for bread'. Consequently, many Sheffield volunteers absented themselves from duty at a political meeting in September 1800 and those who did attend were roundly abused and stoned and one nearly drowned by his colleagues on his return to his employment. One Sheffield unit had disbanded itself in June and another unit at Stafford followed suit in November. Similarly, volunteers near Wolverhampton made it clear to magistrates in May 1800 that while they considered themselves loyal, 'it was never intended by them to give security to the inhuman oppressors, whilst the Poor are starving in the midst of Plenty'.[26]

Volunteers in Birmingham and Ashton under Lyne were also believed to be unreliable and in the following year those at Bolton, if not the entire Lancashire force, were regarded as distinctly suspect. Actual cases of disaffection also occurred widely in the south-west as in corps from Dartmouth, Totnes and Newton Abbot. The Brixham Volunteers were disbanded, their poor discipline being blamed significantly on the low social status of their officers who included a post office official and a tavern keeper. Units were also disarmed at Barnstaple and Plymouth while others refused to sign public declarations reaffirming their loyalty. Nevertheless, there was no indication that volunteers as a whole would have identified with any other kind of disorder and no regulars or militia repeated their indiscretions of 1795.

The subsidence of the food disturbances and of renewed invasion fears during the course of 1801 marked the end of a significant chapter in the development of the auxiliary forces. In January 1798 the forces available to the British government had numbered some 227,000 men of whom 105,000 were militia or supplementary militia, 24,000 fencibles, 15,000 yeomanry or volunteer cavalry and 51,000 volunteers. By January 1801 the establishment of yeomanry and volunteers alone stood at 21,000 and 97,000 respectively although effective strength was somewhat less. The peace preliminaries signed in London in October 1801 and subsequently ratifed at Amiens in the following March saw this numerically impressive force rapidly dissipated. The army was halved, the navy reduced to 70,000 men and the militia and supplementary militia disembodied.

Addington's administration did take the precaution of passing legislation in June 1802 to enable the ministry to accept the continuance of the volunteers and especially the yeomanry. Although retaining their exemption from the ballot, horse duty and hair powder duty – a tax imposed in 1795 and retained until 1869 – these corps were to receive no pay or allowances. Thus, while many did continue their services most did not or did so only with greatly reduced numbers. Further legislation cut the militia to an establishment of 70,000 in April 1802, of which only 9,000 in Scotland and 40,000 in England and Wales would actually be called. It was not anticipated that they would need to be embodied to anything like the extent of the past ten years and, while provision was made for augmentation, it was intended to divide the men into five classes according to age, health and marital status and utilise only the youngest and fittest for a future conflict. A further indication of expected passivity was the curtailment of peacetime training to twenty-one days per annum.

The experience of war had changed little in terms of the evolution of a co-ordinated manpower policy for home defence amid a generally unspectacular war effort in which Britain had achieved little since 1793. The militia remained a less than perfect instrument of partial conscription, which was increasingly resented and succeeded only in depriving the regular army of potential recruits. The militia's unpopularity and the measure of the moral and political evasion of the enforcement of military obligations by successive administrations had been demonstrated by the proliferation of volunteer and yeomanry corps serving under a variety of terms of service and competing, in turn, with the militia for recruits. It would take another six years and the failure of a series of ill-conceived and sometimes desperate expedients to produce an adequate remedy to the problem of harnessing patriotism to obligation under firm central control.

Notes

1 D. Neave, 'Anti-militia riots in Lincolnshire, 1757 and 1796', *Lincolnshire History and Archaeology* XI, 1976, pp. 21–6.

2 I. F. W. Beckett, 'Buckinghamshire Militia Lists for 1759: A Social Analysis', *Records of Buckinghamshire* XX, 3, 1977, pp. 461–69; Bucks R.O., AR 78/77/7; Huntington Library, *Stowe*, STG 1 (7).

3 J. R. Western, *The English Militia in the Eighteenth Century* (Routledge & Kegan Paul, London, 1965), p. 264; HMC *Dropmore* II (1894), pp. 345–6.

4 D. M. Low (ed), *Gibbon's Journal to January 1763* (London, 1929), pp. 192–5 entry for 23 Dec 1762.

5 S. King, 'The Middlesex and Westminster Royal Volunteers, 1779–1780', *Bulletin of the Middlesex Local History Council* XVI, 1963, pp. 3–5; *Norfolk Mercury* 14 Sep 1782.

6 See J. Robertson, *The Scottish Enlightenment and the Militia Issue* (John Donald, Edinburgh, 1985), pp. 128–58.

7 Cf. I. R. Christie, *Stress and Stability in late Eighteenth Century Britain* (Oxford University Press, 1984); H. T. Dickinson (ed), *Britain and the French Revolution* (Macmillan, London, 1989); M. I. Thomis and P. Holt, *Threats of Revolution in Britain, 1789–1848* (Macmillan, London, 1977); E. P. Thompson, *The Making of the English Working Class* (Gollancz, London, 1965); R. A. E. Wells, *Insurrection: The British Experience, 1795–1803* (Alan Sutton, Gloucester, 1983).

8 Western, *English Militia*, pp. 427–9.

9 *The Times* 29 Mar, 11 Apl, 17 Apl and 5 May 1794.

10 The paramountcy of invasion has been stressed by Clive Emsley, *British Society and the French Wars, 1793–1815* (Macmillan, London, 1979), p. 38 and by J. H. Bohstedt, 'Riots in England, 1790–1816 with special reference to Devon' Unpub. Ph.D., Harvard, 1972, pp. 210–14. The theme of insurrection is stressed by J. R. Western, 'The Volunteer Movement as an Anti-revolutionary Force, 1793–1801', *English Historical Review* LXXI, 1956, pp. 603–14. The relationship of urban volunteers and middle-class assertion is explored by Linda Colley, 'Whose Nation? Class and National Consciousness in Britain, 1750–1830', *Past and Present* 113, 1986, pp. 97–117 and J. E. Cookson, 'The English Volunteer Movement of the French Wars, 1793–1815: Some Contexts', *Historical Journal* 32, 4, 1989, pp. 867–91.

11 Army Museums Ogilby Trust, O.T.P. 30 (Acc 553).

12 M. Y. Ashcroft, *To Escape the Monster's Clutches* (North Yorks. County Record Office, Northallerton, 1977), pp. 14, 20–5; N. J. Arch, 'Thomas Lloyd and the Leeds Volunteers', *Journal of the Society for Army*

Historical Research LIX, 1981, pp. 201–6.

13 Army Museums Ogilby Trust, Order Book of West Somerset Yeomanry, 9 Jun 1794.

14 Bucks RO, *Howard–Vyse* D/HV/15/25; British Library, *Dropmore* Add. Mss. 59291; Bucks R.O., *Lieutenancy*, L/Y 2/7 and 5/11; Nottingham University Library, *Drury–Lowe* Dr.N 4/3 and 2/6.

15 P. Mackesy, *War without Victory* (Oxford University Press, London, 1984), p. 78.

16 Hereford and Worcester *RO, Coventry* 705:73 Acc. 2868/4.

17 Berks RO, *Radnor* D/ERa 07; Somerset RO, DD/DR 53; Wilts RO, WRO 361/4; Manchester Central Library, L1/40/4/1; Lancs RO, LM 1/1; Bodleian Library, MS Top Oxon e 241.

18 Cookson, 'English Volunteer Movement', pp. 867–91.

19 Essex RO, L/u 3/2; PRO, HO50/48; Army Museums Ogilby Trust, Muster Book of Westminster Volunteer Cavalry; Oxon RO, *Lieutenancy* L/M XI/iii/1.

20 R. J. Morris, 'Voluntary Societies and British Urban Elites, 1780–1840: An Analysis', *Historical Journal* XXVI, 1, 1983, pp. 95–118.

21 Western, 'Volunteer Movement', pp. 603–14; Emsley, *British Society*, pp. 73–4; Ashcroft, *Monster's Clutches*, p. 50; J. A. Huitson, 'Defence and Public Order in Northumberland, 1793–1815' Unpub. M.Lit., Durham, 1966, pp. 83–5.

22 Manchester Central Library, *Leigh–Philips* M84/1/1/12; Herts R.O., D/EHa.Z5; Wilts RO, WRO 361/4; Bodleian Library, MS Top Oxon e 241.

23 Bohstedt, 'Riots in England', pp. 245–61, 334–5.

24 Wilts RO, WRO 361/4; J. R. S. Whiting, 'The Frampton Volunteers', *Journal of the Society for Army Historical Research* XLVIII, 1970, pp. 14–28; Bodleian Library, MS Top Oxon c 223; Ashcroft, *Monster's Clutches*, pp. 152–5; W. G. Hoskins, *Exeter Militia List, 1803* (Phillimore, Chichester, 1972), passim; Cookson, 'English Volunteer Movement', pp. 867–91.

25 Huitson, 'Defence and Public Order', p. 239.

26 R. A. E. Wells, *Dearth and Distress in Yorkshire, 1793–1802* (Borthwick Institute Papers No. 52, 1977), pp. 29–34; PRO, HO 42/50, Haden to Portland, 10 May 1800 quoted C. Emsley, 'The Military and Popular Disorder in England, 1790–1801', *Journal of the Society for Army Historical Research* LXI, 245/6, 1983, pp. 10–21, 96–112.

4

From expediency to rationalisation (1802–1815)

Bucks Local Militia.

Three Hundreds of Cottesloe.

I _William Welch_ do make Oath that I am by my Trade a _Carpenter_ and have been usually resident in the Parish of _Whitchurch_ in the County of _Bucks_ that I am ——married and that I have no —————— Children —— and that I have no Rupture, nor ever was troubled with Fits; and am no ways disabled by Lameness or otherwise; but have the perfect use of my Limbs; and that I am not a Seaman or Seafaringman. As witness my Hand at _Aylesbury_ the _26th_ Day of _October_ one thousand eight hundred and _twelve_

The Mark X of William Welch

Sworn before me at _Aylesbury_ this _26th_ Day of _October_ one thousand eight hundred and _twelve_

Witness present,

The treaty of Amiens provided but fourteen months of uneasy peace before the conflict between Britain and France was renewed on 18 May 1803. However, the impending breakdown of treaty arrangements had been clear for some months previously and it was as early as 11 March that the Addington administration re-embodied the militia with an immediate extension of the annual training period from 21 to 28 days and a relaxation of the property qualifications for officers. On 28 May the supplementary militia was also re-embodied and thirteen days later came legislation to bring the militia up to establishment more speedily, primarily by fining counties until they had met their militia quota. There was also the first of an almost bewildering variety of other enactments eventually contributing to a total of no fewer than 21 separate acts passed in 1802 or 1803 to raise men either voluntarily or compulsorily for the defence of the country against invasion.

That threat of invasion was to remain a constant factor in British calculations for at least the next ten years and was by no means diminished as popularly supposed by the naval victory at Trafalgar in October 1805. Indeed, British expeditions to Copenhagen in 1807 and to both Walcheren and the Basque Roads in 1809 were intended to damage the French ability to launch a direct attack on Britain by striking at her capacity to gain command of the sea. Just as she had been between 1803 and 1805 Britain was also effectively alone again between July 1807 when the last of her partners in the 'Third Coalition', Russia, concluded the treaty of Tilsit with the French and June 1813 when Britain, Russia and Prussia joined in a 'Fourth Coalition' to which the Swedes, Austrians and others also later subscribed. Despite naval losses in the intervening years and whatever the difficulties that would have been met in attempting actually to man them and to put generally poorly constructed and unseaworthy vessels to sea, the French still had 80 ships of the line as late as 1813 with 35 building compared with the maximum of 113 ships of the line deployed by the Royal Navy for its global duties in 1808–9. However, the period of greatest danger to Britain, of course, was that between 1803 and 1805.

Bonaparte, who had been appointed Consul for life in August 1802 and would be proclaimed Emperor Napoleon I in May 1804, created a new Army of England in May 1803 and maintained it at Boulogne and other camps along the Channel coast until August 1805, by which time it was in excess of 200,000 strong. Doubt has been expressed as to how seriously Napoleon entertained the idea of invasion but the preparations were comprehensive enough. By August 1805 he had lifting capacity for 167,000 men with some 93,000 readily available for the first two waves of any assault. Given favourable weather and tide conditions, an invasion could conceivably have been mounted over a period of just six tides to put the French ashore between Pegwell Bay and Ramsgate with a probable superiority of three to one over those defenders that could have been mustered in the same time scale.[1]

Favourable winds for an attempt persisted for much of the summer of 1803 and suitably calm weather was again experienced in the spring of 1804. An even more critical period for Britain was that between March and August 1805 when Admiral Villeneuve eluded the British naval blockade off Toulon and the British pursuit left the Channel partially unprotected for at least six days. In fact, Napoleon had already decided to march eastwards to counter the military mobilisation by Austria and Russia and thus to abandon the invasion attempt but this was not immediately apparent in Britain. Thereafter, the likelihood of French success was much less since invasion would have required a more comprehensive mastery of the sea than that needed in 1803 but Napoleon certainly seriously revived his ambitions in this regard through his energetic naval rebuilding programmes after 1807.

Thus, there was too great a danger of invasion to be ignored when war was renewed in 1803 and it was always possible that the French squadron in Brest could slip out into the Channel and establish that brief and temporary supremacy that would suffice to allow an attempt to be made. Those advising the British government were acutely aware of the vulnerability of the southern and eastern coasts of England with only 81,000 regular troops available in Britain as a whole and the militia and supplementary militia – together amounting to some 75,000 men – still reforming at a time when in August 1803 the commander-in-chief, the Duke of York, considered 180,000 men necessary for the immediate defence of London alone. One solution was to provide fortifications beyond those existing around important installations such as Chatham, Dover, Portsmouth or Harwich. The two most innovative schemes were the construction of the Royal Military Canal from Shorncliffe to Cliff End and the erection of 103 Martello towers along the coast from Aldeburgh to Seaford although, in each case, the defensive system was not fully completed until 1812.

However, brick and mortar was only a long-term solution to Britain's defensive problems and when the danger was greatest between 1803 and 1805 field works alone such as those dug for the defence of London at Shooters Hill and Brentwood were available. There was also confusion over the continuing viability of the policy of driving the country of population, crops and livestock ahead of any invading force. Originally conceived in 1779 and again mooted in 1796 and 1801, the concept met particular opposition from the lord lieutenant of Sussex, the Duke of Richmond, whose own detailed survey in 1801 had convinced him of the sheer enormity of the task facing county authorities. Accordingly, the policy was effectively abandoned in November 1803 although it was still intended to deprive the French of ready access to horses and draught cattle.

Still another aspect of the defence schemes giving cause for concern was what proved the last flourish of the beacon system. Beacons had been put back into order in some southern counties in 1798 but, even where they were erected, they were in far fewer numbers than in previous times. Moreover, while they were relatively cheap to construct, maintenance and manning was a constant expense and there were frequent false alarms. In late October 1803, for example, the lord lieutenant of Essex, Lord Braybrooke, was moved to advertise in the county press his hope that 'the usual custom of lighting bonfires on the fifth of November may be discontinued at the ensuing anniversary of that day'.[2] None the less, there was still a panic in Chelmsford caused by 'some persons' choosing to burn weeds and bean straw and, in precisely the same way, the GOC of the Northern

District demanded an end to the practice of lighting heath fires after a false alarm at Masham in the North Riding in March 1805. Indeed, the ever-present tensions of the years between 1803 and 1805 can be readily gauged by the frequent occurrence of such alarms. In February 1804, one such major scare was felt throughout the Scottish border country when all the beacons were fired in error, an event impressing itself sufficiently on Walter Scott, then serving as quartermaster, paymaster and secretary with the Royal Edinburgh Volunteer Light Dragoons, for him to include it in his novel *The Antiquary*.

Given the lack of regular troops and fortifications and the pressing nature of the danger of invasion, it is not surprising that Addington's ministry considered a sweeping mobilisation of the population along the lines of the Defence of the Realm legislation of 1798. Accordingly, the other measure enacted along with that for completing the militia on 11 June 1803 was the Defence Act (43 Geo III c 55) requiring lords lieutenant to return the numbers of able-bodied men between the ages of 15 and 60, distinguishing those serving in existing units, those willing to serve and those ineligible for service. Particulars were also required of millers, bakers and the owners of wagons and barges while returns would also enumerate vehicles, livestock, food and forage and those appointed to remove them: the latter requirement, of course, was prior to the abandonment of the driving policy. In most cases the new legislation merely required updating the various forms circulated to localities in 1798, the only substantial variation being the need to record the number and location of bakers' ovens. However, it is indicative of the growing interest in and requirement for the collection of statistical information on the part of authority under the exigencies of war, the Defence Act then being almost immediately superseded by a General Defence Act (43 Geo III c 96) on 27 July 1803.

Apparently suggested to Addington by Pitt and popularly known as the 'Levee en Masse Act' – although hardly equating to that measure of universal conscription introduced by the French National Assembly in August 1793 – the new legislation required yet more returns, dividing males between the ages of 17 and 55 into four classes depending upon age, marital status and the number of children under 10 in order to facilitate preparations for arming and training them. Other information demanded included details of

households, numbers of millers, bakers, stockmen, weapons, livestock, and food and fodder stocks. Indeed, returns were so comprehensive and complex that, at Barnstaple and in the Rowbarrow
hundred of Dorset, the information was reduced to digests with only
summaries forwarded to lords lieutenant while the actual lists were
retained by those appointed captains or superintendents of hundreds
and boroughs under the legislation.

It was anticipated that the first three classes specified in the
General Defence Act, embracing single men aged between 17 and 50
and married men aged between 17 and 30 with two children or less
under 10, would be trained for two hours on a Sunday for a
maximum of 20 days between March and December. Longer
training might be authorised and, in an emergency, those trained
could be assimilated into existing military units or even formed into
new corps. In any case, some would be detailed as pioneers or special
constables. However, it was also made clear that the legislation
would be suspended provided volunteers came forward equivalent
to three-quarters of the first class (single men aged between 17 and
30). Since these were forthcoming – the numbers of volunteers were
actually limited subsequently to six times a county's militia quota –
no training programme was effected. The principle of a liability
wider than that required by militia legislation then lapsed until
briefly revived by the Training Act in July 1806.

Just as the application of the second Defence Act was closely
related to the progress of the revived volunteer movement, so the
Training Act (46 Geo III c 90) reflected what by 1806 had become the
dislike of that same movement on the part of the then secretary of
state for war and colonies, William Windham. Coupled as will be
seen with measures aimed directly at the volunteers, the Training Act
proposed that all males between the ages of 16 and 40 should be
liable to 24 days' training annually to be carried out within 5 miles of
their abode. There would be a remuneration of 1s 0d per day for the
200,000 men selected each year to undergo training but a fine for
those who refused to appear. Training would be carried out by
regular army NCOs and there would be neither uniforms nor
officers, Windham contemplating either incorporating the men into
army or militia in the event of invasion or simply allowing them to
stand as 'armed peasantry'. The sense of outrage engendered among
the volunteers by Windham's policies played no small part in the
collapse of the 'Talents' administration in March 1807 by which

time little or nothing had been done to implement the Training Act beyond perhaps preliminary contacts with suitable regular regiments. Ironically, it remained on the statute book until as late as 1875 when it was finally removed by the provisions of the Militia (Voluntary Enlistment) Act.

It can be readily imagined how far the need to undertake preparations under the terms of such defence legislation naturally placed a considerable additional burden on those at county, hundredal and parochial level already faced with completing the militia and supplementary militia. However, there was yet a further challenge to be met through the attempt to provide for reinforcements to the regular army since the unpopularity of direct recruitment from the militia among the latter's commanding officers had resulted in a firm prohibition on militiamen entering the army being written into the 1802 Militia Act. Thus, on 20 June 1803 more legislation (43 Geo III c 82) proposed to raise an army of reserve – sometimes also referred to as the additional army of England – of 34,000 men in England and Wales and 16,000 men in Scotland and Ireland by ballot of eligible men between the ages of 18 and 45 for service in the United Kingdom or the Channel Isles. Substitution was permitted, in which case service was for five years or the duration rather than just five years for a principal serving in person, and exemption by a fine of £20. The application of the ballot could be delayed if parishes found a number of men equal to two-thirds of its quota willing to serve as parochial substitutes but a fine of £20 for every man deficient of the quota would also be imposed on parishes.

The difficulty for parish officials was that exemption from the army of reserve was extended not only beyond existing militia practice to poor men with more than one child born in wedlock but also to yeomanry and volunteers enlisted before 22 June 1803 and those who had served in the militia. Moreover, since there had already been ballots for the militia and supplementary militia, the price of personal and parochial substitutes rose alarmingly. By early 1804 the average price was £18 in Essex and £24 in Argyll and Bute but in other counties such as Buckinghamshire, Middlesex and Northumberland it had exceeded £30 before the end of 1803 and, in the case of Sussex, reached £50. Insurance clubs flourished once more both locally and nationally. At Stoke Poges in Buckinghamshire, for example, a vestry meeting opened a subscription list for the army of reserve in August 1803 which raised a total of £89 6s 0d, the largest number of subscribers being 45 men who contributed the lowest rate of 10s 6d. Subsequently, outgoings totalled £63 19s 6d to find two £20 fines, a substitute for £23 7s 0d and 12s 6d to defray other costs. At Rochford in Essex, by contrast, parish officials were circulated in January 1804 by Westby & Co of Southwark Repertory offering substitutes who 'will be such as are only of fair Character, while those of a contrary Description (whose only Aim is Desertion and Fraud) will be ever precluded by the Conductors of this Office, whenever they can entertain any reasonable doubt, after due enquiry'.[3]

Unfortunately, there were only too many men whose aim was desertion or fraud, imposing additional burdens on those unable to afford rising prices for substitutes. Another feature of the legislation earning opprobium was the fact that payment of a fine for avoiding service in the army of reserve did not exempt a man from the militia and vice versa. It has been further suggested that the measure as a whole failed to provide the requisite number of recruits for the regular army, which was already suffering through the disparity of its own recruitment bounty of £7 12s 6d with the high prices commanded by substitutes for militia and army of reserve.[4] Nevertheless, by May 1804 when the legislation was effectively suspended on the fall of Addington's ministry, approximately 30,000 men had been raised of whom 19,533 enlisted into the regular army for general service while the army of reserve battalions themselves had been utilised by the Duke of York as second 'nursery' battalions to regular regiments.

It was the intention of the Addington ministry itself to suspend the operation of the army of reserve for a year in the hope of inducing more of those coming forward as substitutes to enter the army instead. However, the evidence of growing parliamentary opposition manifest in his majority falling to just 37 in the vote on this measure on 19 March 1804 played a major part in Addington's decision to resign. Beyond a more aggressive foreign policy, Pitt's approach to defence issues was not noticeably different from that of his predecessor but, determined to improve on Addington's measures, his new ministry swept away the army of reserve by bringing in a curiously hybrid scheme with the Permanent Additional Force Act (44 Geo III c 56) in June 1804.

Designed more to achieve wide political acceptability than to address the actual practical difficulties facing recruitment, this combined the army of reserve and the supplementary militia into a 79,000-strong home service force of men aged between 18 and 45 enlisted for five years or for six months after the conclusion of hostilities on a bounty of 12 guineas. It would both directly feed the army's second battalions and also provide recruits for general service by offering a further bounty of 10 guineas to those who transferred. At the same time, perceived inequities of the ballot and of the rising price of substitutes were eliminated by fixing a parochial quota and requiring parishes to find the men by whatever means they could short of compulsion. Parochial officers would receive a guinea for every man they contributed towards quota but, equally, parishes would be fined £20 for every man short. Moreover, parishes could not accept any man to serve on their behalf who resided over 20 miles away within the same county or over 10 miles away across a county boundary.

It had been hoped to bring in 20,000 men in just two months but by May 1806 the legislation had produced barely 13,000: in Kent only 14 men had been found by November 1804, leaving a county deficit of 1,190.[5] A month later, there were no fewer than 25 counties which had not furnished a single man and still 14 counties in this position as late as May 1806 despite tinkering with the bounties to make the scheme more attractive. But an even greater measure of the failure of the act was the fact that there was a staggering £1.8 million in fines outstanding when it was repealed in May 1806.

It will have been noted that much of the defence legislation enacted between 1803 and 1807 was closely related to the changing status of the revived volunteers. The second Defence Act was suspended where sufficient numbers came forward and the Training Act partially motivated by dislike of them, while the success of other measures such as army of reserve and Permanent Additional Force Act was invariably affected by the exemption granted volunteers. Addington, of course, had already passed legislation to retain yeomanry and volunteer corps in 1802 and on 31 March 1803 invited more to come forward under its provisions with the prospect of qualifying for exemption from the militia for attending only five days' exercise annually and drawing a £2 clothing allowance per volunteer or £60 allowance per troop of yeomanry. However, three months later in what became known as the 'June allowances', pay was offered for up to two days' training per week between Lady Day and Michaelmas and for up to one day a week during the winter to a maximum of 85 days' pay per annum where corps were prepared to serve throughout a military district. None the less, it would appear that there was some official concern that exemption would affect the ballots for the supplementary militia and acceptance of corps was somewhat muted, exemption from the army of reserve only being offered those corps enrolled before 22 June.

In offering pay and requiring service throughout the military district, the June allowances established a different style of volunteering from that which had existed prior to 1803 and this might account for the relatively poor response. Some 14 counties raised no units under the June allowances and many of the new rural corps were apparently raised only under the threat of the levee en masse legislation, the government announcing on 27 July 1803 its willingness to suspend the levee en masse where volunteers came forward equal to three-quarters of the first class specified under the act. However, there was a measure of financial penalty for tardiness in coming forward in that, on 3 August, the 'August allowances' were introduced for corps enrolled since 22 June, offering a clothing allowance of £1 once every three years but only 1s 0d a day for 20 days' training provided a corps was willing to extend its services anywhere. Paradoxically, a so-called Billeting Act (43 Geo III c 121) enacted on 11 August to permit the billeting of yeomanry and volunteers added to the confusion by setting down a minimum of 12 days' training for yeomanry and 24 days' training for volunteers as qualification for exemption from the army of reserve or any other additional force raised.

Part of the difficulty lay in the inadequate organisation of the government machinery whereby documents and decisions were constantly shunted between departments. The deluge of voluntary offers all but overwhelmed the administration and on 18 August the War Office strictly limited acceptance to no more than six times the militia quota. Amid the outcry at the limitation imposed responsibility for the volunteers was passed from the War Office to Charles Yorke as home secretary. However, Yorke had inherited a staff of only 15 which had still not exceeded 19 as late as January 1804 and his office was equally beset by the administrative burden. On 31 August, therefore, he announced that numbers enrolled above the limit of 18 August could be carried as supernumeraries without pay and allowances or exemption from the militia or army of reserve ballots. Further confusion followed in November 1803 when it was proposed that allowances be given for the appointment of adjutants and sergeant majors only where corps were prepared to undertake 85 days' training per annum irrespective of which set of allowances the corps had enrolled under.

The degree of organisational chaos can best be illustrated by the fact that returns furnished to the War Office between December 1803 and February 1804 indicated that 362 units were serving under the June allowances of which 152 were restricted to service in their military district, 108 available for service throughout Britain in the event of an invasion, 56 available for service throughout Britain at any time, and 46 serving under their own terms. A total of 1,165 units were serving under the August allowances but seven of them still specified different terms from those stipulated and only one was prepared to serve anywhere in Britain at any time. In addition, there were 43 supernumerary corps raised under Yorke's concession on 31 August and 11 units which appeared to be serving under no specified terms at all. In at least 31 cases, early amalgamation had resulted in men raised under the June and August allowances serving in the same unit while in the Eastern Regiment of Norfolk Cavalry, each of the six troops served on different terms. Whatever they were entitled to, some 140 volunteer units had also elected to forgo pay and allowances entirely.[6]

Some degree of uniformity was restored by Yorke's Volunteer Exemption Act (44 Geo III c 18) on 20 December 1803, which set the minimum training requirement for exemption from both militia and army of reserve at 24 days per annum. A subsequent Volunteer Consolidation Act (44 Geo III c 54) was passed on 5 June 1804 having originally been introduced during and having contributed to the dying throes of the Addington ministry. Effectively governing volunteer corps until 1863 and yeomanry until 1901, it repealed all the legislation relating to the yeomanry and volunteers so far enacted in 1802 and 1803 and restricted all to 24 days' pay per annum. This also set 24 days' training as the qualifying period for exemption from service in the militia or army of reserve in the case of volunteers and 12 days for yeomanry. The act offered bounties for active or permanent service and, while it vested more effective disciplinary powers in commanding officers, also conferred on volunteers and yeomen the right to resign upon 14 days' notice following some confusion as to the matter in the previous year. Curiously, however, it did not address the differing liabilities of corps originally enrolled under the June and August allowances to serve either only in their own military districts or anywhere in the kingdom.

Given the confusion in government circles it is not perhaps surprising that the same condition should apply in the country as a whole. Indeed, one volunteer company at Iver in Buckinghamshire was so bewildered by the terms offerred that the men refused to take the oath of allegiance for fear of being committed to wider obligations and they were disbanded in September 1803. In Cambridgeshire and Sussex, too, there were apprehensions of volunteers being combined with militia or regulars upon actual service and it was by no means the case that every county could find volunteers equal to three-quarters of the first class specified in the second Defence Act. Generally, Scottish, Welsh and maritime counties did well but those falling short of the required number included Lancashire, Northamptonshire, Somerset, Warwickshire, Wiltshire, Staffordshire and Buckinghamshire despite the offer of the latter's lord lieutenant to give a guinea from his own pocket to every man coming forward to meet the county figure of 3,594 volunteers or yeomen who completed the 20 days' training to qualify as efficient under the August allowances.[7]

In advertising his generosity, the Marquess of Buckingham laid stress on the relief from the compulsory element of the levee en masse to be gained from volunteering and there is no doubt that exemption generally was a powerful stimulus to the revival of the movement as a whole in 1803. In September, for example, the West Somerset Yeomanry took delivery of 500 booklets 'for the information of every Yeoman of the heads of the different Acts of Parliament concerning exemption' while those offering their services for a troop at Dudley in Worcestershire would 'expect to be exempt from the Ballot to the Militia and Army of Reserve'. The antiquary William Upcott, then working as a bookseller's clerk in the capital, had subscribed 2 guineas to insure himself against what appears to have been the army of reserve but found that it did not preclude him from selection for the militia and was 'in a continual state of ferment and trouble'. A remedy presented itself for 'entering into some Volunteer Corps would shield me from all harm'. Unfortunately, Upcott could not afford to join the volunteers but persuaded a friend to subsidise his enlistment in the St James Loyal Volunteers. As far as Upcott was concerned regular attendance for the next three weeks was a necessity only in order 'the sooner to receive the certificate from the adjutant declaring me able to join the rest of the corps, and to render regular attendance unnecessary'.[8]

Generally, therefore, it could be argued that volunteering after 1803 was more self-serving than previously. It now offered more to the poorer elements of society in terms of exemption, pay, clothing and recreational opportunities and this could well have been a major factor in the distinct change of social composition in 1803 previously remarked upon. Nevertheless, there was still clearly a considerable element of patriotism as well as a concern for order and stability and, at the same time, an undeniable fascination for some in belonging to a quasi-military organisation. Upcott noted that some of his fellow recruits enjoyed drill and in London in particular it became fashionable to be seen exercising in the open fields north of Bloomsbury or firing on the ranges at Chalk Farm. Francis Horner, a founder of the *Edinburgh Review*, wrote in July 1803 that 'for ten days past [we] have been drilling most indefatigably; going from Northumberland Street up to the Foundling Hospital Ground twice every day. I have been at it three hours this morning, and my hand shakes so, that you see I cannot write'.[9] Similar testimony to the popularity of drill derives from the correspondence of Charles Kirkpatrick Sharpe of Annandale in Dumfries, who complained in December 1803 that 'a sober-minded Christian' could get no peace when 'Gentlemen and clowns are at it from morning till night' and 'the very cows and hogs at the approach of a hostile cur draw up in battle array, in imitation of the two-legged bumpkins who are spoiling the exercise under every hedge . . .'.[10] Some 12,000 volunteers attended a review in Hyde Park in October 1803 with another 14,000 present on the second day when an appearance was made by the King and exiled French royalty.

Whatever the motivation and despite difficulties in some areas, the number of volunteers and yeomanry had reached over 342,000 effectives in the rank and file by January 1804, of whom some 211,000 served under the August allowances, 67,000 under the June allowances and the remainder under other local terms. Not only was this large number of men more or less unavailable for service in other forces but it was also too sizeable to be easily equipped. The Ordnance Office, which was responsible for supplying arms and equipment to army and auxiliaries, had some 150,000 muskets in store at the time war was renewed in 1803. However, most of these had gone to equip new regulars and the militia and Lord Palmerston estimated in September 1803 that for the volunteers, 'there are scarcely arms sufficient for 5 or 6,000'.[11] While it was originally intended to arm only 25 in every 100 volunteers and to concentrate initial distribution only on those areas most vulnerable to invasion, various extensions and dispensations subsequently granted lifted the requirement from the 66,800 muskets estimated in September 1803 to well over 300,000.

Nevertheless, deficiencies remained and the haphazard distribution either by the Ordnance or lords lieutenant of those muskets made available was a source of much dissension within some counties such as Hertfordshire and Shropshire. In the case of the latter county, only considerable private effort and expenditure enabled corps to equip themselves with firearms. Briefly, between September and December 1803, the Ordnance offered reimbursement at standard contract price to corps buying their own weapons but so many applied to do so that the concession had to be withdrawn on financial grounds. Even where government supplied muskets were available, the ammunition allowance provided for only 24 rounds of ball and 60 blank cartridges per man per year. The government had hoped that most volunteers would be satisfied with pikes, of which some 103,572 had been distributed by April 1804, but it soon became apparent from the reports of lords lieutenant that their issue did almost as much harm to morale as several months' drilling without weapons of any kind.

Adding to the difficulties stemming from the lack of arms and equipment well into 1804 and the confusing array of terms under which individual corps served was the continuing internal governance of corps by mutually agreed rules and resolutions, which might or might not contribute to efficiency. At the inaugural meeting of the Liverpool Independent Rifle Corps on 20 July 1803, for example, it was resolved to exclude anyone below 5 ft 3 in or above 5 ft 10 in in height to achieve 'uniformity' on parade while in August volunteers at Maidenhead in Berkshire copied all the resolutions agreed by a Northamptonshire corps except that they ruled out any Sunday drilling which they disliked. Given the lack of either real powers or established social authority on the part of officers – especially where the social quality of the rank and file had declined – it is not surprising that discipline was often lacking. One example is the Loyal Sandbach and Rode Volunteer Infantry in Cheshire in which no fewer than 16 men had to be fined and six discharged altogether after drunk and disorderly conduct affected four out of the unit's six companies in February 1804. That same year, the commanding officer of the Loyal Horsley and Tetbury Volunteers in Gloucestershire had to remind his men that they should neither be seen walking in the streets of Gloucester out of uniform when on permanent duty nor be seen drunk nor 'pissing against the church'. Their conduct had improved substantially by the following year but in October 1806 there was a near mutiny when the commanding officer 'out of a compliment to them all' offered to lead them abroad, the assumption being that he was volunteering their services for the expedition to Buenos Aires.[12]

While such indiscipline suggests how much broader the social composition of the volunteers became after 1803, it was still the case that many volunteers were by definition those whose commitments would have precluded full-time military training. Thus, orders to units such as the 1st Regiment of the Loyal London Volunteers were still couched in 1804 in such terms as 'the Committee have recommended that the Names of such Members who feel & find it convenient to join the Muster on that occasion be collected, & reported to the Colonel on Wednesday morning next, that he may determine whether the number be sufficient to carry out the Plan with effect'. In the same way the secretary of state for war and colonies, Lord Hobart, had himself called for training when announcing the August allowances to lords lieutenant in 1803 'as far as is consistent with the urgency of the present conjuncture, to local circumstances, and to the course of industry and cultivation'.[13]

Given the difficulties, it is not surprising that a number of leading regulars doubted the volunteers' military effectiveness. Both Major-General Sir John Moore and Lieutenant-General John Simcoe had such reservations. One anecdote recorded of Moore had Pitt, who had raised three battalions of Cinque Ports Volunteers in his capacity as Lord Warden, asking where his corps would be placed in an invasion and being told by Moore that they would be drawn up on a hill 'where you will make a most formidable appearance to the enemy, while I with the soldiers shall be fighting on the beach'. Another military critic was Colonel (later Major-General) Robert Craufurd who felt mutually agreed rules and regulations made for so 'delicate a machine' that the volunteers were unfit for war.[14]

It is significant that Moore, Simcoe and Craufurd were all associated with the development of light infantry formations and tactics for one body of thought suggested that light infantry training would be more appropriate for volunteers than the evolutions of David Dundas's Prussian-style drill manual of 1792. This view was echoed subsequently by the historian Sir John Fortescue. However, whatever the army's shortage of light troops and whatever the inabilities of volunteers to fight in the field without substantial mounted or artillery support, light infantry actually required more training than line troops, not least in musketry. Moreover, Fortescue's general criticism of both militia and volunteers must be viewed in the context of his *The County Lieutenancies and the Army* being published in 1909 with the assistance of a subsidy from the then secretary of state for war, Haldane, whose interests were well served by such a critique.

In fact, Fortescue was at error in implying that the volunteers were left largely to their own devices, for the Duke of York was determined to instil as many military habits as possible despite his lack of formal authority over them. In September 1803 he appointed inspecting field officers to advise the volunteers and yeomanry attending parades and reviews and report regularly on progress. The inspectors could also serve as brigade staff in the event of an invasion, York then instituting a brigade system for both yeomanry and volunteers in May 1804. In October 1803 units in maritime counties had also been given the opportunity of undertaking between ten days' and a month's permanent duty and this was extended to all counties in March 1804 although there was considerable confusion as to the pecuniary reward being offered different corps until the Volunteer Consolidation Act in June granted all the so-called 'marching guinea'. Three months later, there was further encouragement for periods of permanent service by offering ten days' pay for an additional ten days' exercise in the succeeding six months. By March 1804 some 80,000 volunteers had already undertaken permanent service from maritime counties and by June 1804 the total exceeded 100,000.

The relationships between inspectors and the corps were not always cordial but volunteers did improve sufficiently for a number of inspectors to conclude by 1804 that they were fit to act in conjunction with regulars and, as early as December 1803, the distinguished soldier Lord Cornwallis made the point that 'no man, whether civil or military, will persuade me that 300,000 men, trained as the volunteers at present are, do not add very materially to the confidence and to the actual security of this country'.[15]

The dual threat of invasion and the ballot – there had been a marked improvement in Devon after the lord lieutenant had disbanded a battalion of ineffective volunteers in July 1803 and balloted them for the army of reserve – served to stimulate the volunteer movement sufficiently for there still to be 308,973 men serving in the rank and file of volunteers and yeomanry (including over 64,000 in Ireland) in January 1806. However, that same month, Pitt's death brought not only a new administration but also a new secretary of state for war and colonies – Windham – who was implacably hostile to the volunteers for all that he had commanded a volunteer unit himself. In April 1804, for example, Windham had remarked that any offer of voluntary service was 'more liable to spoil than mackerel itself' while his most quoted utterance was that the volunteers were 'painted cherries which none but simple birds would take for real fruit'.[16]

Windham's opposition to volunteers should be seen both in the context of the general suspicion that the volunteers were largely out of central control as well as in terms of his desire to improve the popularity of and the recruitment for the army and militia, the existence of the volunteers having contributed to high prices for militia substitutes and the concomitant uncompetitiveness of regular army bounties. Moreover, Windham believed the volunteers far too expensive, claiming that they had cost over £5 million in allowances since 1803 although, in fact, the actual cost to April 1806 was some £3.4 million. He thus hoped to save £878,000 per annum by reducing pay and allowances while making more men available for the militia and army. Unfortunately, in practice, Windham's measures merely deprived remaining volunteers of any real enducement to efficiency while simultaneously failing to improve recruitment for army and militia.

Windham's principal proposal for the army was to replace enlistment for life by a seven year term of short service for infantry – the initial term was longer for cavalry and artillery – with the promise of increased pay upon re-enlistment and the promise of a pension as a more distant reward. At the same time the militia ballot was suspended for two years from July 1806 with only a limited bounty now being offered in return for voluntary enlistment. The demise of the ballot theoretically removed a significant cause of the militia's unpopularity and, in the process, divested the volunteers of the stimulus of evasion that some now believed their prime motivation.

Originally, Windham had clearly intended to sweep away the volunteers in much the same way that he disposed of Pitt's Permanent Additional Force Act with his own Training Act providing for a system of national military training. In the event, it would appear that the Duke of York persuaded Windham of the military utility of retaining a substantial force of volunteers and they were allowed to survive but only at a price. Thus, Windham removed the inspecting field officers and abolished the June allowances for infantry volunteers, restricting all existing corps to receiving payment on the basis of the August allowances and declining to offer any allowances at all to new corps raised after 24 July 1806. While yeomanry raised on the June allowances retained their allowances in modified form, yeomanry allowances as a whole were severely curtailed and Windham also declined to guarantee any clothing allowances for volunteer corps beyond the current year of 1806. A final measure was to remove the privilege extended in the Volunteer Consolidation Act of volunteer officers ranking equally with those of the army and militia.

Windham's assault had its effect, the returns of those serving in the rank and file falling to 294,378 effectives by July 1807 (inclusive of 65,942 in Ireland) or a net loss of 13,000 men in just 12 months. But, equally, Windham's measures failed to produce more recruits for either the army or militia, whose manpower deficiencies increased respectively from 25,000 to 35,000 and from 8,000 to 18,000 short of establishment. As already recounted, the Training Act was a major disappointment and when the 'Talents' foundered in March 1807 few could have mourned Windham's removal from the War Office. Nevertheless, he had glimpsed the necessity of an all-embracing reform drawing army, militia and volunteers into a more coherent structure and this was certainly the way followed by his able successor in the Portland ministry, Castlereagh.

The real key to a more sensible organisation of the military forces available was the relationship between the army and the militia, the maintenance of the strength of the army becoming an even more vital necessity once Tilsit left Britain thoroughly alone in July 1807. Castlereagh had briefly occupied the War Office for seven months at the close of Pitt's last administration, at which time he had endeavoured to create a 'disposable force' of up to 45,000 infantry and cavalry for ready embarkation. Ultimately, some 30,000 men were committed to North Germany between November 1805 and February 1806 in addition to small expeditionary forces already dispatched to southern Italy and the Cape of Good Hope. With the Permanent Additional Force Act not fulfilling its purpose, the ability fo find British troops for foreign ventures at this time had resulted largely from Pitt's decision to revive the 1799 precedent of enlisting militiamen directly into the line. Since the 1802 act expressly forbade this, enabling legislation had been passed in April 1805 (45 Geo III c 31) to permit the enlistment from a regiment of up to four-fifths of the number borne in excess of the original quota – effectively equalling four-fifths of those added as supplementary militia. Mindful of the opposition of militia colonels to the loss of trained men, safeguards were offered such as the ability of commanding officers to forbid the enlistment of selected men equal to half of the original quota. By such means a total of 10,696 militiamen had been enlisted into the army.

While the expedition to North Germany had achieved little, Castlereagh clearly appreciated the ready reinforcement that had been obtained from the militia. Accordingly, within three days of the decision to send an expeditionary force to Copenhagen, he announced his intention to seek a further 28,000 militiamen for the army including 7,000 from the Irish establishment. Since many militiamen enlisted in 1803 would also be due to reach the end of their term of service in the following year, Castlereagh also proposed to revive the ballot. In the case of the militia in Britain, legislation passed in August (47 Geo III c 57) provided for the enlistment into the army of militiamen in excess of three-fifths of establishment up to five-sixths of the allotted number while further legislation (47 Geo III c 71) allowed for a ballot to be held within three months to make good up to three-quarters of the original 1802 quota. The fine for exemption was raised to £20 while counties, hundreds and parishes were also liable to a £60 fine for every man deficient. Where the full quota was raised, the ballot would be suspended until January 1810.

As a result of the new legislation some 27,505 militiamen were secured for the army but, at the same time, the revival of the ballot also brought what Fortescue aptly described as 'a wild traffic in substitutes',[17] the 26,085 militiamen raised by ballot in England alone including only 3,129 principals. Insurance societies flourished once more and, especially in Wales, the price of substitutes again averaged £40 or more. None the less, Castlereagh had succeeded admirably in augmenting the army and in March 1809 the experiment was repeated with legislation (49 Geo III c 4 and c 53 respectively) again permitting the enlistment of militiamen in excess of three-fifths of establishment and raising replacements initially by voluntary enlistment, for which a bounty of up to 12 guineas would be offered, or, if the quota had not been filled by 1 June 1810 (later extended to 30 June), by ballot. Once the men were raised, however, the ballot would again be suspended until January 1812.

The augmentation of the militia appears to have gone no more smoothly than in 1807 amid the usual opposition to the ballot – one balloted in this year who spent his savings on a substitute was the future railway engineer, George Stephenson, then a colliery brakesman in Northumberland – and some confusion as to the correct interpretation of the finer points of the legislation but 16,429 out of the quota of 28,492 militiamen permitted to enlist had been added to the army by 1 June 1809 to compensate for casualties suffered during the retreat to Corunna and in time for many to be sent to Walcheren.

Invariably, due to opposition from militia colonels, the enlistment of the militia into the line was justified on each occasion on grounds of expediency be it due to the requirements of the Dutch campaign in 1799, the North German campaign in 1805, the desperate situation in which Britain found itself after Tilsit or, increasingly after 1809, the need to maintain the army in the Iberian peninsula. Such opposition was understandable both in view of the indiscipline and drunkenness that often resulted as those transferring to the army expended their bounty money in the shortest possible time and also in terms of the militia being deprived of trained men. Those joining the militia as substitutes for a bounty were equally ready to join the army for a similar bounty but it was also the case that those longest in the militia were usually the most likely to enlist.

That such men were frequently of high quality can perhaps be illustrated by noting that some of the most celebrated accounts of the Peninsular War and Waterloo emanating from the ranks of the army were actually penned by those who had served first in the militia including Private Wheeler, William Surtees, Edward Costello (although his account was ghosted), William Green and Thomas Jackson. In addition, Thomas Morris had been in the volunteers while that most celebrated of soldier authors, Rifleman Harris, had come from the army of reserve. Similarly, one of a handful of early nineteenth-century farm servants' autobiographies to have survived is that of Joseph Mayett, who served in the Royal Bucks King's Own Militia from 1803 to 1815. Equally, however, it should be noted that William Turner, who was executed after the Pentrich rising, had transferred to the army from the militia whilst the leading Cato Street conspirator, Arthur Thistlewood, had been a militia officer. The latter was an appointment also enjoyed by the contemptible Wickham in *Pride and Prejudice*, Jane Austen's work generally having frequent reference to the militia.

In turn, the quality of the men to be found in the militia ensured that it would continue to be seen as an appropriate source for regular recruits given the demands of the commitment to the Peninsula after 1809. Accordingly, Palmerston, who as secretary at war in the Perceval and Liverpool administrations answered for the army in the Commons, maintained Castlereagh's policy. A new bill (51 Geo III c 20) in April 1811 allowed for the reduction of the militia to the 1802 establishment of 70,000 men and for a fixed annual draft of militiamen into the army not exceeding one-seventh of the that quota. More time was also given for filling those vacancies still outstanding from the 1809 legislation with the ballot now suspended until July 1813 once these were filled. Thereafter, in a somewhat unfortunate return to Windham's precedent, vacancies arising from the annual draft to the army would be filled by recruits obtained by voluntary enlistment, of whom up to a quarter might now be boys aged over 14. In addition, further legislation (51 Geo III c 118) provided for the interchange of militia regiments in Britain and Ireland on a voluntary and rotating basis for periods of up to two years at a time with all future militiamen engaged to serve throughout the British Isles.

While the filling of the 1809 vacancies proceeded only slowly, a further 11,453 militiamen entered the army in 1811, 9,927 in the following year and 9,095 in 1813. Additionally, some men in the latter year were specially recruited from 18 militia regiments solely for service in North America in return for a promise of free passage for families and a land grant at the conclusion of hostilities. In November 1813, however, it was proposed (54 Geo III c 1) to obtain an additional 30,000 militiamen by inviting offers from not more than three-quarters of any single regiment to serve anywhere in Europe in return for a bounty of 8 guineas and regular commissions for officers. It was also intended to invite other militiamen to volunteer to serve in provisional battalions under militia officers while yet a further act (54 Geo III c 10) in December 1813 removed the qualifications to universal militia service in the United Kingdom established by the 1811 legislation for the interchange of British and Irish regiments.

Unfortunately, the simultaneous offer of enlisting men into the line as well as forming provisional battalions led to some confusion and there were wide variations in the willingness of men to serve. Only 3,243 men were enlisted into the army between December 1813 and June 1814 while only 2,700 men were obtained for the provisional battalions, of which three were formed in February 1814 drawn from 16 separate county contingents. The three battalions were embarked at Portsmouth in March 1814 but spent over three weeks in the Solent and landed at Pauillac in the Gironde only on 23 April. The French forces had already withdrawn from Bordeaux and, without ever seeing action, the provisional battalions re-embarked on 29 May 1814. According to one somewhat prejudicial account, the provisional militiamen 'were constantly tipsy' while the inhabitants clustered to view their frequent parades and reviews 'not with the idea of gaining any hints as to evolutions, etc., but to gaze on the commanding officers, whom they denominated, "*Les boeufs-gras anglais*" '[18]

One of the difficulties in recruiting the provisional battalions was the resistance to serving except as complete units. In the case of the Denbighshire Militia, for example, only the appointment of their commanding officer, Sir Watkin Wynn, induced enlistment while men were only obtained from the Royal Bucks King's Own Militia, which was serving in Ireland, by virtual coercion as recorded by Mayett: 'the volunteering lasted 28 days during which time we that did not volunteer was very Sharply discipled [sic] for they Continualy [sic] marched us about from place to place and made us do all the duty but we beared it all with patience for we knew it would be all over in a month . . .'.[19]

Undoutedly, there was a much greater willingness on the part of the militia – and, especially, among their colonels – to serve overseas as an entity. Nine regiments had already volunteered for the Peninsula by January 1809 and such offers were repeated regularly thereafter. The Royal Bucks King's Own Militia, for example, volunteered both in 1808 and 1810 while the Royal Carnarvon Militia did so in both 1810 and 1812. However, there was a disinclination to accept offers from regiments which might contain those unfit for foreign service and it was clearly more convenient to the army to be able to direct its militia recruits where they were actually needed without having to accommodate the susceptibilities of independently minded militia colonels.

In this way the militia produced the manpower necessary to maintain the army at strength even if the flurry of additional measures in 1814 suggested that the system was under considerable strain. Militiamen were certainly hastily enlisted into the army during the Hundred Days in 1815 with regiments such as the 3/14th, 42nd and 3rd Guards reputedly filled with militiamen at Waterloo and many of the Guards supposedly still clad in Surrey militia uniforms. But, at the same time, the militia was also still fulfilling its domestic role. The militia was still often deployed on anti-smuggling duties and the more humble duty of guarding prisoners. However, its continuing usefulness was to be demonstrated amid the renewed economic pressures in 1810 leading to the appearance of Luddism in northern counties in the following year, spreading by November 1811 to embrace framework knitters in Leicestershire, Derbyshire and Nottinghamshire, woollen workers in Yorkshire and cotton workers in Lancashire and Cheshire.

With few regulars available, the bulk of the 12,000 men eventually deployed came from the militia. Thus, in May 1812 five militia regiments formed the nucleus of the 3,000 infantry stationed at the camp established at Nottingham while the spread of the disturbances further north resulted in 11 militia regiments (including three from the Nottingham camp) being based on the Kersal Moor camp near Manchester and three in Yorkshire. As related previously, there was some concern that northern militia might prove unreliable but there was no repetition of the major disciplinary problems encountered during earlier food riots. Of course, over ten years had passed and for many militiamen that had meant ten years of steady assimilation into the military life. In this regard, Mayett's autobiography provides a glimpse of the mentality of the ordinary militiaman regularly shunted around from one garrison to another. What is especially informative is that the perspective is of one who was distanced from many of his peers both by his literacy and also by his intermittently strong Baptist faith for the regiment's minority of practising nonconformists 'went by the name of the soapy set ... among the ungodly'. Yet, even Mayett 'carried a very small political universe in his baggage',[20] its parameters closely defined by his reactions to arbitrary military authority and injustice, his frequent illnesses and the overwhelming temptations to which so many of his fellows all too easily succumbed. For Mayett and, one must assume, for the great majority of militiamen being sent to 'fire ball' in Stockport on three occasions had little significance compared with the arduous marching and countermarching in wet weather that accompanied the deployment to the north.

Yeomanry, of course, were also employed against the Luddites in Nottinghamshire, Derbyshire, the West Riding and Leicestershire and, to a lesser extent, in Lancashire; in fact, the South Notts Yeomanry were out on duty for nearly three months. A volunteer corps also saw duty at Mansfield but this was very much an exception, for the second crucial plank in Castlereagh's extensive reorganisation after 1807 had been the creation of an entirely new military force to replace the majority of the volunteers.

Aware of the fact that no fewer than 110 out of the 558 non-Irish MPs in the Commons were volunteers – 77 of them commanding officers – Castlereagh had initially acted to reverse Windham's decisions by restoring inspecting field officers in July 1807 and granting all corps the August allowances in the following month. However, it was not Castlereagh's intention to leave the volunteers unreformed. In fact, Lord Grenville had contemplated introducing some new form of permanent training to substitute for the volunteers and Castlereagh himself thought along similar lines with the intention of creating a 'sedentary militia' by training all men aged between 18 and 30 and then balloting from them 200,000 men in England and 100,000 in Scotland for a term of three years' service in which they would undertake a further 28 days' training annually. The volunteers could then be gradually reduced as the sedentary militia increased, a force that had threatened to escape central control thus being replaced by one firmly under central control and military discipline.

There were a number of amendments to Castlereagh's legislation and the bill (48 Geo III c 111) passed on 30 June 1808 established what was now to be called the local militia. This and the volunteers together would total no more than six times the 1802 militia quota or 308,934 men in Britain as a whole. Volunteers were encouraged to transfer to the local militia in return for a 2 guinea bounty and individuals could also enlist on the same terms. In addition, a 'marching guinea' would be paid at the first annual training, which would be for 28 days annually during the four-year term of enlistment. In subsequent years a further 10s 6d would be paid for 'necessaries' while any overall mobilisation of the local militia would also be accompanied by payment of a guinea.

Deficiencies would be made up by ballot among those aged 18 to 30. No substitution was to be allowed and there were heavy fines on a sliding income scale for evasion and imprisonment for those failing to pay fines. Some limited exemption was granted including to those who had served in the army of reserve and to regular militiamen, and local militiamen themselves would be exempt from the militia ballot both during their service and for two years thereafter. They would normally venture no further than an adjoining county but would be liable to serve anywhere in Britain in the event of invasion or insurrection and could be called out for up to 14 days – counting against annual training – to suppress riots. Furthermore, local militiamen could transfer to the regular army at any time outside the annual training period with the vacancies being made up either by voluntary means or ballot: in the event, probably no more than 20,000 and possibly as few as 13,000 did so between 1809 and 1813.

The often heavy financial burdens now falling on volunteer officers, some of whom had only originally joined under the threat of the levee in 1803, persuaded many that they should agree to transfer to the local militia, especially as some saw the prospect of advancing themselves in what was almost an exercise in recruiting for rank. In fact, the pecuniary rewards were few and a number of lords lieutenant also took it upon themselves to regulate the entry of volunteer officers, who were not required to fulfil the property qualifications applied to new candidates. Thus, it might be said that the traditional elite re-asserted the control they had lost over the volunteers. In Leicestershire the Duke of Rutland declined to appoint a commanding officer to the Loughborough battalion for four years on the grounds that no one was qualified and in 1813 offered only an ensigncy to another local militia lieutenant-colonel seeking a commission in the regular militia. Certainly Castlereagh himself wished to restrict the eligibility for commissions but the propertied had long ceased to serve willingly in the volunteers and, while there was an increasing attempt to weed out volunteer officers in succeeding years, the local militia was to remain highly dependent upon those who were or aspired to be of the middling class. Indeed, the subsequent amending legislation in 1812 prohibited officers or those on the permanent staff of the local militia from retailing alcohol, several officers in Lancashire having been indicted for keeping taverns. Another indication, perhaps, of the lesser regard in which the local militia was held was the fact that, compared to the 77 volunteer commanding officers who had sat in the Commons, only 37 local militia commanding officers were MPs in 1809 although their number did include Palmerston.

While volunteer officers might be prepared to transfer, this was by no means universally true of the rank and file of the volunteers, urban members in particular apparently finding that other voluntary organisations or societies would now better serve their social requirements. In the North Riding, for example, Lieutenant-Colonel Sir George Cayley threatened to resign when only a quarter of the men of his Pickering Lyth corps volunteered to transfer to the local militia and by November not one complete corps out of 22 in the riding had transferred and only seven had partially done so. Similarly, 1,429 men had to be found by ballot in Buckinghamshire despite numerous appeals to the loyalty of the volunteers by the Marquess of Buckingham and, in neighbouring Northamptonshire, the subdivisions of Towcester and Wellingborough had to ballot for 45 and 56 per cent of their quota respectively. There was an even more marked reluctance in counties where the volunteers were strong or the politics Whiggish such as Cheshire, Essex, Lincolnshire, Norfolk, Surrey, Sussex and Kent. In the latter county a total of 5,074 men had to be ballotted for since only 2,702 had come forward voluntarily and it would appear that opposition to the local militia in Kent was persistent thereafter. However, some counties such as Carmarthenshire, Caernarvonshire, Denbighshire, Devon and Wiltshire had few vacancies to make up and, overall, the numbers balloted amounted to 32,810 men across 76 of the 87 counties of England, Wales and Scotland. Approximately 125,000 volunteers transfered and, with the addition of civilians enlisting voluntarily, the local militia attained a strength of 195,161 men by 1809.

A sample of 4,878 local militiamen drawn from surviving enrolment details from the counties of Buckinghamshire, Cheshire, Essex, Kent, Lancashire and Northamptonshire suggests that those obtained for the local militia from whatever source were about equally drawn from artisans and retailers (51.1 per cent) and unskilled men or servants (43.8 per cent) although there were considerable variations from county to county.[21] Perhaps not unexpectedly, the landed and professional classes were little represented in the rank and file of the local militia. The labourer poet of Northamptonshire, John Clare, who volunteered for the local militia, certainly recorded of his peers gathering for their first training that 'a more motley multitude of lawless fellows was never seen in Oundle before . . .'.[22] Similarly, it would appear that many of those enlisted in Lancashire were the Catholic poor despite the fear of arming that section of the community entertained in some quarters. The actual demand on the overall male population was relatively limited but the concentration of the ballot among those aged between 18 and 30 made it appear more so, even if this also reduced the amount parishes might expect to expend on family allowances when the local militia was called out for duty.

It would seem that it was anticipated that, in performing its annual duties, the force would not only rehabilitate the image of militia obligation generally but also revive popular loyalism. Certainly, it was assumed that, since local militiamen would be under more formal discipline, they would prove more reliable than volunteers. Unfortunately, rather in the manner of the militia legislation in 1757 or the supplementary militia legislation in 1796, the government's purpose went largely unexplained. There were some fears that local militiamen might be compelled to serve overseas once they had taken the customary oaths while there was also confusion over the 'marching guinea' since, in reality, men were only entitled to receive any surplus remaining after the provision of 'necessaries'. Those forcibly balloted for the local militia would have had their own cause for resentment while former volunteers were likely to misunderstand the nature of the disciplinary code to which they were now subject, not least their liability to suffer the lash. The relatively lowly social status of some former volunteer officers who had received local militia commissions might also render them less able to impose authority where discipline could no longer rest on mutual consent. Commissioned urban tradesmen, for example, might suffer economic loss if they were deemed to deal too harshly with those of their customers temporarily in uniform. It has also been suggested that the uneasy juxtaposition of middle-class officers, officers or others aspiring to respectability and unskilled labourers resulted in a kind of incipient social conflict which could only contribute to the difficulty of imposing discipline during the short period of time for which the local militia was assembled for its annual training.[23]

Thus, the first annual training of the local militia was attended by serious disciplinary difficulties in at least 14 of the 147 regiments called out in June 1809. At Reading, the Royal Berkshire Local Militia was incited to lay down its arms by members of the Reading Loyal Volunteers who, having been dismissed from their own parade in honour of the King's birthday earlier in the day, had apparently spent the intervening period in the local hostelries.[24] At Taunton and in the case of the Archenfield Local Militia in Hertfordshire, the disturbances extended to the participation of local inhabitants while, in what became a case of some notoriety, the King's German Legion was employed to restore order to the Cambridgeshire Local Militia at Ely. Cobbett's savage condemnation of the use of German troops and the subsequent floggings of local militiamen in the columns of the *Political Register* earned him a two-year prison sentence for seditious libel.

There were at least 11 more disturbances during the 1810 training, of which the most serious were those involving the West Mendip Local Militia at Bath, the 2nd Wiltshire Local Militia at Devizes and the Upper Tivy Local Militia at Aberystwyth. It is possible that these disturbances may have been partly influenced by the Burdett agitation and, perhaps not surprisingly, there were fears that the local militia would not prove sufficiently reliable to perform its role in aid of the civil power. Thus, in May 1810 Warwickshire magistrates declined to send local militia assembled for its annual training to deal with a food riot in Birmingham while a troop of the Staffordshire Yeomanry was also called out lest the loyalties of local militiamen be subverted by a similar riot in Wolverhampton. In fact, the West Staffordshire Local Militia proved perfectly reliable, conceivably because they were better paid, fed and clothed than the rioters.

Similarly, the pay and allowances enjoyed on duty by local militiamen in Lancashire exceeded the wages they could earn in civilian employment and may have contributed significantly to their reliability during the Luddite disturbances despite the doubts about the potential loyalty of the many weavers, spinners, colliers and mechanics serving. Indeed, by successive partial embodiment from all six Lancashire regiments, a standing force of upwards of 350 men was kept permanently available in the county from May 1812 onwards. All four Nottinghamshire regiments had been called upon in November 1811 and the government had no hesitation in bringing out the West Riding local militia in face of the reluctance of the local magistrates. Cheshire local militiamen were similarly employed in spite of local misgivings. Local militiamen were potential targets for subversion and their depots also offered opportunities for the acquisition of weapons. In fact, there was a raid on the local militia armoury at Sheffield while the commandant and ten NCOs of the Bolton Local Militia successfully defended their armoury against a mob for two days. Generally, however, the local militia passed the test, the murder by luddites of a local militia NCO and his woman companion in Manchester in May 1812 seemingly only strengthening the force's commitment to order.[25]

Further indications of the commitment of the local militia were the offers received in 1811 from units in Cornwall, Banff and Berkshire for service either out of the county or even overseas. However, in the following year major amending legislation was required when it was only belatedly realised that men were not necessarily going to re-enlist willingly at the expiry of their four years' term of service. There had been some minor amending legislation in both 1809 and 1810 and a certain desire for economy had also become apparent with the reduction of the permanent staff of the local militia in 1810 and the effective reduction of annual training for trained men to 15 days in 1809 and to 14 days in 1811. The new Local Militia Consolidation Act (52 Geo III c 38, 68) of April 1812 set the force's strength lower at 193,912 men and made provision for a parish bounty for all those aged between 18 and 30 with no more than two children who were prepared to prolong their service.

In effect, the government was now allowing a form of substitution while the local militia would still be competing with the regular militia for the youngest age groups even though the new legislation now reduced the militia exemption for new recruits to just one year after the expiry of their term of service. Nevertheless, further amendments to the local militia arrangements were made to enable the authorities to use the force more flexibly. Thus, in December 1813 legislation was enacted to allow the local militia to serve outside its own county for up to 42 days per annum. However, there appears to have been some suspicion encouraged by employers, who were often reluctant to take on local militiamen, that overseas service was intended. Consequently, only 18,425 men came forward in January 1814, only eight regiments were ordered out in March and only six actually completed a full 42 days' garrison service. The 1813 legislation for taking up such offers was due to expire in March 1815 but the planned extension lapsed with Napoleon's abdication in April 1814, only to be hastily revived with his re-appearance from Elba in March 1815. It reached the statute book on 7 June 1815 – just eleven days before Waterloo.

At the time that the authorities had been seeking offers of out-county service in 1814, the purpose had been represented as releasing regulars for the campaign in the Peninsula when it had actually released regular militia for Ireland. In the same way, the continental campaigns had also provided the means by which remaining volunteer corps were finally disbanded, it being announced on 17 March 1813 that their muskets were needed to sustain the Prussian uprising against the French. However, the existence of the local militia was also advanced as precluding the need for more than a handful of volunteer corps and clothing allowances had been withdrawn as early as June 1809 although under the local militia legislation in April 1810 the minimum training period required for exemption of volunteers from the ballot had been reduced to 18 days per annum. By March 1812 the volunteers had already declined to a strength of just 68,643 officers and men and after March 1813 only a few corps survived in Middlesex, Surrey, Northumberland, Kent, Gloucestershire, Devon and Hampshire.

No such policy of allowing units to wither on the vine was applied to the yeomanry, which was regarded as far more reliable than urban volunteer corps, and in October 1813 regular cavalry pay was extended to all yeomen prepared to undertake at least 12 days' annual training. Moreover, the yeomanry was to survive the dismantling of the wartime forces. In the case of the local militia, only those regiments not called out for training in 1813 were notified of an intention to train them in 1814 but none were called out and half the permanent staff of NCOs were paid off in May 1814 with the remainder paid off in April 1816. The local militia ballot was formally suspended the following month when the local militia stood at 183,214 officers and men. This suspension was then renewed annually until 1836, at which time the force was finally abolished although the 1812 legislation was actually to remain on the statute book until 1921. Militia training was also suspended in 1815 and the militia forbidden to recruit by beat of drum although the permanent staff was retained.

Naturally enough, the end of almost 20 years' continuous war was attended by some considerable problems of adjustment given the scale of the effort required to wage the war. Indeed, it has been calculated that in 1809 between one in nine and one in ten of the able-bodied male population of Britain and Ireland was serving in army, navy or militia. With the addition of those serving in the local militia, yeomanry and volunteers the proportion rose to perhaps one in six of the able bodied male population, representing a higher proportion under arms than in either France or Austria and absorbing about a fifth of the increase in the United Kingdom's male population during the war years.[26] However, in 1815 it inevitably implied a flood of newly demobilised soldiers and regular militiamen on the labour market: in fact, East Midlands employers had urged the disbanding of the militia in Derbyshire, Lincolnshire and Nottinghamshire in April 1814 with the intention of breaking the combination of local framework-knitters. Yet, at the same time, demobilisation did lift the burden from parishes and counties of paying out allowances to the families of militiamen and local militiamen. Thus, the amount paid annually by Buckinghamshire to support the families of out-county substitutes doubled between 1800 and 1820 while a figure much publicised by opponents of the militia in the 1840s was the £29,096 5s 6d supposedly spent by the parish of Marylebone on family allowances between 1800 and 1815. In 1809 Middlesex had actually been taken to court by Warwickshire for failing to pay for its substitutes' dependants sufficiently promptly.[27]

Perhaps the most significant feature of the demobilisation process, however, was the suspension of the ballot for the local militia following that effected some years earlier in the case of the regular militia. In each case, of course, the ballot was suspended rather than abolished but, if there was one clear lesson from 20 years' experience of administrative expediency with regard to the auxiliary forces, it was the almost universal distaste for compulsion. At the same time, the Revolutionary and Napoleonic wars had laid down certain patterns of military response to the threat of invasion. Volunteer corps might not command the widespread respect of professional soldiers or politicians but they did reflect a preference for a particular form of amateur soldiering among the middling elements of society or those aspiring to that status which readily suited the more assertive nature of emerging urban society. Conceivably, despite the occasional unreliability of volunteers, it was also a form of military organisation that might induce loyalty to the status quo.

Equally, yeomanry corps suggested not only an additional and attractive pastime for county society and those who aspired to be assimilated within it but also a wholly reliable military instrument at the service of local privilege. At county level, the militia, which had amounted to about a third of the country's land forces as a whole and over half those available for home defence, still performed a social and economic function and still provided opportunities for status and patronage. However, of all the auxiliary forces to survive through or emerge from the wars, it was the militia that was most threatened not only by the hostility to the ballot but also by the increasing assumption among soldiers and politicians that it served only as an adjunct to the army. In essence, the wartime experience had undermined both the militia's independence and its acceptability.

Notes

1   R. Glover, *Britain at Bay: Defence against Bonaparte, 1803–1814* (Allen & Unwin, London, 1973), pp. 13–29.
2   Essex RO, Q/SBb 393/76, Braybrooke to Cawkwell, 25 Oct 1803.
3   Bucks RO, PR 198/3/2; Essex RO, D/P 129/17/5.
4   The Hon. J. W. Fortescue, *The County Lieutenancies and the Army, 1803–1814* (Macmillan, London, 1909), pp. 73–4; Glover, *Britain at Bay*, pp. 134–6.
5   P. Bloomfield, *Kent and the Napoleonic Wars* (Alan Sutton for the Kent Archives Office, 1987), p. 43.
6   Bucks RO, D86/31/55; PRO, HO 50/61, Grenville to Yorke, 19 Sep 1803.
7   P. Haythornthwaite, 'The Volunteer Force, 1803–1805', *Journal of the Society for Army Historical Research* LXIV, 260, 1986, pp. 193–204.
8   Army Museums Ogilby Trust, Order Book of West Somerset Yeomanry, 24 Sep 1803; Hereford and Worcs. RO, Mss 705:73 Acc 2868/4, Ward to Coventry, 4 Oct 1803; British Library, Add Mss 32558, Upcott Diary for 16 Aug 1803 quoted in E. M. Renn, 'British Civil and Military Preparations against Napoleon's Planned Invasion', Unpub. Ph.D., Florida State, 1974, pp. 378–9.
9   Leonard Horner (ed), *Memoirs and Correspondence of Francis Horner, M.P.* (John Murray, London, 1843), p. 225 quoted in Renn, 'British Civil and Military Preparations', p. 271.

10 Sharpe to Newton, 5 Dec 1803 quoted in A. D. Harvey, *English Literature and the Great War with France* (Nold Johnson, London, 1981), pp. 8–9.

11 Palmerston to Cholmeley, 22 Sep 1803 quoted in Ashcroft, *Monster's Clutches*, p. 71.

12 AMOT, Minutes of the Liverpool Independent Rifle Corps, 20 Jul 1803; Berks RO, Radnor Mss, D/ERa 08/1, Pollock to Radnor, 21 Aug 1803; Cheshire RO DJW 1/113 Minutes of Court of Inquiry of the Loyal Sandbach and Rode Volunteer Infantry, 23 Feb 1804; C. C. Goodwyn Esq, Log Book of Sergeant Major Goodwyn, Tetbury Loyal Volunteers, 31 May 1804 and 18 Oct 1806.

13 AMOT, Orders of 1st Regiment, Loyal London Volunteers, 10 Aug 1804; Bucks RO, Way Mss, D/W 88/9.

14 Bloomfield, *Kent and the Napoleonic Wars*, p. 47; Fortescue, *County Lieutenancies and the Army*, p. 125.

15 Quoted in Glover, *Britain at Bay*, p. 45.

16 Renn, 'British Civil and Military Preparations', p. 220; Glover, *Britain at Bay*, p. 143.

17 Fortescue, *County Lieutenancies*, p. 195.

18 *The Reminiscences and Recollections of Captain Gronow* (John Nimmo, London, 1900) II, pp. 217–19.

19 Ann Kussmaul (ed), *The Autobiography of Joseph Mayett of Quainton, 1783–1839* (Bucks Record Society No. 23, 1986), p. 55.

20 Kussmaul, *Autobiography of Joseph Mayett*, p. xxi.

21 S. C. Smith, 'Loyalty and Opposition in the Napoleonic Wars: The Impact of the Local Militia, 1807–1815', Unpub. D.Phil., Oxford, 1984, pp. 142–205.

22 J. W. and A Tibble (eds), *The Prose of John Clare* (Routledge & Kegan Paul, London, 1951), p. 47.

23 Smith, 'Loyalty and Opposition', pp. 42–141.

24 Berks RO, *Radnor*, 025.

25 Smith, 'Loyalty and Opposition', pp. 266–84.

26 Emsley, *British Society and the French Wars*, p. 133; Harvey, *English Literature*, p. 5.

27 Bucks RO, Q/FBM/1–3; Ibid., T/A 5/1; Emsley, *British Society and the French Wars*, p. 144.

5

Decline and revival (1815–1858)

It was not perhaps surprising that the conclusion of the Revolutionary and Napoleonic wars should be accompanied by a desire for military retrenchment. Economic considerations, therefore, were of some consequence in shaping the development of the auxiliary forces in the post-war decades. However, even if surviving in a seemingly moribund condition, auxiliary forces still functioned as social institutions irrespective of the continuing role in aid of the civil power also required of the yeomanry in particular amid the years of social, economic and political unrest that followed Waterloo. Inevitably, that task was attended by political controversies and the same was also true of the role auxiliaries might play in defence of the country against invasion as an increasing perception of national danger in the 1840s prompted first debate and then a major revival of both militia and volunteers in the 1850s.

Domestic events between 1815 and 1848 had a strong element of economic determinism especially liable to trigger disturbances amid the other consequences of often complex change in town and countryside alike. Certainly, although the interpretation of available statistics is open to dispute, crime generally increased in the first half of the nineteenth century with the peak of committals for all offences in years such as 1817, 1819, 1832, 1842 and 1848 when economic difficulties were acute.[1] Those years also tended to witness actual disturbances such as the blanketeers' march and the Pentrich rising in 1817, 'Peterloo' in 1819 and, in 1842 and 1848, various manifestations of chartism, which had been experienced first between 1837 and 1840 and had embraced an apparent attempted insurrection at Newport in Monmouthshire in November 1839. While 1832 itself did not ultimately prove a year of particular crisis in terms of public disorder, it did follow two such crisis years. Over a thousand separate incidents spread over 20 southern counties comprised the 'Swing' disturbances in the winter of 1830–1 while reform agitation spawned many disturbances in 1831 including serious riots at Nottingham, Derby and Bristol in October and what had amounted to a near insurrection at Merthyr Tydfil in June.

In fact, although Britain remained a disorderly society, most crime in the first half of the nineteenth century was non-violent. Moreover, many instances of disorder incorporated a distinctly ritualistic element which looked back to the eighteenth century or before while both the agitation for parliamentary reform between 1830 and 1832 and the demands of the chartists were accompanied far more by the rhetoric of menace than by actual violence. Even after Newport in 1839, the subsequent prosecution case failed to prove that there had been an intention of insurrection and the substance of most alleged plots between 1815 and 1848 remains elusive.

Similarly, it can be noted that few troops were required to disperse those few disturbances which did seem to have more than rudimentary purpose or organisation. A single volley by a detachment of the 45th Foot, for example, sufficed to suppress between 4,000 and 5,000 chartists at Newport in 1839 and, in fact, deaths at the hands of the forces of order were comparatively rare in Britain between 1815 and 1848. South Wales arguably saw the worst violence but troops still only opened fire on three occasions between 1815 and 1831, killing one person in 1816 but then between 16 and 25 at Merthyr Tydfil in 1831 and between 12 and 20 at Newport in 1839. None the less, successive administrations frequently confused pressure for reform with threat of revolution and, on occasions, it did appear to government or establishment that the forces available were not adequate to preserve order. Yet, paradoxically, the lack of available force was itself often a consequence of the economic retrenchment in which ministers indulged. Thus, while the Whigs would have reduced military expenditure even more substantially, the Liverpool administration was equally concerned to seek economies once it was clear that large military forces were no longer required after the end of hostilities in 1815.

Accordingly, the regular establishment was cut to 149,000 officers and men in January 1816 and to 123,000 in the following year, of whom just 28,000 and 26,000 respectively were to be stationed in Britain. In practice, of course, the actual number of troops under arms was likely to be even smaller and, when major disorder necessitating reinforcement from Britain erupted in Ireland in 1821, the home garrison was left with just four cavalry and four infantry regiments. Similar reductions affected the Royal Navy, which had but 14 line of battle left in commission by 1817.

The militia might have suffered just as severely but for the fact that its estimates were determined by a select committee of the Commons rather than by the secretary at war. Among MPs there were rarely fewer than 50 or 60 militia officers in any one year between 1815 and 1860 – the only real exception was the period between 1832 and 1835 – and, with the addition of further militia officers in the Lords, the militia interest was formidably placed to resist reductions. Moreover, if they could not achieve their goal of raising the regular establishment then leading soldiers such as Wellington and Hardinge were prepared to support the militia as the best alternative available. Palmerston viewed the militia in much the same way and William IV was also a firm supporter of the militia although apparently from the mistaken belief that the Crown retained real authority over the force.

Thus, the militia vote was never less than the £306,000 secured in 1816 and successive administrations held back from challenging the force's independence from the army, no recruiting of militiamen into the line being permitted until the Crimean War. The militia was no longer widely perceived as having any contemporary significance as a constitutional check on the army – a point made by Palmerston in 1836 – but it did remain of the utmost importance as a social institution, especially at county level, and this explains the determination with which the militia interest defended its position at Westminster. The Duke of Buckingham and Chandos's regiment – the Royal Bucks King's Own Militia – may serve as illustration. For all that the militia had little real existence beyond its permanent staff – particularly after 1831 – militia appointments still continued to be made in Buckinghamshire as elsewhere. Indeed, 15 were made in the county's regiment between 1815 and 1852 although as late as 1850 there were still six officers serving who had been with the provisional battalion at Bordeaux in 1814 and two – both over 70 years of age – who had seen war service with the 14th Foot. But above all, property qualifications were still required until 1869 and the added importance of county status was amply demonstrated by the Duke's unsuccessful attempt in 1831 to remove three officers whose assumption of mercantile occupations he judged unsuitable. Militia appointments generally were still an instrument of patronage at a time when aristocratic influence was coming under increasing attack in other spheres and this also extended to the permanent staff.

The variety of tasks performed by the latter could go well beyond any purely military function as may be judged by the composition of the corporation of Buckingham in 1830, which also corresponded with the electorate for this pocket borough. There were 13 electors of whom one was the paymaster of the Royal Bucks; another the quartermaster; a third the adjutant, who also performed the duties of town clerk; and a fourth the former adjutant. Small wonder that the second Lord Carrington reputedly paid an ailing Duke some £2,000 for the colonelcy in 1839 and, when becoming lord lieutenant on the Duke's death shortly afterwards, took but four days to transfer staff and headquarters to his own seat at Wycombe Abbey from the barracks built in Buckingham in 1802. The symbolism was not lost on the Duke's uncle, Thomas Grenville, who complained that the new colonel was the son of a man who 'thirty years ago was a stranger to the County without an acre in it'.[2] Indeed, when Carrington died in 1868 and the third Duke of Buckingham and Chandos succeeded to the lieutenancy he immediately enquired into the legality of the transfer of headquarters 29 years previously.

None the less, the militia could not wholly avoid change. One reason was the decline in its customary parliamentary strength between 1832 and 1835 but there was also the enduring unpopularity of the ballot. A new ballot was ordered in July 1816 but actual training suspended annually until April 1820. However, training was then ordered in 1821 and again in 1825 when the term of service was extended to five years. Direct enlistment by beat of drum had been suspended in 1815 and while substitution was still possible it had actually become harder for the lower elements of society to evade the ballot without considerable cost. A major contributory factor was that insurance societies had all but died out and, to judge by what happened in both Middlesex and Suffolk, any revival of the societies in the 1820s was forestalled by the effective control wielded over substitution by permanent staff and regimental surgeons, who now simply rejected on medical or other grounds any substitute not procured directly from themselves.

It was not perhaps surprising in the circumstances that some 14,000 out of the 17,000 men balloted in Middlesex in 1820 – the actual number required for service was just 3,000 – attempted to present a case for exemption. As before, those actually compelled to serve were likely to be labourers, a status registered for 69.4 per cent of the 59 men enrolled in the Bullingdon subdivision of Oxfordshire between March and May 1822, 82.4 per cent of a total of 74 men enrolled in Buckinghamshire in April and May 1821 and for 90.6 per cent of the 96 men drawn in the Newport hundreds of the same county in May 1825.[3]

Another ballot was ordered in October 1828 but legislation in the following year authorised its suspension for a year at a time largely as a consequence of a 40 per cent reduction in the permanent staff – numbers in Britain actually fell from 3,384 to 2,118 or by 37 per cent – effected by the Wellington administration in April 1829. It is not entirely clear why the reduction occurred, especially when Wellington had previously expressed himself satisfied with the existing system. However, the most likely explanation would appear to be the way in which some permanent staffs in English and particularly Irish militia regiments commanded by Protestant ultras such as the Duke of Rutland, Lord Rolle or the Earl of Westmeath had become closely identified with Orange lodges or Brunswick clubs. Indeed, some Irish staff seemed little more than 'armed protestant gangs' being unwillingly subsidised by the government.[4] Thus, Wellington's growing irritation with the ultras amid the Catholic emancipation crisis brought retribution down upon the militia as a whole.

In fact, a new ballot was announced by order in council on 29 December 1830 in the wake of the domestic reform crisis and the fall of the French Bourbon monarchy, which had triggered other insurrectionary movements across Europe. It was intended to assemble the militia in February 1831 and train them during the summer but considerable problems arose from the lack of staff and equipment, the increasing unfamiliarity with militia procedures and legal complications associated with the suspension of the ballot in 1829. Indeed, the attempt to ballot and train the militia amounted to an 'administrative disaster of the first order'[5] even without the additional difficulty consequent upon the emergence of opposition from the newly formed national union of the working classes.

Established in 1830, the NUWC urged working men to claim exemption from the new ballot on the grounds that military service should not be required of those deprived of the franchise. One of its leaders, William Lovett, also successfully contrived – at the second attempt – a confrontation with Marylebone magistrates and was fined £20 for non-compliance on pain of having goods to the same value seized and publicly auctioned if he defaulted. Agitation on Lovett's behalf extended to radical parliamentarians and the capital's auctioneers all declined to handle the sale when Lovett duly defaulted so that the goods had to be disposed of privately. Ostensibly, Lovett's stand had little result since the only actual overt resistance to the ballot was the tearing down of a list at Sleaford in Lincolnshire and, in any case, the government had already decided in July 1831 that the ballot would be suspended some two months before Lovett's second court appearance.

Nevertheless, Lovett's case became associated in the collective mind of the political establishment with the greater upheavals of the autumn of 1831 to such an extent that support for compulsion appeared the equivalent of committing political suicide. Moreover, both the myth that a single individual's action had staved off compulsion – it was the last militia ballot ever attempted – and also the moral logic of Lovett's premise in equating military service with the reward of the franchise proved infectious. In fact, as early as 1816 Samuel Bamford had pointed out that the militia lists provided a ready basis for electoral rolls and, of course, the forms of universal conscription adopted by continental states such as France in 1793 and Prussia in 1813 had equally embodied the ideal of obligation being rewarded with full political participation for all that the concept of a 'nation in arms' had then come under sustained attack from restored monarchies. Thus, the NUWC's theme was to be echoed by a variety of working-class organisations that emerged in the late 1830s and 1840s such as the chartists and the anti-corn law league, the chartist *Northern Star* first employing the subsequently familiar slogan of 'No Vote, No Musket' in January 1846. At the same time, the militia was also subjected to the wider moral challenge to militarism evinced by nonconformist groups which, while not dissimilar to condemnation of the supposedly dire effects upon men of militia service in earlier centuries, was considerably more vehement in tone.

As already indicated, the militia also became exceedingly vulnerable when the number of its MPs fell from 64 to effectively just 15 after the election of December 1832 and, in the following autumn, the new secretary at war, Edward Ellice, proposed a further reduction in the militia permanent staff. While the outrage of the

King and entrenched militia colonels in the Lords sufficed to effect a compromise whereby the plans were presented to a militia committee of the Commons in May 1834, Ellice secured from a committee no longer dominated by militia representatives a thorough inspection of the permanent staff by regulars. Almost two-thirds of the militia's staff were reported as unfit but, in the event, there was no time to introduce legislation before the administration fell in November 1834. The subsequent election saw many militia MPs returned once more but when the Whigs again assumed the mantle of government in April another secretary at war, Henry Grey, Viscount Howick returned to the attack by proposing the total abolition of the militia staff and the permanent suspension of the ballot. In fact, the militia interest in the Lords proved too strong for the Whigs, who were compelled to reduce the measure to one of merely removing inefficient staff since William IV only agreed to give the royal assent to the emasculated bill in September 1835 on the understanding that proposals would be brought forward in the next session for establishing a more efficient militia system. Howick, Lord John Russell and others subsequently evolved a number of proposals for wider militia reform but although the Whigs retained office until 1841 all such plans were effectively shelved upon the King's death in June 1837.

If the Whigs had little regard for the militia, they had even less for the yeomanry whose high profile in aid of the civil power through the immediate post-war decades had hardly endeared it to those radicals who viewed it as a wholly Tory creature. It was not therefore surprising that a reduction in the yeomanry was announced by Russell in March 1838 ostensibly on the grounds that it would be too costly to maintain the existing force of just over 18,300 officers and men whose reclothing by the government was due. Figures vary but between 4,500 and 4,700 yeomen were struck from the establishment while others resigned in protest as in West Kent where the reduction of the Cobham and Tonbridge troops brought the mass resignation of the Dartford and Sevenoaks troops to leave only those at Chiselhurst and Oxonhoath. However, it was also the case that nine corps with approximately 680 men had been allowed to serve on without pay.

None the less, it was not just the Whigs who reduced the yeomanry for the Tories had done so even more drastically in December 1827. In fact, while also underlining the significance of economic considerations in determining post-war military policy, the earlier Tory reduction illustrates that nothing in regard to the yeomanry – about which much is still obscured by the absence of detailed research – is quite as straightforward as it might appear. Apparently taken purely on economic grounds, the 1827 decision was that all those corps not called out in aid of the civil power in the previous ten years should be cut from the establishment. This fell from 24,288 to 10,705 officers and men although, as was to occur in 1838, units were allowed to continue their services at their own expense. In all, of 62 corps or regiments, 24 were disbanded, 22 retained and 16 chose to maintain themselves.

Those corps which had not been called out frequently had primarily been those in southern England and, ironically, it was then those very counties that were affected by the 'Swing' disturbances in 1830 with the result that a number of yeomanry corps were either brought back on to the official establishment or raised anew. Much the same was to happen after the 1838 reductions for the threat of chartism saw the Tories bringing back on to the establishment in 1842 six of the nine corps that had maintained themselves over the previous six years. While some corps were actually disbanded, they also presided over an increase of some 950 men in the yeomanry force as a whole by December 1842. In exactly the same way, the force had increased to the heights of the 62 separate corps of 1827 through the fear of disorder in the period between 1817 and 1819 and it had actually mustered over 28,000 officers and men in 1820.

Although the cost of the yeomanry had risen by 45.7 per cent between 1816 and 1821,[6] only a small proportion was directly attributable to duties in aid of the civil power – it was barely 7 per cent of the total in 1819. Thus, while it was clearly cheaper to employ regulars who would not receive any additional pay, the frequent charge made against yeomanry that they were simply too expensive when used in aid of the civil power was patently false. Moreover, it is clear that even the force as a whole was cheap since the annual capitation grant of £1 10s 0d given for every efficient man from 1817 onwards to meet the cost of uniform and equipment expenses fell far short of actual requirements. This was despite the fact that potentially more men could achieve the requisite efficiency, the former necessity of performing 12 days' continuous service per annum having been reduced by legislation in 1816 (56 Geo III c 39) to eight days inclusive of two days travelling to and from the place of

exercise. Accordingly, the yeomanry continued to be highly dependent upon the generosity of its own members. One example was
when a new squadron was raised in Worcestershire in February 1832
and advanced three years' capitation grant: Lord Plymouth was still
compelled to find £6,200 himself to equip the troop properly. Later,
the Earl of Dudley was said to have spent at least £4,000 a year of his
own money on the Worcestershire Yeomanry between 1854 and
1871 and it is also the case that the second Duke of Buckingham and
Chandos's bankrupcy in 1848 was partly hastened by his massive
contribution to maintaining his regiment, not least when it had been
continued outside the official establishment between 1827 and
1830.[7]

In financial terms at least, there was little return on such expense
but, of course, there were other returns. In many respects the
yeomanry was far more visible within the local community than the
militia after 1815. Not only was the yeomanry seen during its annual
training, which often involved entertaining 'trials of speed' or 'trials
of skills' for spectators, but on many other county occasions. On the
one hand, this generated some trade – the towns of Beaconsfield
and High Wycombe in Buckinghamshire, for example, actively
competed for the annual visit of the First or Southern Regiment of
the county's yeomanry in 1825. On the other, the decorative function of yeomanry conferred social position. In the case of the second
Duke of Buckingham and Chandos, who commanded the 2nd Regiment of Bucks Yeomanry Cavalry from 1839 to 1861, it had often
been remarked how as a young man he had enjoyed displaying
himself at its head and quite clearly the investment was reflected in
the considerable status the Duke believed he derived from military
leadership in the county. Ever larger yeomanry reviews were staged
at his seat of Stowe and the Duke also took considerable pleasure in
using his position to issue orders to his son, the Marquess of
Chandos, who commanded a troop and was determined to save the
family fortune in spite of his father, to attend to his yeomanry
duties.[8] The latter circumstance was perhaps untypical but the social
and political function of the yeomanry in relation to the county
establishment in Buckinghamshire was surely not far different from
that pertaining elsewhere.

In terms of its contribution to public duty, the yeomanry actually
performed many varied tasks including, for example, fire fighting in
Wiltshire in 1839 and frequent wreck protection duty in Devon. But,

of course, the most enduring image of the yeomanry is indeed that of a class-ridden instrument riding down the people as echoed in Russell's oft-quoted remark during the debate in April 1838 on the reduction of the force that 'for his part he would rather that any force should be employed in case of local disturbance than the local corps of yeomanry' or Sir Charles Napier's equally well known statement of August 1839 that 'if the Chartists want a fight, they can be indulged without yeomen, who are over-zealous for cutting and slashing'.[9]

Certainly, there are indications of the conservative political motivation of some yeomen. In Wiltshire the Hindon troop was known locally as the 'Wiltshire Cossacks', the large number of supposedly 'Independent Horsemen' who accompanied John Benett to the county hustings in 1818 and 1819 being yeomen in mufti. Benett failed to secure election in 1818 but he was successful in 1819, a silver claret jug presented to one of his supporters recording that the 'names of the Wiltshire Cossacks will live for ages in the hearts of all who may value the Independence of the County of Wilts and be more imperishable than the metal on which this is inscribed'.[10] Perhaps significantly, the only death inflicted by yeomen during the 'Swing' riots occurred on 25 November 1830 during the running battle fought between the Hindon troop and a mob intent on destroying machinery at the estate owned by Benett, who continued to represent the county in the Tory interest until 1852. Ultras were also numbered among the yeomanry's officers including Michael Sadler, Sir Richard Vyvyan and Sir H. P. Willoughby.

Above all, there is the issue of the 11 dead and some 400 injured attributed by the Metropolitan Relief Committee to 'Peterloo' on 16 August 1819 and the role of 40 members of the Manchester and Salford Yeomanry Cavalry in dispersing a crowd usually estimated at around 60,000 strong. There seems little reason to doubt that there was considerable mutual antagonism between the Manchester reformers and those who had formed the yeomanry there in June 1817 in response to radical agitation, the *Manchester Observer* representing the yeomen as 'fawning dependents of the great, with a few fools and a greater proportion of coxcombs who imagine they acquire considerable importance by wearing regimentals'. In this regard much has been made of the details for 80 of the 101 men of the corps published in the Manchester press in August 1822 whereby emphasis has been placed on the 11 cotton manufacturers and merchants, the 13 publicans and the many shopkeepers. One standard modern account characterises the manufacturers and merchants as most likely to have been Pittites, the publicans as in fear of losing their licences unless they supported the magistrates and the shopkeepers as those catering for the 'better class'. Other accounts display an utter contempt for the presence in the yeomanry of men like the seven butchers and two cheesemongers.[11]

In so far as this seemingly echoes the attitude of the contemporary radical press then it can be argued that, in such an atmosphere, it is not improbable that there was an element of scores being settled once the yeomanry became involved in the crowd. None the less, it must be pointed out that there were 39 different occupations listed for the corps and that while 19 were professional or businessmen and 36 tradesmen (23.7 and 45 per cent respectively), 18 were craftsmen or artisans (22.5 per cent) and six manual workers (7.5 per cent). Moreover, those occupations counted are for original members of the corps whereas there were actually a number of substitutes serving on their behalf whose status was presumably lower. And, in any case, to quote one analysis of the event, it seems unlikely that 40 men 'had decided to wage class war on the packed thousands present on St Peter's Field' in any premeditated way.[12]

In fact, there can be few events so well documented as Peterloo and yet so difficult to unravel from the tainted nature of the evidence presented by protagonists on both sides. Accounts of what happened as the yeomanry moved through the crowd to apprehend Henry Hunt are totally conflicting and the whole affair is generally acknowledged to have lasted barely ten minutes. There does appear a measure of agreement that Hunt and another radical had been secured before yeomen and crowd came into conflict at which point a contingent of the 15th Hussars, who had since arrived, were committed to extricate the yeomen whose difficulties were conceivably due to poor horsemanship. While evidence of whether it was yeomen or regulars who used the flat rather than the edge of their sabres is as conflicting as most other aspects of Peterloo, some deaths were undoutedly caused by the regulars. At least one death also occurred as men from the 31st and 88th Foot continued to clear the streets and it is highly likely that other injuries claimed for Peterloo occurred during those succeeding hours. It must also be pointed out that the crowd itself was not entirely pacific since many were clearly armed to the extent of bearing clubs or sticks and, once the conflict erupted, the troops were also stoned. Indeed, it was claimed that 67 soldiers had been injured during the incident and its aftermath as were 20 horses including 11 belonging to the yeomen.

For the yeomanry, however, Peterloo – the name was coined by the *Manchester Observer* on 21 August – was to become a haunting slogan: two weeks later, the Warwickshire Yeomanry found themselves taunted as 'Manchester butchers who cut up women and children'.[13] Indeed, there were to be occasions thereafter when the yeomanry's perceived lack of impartiality could be said to have risked even greater disorder by their presence in aid of the civil power than their absence. Thus, yeomanry detachments were often stoned or otherwise attacked as at Manchester in 1826, Stoke on Trent in 1837, Birmingham in 1839, Chard in 1842 and Exeter in 1846 although in Birmingham the antagonism arose partly from the yeomanry being seen to act as a county force in an autonomous borough. Earl Grosvenor was to claim in 1838 that the actual existence of the yeomanry was more important to stability than its active use but in some cases yeomanry were sent away by magistrates fearful of the effect of its very appearance.

However, there is evidence to suggest that, in certain circumstances, the yeomanry was by no means merely a simple and unthinking instrument of Tory or class oppression. In August 1820, for example, the Hon. William Lamb, the future Lord Melbourne, reported to the Home Office that many in his own Hertfordshire troop sympathised with Queen Caroline and might not be prepared to act against rioters displaying similar ideas. Between 1830 and 1832 even more doubts were expressed as to the absolute loyalty of the yeomanry. In East Sussex, for example, Lord Egremont discovered that sympathy for the 'Swing' rioters among farmers or at least tenant farmers was such that it was impossible to raise new yeomanry to meet the crisis. Similarly, attempts to raise yeomanry in Kent also foundered, a meeting chaired by Lord Winchilsea at Canterbury in October 1830 bringing demands for the reduction of public offices and one chaired by Lord Clifton at Rochester in November actually resulting in a resolution that rents and tithes be reduced. In terms of the reform crisis, similar refusals to join the yeomanry were met at Birmingham in 1830, Carmarthen in May 1831 and Cheltenham in 1832.

In March 1831, Captain Assheton-Smith of the Andover troop felt compelled to seek the advice of Wellington, who served as lord lieutenant of Hampshire from 1820 to 1852, amid much talk among his men which indicated their unwillingness to suppress any reform agitation. Assheton-Smith had tried to persuade his men that 'no Political Consideration must weigh with us' since they 'were enrolled for the purpose of suppressing Riot, wherever it may be or from whatever cause it might arise'. However, a number of men had then threatened to resign and he could 'never trust them much after what has occurred'.[14] The Duke advised that political discussion should be avoided at all costs and precisely the same course was urged by the lord lieutenant of Buckinghamshire in June 1831. None the less, members of the Hertfordshire Yeomanry certainly appear to have resigned when the Whig prime minister, Grey, offered his own resignation in May 1832 as did some 30 members of the Wolverhampton troop in Staffordshire while, in the Salisbury troop of the Wiltshire Yeomanry, Lord Arundell, who had voted against reform, was faced with a remonstrance from the sergeant major and 30 men opposed to his position. Eight of them resigned but so did a cornet whose support for Arundell became untenable and Arundell himself soon retired. In Yorkshire, Lord Wharncliffe had been faced with a similar round robin in October 1831, which led to the resignation of 22 men from the Doncaster troop and elements of the Dorset Yeomanry were similarly considered unreliable at that same time.

It was also alleged by a regular officer sent to assume control of the situation that, when a major and 34 men of the Swansea and Fairwood troop of the Western (Swansea) Division of the Glamorgan Yeomanry gave up their weapons to rioters near Merthyr Tydfil on 4 June 1831, it had been 'more a willing than a compulsory surrender'.[15] However, while the incident was a further and embarrassing blow to the reputation of the yeomanry, it would appear that the men, whose corps was shortly afterwards disbanded, were effectively ambushed by some 400 miners as they rode through a defile between slag heaps with the hapless officer enticed forward and seized so that his men felt obliged to surrender. Yet, at the same time, other Glamorgan yeomen had performed creditably in covering the retirement from the town of a detachment of the 93rd Highlanders two days earlier and they spearheaded the reoccupation of Merthyr on 6 June.

Other apparent failures were not always those of the yeomen themselves. Thus, when Bristol was literally consumed by reform riots on the night of 30 October 1831 the Dodington and Marshfield troop of the Gloucestershire Yeomanry left the city after two frustrating hours when they could not find a local magistrate to authorise any action and the regular subsequently cashiered for his manifold failures declined to allow one of the yeomen who was a magistrate to remove his uniform and read the Riot Act. The Bedminster troop of the North Somerset Yeomanry was similarly ignored and also retired while the same regiment's Bath troop was unable to reach the city when disturbances broke out in Bath itself. Again, yeomanry from Gloucestershire, Somerset and Wiltshire all assisted in restoring order in Bristol on succeeding days.

Nevertheless, there was the considerable difficulty for the yeomanry in meeting any disturbances of its actual geographical location and the disruption to civilian occupations attending such duties. In 1839, for example, which marked the beginning of the chartist disturbances in the industrial north and Midlands, the yeomanry of Worcestershire, Warwickshire and Staffordshire mustered 1,886 officers and men in 25 different troops and that in Derbyshire, Nottinghamshire and Leicestershire totalled 1,450 men in 20 troops. However, Lancashire which was larger than the three West Midlands counties put together had but 171 yeomen in three troops and County Durham not a single yeoman. South Wales was also bereft of yeomanry. In 1819 there were just 133 yeomen in Glamorgan and none at all in Cardiganshire while all the Welsh yeomanry were struck from the official establishment in 1827. Troops in Pembrokeshire and Denbighshire continued at their own expense and new corps were raised in 1831 but only those in Pembrokeshire then survived the Whig reductions of 1838.

A factor in the weakness of the yeomanry in south Wales was the absence of farmers who were generally supposed to be the backbone of the force. But, as the composition of the Manchester and Salford Yeomanry Cavalry has already indicated, it was not a foregone conclusion that the post-war yeomanry would be dominated by the farming community any more than that had been true of the yeomanry during the late war. In December 1817, for example, of 172 men of the Western Regiment of Oxfordshire Yeomanry only 51 (29.6 per cent) were farmers with the balance including a substantial contingent of tradesmen (19.1 per cent) and artisans (30.2 per cent). Three years later what had now become the Northwestern Regiment and 242 strong was not markedly different with farmers representing 30.4 per cent, tradesmen 24.3 per cent and artisans 32.6 per cent. In neighbouring Buckinghamshire those identifiable from lists of 61 men of B Troop and 54 men of C Troop of the 2nd Royal Bucks Regiment of Yeomanry Cavalry in January 1845 and May 1846 respectively show a similar division between farmers and tradesmen if not the same reliance upon artisans or craftsmen. In the former troop, 30 men (49.1 per cent) can be identified as farmers and 10 men (16.3 per cent) as tradesmen and, in the latter troop, 20 men (37 per cent) can be identified as farmers and 14 as tradesmen (25.9 per cent). In the Hawarden Troop formed in Flintshire in February 1831, the proportion of farmers was far higher, two lists for March and July of that year showing 41 of the 57 members as farmers or farmers' sons (71.9 per cent).[16]

Where there was any degree of dependence upon the farming community it was found that disturbances often occurred at just those times most inconvenient to the demands of the agricultural year but, in any case, few yeomen could undertake prolonged service without disruption to their civilian calling. In April 1820, for example, Scottish yeomanry found it difficult to respond adequately to widespread disturbances due to bad weather having delayed the annual ploughing although 16 men of the Kilsyth Troop of Stirlingshire Yeomary and an equal number of regular cavalrymen fought and dispersed 35 armed men marching on the Carron iron works near Falkirk in the so-called 'Battle of Bonnymuir'. In the following year the sacrifices of yeomen who were also his tenants when called out for guard duties in London during the coronation of the unpopular George IV in July 1821 at a busy time of year prompted the second Marquess of Buckingham to suspend payment of rents due at Michaelmas until the following Lady Day. Nine years later in the midst of the 'Swing' disturbances of December 1830 in the county, only four men from one troop were able to answer an urgent summons to the village of Whitchurch.

Yet, despite these problems, the yeomanry did manage to perform long spells of duty at times of crisis. In 1822 yeomen from 12 different English corps were called out in aid of the civil power on 19 separate occasions and in 1826 men from 13 different corps were on duty at 16 different times. Following the Whigs' reductions in 1838, northern and Midlands yeomanry were not inclined to co-operate in the plans of Sir Charles Napier, who commanded the northern district from 1839 to 1841, for permanent yeomanry duty in face of the chartist challenge but their efforts were still considerable and both Napier and Lieutenant-General Sir Thomas Arbuthnot, who took charge of both the northern and Midlands districts in August 1842, were given direct powers to summon the yeomanry rather than applying for them through the Home Office. In 1842, which proved to be the year of greatest strain, 84 troops from 18 separate corps were on duty in 15 English, Welsh and Scottish counties for a staggering total of 338 days. In the case of both Worcestershire and Ayrshire no less than 71 days' service was required. But in some counties there were almost continuous demands between 1815 and 1848. In that period the Cheshire Yeomanry was called out on 18 occasions but the busiest force was undoutedly that of Staffordshire, the Himley troop alone being out for 23 days' continuous service in 1823 and 25 days in 1842.

Despite its faults, the general utility of the yeomanry at times of major crisis such as 1842 or in 1848, when even the Whigs were prepared to employ it in the interests of order, contributed to a certain ambivalence on the part of politicians to the force. The Whig secretary at war, Macaulay, praised the yeomanry in 1840 as did the Tory home secretary, Graham, in 1843 although the latter also entertained reservations concerning the difficulties of reconciling military duty with the demands of agriculture. Wellington, too, had grave doubts as to the desirability of yeomen continuing to regulate their own affairs to the extent of electing officers but also chose to view the yeomanry as a unifying element between the landed and middle classes which posed no risk to established authority. Accordingly, he opposed the Whig reductions in 1838, particularly as he believed that they were designed to speed the creation of a professional police force under central rather than local control. Indeed, as has been suggested, the yeomanry was admirably suited to a vision of an unpoliced and hierarchical rural society. But many of the disorders with which the yeomanry was confronted arose from the pressures of industrialisation and urbanisation and, as Peel remarked in July 1826, the situation required 'something less cumbrous and expensive than Yeomanry, but of a more permanent and efficient character than special constables'.[17]

Certainly, special constables were no real alternative to yeomanry since they tended to suffer from the same kind of defects and, despite periodic legislation encouraging their enrolment, they were rarely effective. Even less response was to be expected from that older manifestation of civic obligation, the posse, which was occasionally summoned as in Berkshire in November 1830, Bristol in October 1831 and Lanarkshire in August 1842. During the 'Swing' disturbances semi-feudal bands of retainers were also organised on some estates but, of course, this was hardly a solution to the problems of public order.

Invariably, local magistrates demanded regulars but, as already indicated, few were stationed in Britain. The only other approximation to regulars were army pensioners, who may have amounted to between 70,000 and 80,000 men by the 1840s. Invalid companies had existed during the Napoleonic wars and veterans battalions were also briefly organised between 1819 and 1821. Pensioners were subsequently encouraged to come forward as special constables but consideration was given as early as 1830 to a more durable organisation for at least those pensioners aged under 55 and this culminated in legislation in August 1843 to raise a force of 10,000 enrolled pensioners to be trained for eight days annually. But, by 1848, the force was still only 8,720 strong and even the addition of naval and East India Company pensioners in 1846 and 1848 respectively left it well short of its increased 30,000 establishment: the 14,000 or so remaining enrolled pensioners were absorbed into the army reserve in 1867.

Based on his experience as Irish secretary between 1812 and 1818, Peel's favoured solution, of course, was a centralised constabulary but, as already noted with respect to Wellington's preference for yeomanry, a centralised constabulary was regarded as an unacceptable challenge to local control exercised through magistrates and, indeed, as a manifestation of the absolutism supposedly represented by continental gendarmerie. Equally important was the fact that England was not actually unpoliced outside London and that the variety of forces which did exist appeared quite capable of dealing with the relatively low level of what might be regarded as ordinary crime.

None the less, the considerable strain placed on the Metropolitan Police, which attained a strength of 3,314 in 1830, by its additional role as a kind of national riot squad necessitated consideration of organised policing in rural areas and unchartered conurbations such as Birmingham and Manchester. However, while Birmingham, Manchester and Bolton were the subjects of separate policing legislation in 1839, the Rural Constabulary Act of the same year was merely permissive of county constabularies and left control in local hands. By 1851 only 28 out of 56 English and Welsh counties had formed such county police and, outside of boroughs, there were only 7,381 men serving in such forces. Even when the fears aroused by the effect of the suspension of transportation as a punishment in 1853 and of the demobilisation of Crimean veterans combined with growing apprehension of invasion to result in the mandatory provisions of the County and Borough Police Act of 1856, local control was preserved.

Yet, the creation of police forces in those counties and boroughs which had not previously had them under the 1856 legislation did herald a marked decline in the use of yeomanry and other auxiliaries in aid of the civil power since the imperative behind the growing acceptance of police was public order rather than crime. Indeed, the new police emerged in the context of a growing desire shared by landed and middle class alike for an orderly society amid an increasing prosperity, which was itself to eradicate many of the social and economic pressures that had directly stimulated disturbances in the recent past. Economic success combined with paternalism and the discipline of industrial wage labour served to promote social order in many previously turbulent areas. In the process, a greater confidence emerged which saw the steady abolition of capital penalty for all but murder and treason. Indeed, regulars and auxiliaries were to be rarely employed in aid of the civil power between 1848 and the threat posed by fenian activity in 1867.

But if the transition to an orderly society steadily eliminated one role for auxiliaries, another was to result when the marked admiration for science, progress and achievement which played such an integral part in the transformation of attitudes was itself seemingly to pose a threat to progress and prosperity through the challenge of technology to Britain's security. That challenge came from the often exaggerated but none the less real progress of France towards the construction of the world's first sea-going armoured ironclad fleet, a project made feasible in the 1840s by the simultaneous developments of steam power, the screw propeller, rifled ordnance and armour plate. Notwithstanding the alliance between Britain and France during the Crimean War, there were frequent clashes of Anglo–French interests in the 1840s and 1850s. In May 1844, for example, in the midst of a dispute over the status of Tahiti, a widely publicised pamphlet by the Prince de Joinville, son of King

Louis Philippe, forcibly argued the advantages France would have enjoyed by having steam powered warships able to challenge British naval superiority. Two years later France announced a naval building programme of 93 million francs and, although it initiated a naval arms race that the French could not ultimately win, it still seemed a likely indication of French intentions.

Added impetus for French naval expansion and British concern derived from the enthusiasms of Louis Napoleon, whose seizure of power in December 1851 once more raised the spectre of Napoleonic ambition. It is far from clear what Napoleon III, as Louis Napoleon became in November 1852, hoped to gain from a massive naval programme announced in August 1855 which was clearly beyond French financial and technological capabilities but the emperor's character and intentions were equally enigmatic. The effectiveness of shell projectiles upon wooden ships, spectacularly demonstrated during the Crimean War by the destruction of the Turkish fleet at Sinope in November 1853 and again by the damage inflicted on the Allied fleets before Sebastopol in November 1854, underlined the almost revolutionary change in naval warfare and what appeared the inherent unpredictability in a rapidly changing naval and military environment of the outcome of any Anglo–French conflict. In reality, steam had not 'bridged the Channel' in the way Palmerston implied in a celebrated speech in June 1845, the Royal Navy not only always retaining a working superiority in battleships and steamers but also planning an offensive strategy in the event of war. However, the naval case was not well presented and continuing anxieties were fed by a national popular press virtually created out of the Crimean War. And, indeed, a society newly emerging from the implied threat of chartism and social chaos proved highly susceptible to the phenomenon of the invasion 'panic', Richard Cobden coining the term, 'The three panics', to describe those of 1846–7, 1851–2 and 1858–9.

Not unexpectedly, leading soldiers such as Wellington and the inspector-general of fortifications, Sir John Fox Burgoyne, who commanded more credibility than their naval counterparts, looked for a rapid augmentation of the number of regulars permanently stationed in Britain. Estimates as to the likely scale of any French invasion force ranged from 15,000 to 200,000 but, in any case, the professional military forecasts of the probable outcome of invasion were almost universally pessimistic. One letter from Wellington to Burgoyne, the publication of which by the *Morning Chronicle* in

January 1848 prolonged the 'first panic', for example, contained such emotive phrases as 'we are not safe for a week after the declaration of war'.[18] Nor were Wellington and Burgoyne alone in playing Cassandra, Sir Francis Head's pamphlet *The Defenceless State of Great Britain*, published in 1850, being particularly influential in arousing fears of the French danger.

However, whatever the likelihood of invasion, the position as regards regulars would not be improved given that any substantial increase in the establishment was politically unacceptable. In any case, the size of home army recommended by soldiers varied almost as much as the estimate of the French invasion force. There was also the fact that each 'panic' was of relatively short duration so that, for example, the fall of Louis Philippe's government in February 1848 not only resulted in a rapid decline of public apprehension but also made Wellington's letter appear unduly alarmist, an accusation also levelled at Head's pamphlet at least until Louis Napoleon's coup revived the debate.

Another possible response to the perceived danger was the construction of fortifications. This certainly posed fewer constitutional difficulties than an increase in the military establishment but still implied considerable expenditure and did not reduce the need for manpower. Nor was sufficient manpower released for service at home by the application of a policy of raising more local forces in the colonies. Increasingly, therefore, politicians returned to the subject of militia reform which, since 1837, had only really been addressed in the Channel Islands during the service of Sir William Napier as lieutenant governor of Guernsey, although the greater militia liability of the male population there from the age of 16 onwards was unlikely to be welcomed in Britain.

In fact, Welllington, Burgoyne and Hardinge had all recognised the need to supplement the available regulars with a reformed militia. The question, of course, was what precise direction reform should follow and the militia debate of the 1840s was to be played out against a background of conflicting pressures. On the one hand, the militia interest tirelessly advocated revival through such means as militia clubs and a vigorous letter-writing campaign in the military press while, on the other, outright abolitionists drawn from the ranks of the chartists and peace society not only co-operated with each other in 1846 but came together two years later with the anti-corn law league in the so-called national defence committee, attracting often sizeable crowds to public meetings.

In all, there were to be four separate phases in the reform of the militia between 1845 and 1852. Initially, it was the powerful combination of Wellington and Palmerston which, in the summer of 1845, persuaded Peel – himself no friend of the militia – to task Sidney Herbert at the War Office and Sir James Graham at the Home Office with producing a workable scheme of reform. They concluded in August 1845 that the ballot should be revived and that all necessary steps could be taken to put the machinery in order prior to actually seeking parliamentary approval in the autumn. However, it would appear that Peel remained unconvinced of the viability of the legislation Herbert and Graham subsequently prepared for a 100,000 strong force drawn from those aged 18 to 40 to be enlisted for seven years and trained for up to three months annually. In the event, the corn laws crisis led to the fall of Peel's administration before any decision was reached on whether or not to introduce the bill.

Russell, who succeeded Peel as prime minister, proved rather more amenable to continuing pressure from Wellington and Palmerston, who appeared to favour carrying through the Herbert/Graham scheme. However, Russell was also presented in December 1847 with an alternative scheme advocated by his secretary at war, Fox Maule. Influenced greatly by the army reformer Alexander Tulloch, Maule envisaged what could be regarded as a regular militia of 50,000 unmarried men under the age of 30 to be raised by ballot when war appeared likely and then trained for up to 60 days at a time. But there would also be a permanent 150,000-strong local militia or 'army of reserve' again raised by ballot. The local militiaman would be liable to 28 days' training in the first year of service and 14 days in subsequent years but service would only be within the county. Russell then came up with a compromise in January 1848 of a 200,000-strong force (150,000 in Britain and 50,000 in Ireland) of regular and local militia to be raised by annually balloting 40,000 men aged between 18 and 25, the individual serving for five years and undertaking three years' service in the regular militia and two years in the local militia. The militiaman would be trained for 28 days in each of the first two years, for 21 days in the third year and for 14 days in each of the fourth and fifth years when he would no longer be liable to leave his county except in the event of an imminent invasion. Such a complicated scheme found few supporters, especially when Russell proposed to meet the expenditure by increasing income tax from 7*d* to 1*s* 0*d* in the pound. But, in any case, the scheme having been introduced to the Commons on 18 February 1848, militia reform immediately dropped from the political agenda when revolution broke out in Paris four days later and Louis Philippe abdicated on 24 February.

The opportunity to address militia reform for a third time arose only in the wake of the second 'panic' following Louis Napoleon's coup in December 1851. Russell was again faced with conflicting positions among his ministers but Palmerston's dismissal from the government in December inclined the prime minister once more towards the idea of a local militia. Building on this aspect of Maule's 1847 scheme, Russell now proposed raising 72,000 men in the first year by a combination of voluntary enlistment and ballotting among those aged between 20 and 23, increasing the total to 100,000 in the second year and eventually to 150,000 with the ballot subsequently applied as necessary to those aged between 20 and 21. The term of service would be five years with 28 days' training in the first year and 14 days annually thereafter and a liability to go out county only in the event of imminent invasion. It was powerfully attacked by Palmerston, who proposed an amendment to regulate the militia on the basis of the 1802 legislation, in what is usually regarded as a 'tit for tat' for his dismissal from the Foreign Office but actually reflected deep division on the future of the militia. On 20 February Palmerston's amendment was passed by 134 votes to 125 and Russell resigned.

By the nature of its assumption of office, the Derby administration was very much committed to finding a solution to the militia problem but, in effect, on the basis of the 1802 legislation. It was clear, however, that the principle of compulsion was no longer acceptable. The same was equally true of the United States where eight states abandoned it for militia service between 1840 and 1851 and it is noticeable that, given the moribund state of the English militia since 1831, much of the alleged evidence of the corrupting effects of militia service used by English abolitionists was derived from American example. Canada had also established a voluntary militia in 1846. Fortunately, the legal skills of the new occupant of the Home Office, Spencer Walpole, were equal to the task of escaping the undoubted unpopularity of compulsion by interpreting the exceptional circumstances permitting voluntary enlistment sometimes presented in the ballot clauses of past militia acts as the real intent of such legislation. This convenient fiction enabled the government to stress that the ballot would only be applied if voluntary enlistment failed but, in other respects, the force was little different to the basic concept of the eighteenth-century militia.

It was proposed to raise 80,000 men in England and Wales from those aged between 18 and 35 to serve for five years and undertake 21 days' training annually, although this could be extended to 56 days in emergencies. In the first year of operation, 50,000 men would be sought and 30,000 in the second year, county quotas being fixed on the basis of one man for every 174 males in the first year and one in every 286 males in the second year as enumerated in the most recent 1851 census. To induce volunteers, a bounty of £6 was offered, of which 10s 0d would be paid on enrolment, 10s 0d after the first annual training and the remainder in monthly instalments of 2s 0d. One guinea would be paid daily during the first four annual trainings, with the remuneration increasing to £1 16s 0d during the last training.

The legislation was not without its critics, especially among radicals who argued that the burden would once more fall on the lowest elements of society. In all over 200 hours were spent on the bill involving 32 divisions in the Commons alone but parliamentary opposition was effectively eroded when Russell's attempt to throw the bill out on its second reading went down by 315 to 165 votes on 26 April. The collapse of chartism appeared to offer little support for the view expressed by some opponents that the lowest elements of the population could not be trusted if trained in the use of arms. There was also a growing belief in some quarters that the effect of military training upon the individual was more likely to result in moral regeneration than degradation even if many regarded the militia itself as incapable of effecting such a transformation. Indeed, Walpole actually proposed granting the franchise to any militiaman with two years' satisfactory service but this was quickly withdrawn by his Cabinet colleagues.

Although the new Militia Act (15 and 16 Vict c 50) finally received its royal assent on 30 June 1852, there was still considerable opposition to be overcome before its provisions could be effected. Over 800 petitions had been presented against the bill during its passage through parliament, the response being particularly vehement in manufacturing areas where it was believed that enrolment would seriously disrupt the industrial labour force. Radical and pacifist propaganda made much of this as well as raising older themes such as the moral and social evil represented by military service and the opportunities for increased government and aristocratic patronage that would arise from the establishment of the militia. One especially effective aspect of the anti-militia campaign was the stress laid on the possibility of militiamen being flogged: waged primarily through graphic posters, these were all the more effective in Wales for being printed in Welsh when the government's own recruiting literature was only made available in English.

However, an even more carefully calculated tactic was to induce friendly societies to invoke long forgotten clauses in their constitutions forbidding the payment of benefit to those involved in military service. This had mattered little during the Napoleonic wars when such societies had had comparatively few members but by the mid 1850s they embraced almost half the population. In Buckinghamshire, for example, three newly enrolled privates petitioned their commanding officer, Lord Carrington, in November 1852 when refused benefit by societies in Sherrington, Langley Marish and Stoke Poges. Carrington discovered that there was no legal remedy although his public announcement that he would compensate the men from his own pocket was sufficient to shame at least the Sherrington society into readmitting one of them.[19] There were similar problems in other counties and in the following year a clause was inserted into legislation formally suspending the possibility of a ballot (16 and 17 Vict c 133), which allowed recourse to magistrates by those militiamen refused benefit.

Irrespective of the intention to avoid any ballot, the fact that the threat could be suspended as early as September 1853 was indicative of the ultimate failure of the opposition to prevent the militia being raised. None the less, this result was not attained without a considerable effort to complete quotas in the autumn of 1852 after many initial difficulties in both manufacturing and rural areas deriving from a generally healthy economic situation in which demand for labour had pushed up wages. The problem had also been compounded for the lieutenancies by the effect of the radical campaign, which virtually compelled them to prove that militiamen could be found from among the more respectable elements of local society. The government itself expressed a desire that householders could be induced to come forward and certainly it would appear that considerable care was exercised in recruiting the militia. In Buckinghamshire, Carrington insisted on recruits being checked against police records, personally interviewed each man prior to attestation and provided each with 3s 0d from his own pocket by way of establishing a personal loyalty. Similarly painstaking methods were employed in such counties as Caernarvonshire, West Sussex, the North Riding and Somerset.

Curiously, and to the astonishment of contemporaries, it actually proved easier to recruit in manufacturing than in rural areas once the county community rose to the radical challenge but there was something of a denouement during the first annual training period in 1853 when large numbers of attested militiamen in manufacturing areas simply did not appear. In all only 5,175 out of 38,585 men called for training in 52 different regiments failed to come out but 3,924 of these defaulters were drawn from just 14 regiments. However, while many had clearly attested for the bounty, there could be other reasons for non-appearance. In Hampshire, for example, a total of 47 men could not be found but it transpired that, of these, no fewer than 14 were serving prison sentences, six had left the county, two were at sea, two were dead, one had enlisted in the army, one was a vagrant and another had been found employed as a railway porter at Waterloo.

This might imply that, not for the first time in its history, the militia's social composition fell short of the government's ideal. Moreover, figures available for Hampshire and Oxfordshire show a traditional dependence upon youthful agricultural labourers amounting, for example, to 79.5 per cent of the 142 men enrolled in the Oxford Subdivision in August 1852 and to 84.4 per cent of the 251 men enrolled for the two Hampshire regiments between December 1852 and March 1853. In each case the average age of all the militiamen was just over 20 years. The Royal Bucks King's Own Militia was also reported as being nine-tenths agricultural labourers in November 1852 and, whatever Carrington's view as to the quality of man required, at least one of his deputy lieutenants cheerfully reported in April 1853 that he was circulating recruiting literature 'amongst the Peasantry of my district'.[20]

Yet, it would appear that the Irish vagrants many had predicted would form the majority of the militia were avoided and, for all that the annual training period was hardly compatible with regular employment, those militiamen enrolled in 1852 and 1853 were generally more respectable than had been imagined. Certainly, there were few instances of trouble during the training when, more often than not, the men had to be billeted on innkeepers and the number of memorials forthcoming from towns in praise of the men's conduct was impressive given the vested interest of the militia's opponents in exploiting any incidents. Undoubtedly, an important factor was the special effort made by commanding officers such as Carrington to make militia service a vehicle for moral paternalism. He was not alone in expounding the benefits of temperance, industry and the desire for self-improvement, a process assisted by the generous distribution of religious tracts, compulsory church attendance and the provision of a regimental school to teach reading and writing. Similar arrangements were made in other regiments and, indeed, the secretary at war, Beresford, had circulated militia regiments in December 1852 with details of the range of educational material available for purchase. The militia, therefore, had been created in the image of 'a half way house between a sunday school and a superior mechanics' institute'.[21]

The good behaviour of the militia in 1853 certainly reinforced the notion that military service could be morally beneficial as had the widely reported courage of those regulars shipwrecked on the *Birkenhead* off South Africa in February 1852. But it was also the case that support for the militia among local communities derived from the positive advantage arising from the raising and training of the militia. Many regiments, for example, entertained with their band concerts but tradesmen and especially innkeepers also stood to make profits. And, of course, there was the question of appointments, though, in this respect, the militia did bear out the radicals' charges in that commissions remained very much the preserve of landed county society. Although some older officers were eased out in 1852, no major reconstruction of the militia's officer corps occurred with around 60 per cent having been commissioned before the revival. Many clamoured for commissions but wealth and county connections remained paramount. Thus, there are examples in many counties of professional men – merchants, stockbrokers, solicitors – failing to obtain appointment, one such example being the Marquess of Salisbury's cutting rejoinder to one misguided applicant in October 1852 that employment in the General Screw Steam Navigation Company was an 'insuperable obstacle' to a militia commission.[22]

Among those also subjected to effective discrimination were former regular officers, whom the government had wished to encourage by exemption from property qualifications. However, only 225 former regulars appear to have been appointed to the militia in 1852, the militia interest being as determined as ever to remain independent of the army. What could not be anticipated was the outbreak of the Crimean War, the despatch of an expeditionary force and the protracted military operations coupled with the primarily naval war fought out in the Baltic representing the first real occasion on which British politicians were confronted with the difficulties of reconciling competing demands for manpower between the armed forces and industry.

At least a quarter below its peacetime establishment with a system intended to meet the defensive needs of Britain and the empire rather than a major war against a European opponent, the army was ill prepared to find the initial 26,000 men required for the Crimea. Rural depopulation and large-scale emigration from Scotland and especially Ireland had already reduced the army's ability to recruit but there was now also the competition of the high wages being offered by manufacturing industry and even agriculture faced with labour shortages. One solution was the employment in the Crimea of mercenary formations recruited from Poland, Switzerland, Italy and the German states and another to release more regulars for the field army by raising a civilian labour force. However, it was inevitable that any previous desire to utilise the militia only in its own independent role in home defence should, in the words of a circular of 20 November 1854 once more authorising recruiting direct from the militia into the line, 'yield to the necessity of strengthening Lord Raglan's army'.[23]

There were those such as the Duke of Newcastle, and that perennial opponent of a voluntary militia, Earl Grey (formerly Howick) who believed that passing potential regular recruits through the militia unnecessarily delayed their reaching the army. However, a more substantial body of opinion extending to Fox Maule (now Lord Panmure), Herbert, Russell, Hardinge, Raglan and the Prince Consort viewed the militia as a ready source of augmenting the army. While no invasion could be said to be imminent, the government had received sufficient encouragement from militia colonels to authorise the embodiment of those regiments prepared to offer their services in May 1854 with many taking over garrison duties in Britain from

July. In April a 10*s* 0*d* bounty had been offered to those willing to enlist in the army but the now traditional objection of militia colonels to recruitment into the line was met by stipulating that men would only be released with the permission of commanding officers.

However, as the manpower crisis increased dramatically through the autumn, such luxury could no longer be afforded and the November circular authorised recruitment up to 25 per cent of a regimental establishment with the added enticements of an additional £1 bounty over and above the regular recruitment bounty and recruiting for rank at the rate of one regular ensigncy for every 75 militiamen going to the line. At the same time the number of regiments embodied was doubled – 61 regiments were eventually embodied during the war – while legislation announced in October and carried through early in 1855 (18 & 19 Vict c 1) had also enabled the government to take up offers from up to 75 per cent of a regiment's establishment willing to volunteer for up to five years' overseas service, a subsequent circular seeking definite offers for garrison duties in the Mediterranean. In fact, over 30 regiments volunteered for such overseas service and three for service in the Crimea but, in the event, only ten were dispatched to garrison on Gibraltar, Malta and the Ionian islands. The Scottish and Irish militias were also revived purely as a mechanism for channelling manpower into the army.

As during the Napoleonic wars, volunteering to go overseas as a complete unit was a very different matter as far as militia colonels were concerned to having a unit constantly drained of its trained manpower. Accordingly, although 12,265 militiamen passed into the army during 1854 – 5,703 of them prior to the November circular – and possibly 33,000 during the war as a whole representing perhaps over three-quarters of the army's total wartime recruits, the process was not accomplished without some friction. Counties whose militia colonels were closest in friendship to the secretary at war, Herbert, such as those in Berkshire, Hampshire and Wiltshire appear to have responded best to the appeal to send men to the line but all attempted to send as few as possible.

What compounded the difficulties for the militia colonels was Grey's persistence in pressing a promise he had extracted from Newcastle at the time of the militia's first embodiment that men should be released after the expiration of 56 days' service unless they specifically volunteered to remain. Having failed to get action in the autumn of 1854, Grey again raised the issue in February 1855 and his allegations that faith had been broken prompted near mutinies in at least nine regiments. Shrinking from keeping the militia filled through the ballot, the secretary of state for war in Palmerston's new administration, Panmure, announced the so-called 'act of grace' whereby those who had enlisted prior to embodiment were offered their release or a £1 bounty if they chose to remain. Some 11,909 men resolved to stay but 16,769 men took their discharge, the majority apparently the very married householders with dependants regarded by government as the ideal militiamen.

The loss of such men and, indeed, the constant drain to the line changed the nature of the militiaman as ever younger recruits of ever lower social status filled the vacancies. Embodied service itself was becoming increasingly unpopular, especially in Dublin and the new hutted encampment at Aldershot. There was also concern that families could not sustain themselves on a militiaman's pay and allowances and, coupled with a less disciplined kind of recruit, frustrations were manifested in a growing number of disturbances involving militiamen through 1855 and 1856. On Corfu, for example, men from three militia regiments were involved in what amounted to a three-day battle amongst themselves for control of the streets while similar drunken brawls occurred as far apart as Reading, Colchester, Plymouth, South Shields and Southampton. At the same time, an increasing turnover amongst junior officers also contributed to the general decline.

The militia was disembodied in May 1856 but within a short time the outbreak of the Indian mutiny again created a manpower shortage in the army: indeed, the regular garrison in Britain was reduced to just 14 battalions. Consequently, some militia regiments were again embodied in August 1857: approximately 30,000 men had been embodied by February 1858, of whom some 20,000 were once more serving in the Mediterranean under temporary enabling legislation (21 & 22 Vict c 85). Moreover, in December 1857 permission was once more given for direct recruitment into the line with a limitation fixed at 17 per cent of establishment: in all, 8,000 militiamen did so. However, the reduction of the militia to a mere draft-finding body for the army was hardly likely to arrest the seeming distintegration of the militia. In 1857 only 1,500 out of 12,000 time-expired men had decided to re-enlist and the government chose to postpone the annual training that year until after the general election for fear of losing seats through its unpopularity. Two years later, under 29,000 men out of a total force of 80,000 appeared for that year's annual training.

In May 1858 the recently formed home defence committee recommended that a royal commission should further consider the position of the militia but its intention was actually to bind the militia even more firmly to the army. Once more, the militia interest rallied itself and succeeded in dominating the commission, resisting pressure from Grey and others for wide terms of reference. The resulting recommendations in March 1859 hardly addressed the increasing problems revealed by the commission's own minutes of evidence and were but minor suggested adjustments, of which the most important was an increase of the training period from 21 to 28 days annually.

Herbert, who became secretary of state for war in Palmerston's new administration when that of Derby was overthrown on a vote of confidence in June 1859, apparently contemplated a revival of the ballot but went little further than overhauling the ballot machinery in minor legislation resulting from the recommendations. None the less, he did move in other ways in an attempt to preserve the militia. In February 1860 an additional inducement of a 10s 0d gratuity was offered to those re-enlisting after five years' service and in April Herbert disembodied the militia once more. Following extensive consultation with militia colonels, he also took the step in June of prohibiting the recruitment of militiamen into the line. It was too late for, by 1860, another challenge to the militia's viability had arisen with the establishment during the 'third panic' of 1858–9 of a popular solution to Britain's military weakness in the form of the revival of the volunteer movement.

In fact, the movement had never wholly died. In 1820 surviving or newly raised volunteer corps mustered 216 officers and 1,156 men, mostly in Scotland. A number of these were called out in aid of the civil power in 1820 and they were still mostly in existence in 1825: one unit at Greenock appears to survived until 1841. A handful of volunteer corps also existed in England at different times. One at Bath, for example, saw duty in aid of the civil power in both 1817 and 1819 but it had disappeared by 1826. The two best documented are those at Newcastle-under-Lyme and Leeds. That at Newcastle-under-Lyme was raised in October 1819 in the wake of Peterloo when some 62 men were enrolled in four companies but the corps was subsequently disbanded in August 1823. Similar fears prompted the establishment of the Leeds corps in January 1820 and, excluding its 20-strong committee, the 82 men enrolled included five professional men, 24 tradesmen and 22 artisans or craftsmen. As in the case of the Newcastle volunteers, the unit does not seem to have survived beyond 1823 and in May 1826 it was noted that only the King's Cheshire Volunteers had claimed any clothing allowance in the past six years.[24]

At the time of the 'Swing' riots and reform agitation in 1830–1 voluntary associations may have existed in Edinburgh and Glasgow while a volunteer 'mounted constabulary' was raised at High Wycombe in Buckinghamshire and night patrols and farm guards mounted at Chesham and Upton cum Chalvey. However, a distinct awakening of the volunteer spirit can be detected in the responses to Russell's decision in early 1839 to invite lords lieutenant to raise associations to protect life and property during the first wave of chartist disturbances. In May offers were accepted in Staffordshire and at Cockermouth, Monmouth, Loughborough, Bath, Bradford, Mansfield, Pontypool and Derby although it is not clear whether all these resulted in the actual formation of an association. Russell was prepared to issue arms temporarily to such units but it was made clear that the 'object was to provide a necessary supply of arms for the well disposed, who would come forward and associate to defend life and property against disturbers of the public peace'.[25] What was not intended was that any of these associations should become permanent volunteer corps and, accordingly, firm offers of this nature were turned down.

A few volunteer horse patrols were undertaken in Staffordshire and Cheshire in 1842 and some kind of volunteer units also seem to have existed at Salisbury until 1840 and at Uxbridge until 1843 but it was the invasion debate of the 1840s and 1850s that thoroughly brought the volunteer issue back to prominence although it was clear that many soldiers and politicians saw little value in volunteer corps. Certainly, no serving soldier in a position of responsibility seriously contemplated the revival of the volunteers. In particular, Burgoyne and others believed that the kind of gentlemanly volunteers envisaged would prove unequal to the discipline and hardship of a campaign although a role might be found for riflemen in warding off localised raids. The Duke of Cambridge, who became commander-in-chief in 1855, was equally opposed to volunteers of whom he spoke in 1857 in terms of a 'very dangerous rabble' and 'unmanageable bodies that would ruin our army'.[26] It was a view largely shared by politicians such as Palmerston and Panmure.

Yet, for all the opposition to volunteering amongst the military and political establishment, the popular demand grew steadily through the 1840s and 1850s. Indeed, while only two organs of the press consistently supported the militia in these decades and only a handful of writers or military journals advocated some form of conscripted reserve army, volunteers received overwhelming support from press and pamphleteers. At least twenty-five individuals penned pamphlets in support of a revived volunteer force between 1845 and 1852 and press support ranged from the chartist *Northern Star* to middle-class mouthpieces such as *The Examiner*, *Manchester Guardian* and *The Daily News*.

Still other volunteer advocates emerged in the 1850s while the cause was also taken up by *The Times* whose advocacy of national defence issues might possibly have derived from a desire to preserve beneficial paper duties which would otherwise have been relinquished if a peacetime rate of expenditure was restored.[27] Some individual writers doubtless saw similar profit in financially rewarding populism and it was also the case that there were many individuals eager to claim the distinction of having personally revived the volunteers. Indeed, a lively controversy arose in the closing months of 1860 over who had the best claim, contemporaries generally recognising three men as leading contenders – Hans Busk, Alfred Bate Richards and Nathaniel Bousfield. The claims of Busk, who was instrumental in rejuvenating the Victoria Rifles in 1858; Bousfield, who founded the Liverpool Drill Club in 1855; and Richards, who became secretary to the so-called national and constitutional defence association in the same year of 1855, have been examined elsewhere.[28] Suffice it to say that careful investigation by Sir Duncan MacDougall, whose own role in the advocacy of volunteers was far from negligible, concluded in September 1861 that no single individual could claim to have originated the volunteer movement.

Of course, there was also the example of many of the existing volunteer organisations in the United States, the colonies and Switzerland by the late 1850s and the experience of many British officers in leading irregulars in the Carlist wars in Spain, the Maori wars and the Indian mutiny. This experience in particular suggested that volunteers armed as riflemen and making use of natural cover would be effective in audacious operations against the rear or flank of invading forces. It was argued that this role in itself required more intelligence than was likely to be found amongst militiamen and, in fact, volunteers would be better trained because they could devote more time to training in leisure moments than a militiaman restricted to three or four weeks' training in summer.

Volunteering also appealed to radicals since it not only avoided apparent militarisation of the working class through militia service and the disruption of the domestic economy but also suggested a people's movement free of the aristocratic domination of the militia. Moreover, a large number of volunteer advocates ranging from the leader writers of the *Northern Star* on the left of the political spectrum to those on the extreme right such as Richards viewed volunteering as a means of arresting a perceived national degeneration in industrialised society. It is a theme linked not only to the way in which some had seen the militia as such a vehicle of social engineering but also conceivably to the almost Darwinian terms in which the outbreak of the Crimean War was viewed and to the growth of the 'cult' of the Christian hero evident at the time of the Indian mutiny.

But however popular, the cause of the volunteer met with a singular lack of success between the mid-1840s and 1858. In January 1848, for example, a central volunteer committee, which included both Thomas Hughes and W. H. G. Kingston as members, was formed in London but Kingston's offer to form a corps was no more successful in eliciting a favourable government response than the eleven others received at that time. It is arguable that the dockyard battalions authorised by Russell in April 1847 and which attained a strength of over 9,000 men by March 1848 were the real forerunners of the revived volunteers but few of the volunteer advocates recognised them as such and the Royal Naval Coastal Volunteers (later the Royal Naval Artillery Volunteers) established in April 1853 were actually a maritime militia eventually incorporated into the Royal Naval Reserve in the 1880s.

The 'second panic' prompted 15 offers to form corps in January and February 1852 and there were a further 22 in the course of the next two years. The home secretary in Russell's administration, Sir George Grey, appears to have had no particular objection to volunteers on the grounds that they would not compete with the militia and he accepted offers of corps or rifle clubs at Cheltenham, Hull,

Bridport and Exeter and from the sports club at Hanover Park, Peckham. However, after Russell's resignation, the incoming Derby government took the view that volunteers would only be required if the intended militia bill proved a failure. Consequently, Spencer Walpole, who also feared both the potential social divisiveness of middle-class volunteer units and increased budget demands generated by them, turned down new offers as did lords lieutenant. Walpole did feel obliged to honour Grey's acceptance of that at Exeter as it appeared an area at exceptional risk. Accordingly, the Exeter and South Devon Rifle Corps was accepted on 26 March 1852 – its first officers were commissioned on 4 January 1853 – to become the premier volunteer unit in the country apart from the Honourable Artillery Company.

One other corps also had its officers commissioned on the same day as that at Exeter although it would appear that it was not formally organised until July 1853 – the Victoria Volunteer Rifle Corps. Formed as the Royal Victoria Rifle Club in 1835, the unit claimed a direct connection with the Duke of Cumberland's Sharpshooters which, in turn, were said to have survived the general dissolution of the volunteers at the close of the Napoleonic wars although apparently also in the form of a rifle club. Although organised with 300 men in four companies, the Victoria Rifles dwindled to just 35 effective members by 1858 when Busk became involved in its revival but the rifle clubs accepted by Grey in 1852 appear to have prospered and more were formed including Bousfield's drill club at Liverpool in 1855.

All such groups were drawn from essentially upper middle class elements, the Exeter corps founded by the superintendent of the Exminster Lunatic Asylum, Dr (later Sir) John Bucknill, being designed to accommodate those unable to join either militia or army such as gentlemen, professional men, merchants, tradesmen and 'other respectable inhabitants of their respective districts'.[29] Similarly, the Liverpool club was drawn from younger members of the cotton trade and the relatively exclusive nature of corps and clubs was reflected in the expenses required since it had been clear ever since Sidmouth had reiterated the policy in August 1820 that volunteers could expect no government funding. Thus, the Peckham club had an initial outlay of £14 on uniform and £6 on rifle while the estimated cost of uniform and equipment at Exeter in 1857 was 12 guineas.

There was an idea that the formation of more volunteer corps could free regulars for service overseas and the campaign for volunteers drew renewed inspiration from the Indian mutiny with even suggestions that they should be sent to cruise the Indus and Ganges in armed boats. But such arguments singularly failed to impress either soldiers or politicians while yet another alternative was seen in the militarisation of the new county constabularies as advocated by such chief constables as those in Essex, Kent and Hampshire. At the close of 1857, therefore, there seemed little chance indeed that volunteers would ever be accepted as a permanent addition to the country's defensive forces. What changed the attitudes of at least the politicians, however, was the occurrence of the 'third panic' of 1858–9, which was to culminate in the authorisation of the creation of volunteer corps on 12 May 1859 and, thereby, the re-establishment of the auxiliary forces' triumvirate of militia, yeomanry and volunteers.

Notes

1   C. Emsley, *Crime and Society in England, 1750–1900* (Longman, London, 1987), p. 32.

2   B. Keith-Lucas, *The Unreformed Local Government System* (Croom Helm, London, 1980), pp. 16–17; Bucks RO, *Morgan–Grenville Mss*, D55 AR 40/63, Grenville to Chandos, 22 Jan 1839.

3   Huntington Library, *Stowe Mss*, STG Military Box 2 (4, 5); Bucks RO, *Lieutenancy*, L/Md 5/7 L/V 2/7; Oxon RO, *Lieutenancy*, L/M, II/iii/1.

4   Duncan Anderson, 'The English Militia in the Mid-Nineteenth Century: A Study of its Military, Social and Political significance', Unpub. D.Phil., Oxford, 1982, p. 221.

5   Ibid., p. 224.

6   Extracted from *BPP* 1829 (318) XVI. 177.

7   Marquess of Anglesey, *A History of British Cavalry* (Leo Cooper, London, 1973), I, p. 78.

8   D. & E. Spring, 'The Fall of the Grenvilles, 1844–48', *Huntington Library Quarterly* XIX, 2, 1956, pp. 165–90.

9   *Hansard* 3rd ser., XLII, col. 651, Russell, 27 Apl 1838; Lt. General Sir William Napier, *The Life and Opinions of General Sir Charles Napier* (Murray, London, 1857), II, p. 73 quoting Napier's journal for 15 Aug 1839.

10   J. & P. Drury, *A Tisbury History* (Tisbury Books, Tisbury, 1980), p. 60.

11   Joyce Marlow, *The Peterloo Massacre* (Rapp & Whiting, London, 1969), p. 98; Donald Read, *Peterloo* (Manchester University Press, 1958), pp. 80–82.

12   K. O. Fox, *Making Life Possible* (Privately printed, Kineton, 1982),

pp. 166–7.

13   P. J. R. Mileham, *The Yeomanry Regiments* (Spellmount, Tunbridge Wells, 1985), p. 16.

14   PRO, HO 50/363, Lamb to HO, 16 Aug 1820; Southampton University Library, *Wellington Mss*, 4/1/3/2/57, Assheton-Smith to Wellington, 13 Mar 1831 and Wellington to Assheton-Smith, 14 Mar 1831.

15   G. A. Williams, *The Merthyr Rising* (Croom Helm, London, 1978), p. 154.

16   Oxon RO, *Lieutenancy*, L/M VI/i/1; Huntington Library, *Stowe Mss*, STG Military Box 3 (3), 4 (1); Clywd RO, D/HA/1262.

17   A. Silver, 'The Demand for Order in Civil Society: A Review of Some Themes in the History of Urban Crime' in D. J. Bordua (ed), *The Police: Six Sociological Essays* (Wiley, New York, 1967), pp. 1–24.

18   The Hon. G Wrottesley, *The Life and Correspondence of Field Marshal Sir John Fox Burgoyne* (Richard Bentley & Son, London, 1873), I, pp. 444–51.

19   Bucks RO, *Carrington* 28/A/2.

20   Hants RO, *Lieutenancy*, L.L. 26 (including Oxfordshire correspondence), 27, 28; Bucks RO, *Carrington* 28/A/1, Bernard to Carrington, 11 Apl 1853.

21   Anderson, 'English Militia', p. 354.

22   Ibid., p. 77 quoting Salisbury to Goldsworthy, 28 Oct 1852.

23   Bucks RO, *Carrington* 28/B/11, Circular of 28 Nov 1854.

24   Staffs RO, D 1460, Declaration of Loyal Inhabitants, 20 Oct 1819; Emily Hargrave, 'The Leeds Volunteers, 1820', *Miscellanea 7 of the Thoresby Society* 24, 1919, pp. 451–68; PRO, WO 43/258, List of volunteer corps, 4 May 1826.

25   PRO, HO 41/14, Phillips to Dundas, 28 May 1839.

26   W. Verner, *The Military Life of HRH George, Duke of Cambridge* (Murray, London, 1905), I, pp. 162–7.

27   J. R. Vincent, *The Formation of the British Liberal Party, 1857–68* (2nd edit., Pelican, Harmondsworth, 1972), p. 99.

28   Beckett, *Riflemen Form*, pp. 13–16.

29   Devon R.O., *Seymour of Berry Pomeroy Mss*, 1392 M/Box 18/12.

6
The volunteer triumphant (1858–1899)

While invasion panics in Victorian England tended to be transient affairs, they often had enduring consequences and, in this respect, the 'third panic' of 1858–9 undoubtedly had the greatest impact of all. Those of 1846–8 and 1851–2 had certainly led to the revival of the militia but that force, like the yeomanry, had relatively little popular appeal, not least for the increasing majority inhabiting urban areas, which constituted some 58.7 per cent of the population by 1861. In essence, the existing auxiliary forces were as unrepresentative of society as the regular army in which, as the royal commission on purchase had phrased it in 1857, the middle classes 'had no place . . . under the present system'.[1] In 1859, however, what was tolerated by government in the expectation of it providing a purely temporary response to crisis – a revival of the volunteer movement – was to prove arguably the most significant of the auxiliary forces of the Victorian era in terms of its effect upon social, political and military affairs. Certainly, by the beginning of the twentieth century a far larger section of society had become exposed to military values than would have been possible before 1859.

The immediate cause of the 'third panic' was the repercussions in France of a bomb plot attempt upon the life of Napoleon III by an Italian refugee, Orsini, on 14 January 1858. Orsini had close connections with fellow exiles in London and his bomb had allegedly been made in Birmingham. The resulting agitation appeared genuine with the publication of highly inflammatory addresses congratulating the emperor on his escape. However, Palmerston's attempt to placate the French by introducing a conspiracy to murder bill making it a felony rather than merely a misdemeanour to plot murder abroad from England was defeated on its second reading and he resigned. Once again prime minister, Derby was far more inclined to review military and naval arrangements in the light of continuing rumours of French hostility particularly given the rising tension in Europe. Indeed, war was to break out between France and Austria–Hungary on 3 April 1859.

Derby's initial concern had been to increase naval expenditure but the secretary of state for war, General Jonathan Peel, had established the home defence committee in May 1858 and, of course, instituted the royal commission on the militia. In March 1859 a select committee on military organisation also began its deliberations into the effects of the administrative changes wrought in 1855 after the Crimean debacle, the most significant of which from the point of view of the auxiliary forces had been the transfer of responsibility for them from the Home Office to the new War Office. It was thus Peel rather than the home secretary who would now determine the policy towards any volunteer offers but the conclusions to be drawn from military advice to Peel's various enquiries were hardly likely to encourage acceptance.

Cambridge, who chaired the home defence committee, voiced familiar doubts as to the utility of volunteers as did Burgoyne in another of his memoranda in June 1858. Both repeated their criticisms of irregulars to the select committee while the only two regular witnesses before the militia commission both took the opportunity to deliver some well directed blows at any suggestion of raising volunteers. Similarly, the royal commission on national defences, established in August 1859, would also report in February 1860 that volunteers could be seen only as a partial remedy to the numerical inferiority of those forces available for home defence.

None the less, whatever general military opinion, the demand from the public for volunteers grew steadily. A meeting of the national and constitutional defence association convened by Alfred Richards at St Martin's Hall, Long Acre on 16 April 1859 initiated an increasingly hysterical press campaign, notably in the columns of *The Times* whose articles were widely reproduced.

Volunteers were projected as not only cheaper than regulars but also more likely to instil the country at large with military knowledge. There were indications of support outside London, the campaign culminating on 9 May in the publication of Tennyson's celebrated poem, 'The War', in *The Times* seemingly mirroring the mood of many with its suspicion of France, its concern to prepare for eventualities and the resounding call, 'Riflemen Form'.

On 12 May Peel issued a circular authorising lords lieutenant to raise volunteers under the 1804 Volunteer Consolidation Act, later claiming that it was solely in response to popular opinion. Certainly, Peel and his colleagues did not fear invasion but some concession had to be made to popular pressure given the government's debt to the anti-Gallic feeling that had brought it to power and Peel believed that it would be impossible to resist the demand for volunteers. No further increase in military expenditure would be acceptable either to public or parliament while the militia's failings had been made all too clear by the recent royal commission. By contrast, accepting volunteers had the overriding advantage of satisfying public opinion at absolutely no cost since any units would be self-supporting. There was no longer any real fear of entrusting the 'people' with arms but, in any case, no government arms would be issued and only the wealthy could buy their own weapons. Moreover, those capable of affording such expense were unlikely to be those liable to join either army or militia. Even more important, there was every reason to suppose that the novelty and enthusiasm would soon wear off and the whole movement collapse.

The lack of interest in the terms of volunteer employment is amply illustrated by the circular, which was no more than a selection from the provisions of the 1804 legislation. In return for the empty reward of ballot exemption, the volunteer must participate in at least eight drills in four months or 24 in a year although the ability to resign on 14 days' notice was also included. All arms, equipment, ammunition and expenses would be borne by the men themselves with property vested in commanding officers, who would be appointed by lords lieutenant. Any subscriptions and disciplinary fines would be recoverable under the by-laws of the unit before magistrates. However, the circular did not actually define the purpose of the new volunteer corps and it was left to the Prince Consort, who was conscious of the need to do so, to submit draft 'Instructions to Lords Lieutenant' to Peel on 20 May.

Issued on 25 May, this second circular was a considerable improvement in outlining a purpose for volunteers in inducing 'those classes to come forward as Volunteers who do not, under our present system, enter either the Regular Army or the Militia' and in defining a military role for volunteers as riflemen operating in closed country 'to hang with the most telling effect upon the flanks and communications of a hostile Army'.[2] Some basic drill lessons were also listed with the recommendation that training should not interfere with private avocations and should concentrate in the first instance on imparting the use of the rifle during leisure hours. However, the second circular still did not reveal any copious concession on the part of the administration and, while Peel was now prepared to issue ammunition from government stores at cost price, he declined to respond to appeals from volunteers in Cornwall to provide arms and ammunition gratis. Indeed, he later remarked significantly that the government had intended a drilled but unarmed population with arms made available only in an emergency.

At this point other events intervened with the new Liberal coalition effected on 6 June 1859 bringing down Derby's ministry on a motion of confidence four days later and returning Sidney Herbert to the War Office with Earl de Grey and Ripon as his under-secretary. As a firm advocate of the militia, Herbert was by no means favourably disposed towards the infant volunteers but de Grey, to whom he devolved responsibility for the force, was a personal friend of such leading volunteer enthusiasts as Richards and Thomas Hughes and it is clear that his influence was of considerable importance in establishing its viability. With one brief interval de Grey remained under-secretary until 1863 and then himself served as secretary of state until February 1866.

The first fruit of the new partnership was the announcement on 1 July 1859 that 25 long Enfield rifles would be issued for every 100 volunteers on condition that corps undertook to provide a safe range, secure custody, and a set of approved rules while also making themselves subject to periodic military inspection. Instructors were to be made available from the militia staffs and courses opened to volunteers at the Hythe musketry school. Artillery volunteers, who had been authorised by the second circular, would also gain free ammunition and access to guns for practice. On 13 July Herbert confirmed the arrangements for volunteers in another circular, which specified that volunteers would be liable to serve anywhere in Britain in the event of actual invasion or appearance of an invading force on the coast or in the event of rebellion or insurrection as well as adding to earlier conditions the need to obtain the lord lieutenant's approval of the proposed uniform. A War Office rules committee was also established from among leading volunteers and reported on 10 August with a set of model rules for corps.

Both Herbert and de Grey professed to wish that the volunteers should become something of more tangible military value than mere rifle clubs but, while still intending to prevent the volunteers from becoming too great a charge upon public funds and thereby maintaining a convenient fiction of the self-sufficient 'character' of the volunteers, the assistance offered by Herbert and de Grey also enabled them steadily to increase government control. Accordingly, uniformity of arms calibre was achieved by the issue of remaining rifle requirements by December 1859; enforcement of uniform codes; the appointment of adjutants in February 1860 and the authorisation of a battalion structure in March 1860 either in the form of 'consolidated' battalions where corps were in close proximity or, primarily in rural areas, as 'administrative' battalions in which corps retained their own identity but combined 'to effect a unity of system in correspondence, drill, inspection and returns'.[3] Following the recommendations of the select committee on military organisation, an inspector general of volunteers was appointed on 22 January 1860.

The rationalisation of the volunteer force was not entirely without cost to the War Office. Just as the enactment of the new militia system in 1852 had claimed the full attention of six clerks in the old secretary at war's department so the staff dealing with the volume of volunteer correspondence in the War Office had to be increased from five to 15 clerks by the end of 1860. However, the extension of official control was all the more necessary given the unexpectedly rapid growth of the movement, particularly in the autumn of 1859 and spring of 1860. The first reliable figure is the 161,239 officers and men officially recorded as enrolled for 1861, representing an average monthly increase of 7,000 recruits over the two years to May 1861. By this time, 747 separate rifle corps had been formed of which 133 had been formed in 1859 and 578 in 1860. The official figures for 1861 revealed a ratio of volunteers per 100 of population of 0.6 in England and Wales and 1.1 in Scotland, where volunteering was always to enjoy a proportionally higher hold on the population. The same ratios were recorded for England and Wales in both 1871 and 1881 but the Scottish ratio had by then increased to 1.3 per 100 of population.[4]

It would be wrong to imply that the formation of the volunteers went without challenge in the localities in 1859 and 1860, pacifists circulating pamphlets deploying much the same kind of rhetoric as in the militia agitation of the 1840s. Moreover, in the public meetings commonly held to discuss the formation of volunteers, some of those attending in northern towns such as Huddersfield, Rochdale and Oldham voiced a belief that volunteering represented an attempt to kill interest in reform. However, the public mood was clearly against such argument, and the volunteer movement was widely supported by both the established Church and, perhaps even more crucially, by women who were active in presenting bugles and colours to new units and raising funds. Occasionally, the public meetings raised fears for property or of the ballot but the overwhelming message was suspicion of France and the need to be prepared for any eventuality.

In fact, while the Franco–Austrian war was concluded in July 1859 fears of French ambition remained just as great in Britain. A survey of 'war scare' articles in the *Saturday Review*, for example, reveals that while 15 such articles had appeared in 1858 and 47 in 1859, there were 44 in 1860, 33 in 1861 and still 25 in 1862.[5] Certainly, there was no decrease in French naval expenditure and the French launched the first seagoing ironclad, *La Gloire*, in November 1859. Even Palmerston had grown wary of Napoleon III and, against the financial opposition of Gladstone at the Exchequer, he fully supported the massive fortification programme advocated by the royal commission on national defences. Moreover, by 1861 there were indications of approaching conflict with the United States, Britain subsequently maintaining large numbers of regulars in Canada during the American civil war.

Such continuing tensions were a major stimulus to volunteer recruiting, one overt sign of permanency being the creation in November 1859 of the national rifle association along the lines of the Swiss *tir federal* to promote the movement and encourage rifle shooting as a pastime. Appropriately perhaps, the medals awarded at the first annual meeting held at Wimbledon on 2 July 1860, which was opened by the Queen, bore the image of a mediaeval archer and a modern rifleman standing together with the motto, 'Sit per-petuum'. In a relatively short period of time, therefore, any thoughts that this comparatively large, spontaneous and patriotic national response would prove but a temporary phenomenon were quickly dispelled although, as it developed, the volunteer force was also to bear increasingly less resemblance to the exclusive middle-class clubs envisaged by many of its original advocates.

That initial ideal is readily apparent in the rules adopted by most early corps, which like those of the Napoleonic volunteers, defined a preference for maintaining exclusiveness by the barrier of expense. Thus, there were usually provision for honorary and enrolled members, entrance fees of perhaps half a guinea, proposing and seconding of members and annual subscriptions usually ranging from one to three guineas. There was to be essentially no difference between officers, who initially were often elected, and men with all eligible to serve on finance committees and annual accounts published for general scrutiny and discussion. Discipline was simply expected of gentlemen and would be enforced only by petty fines.

In addition, of course, there were the costs of uniform, which often exceeded £4, and of equipment, which would push the overall cost even higher. Thus, the total cost of joining could range from £7 10s at Trowbridge at the lower end of the scale to an average £10 at Maidstone and to £14 7s 6d in the particularly exclusive London Rifle Brigade. In a general economic situation in which, for example, a Liverpool dock porter earned 3s 6d a day – the average cost of the uniform alone in the city corps was £4 13s 6d – or in which rural labourers could earn between 9s 0d and 12s 0d a week depending upon season, it was generally agreed that about 18s 0d per week regular wage was the lowest income level at which volunteers should be recruited without competing directly with the army or militia.[6]

None the less, one reason why lords lieutenant strongly associated with the militia such as the Marquess of Salisbury in Middlesex and the Marquess of Winchester in Hampshire proved especially obstructive to would-be volunteers was that the force did compete with the militia. On the one hand, many younger members of the landed classes who might otherwise have sought militia commissions were now attracted to the volunteers who, whether in urban or rural areas, showed a distinct preference for placing themselves under aristocratic command. In the metropolis, for example, such officers often remained long after most of their fellows had departed from provincial corps, those commanding regiments in 1860 including Earl Grosvenor, Viscount Bury and Lords Ranelagh, Radstock, Elcho and Enfield. It has been argued that the volunteers represented an 'anti-militarist' middle-class challenge to the aristocratic and landed dominance of the militia and army and, of course, those excluded from militia or regular commissions could and did find an outlet for their military aspirations in the force.[7] As will be indicated later, it was also the case that some volunteers did decisively reject any question of regular interference in the movement. However, it would appear that the influence of what Matthew Arnold, who joined the Queen's Westminsters, regarded as a reflection of 'hideous English toadyism'[8] in so readily placing the nobility in command was the more pervasive influence.

Notwithstanding the middle-class image, the volunteers also competed with the militia by attracting the kind of respectable working-class men who had declined to re-enlist in 1857 since, from the very beginning, leading volunteers such as Richards and Elcho believed artisans should not be excluded lest the movement decline from relying on too narrow a social base. Volunteers frequently recruited well in areas where the militia had fared badly and it is probable that the resistance to artisan volunteers or corps voiced by such lords lieutenant as Salisbury, Lord Hardwicke in Cambridgeshire and Lord Exeter in Northamptonshire was motivated rather more by their likely effect on militia recruitment than by Salisbury's stated concern in one long-running battle in Middlesex that an artisan unit would 'place upon its class the stamp of inferiority to another'.[9]

The volunteers were, therefore, immediately more diverse in social composition than might have been anticipated. In rural areas, where difficulties often arose from the scattered nature of the population, some corps still resembled the bands of neo-feudal retainers seen in earlier manifestations of the volunteer tradition with a proliferation of tenants or estate employees as at Althorp in Northamptonshire, Maiden Bradley in Wiltshire, Woburn in Bedfordshire, Alnwick in Northumberland and on the Zetland estate in the North Riding. Much also depended upon the attitude of the farming community in counties such as Oxfordshire, Northamptonshire, Somerset, Kent, Wiltshire and Cornwall and, indeed, the farming and hunting community were also drawn into the 30 or so mounted units raised as light horse or mounted volunteers – usually where yeomanry did not already exist – but few survived beyond the 1860s.

Most rural units were concentrated in the small market towns. In the latter volunteers embraced a broad cross-section of the local community though, if landed gentlemen were not available, leadership noticeably devolved upon solicitors or others trained in the legal profession. Occasionally, there might be a large residential middle class but, more usually, rural units had a predominance of professional men and tradesmen with a sprinkling of artisans or craftsmen as was the case in such corps as those at Northampton, Dorchester, Weymouth, Wells, Reigate, Salisbury, Canterbury, Chepstow, Winslow in Buckinghamshire and Toddington in Bedfordshire. In Oxfordshire, where it is possible to reconstruct the entire volunteer force of 379 men in seven units (excluding the university corps) in 1859–60 – those at Oxford, Banbury, Henley, Witney, Deddington, Bicester and Thame – approximately 43.7 per cent could be regarded as lower middle-class tradesmen, clerks or craftsmen/artisans with 33.8 per cent upper middle-class professionals or farmers.[10]

However, most volunteers, be they middle class or artisan, were to be found in large urban centres, the most favourable environment being where wealth, youth and the middle classes were found to coincide although it was also in the great urban centres that the majority of the purely artisan corps were raised. Thus, over 50 corps were raised in Middlesex, 12 in the Tower Hamlets and five in the City. By the end of 1859 Merseyside alone had furnished over 4,000 volunteers in 26 separate corps while, by June 1861, Newcastle, Hull and Birmingham had each raised over 1,000 volunteers and Manchester some 3,700 volunteers. Yet, the key note of the larger urban centres was variety since so many individual companies and interests combined to form a composite whole.

Corps in London ranged from some of the wealthiest and most exclusive units in the country to the poorest. Among the former were the 11th Middlesex (St George's) RVC with companies drawn from Bond Street, Grosvenor Square, Hanover Square and Belgravia; the 23rd Middlesex (Inns of Court) RVC and the 38th Middlesex (Artists' Rifles) whose members included Val Prinsep, G. F. Watts, Edward Burne-Jones, Dante Gabriel Rossetti, William Morris, John Millais and Frederick Leighton. By contrast, Thomas Hughes raised the 19th Middlesex RVC from pupils of the Christian socialist working men's college in Bloomsbury and from artisans, clerks, warehousemen and shipmen while the cartoonist George Cruikshank's 48th Middlesex (Havelock's Temperance) RVC, after purchasing uniform and accoutrements 'acknowledged themselves unable to contribute money sufficient to defray the legitimate and absolutely necessary expenses of the corps'.[11] The same extremes were to be found in Liverpool where the volunteers also reflected ethnic divisions resembling the immigrant companies common in the American volunteer movement of the 1840s and 1850s.

Outside the capital, there was less evidence in urban areas of leadership by the landed elite, and volunteers looked for leadership to manufacturers and merchants such as the shipowner James Walter, and the colliery owner James Bourne, in Liverpool; the coal owner Edward Potter, in North Shields and Tynemouth; and the chemical works manager Henry Allhusen, in Gateshead. In Leeds, where the level of municipal support for the volunteers was to remain consistently high, volunteering was apparently viewed by the leaders of the metal and machine trades and the wool trade as an opportunity to challenge the hold of the textile trade on council chamber and city affairs by demonstrating their own commitment to the community.[12]

However, it should be noted that the urban leadership in Leeds was predominantly Tory and anglican and urban volunteering was always strongest among similarly Tory and anglican urban elites in Lancashire towns such as Blackburn, Bolton, Bury, Preston and Warrington. Those who might be termed moderate nonconformist manufacturers such as Edward Akroyd, worsted manufacturer, Liberal MP for Halifax from 1865 to 1868 and a prominent member of the volunteer interest in the Commons, or his fellow worsted manufacturer, W. E. Forster, the Quaker who sat as MP for Bradford from 1861 to 1886 and raised the 23rd West Riding RVC from his own mill hands, were occasionally prominent, but nonconformist employers were generally opposed to the movement. This was certainly true of spinning manufacturers and mill owners in Manchester, Rochdale and Huddersfield and indications of such opposition continued to appear.

For the most part, however, officers in centres such as Liverpool and Manchester were drawn from professional men from the commercial and financial worlds rather than from the legal profession as was common in the countryside. Similarly, in London a surviving set of commissioning forms for 413 officers from nine Middlesex rifle corps and 178 officers from three artillery corps between 1860 and 1872 reveals that, of the 300 rifle officers whose occupations are known, 53 per cent were professional men and, of the 170 known artillery officers, 67.7 per cent were also professionals. Of the remainder 20.3 per cent and 16.6 per cent respectively were tradesmen and clerks. Of the professional men among rifle officers the largest group were employed in finance or insurance (20 per cent) and, in the case of artillery officers, the largest group was engaged in educational, medical or clerical supervision (24.3 per cent).[13]

In terms of rank and file most metropolitan corps appear to have relied on a strong core of lower middle-class men with the predominance of tradesmen in the rural areas giving way to a dependence upon clerks. Nevertheless, as in the country as a whole, a distinct change became apparent as early as 1862 with just that decline in enthusiasm that ministers had predicted in 1859. Time was one crucial factor but another was expense since there had often been unnecessary extravagance at the start and the level of public subscription received initially simply could not be maintained: in the 1st Warwickshire (Birmingham) RVC, for example, the deficit on the years 1860–2 amounted to £1,464 12s 0d. Faced with declining public financial support in 1861 and 1862 volunteer agitation began both within and outside Westminster for government pecuniary aid and it was the royal commission appointed in May 1862 in response to that agitation that first provided evidence of the changing composition.

In Liverpool, for example, the professional element was found to have declined substantially with a unit such as the Nathaniel Bousfield's 1st Lancashire RVC, which had originally contained sons of gentlemen, professional cotton brokers and merchants, now dependent upon tradesmen and artisans. In Manchester between 2,000 and 3,000 volunteers were artisans and between 6,000 and 7,000 in Glasgow. Elsewhere the picture was much the same and some rural units were even beginning to recruit agricultural labourers. Evidence from 1862 onwards illustrates a continuing process of change with volunteers becoming younger and more working-class. In the case of the 1st Lincoln (City) RVC the proportion of artisans and labourers serving increased from 32.6 per cent in the period 1859–63 to 64.5 per cent in 1864–68, 76.5 per cent in 1869–73 and to 83.3 per cent in 1884–8. The Bury Departmental Committe confirmed the trend in 1878 and the Norfolk Commission in 1904 produced figures based on replies by 218 volunteer commanding officers revealing that 35.5 per cent of the force's rank and file were artisans, 12.8 per cent town or agricultural labourers, 6 per cent miners and 12.9 per cent factory hands. Only 3.2 per cent were self–employed although 1.8 per cent were professional men and 9.6 per cent clerks.[14]

Clearly, there is a certain paradox in the fact that the middle class quickly deserted the volunteers but the movement survived the loss of its creators. Indeed, despite the frequently voiced fears of volunteers themselves and an average turnover of 25 per cent per annum, there was an overall steady rate of growth. The force topped the 200,000 mark in 1878 and continued to enjoy the support of nearly a quarter of a million men for much of the period thereafter, the peak strength being the 288,476 officers and men recorded in 1901. There were net increases in the force under the impact of international crises such as the Balkan crisis in 1877–8, Penjdeh and the Sudan in 1885 and the South African War but not all international or domestic invasion scares had the same effect after 1859 and such gains were usually temporary, notably among officers who had a greater burden of expense to consider. Moreover, the general public attitude towards the force that prevailed during periods of international calm was also somewhat unhelpful in maintaining strength.

To a certain extent, volunteers brought difficulties on themselves, their military pretensions and fanciful uniforms in the early years often inviting public ridicule. However, the popular press and even some politicians also fostered the gibes reminiscent of those directed at volunteers or militiamen in earlier times, the most celebrated – the *Punch* cartoon, 'Who Shot the Dog' – ironically appearing in a journal which generally supported the movement. But, at the same time, the volunteers' need for drill space and ranges also led to friction where the public believed common rights threatened and there were some unseemly clashes such as that between volunteers and crowds in Regent's Park on Whit Monday, 1861. Volunteers were actually banned from Hyde Park in 1880 and 1881 and such treatment at the hands of central authority was repeated by many local authorities although it can be noted that, as in previous times, certain localities could benefit from the volunteer presence. In particular, the great Easter Monday reviews organised by the metropolitan corps at such venues as Brighton and Portsmouth between 1861 and 1877 attracted considerable trade – volunteers and their families apparently spent over £50,000 at Brighton in 1863 – and representatives of rail companies and towns regularly advertised their facilities to metropolitan commanding officers.

Indeed, trade was one facet of an interdependence between auxiliaries and the local community in Victorian Britain embracing not only the level of financial assistance sought and given but the way community pride and status could become intimately bound up in auxiliary unit affairs. In Buckinghamshire, for example, the inhabitants of High Wycombe greatly resented the disbanding of its volunteer company in 1871 for firing off ammunition indiscriminately after a field day. The same sense of local outrage accompanied the disbandment of the 18th Hants (Basingstoke) RVC in 1864 after its men refused to be broken up to reinforce other units at a Guildford review.

No public function at local level in the second half of the nineteenth century was really complete without an auxiliary presence and few weekly issues of the provincial press went by without some record of their activities. However, it was equally the case that the auxiliaries could provoke local hostility by their own actions, not least lapses of discipline, and a particular difficulty for the volunteers was also the virtual ostracism of their officers in many areas of society, which increased as vacancies were filled with those who might previously have seen non-commissioned rank as the limit of their ambitions. Satirical magazines poured scorn on the allegedly low breeding and poor professional standing of such officers while society journals, military journals and much of the press habitually declined to recognise volunteer rank in reports, the attitude being summed up as 'a greengrocer presented with a major's commission is a greengrocer pleased'.[15] In March 1860 the Queen received 2,000 volunteer officers at a special levee but this was never repeated and it was only in 1890 that volunteers were placed on the same footing as militia and yeomanry officers with respect to presentation at court.

Ironically, even the volunteers' successes worked against them in the long run. In 1863 the government under the influence of de Grey responded to the financial problems of the volunteer force and the recommendations of the royal commission by agreeing an annual capitation grant of £1 per man with an additional 10s 0d for extra efficiency. Incorporated in the Volunteer Act of 1863 (26 & 27 Vict c 65) the standard was established as attendance at nine drills and the annual inspection for the basic capitation grant and firing off 60 rounds at a target for the additional 10s 0d. After 1863 government declined to accept the view that a bargain had been struck whereby, if the volunteers found the grant insufficient, it would be reviewed and, as secretary of state in 1867–8, Sir John Pakington refused to bow to pressure to increase the capitation grant. However, the basic grant was increased to £1 10s 0d in 1869 and to £1 15s 0d in 1887 with other allowances also increased but at the price of efficiency requirements being correspondingly tightened, the musketry standard for one being raised in 1869, 1887 and 1889. Even more significantly, drills required of new recruits climbed to 60 in the first two years following the recommendations of the Bury committee in 1878 and, from 1896, 12 rather than nine were required in the third and fourth years of service.

Such increasing commitment conflicted immediately with the civil occupations of many volunteers, the relationship between auxiliaries and employers being another level of interdependence. Conscious of the need to effect co-operation with employers, leading volunteers such as Elcho, Grosvenor and Thomas Hughes had sought agreements in the metropolis in September 1860 for earlier Saturday closing. This was followed in 1866 by the first half-holiday experiments with 30 to 40 prominent metropolitan employers but the increasing government requirements undermined the volunteers' efforts and by 1881 the *Volunteer Service Gazette* concluded that most employers were now opposed to the movement and even government itself often refused to release civil servants.

At the same time, the success of the early closing movement, which volunteers like Elcho and Hughes had wholeheartedly supported, also backfired against the force. The passing of the Bank Holiday Act in 1875, for example, gave the railway companies sufficient civilian traffic to refuse to convey the volunteers and forced the cancellation of the Easter review in 1874 and 1875 and its final abandonment in 1878. Moreover, while the volunteer movement itself opened up new recreational opportunities in Victorian Britain, the growth of sport which the volunteers helped to encourage contributed to their recruitment difficulties by offering rival attractions.

Yet, it was primarily as a recreational pursuit that the volunteer movement appealed to the artisan and thereby survived, particularly as the disciplined pursuit of leisure endowed volunteering with a strongly moral purpose. Even the activities dictated primarily by military necessity such as musketry became the focus for unashamed social intercourse. County rifle associations began to appear in the mid-1860s, organising annual matches with accompanying dinners or entertainments. The annual Wimbledon meeting of the national rifle association was the climax of the shooting year and the NRA also arranged the visit of 11,000 volunteers to the Belgian *tir federal* in 1866. The annual training camps, which began to be held from 1864–5 onwards, served to introduce volunteers to some of the privations of military life but also provided rich diversions such as that at Althorp in August 1864 which offered athletics, shooting matches, pony races, cricket and music hall.

Camps, reviews – notably the royal reviews of 1860, 1863, 1866 and 1881 – or the volunteers' promotion of the grand military tournament and assault at arms, first held in 1880 and which still survives as the annual royal tournament, also offered spectacle to the public. Crowds such as the 40,000 to 50,000 who visited the midland counties review at Warwick in July 1861 or the estimated 150,000 to 200,000 watching the Knowsley review the previous year were as large as if not larger than those who had attended similar events fifty years before while volunteer bands were as important in stimulating amateur music making as they had been in the Napoleonic era. Activities of financial necessity such as fund-raising balls, concerts, bazaars and theatrical performances also added to the entertainment available through the volunteers as did the activities purely internal to units such as dinners, prize givings and the variety of clubs that sprang up attached to corps or companies. Indeed, volunteer athletic and football clubs were especially important in popularising sports previously confined to the wealthier classes. Just as it has been noted that many public houses adopted names connected to the volunteers, implying at the very least the companionship of the movement[16] so, too, did the volunteers found many new masonic lodges although lodges were also associated with eighteenth- or early-nineteenth century militia or volunteers.

The influence of what has been called 'social inheritance'[17] – men joining because their friends had done so – can be no more discounted in discusing the motivation for volunteering than patriotism. But, even if volunteer commissions were believed to offer little social prestige, it was also the case that what might be regarded as patriotic recreation had an additional moral quality viewed as advantageous to volunteer and employer alike. It is no accident that men like Matthew Arnold, Thomas Hughes and Samuel Smiles were such strong supporters of a movement in which drill, discipline and healthy exercise were held to promote habits of order, obedience, cleanliness and punctuality as well as social harmony. Witnesses before the royal commission in 1862 testified to the success of the volunteers in reclaiming the idle and dissipated and it was suggested that a volunteer was worth 3s 0d a week more to a jobbing master than an ordinary employee. Much the same arguments were used for the creation of the many public school cadet corps that came to be attached to volunteer units and this spread in the 1880s with independent cadet corps and battalions in Birmingham, Liverpool, Manchester, Glasgow and London seeking to exercise a moral influence over working-class boys: both William Smith, who founded the Boys' Brigade in 1883, and Walter Gee, who founded the Church Lads' Brigade eight years later, were also volunteers.

The moral and social benefits perceived in volunteering certainly implied a measure of social control and conditioning of the working class by the middle class. While there is little evidence of employers coercing men into enrolling into those corps raised at their industrial enterprises in 1859 or 1860, there were instances in which volunteer discipline was maintained under pain of dismissal from civilian employment as in the case of London and North Western Railway Company employees in Buckinghamshire, Cunard employees in Liverpool, Tetley employees in Leeds and Post Office employees in Middlesex. The general decline of support among employers tended to reduce the likelihood of the factory floor being simply reproduced on the parade ground and, of course, the discipline and subordination of the work place was in itself a dominating factor in much working-class experience. More commonly, however, the volunteers were exposed to a a more subtle degree of social control.

The cadet battalions were but one means by which groups like the charity organisation society, which was closely connected with the largest cadet battalion in Southwark, pursued the reinforcement of social conformity by consciously attempting to penetrate the leisure of the disadvantaged working-class adolescent as an antidote to restlessness and parental vice. In fact, it would appear that those susceptible to the appeal of such organisations tended to be upwardly mobile youth in the suburbs for whom participation is said to have conferred a *rite de passage* between the classes. Similarly, it has been suggested that Victorian clerks in Manchester and Liverpool were able to associate with their employers in uniform in a way which compensated for declining opportunities of upward mobility. Seeking respectability through participation has also been noted as a characteristic of the 'labour aristocracy' itself in Edinburgh and the London boroughs of Deptford, Greenwich and Woolwich, the volunteers representing a way in which skilled men might distinguish themselves from their fellows and stake a claim to respectability.[18]

But whatever the social role of the volunteer movement, its *raison d'être* was to resist possible invasion and here its practical military potential was in some doubt at least as far as most professional soldiers were concerned. Regulars rarely comprehended the special problems facing auxiliaries held together by mutual consent rather than a strict code of discipline. In the case of the volunteers, the notion of drill and discipline was extremely rudimentary at first and not assisted by the election of officers – when all those aspiring to command had left the room during the ballot in one Edinburgh company in 1859, the remaining three members had elected themselves – and the often distinct lack of subordination displayed by such officers. The regular inspectors called to officiate at volunteer inspections, sham fights and reviews seldom stimulated volunteer energy in the right direction. It was also unfortunate that some of the worst instances of volunteer indiscipline or confusion occurred at or after such public performances – de Grey was forced to issue a circular in August 1861 condemning the practice of firing rifles out of railway carriage windows – although some resulted from the fact that the men were often attempting to execute drill movements in the midst of even more undisciplined crowds.

Nor did the performance of auxiliaries abroad suggest to regulars that the volunteers could hope to improve although the evidence regulars cited was highly selective. Thus, volunteers pointed to the success of a confederate army, which could be said to be less well disciplined than themselves, at the first battle of the American civil war at Manassas in July 1861. Regulars preferred to use the example of the rout of the union army in the same battle as more indicative of the likely fate of volunteers in the field. Similarly, although irregular forces enjoyed military successes in Canada, New Zealand and Italy, it was the setbacks like the collapse of Garibaldi's army at Mentana in November 1867 or of the *garde mobile* in France in 1870 that were seen as most significant by a generally hostile military press campaign, which reached its height in the period between 1868 and 1871.

There was perhaps a sense in which the volunteers, controlled through the War Office, fell victim to the general struggle which had ensued between it and the commander-in-chief at the Horse Guards. But, much of the regular criticism was also conceived in a spirit of narrow professionalism such as the constant sniping between 1866 and 1871 at the idea of volunteers successfully operating field artillery as opposed to static garrison artillery. This culminated in the refusal by Edward Cardwell as secretary of state to allow the maintenance of horses, harness or field guns of units such as the 1st Middlesex AV and 1st Newcastle AV to be paid for from the capitation grant. In rather the same way, regular evidence presented to a committee on the yeomanry established by Frederick Stanley in April 1875 was instrumental in removing the horse artillery troops of the yeomanry in Buckinghamshire and Essex, the dismounted rifle troop in Northumberland and the rifle troop raised in Wiltshire in 1859 to ride in specially constructed carriages.

But the fault was not all one way since some volunteers were equally blind to the limitations of civilians only temporarily in uniform and inspired at least initially by the concept of a free assembly of social equals, who were not only unpaid but capable of resigning at short notice. A recognised 'advanced school' of younger officers emerged in the 1870s seeking greater commitment as the price of greater integration with the army without regard for the crucial factors of time and civilian employment but an earlier manifestation of progressivism, most closely identified with Lord Ranelagh, had taken a rather different course in seeking total independence.

It was Ranelagh's suggestion in November 1860 that the metropolitan volunteers – he commanded the 2nd Middlesex (South Middlesex) RVC – should hold a review at Brighton on the following Easter Monday. However, both Elcho and Bury took the view that it was too early to undertake projects on such a scale and, while Bury led an official contingent of volunteers to Wimbledon, Ranelagh took off 4,000 or so to Brighton. Ranelagh had been equally instrumental in a resolution passed by the metropolitan commanding officers in April 1860, which had the effect of prohibiting regulars from commanding at volunteer reviews, but in a stormy meeting in April 1861 it was decided to invite regulars to command in future. Ranelagh appeared to accept the decision but then tried to overturn it in February 1862 and in June publicly quarrelled with a regular sent to supervise a sham fight at Panshanger. In the following year he was again accused of trying to dictate venues for reviews to his fellow metropolitan commanding officers while, in January 1868, he caused further controversy by describing the volunteers as a 'sham' army and clarifying his meaning the following month by calling for the volunteers to be 'a distinct and separate force from the Army'.[19]

An element within the chord that Ranelagh struck among some

volunteers and parts of the press was the assertion of middle-class identity through an overt challenge to traditional military authority as represented by Horse Guards. Many of those involved in the volunteers were still effectively excluded from regular or militia commissions and volunteers were also to be found among those advocating the reduction of military expenditure and wider military reform although it should be noted that others like Elcho and Bury were strongly opposed to the abolition of purchase in the regulars and Ranelagh may also have found some of the support he engendered from organs such as *The Morning Star* and *The Herald of Peace* for a 'people's army' personally distasteful.

Ironically, the very existence of the volunteers may have had a detrimental effect upon military reform in that their claims to represent the nation's real military reserve conceivably delayed the establishment of an army reserve until 1867. As will be seen, that reserve was in any case totally inadequate and the only effective means by which Britain could have matched the manpower available to continental powers such as Prussia, whose series of stunning victories in the cause of German unification in 1864, 1866 and 1870 gave considerable pause for thought, would have been through the adoption of continental-style conscription. One regular, Robert Home, who was to be responsible for the British army's first mobilisation scheme in 1875, believed the volunteers would prove a means of uniting army and people and so pave the way for conscription. But as Elcho, who was himself later converted to the cause of conscription, realised, the volunteers' existence was a further argument against the ballot rather than an additional factor in its favour.

One frequent claim by volunteers was that what they lacked in discipline they made up for in intelligence and certainly they were to provide a fertile breeding ground for new ideas. Nineteen units had machine guns by 1893 and volunteer units had also experimented with mounted infantry and cyclists. Likewise, volunteers were involved in the development of the service rifle, of more sensible uniforms and in the eventual reform of the regular army's drill book. Similarly, at a time when large-scale manoeuvres by regulars were rare – none were held in England between 1853 and 1871 or between 1873 and 1898 and another prominent volunteer, Robert Loyd-Lindsay, was instrumental in encouraging those that were held between 1871 and 1873 – the volunteers alone offered regulars the opportunity of handling large bodies of men in peacetime.

The emergence of a younger generation of volunteer officers in the 1870s or ex-regulars like Howard Vincent, who commanded the Central London Rangers from 1875 to 1878 and the Queen's Westminsters from 1884 to 1908, resulted in a general movement towards greater organisation, discipline and commitment and there were internally generated attempts to improve the military education of officers through such means as the Manchester tactical society founded by Henry Spenser Wilkinson and fellow volunteers in 1881. In turn, this influenced the introduction of a tactical examination in 1882 and popularised wargaming. Volunteers also endeavoured to create services which they conspicuously lacked, adding a railway staff in 1865 and a medical staff in 1885 although various efforts to organise a transport service were less successful.

The precise role of the volunteers in national defence also came to be a matter of controversy as some sought to extend their utility beyond meeting any invasion despite the difficulty of reconciling such commitment with employment. As early as December 1861 two units offered to serve in Canada in the wake of the Trent affair and offers of both home and overseas garrison service were made in 1878. However, legislation did not permit even limited offers of garrison service, which were again turned down in 1885. The exception was the despatch of two officers and 100 men from the 24th Middlesex (Post Office) RVC to Egypt in 1882 to perform the duties of an army post office corps. Subsequently, the battalion formed two field telegraph companies and one officer and 32 men from the corps were subsequently sent to Suakin in March 1885 while some 40 men from the 1st Newcastle and Durham and the 1st Lancashire engineer corps also went to Suakin on railway duties.

The actual number of offers made by volunteers in 1878 and 1885 was relatively small but the climate of opinion was changing all the time. In 1888 there were still so many doubts expressed that the secretary of state, Edward Stanhope, dropped a clause from his national defence bill by which volunteers could have been called out when the militia was embodied in cases of imminent national danger or emergency rather than just upon actual or apprehended invasion. By 1895, however, volunteers favoured a wider interpretation of their duties and the Volunteers (Military Service) Act in July followed the recommendations of an earlier select committee in allowing volunteer offers of service to be accepted once the militia was embodied although it still did not permit service overseas.

The use of postal and engineering volunteers overseas, however, was a measure of growing contact between regulars and the volunteers by the late 1870s and early 1880s. This arose partly from the organisational changes of localisation introduced by Edward Cardwell in 1873 and territorialisation introduced when Hugh Childers was at the War Office in 1881 but there were also considerations of official necessity. Thus, volunteers were to be given an increasing role in the mobilisation schemes for home defence. In the first scheme of 1875 40,000 volunteers or approximately one quarter of the force were allocated to garrisons although there was some likelihood that they might also be used locally for a more mobile defensive role and, by 1878, there was some suggestion of coastal brigades in addition to garrisons.

Increasingly projected as a viable and cheap 'second line', 97 out of 209 volunteer battalions, including 21,000 men in defence of London, were utilised in the mobilisation scheme of 1886 while that of 1888 took a major step forward in proposing to organise 18 volunteer brigades of six battalions each in large camps at Aldershot, Caterham, Chatham, Tilbury, Warley and Epping occupying a line between the immediate defences of London and the two regular army corps operating to the south. The defence of London itself was also entrusted to volunteers in fixed fortifications. Volunteer engineers had already been used to supplement the manpower available for submarine mining defences of mercantile ports from 1884 onwards and additional submarine mining companies and position batteries were now raised to meet deficiencies in the mobilisation scheme.

While growing numbers of regulars were prepared to help the volunteers by the late 1870s and 1880s, much still depended upon their good will and it must be said that localisation and territorialisation were not always successful in promoting co-operation. Cardwell had aroused the animosity of volunteers from the beginning by initially refusing to increase the capitation grant and then coupling the increase to 30s 0d in 1869 with greater requirements. Similarly, the certificate of proficiency introduced in 1870 for officers and non-commissioned officers through attachment to army, militia or schools of instruction, which could earn an additional 5s 0d capitation grant, was made compulsory in May 1872 and Cardwell also now insisted on a compulsory brigade drill each year and on a minimum level of volunteers being present before drills could count towards efficiency.

Even less welcome were the implications of Cardwell's major reforms, not least in their assault on one of the few remaining military functions of the lieutenancy. By the Regulation of the Forces Act of 1871, all auxiliary commissions were to be issued by the Crown rather than by the lord lieutenant although the lieutenancy would be able to make recommendations on first appointments. Under the same legislation, volunteers brigaded with militia or regulars were made liable to the provisions of the Mutiny Act. The Localisation Act applied to the force in April 1873 then placed volunteer units into new sub-districts with two 'linked' regular battalions and two militia battalions centred upon a brigade depot. Responsibility for the inspection and training of volunteers was now vested in the regulars commanding the depots while volunteer adjutants, who would be progressively replaced by regulars on attachment, were gazetted as regular captains and given additional depot and recruiting duties.

It is clear that many depot commanders did not take sufficient interest in the volunteers under their supervision and the same was sometimes true of GOCs of districts. The Bury departmental committee in 1878 – both the under-secretary of state for war, Bury, and the financial secretary to the War Office, Loyd-Lindsay in Disraeli's administration, were, of course, volunteers – endeavoured to promote greater assimilation of volunteers within the Cardwell system by consolidating administrative battalions but it was Childers who brought full territorialisation into effect in July 1881. Thus, volunteer battalions were translated into volunteer battalions of the new territorial regiments comprising both regular and militia battalions. The renumbering and retitling was not always popular and, in the case of metropolitan units, arbitrary division between the depots of the King's Royal Rifle Corps and the Rifle Brigade at Winchester and the depots of the Royal Fusiliers and Middlesex Regiment in London was hardly conducive to rational military organisation and training.

But, if the reforms instituted by Cardwell had many implications for the volunteers, the same was even more true of the militia, which was increasingly being subordinated to the regulars. One factor was the glaring inadequacy of the army's reserves when compared to those of continental armies coupled, in the mid-1860s, with something of a recruiting crisis. Herbert had established an army reserve in 1859 from men taking early discharge but fewer than 3,000 had enrolled by 1866 when a royal commission chaired by Panmure, now Earl of Dalhousie, not only recommended using the militia as the basis for a properly organised reserve but also called for the abandonment of Herbert's prohibition on recruitment into the line. Both recommendations found favour with General Peel serving another term at the War Office in Derby's third administration. Accordingly, militia recruitment into the army was reopened in May 1866 and in the following March Peel unveiled a new reserve scheme allowing for a first reserve of 50,000 men earmarked for overseas service and a second reserve of 30,000 men for home defence, the militia being invited to contribute up to 30,000 men to the first reserve in return for a bounty. So little inducement was offered to either regulars or militiamen that by 1870 the scheme had enrolled only 19,916 militiamen and 20,467 regulars, of whom the vast majority enlisted for the second rather than the first reserve.

Cardwell sought to build a 60,000 strong reserve by introducing short service embodying periods in both the line and the reserve which would enable vacancies in home battalions to be filled upon mobilisation. It was additionally intended that the militia should feed both men and officers to the army, a development further encouraged by the close affiliation of militia and line under localisation. Militia officers had been eligible to attend Hythe since 1862 and in 1870 Cardwell also extended to them as well as to volunteer officers the opportunity to attend regular schools of instruction. In the same year Cardwell also attempted to stimulate Peel's militia reserve, which he had retained, by promising a regular commission for every 100 militia reservists upon actual mobilisation for service. However, it was the ability of militia officers to pass into the line which became the most crucial aspect of the new integration.

In March 1869 Cardwell had already announced the abolition of the militia property qualifications, seemingly opening the officer corps to newcomers – and, indeed, to half-pay regular offficers – in the same way that the abolition of purchase in 1871 suggested the opening of the regular officer corps. Abolition made it far easier to integrate regular officers with auxiliaries, who were not subject to purchase although a few volunteer adjutancies had changed hands illegally for money since 1859 and militia adjutancies had regularly done so. But the important step for the militia was the general order in February 1872 offering each militia regiment with at least ten companies an annual nomination for a regular commission from among those subalterns aged between 19 and 22 who had attended at least two annual trainings and passed an examination in their professional duties. Thus, the militia rapidly became a backdoor route to a regular commission for those failing to achieve admission to Sandhurst or Woolwich where nominations were few and competition fierce. Examples of those finding salvation in the militia are the future field marshals Sir Henry Wilson and Sir John French and the future Marshal of the Royal Air Force, Lord Trenchard.

Some of the most prominent defenders of militia independence had died in the 1860s and Cardwell's publicly expressed assumption in 1872 that the militia was now simply an auxiliary to the line went largely unchallenged. Similarly, a militia committee established under the chairmanship of Lord Harris in 1889 to review the relationship with the army even recommended changing its title from the militia to the reserve to the line although it also commented on the number of officers who were no more than 'birds of passage'. Certainly the militia was now a vital adjunct to the line, the 327,496 men passing to the army from the militia between 1882 and 1904 representing 35.4 per cent of the army's manpower requirements in the same period. Indeed, service in the militia frequently brought men up to the physical standards required of the army. The force also became something of a temporary refuge for the unemployed at times of economic depression, the term of service having been increased from five to six years in 1873 and the annual training from 21 to the more traditional 28 days in 1875. The effect of both pressures on the militia may perhaps be gauged from the calculation that, of every 20 militia recruits between 1894 and 1898, seven joined the army, four deserted, five were discharged and only four completed their term of service. As for the militia's social composition, of 106,153 men enrolled in 1898, 30.7 per cent were agricultural labourers, 18.2 per cent mechanical labourers, 11.9 per cent miners, 3.3 per cent fishermen and only 9.3 per cent artisans. The figures produced by the Norfolk commission for 1904 were broadly similar with fishermen now representing 4 per cent, miners 10 per cent and artisans 11 per cent but mechanical labourers 21 per cent and agricultural labourers down to 22 per cent.[20]

In 1870 it became possible to call out the militia for imminent national danger or emergency and provision was made in the Militia (Voluntary Enlistment) Act of 1875 to accept voluntary offers from units to serve at Gibraltar and Malta and in the Channel Isles, the

1882 Militia Act (45 & 46 Vict c 49) reconfirming the 1858 legislation in specifying that at least 75 per cent of the men must do so but that the remainder could not be sent overseas against their will. In fact, no militiamen served overseas between the end of the Indian mutiny embodiment and the South African War although five militia infantry battalions and a militia garrison artillery brigade were embodied during the war scare between March and September 1885.

Nevertheless, at the very least both volunteers and militia had a defined role of sorts in national and even imperial defence. The same was hardly true of the yeomanry, which was left virtually unscathed by the Cardwell reforms. Indeed, after the passing of the Volunteer Act in 1863, the yeomanry alone remained subject to the provisions of the 1804 legislation. As a result, few changes were effected in the yeomanry's organisation with not even minimum numbers laid down for troops, squadrons or regiments until 1875 despite recommendations on establishments by an earlier yeomanry committee in 1861. As remarked earlier, the 1875 committee did recommend the removal of attached horse artillery and dismounted sections but both the 1861 and 1875 enquiries as well as yet another yeomanry committee in 1892 confirmed the now traditional eight days (inclusive of two days for travel to and from the specified location) as the annual permanent duty. Often, however, the annual training was dispensed with as in 1849, 1851, 1857, 1860, 1861 and 1879 on the grounds that the force had been judged efficient previously. The 1875 committee did recommend an additional two days' training in the form of troop drills but both this and another recommendation that a yeoman should give six months rather than 14 days' notice of resignation was rejected. The Bury committee in 1878 had similarly failed to get its recommendation that volunteers should have a fixed term of enlistment accepted, although a few yeomanry and volunteer units did institute three-or-four year terms of service in an effort to promote continuity.

Cardwell placed the yeomanry under military law whilst on training and exercise or in aid of the civil power but otherwise made no changes to the force's status and it was only in 1888 that Stanhope's National Defence Act made it liable to serve anywhere in Great Britain upon the embodiment of the militia. Following the 1892 recommendations, an annual capitation grant of £1 was introduced and from January 1893 yeomanry regiments were paired in brigades in the expectation that brigade training would take place every three years. However, brigading came at the price of individual regiments losing their adjutants who were now attached only to brigades and the idea of brigade camps was then abandoned in 1898. Moreover, the training that did take place was rarely realistic and, in fact, the yeomanry was to prove highly resistant to the introduction of musketry requirements and wedded to cold steel. Its strength, which had varied considerably mid-century, then steadily declined from the 15,773 officers and men of 1871 to only 11,891 in 1899 and even this did not reflect the actual number likely to appear at annual training: in 1878 only 10,508 had done so and only 8,829 did so in 1899. The yeomanry also cost proportionally more than the other auxiliary forces, the average annual cost of a volunteer to the state in 1882 being £1 13s 1d compared to a yeoman's £6 7s 5d.[21]

Yet the yeomanry remained especially influential in local society. In 1849, for example, the Leicestershire yeomanry had mustered three MPs among its officers while in the 1880s the Queen's Own West Kents had not only six MPs but two peers. In 1902 an official estimate put the annual cost of being a yeomanry officer at least £100 above the available pay and allowances and it is not perhaps surprising to find F. H. Cripps, the son of Lord Parmoor, recounting in his memoirs as atypical of yeomanry encampments the night that two Oxfordshire yeomanry officers, F. E. Smith and Winston Churchill, lost £1,000 between them playing chemin de fer with Cripps and two fellow officers of the Royal Bucks Hussars, Evelyn de Rothschild and the son of Lord Rosebery, Neil Primrose.

The presence of the Rothschilds in the yeomanry in Buckinghamshire is in itself suggestive of another important role which the auxiliaries as a whole and the yeomanry in particular appear to have played as an entrée to local county society. Indeed, the Royal Bucks Hussars became known as the 'Flying Foreskins' from the number of emerging Jewish families associated with it such as the Rothschilds and the Lawsons. In Buckinghamshire at least, if not elsewhere, militia and volunteers provided a similar route by which the second if not the first generation of newcomers sealed a commitment to the county and many men held dual commissions or passed through more than one of the branches of the auxiliary forces without making any apparent social distinction between them.[22] Only further research will show how far this was replicated in other counties.

Wealth alone would not necessarily confer acceptance in the

yeomanry since county status counted far more, this tending to preclude ordinary regular officers from yeomanry rank and contributing to the growing shortage of officer candidates. But the aristocratic presence equally attracted able regulars to seek periods of attachment as adjutants such as Sir John French and Adrian Carton de Wiart. In many other respects it also appeared that little had changed. In 1872 the third Duke of Buckingham and Chandos had reminded one of his tenants that he was required to provide draught horses for his regiment's horse artillery and, as late as 1893, Colonel Egerton-Warburton of the Cheshire Yeomanry gave one of his tenants notice to quit on the grounds that he required them to be both anglicans and yeomen. In counties such as Warwickshire, Northamptonshire and Leicestershire the force still depended largely on the farming community and even as late as 1901 the distribution of the four squadrons of a new yeomanry regiment raised in Essex matched that of the four hunts in the county.

But, in reality, the yeomanry was changing by the end of the nineteenth century and in 1901 new urban-based yeomanry regiments were raised such as the Westminster Dragoons and the Surrey yeomanry with a new horse allowance of £5 to assist in the hire of mounts. Indeed, while 74 per cent of yeomen had ridden their own horses in 1876 and still 70 per cent in 1899 a position was reached by 1903 in which only 50 per cent of yeomen did so. To some extent this reflected the fact that the country's horse population had itself declined – it was to do so by 11 per cent alone between 1904 and 1910 under the impact of the motor car – but cycles had begun to appear in increasing numbers even before the South African War. Thus, in 1904 the yeomanry's representative in the War Office's auxiliary forces branch was to complain that 'a large number of yeomanry are really townspeople with no intimate knowledge of, or feeling for, horses'.[23]

There was another sense, too, in which times had changed by 1899 for the yeomanry had long ceased its role in aid of the civil power. This was a result not only of the development of county constabularies after 1856 but also of the problems presented by the creation of the volunteers three years later. There is no doubt that local political allegiances played a part in appointments to the auxiliary forces as a whole in the latter half of the nineteenth century for all that volunteers in particular held that partisan disputes were destructive of that social harmony they claimed to promote. Moreover, Herbert found it necessary to impose a ban on volunteers in uniform attending any meetings without an ostensibly military purpose or assembling at all between the issue of election writs and an election after volunteers had escorted Palmerston to the poll at Tiverton in April 1861.

The spirit of Herbert's circular was more or less maintained but, perhaps inevitably, there were occasional breaches of the ruling and, from time to time, volunteers were implicated in partisan activities. There was an attempt, for example, to involve the movement in the renewed agitation for the extension of the franchise in the mid-1860s, Elcho being mobbed by pro-franchise demonstrators after one Hyde Park parade in June 1866 for his alleged double standards in arming men to whom he denied the franchise. Similarly, some radically minded volunteers were dismissed in 1871 for threatening to defy a ban on welcoming the French republican, Jules Favre, to England in uniform while, as late as 1886, some 34 men of the 1st Inverness RV offered their resignations in protest against the employment of regulars to collect rates on the island of Skye. By contrast, volunteers were connected with what might be termed street Toryism in Exeter in 1860 and Cheltenham in 1866 and the ever-closer identification between Conservatism and patriotism from the 1870s perhaps implied at least a tacit acceptance of Conservative principles among those who enlisted, for example, during the war scare in 1878. Indeed, some volunteers were involved in the promotion of jingoism in 1877–8 and it has also been suggested that the movement generally contributed to an emerging uniformity of Conservative and anglican belief amongst a previously diverse industrial employer elite.[24]

None the less, it was comparatively unusual for volunteers to be seen to make overtly political gestures and considerable uncertainty had arisen in respect to any possible role in aid of the civil power. Volunteers were first employed in such a role at Weston-super-Mare in April 1861 when an unlikely riot broke out between the supporters of protagonists in a divorce case but there were then incidents for which volunteers were called out at Chesterfield in 1862 and at Guildford in 1863. However, it was the issue of the safety of volunteer armouries during the fenian threat in 1866–7 which finally prompted government action. Precautions were ordered at armouries in December 1866 and then in February 1867 the 6th

Cheshire RVC were called out and sworn in as special constables to prevent fenians from seizing Chester Castle before the arrival of regular reinforcements. The exact legal implications alarmed volunteers and government alike and circulars were issued in June and October 1867 indicating that volunteers could not be utilised for such duties other than as individuals acting as specials although they might use their military knowledge to combine and they could be armed in cases where riots were aimed at insurrection, felony or subversion of authority or if armouries were under attack.

Further fenian activity in 1867 and early 1868 saw volunteers out in Birmingham, Sheffield, Salford and Sidmouth but the circulars largely precluded the use of volunteers in aid of the civil power thereafter. The doubts expressed as to the wisdom of employing auxiliaries equally applied to the yeomanry and November 1867, when four troops of the Devon Yeomanry were used during food riots in Exeter and Teignmouth, marked the last occasion on which yeomen were so employed although they remained theoretically available for aid to the civil power. The militia, of course, was rarely available accept in terms of its permanent staff and there appear to be few instances of its use even being contemplated.

After 1867, therefore, auxiliaries mostly avoided open conflict with their fellow citizens but their largely negative attitude towards partisan involvement in politics was not repeated at Westminster where auxiliary force representatives were diligent in bringing any grievances to the attention of successive secretaries of state for war. The sheer number of MPs holding actual, former or honorary rank in the auxiliaries was considerable. In 1861 there were 48 such MPs connected to the volunteers alone with an additional 51 connected to the militia and 43 to the yeomanry. As in the case of other identifiable parliamentary interest groups such as the railway interest, there was in reality a considerable difference between the nominal total and those that actually constituted an effective interest. Thus, to take the volunteers, only 15 of the 48 MPs could really be considered to be active in the force's interests. Similarly, when between 1868 and 1880 there were 130 volunteers in the Commons, the effective interest numbered only 34 at most. Moreover, co-ordination was made difficult from the varying political persuasions of volunteer representatives – in 1869, for example, 52 sat in the Conservative interest and 78 for the Liberals – and the often differing perceptions of local requirements. Whereas other interest groups often possessed some kind of central organisation and even premises the volunteers had only the periodic meetings of the metropolitan commanding officers and were reluctant to contemplate the kind of permanent parliamentary monitoring body proposed for them by Ranelagh in 1870 which might have offset the steady growth in party discipline reducing the ability of private members to obstruct legislation effectively.

Indeed, it was only the assimilation of peripheral interest groups within the main parties in the 1870s and 1880s which offered a solution to the problem and, like the railway interest, the volunteer interest at Westminster was to become increasingly identified with the Conservatives in line with the general trend towards an alliance of landed and business interests in late Victorian politics. Certainly, there was a clear decline in the number of Liberal volunteers and Liberal military and naval MPs generally after 1869 so that, by 1890, 70 per cent of the total of volunteer MPs were Conservatives and 84 per cent of the effective interest. A volunteer member, Arthur Brookfield, became secretary of a revived service members' committee at Westminster in the 1880s with a militia officer, Sir James Fergusson, as chairman while an institute of commanding officers of volunteers also emerged to replace the old meetings of the metropolitan commanding officers as a far more effective focus of volunteer opinion.

Yet, despite the difficulties, the volunteers were not entirely without political success during the earlier phase of their existence as an interest group. A combination of parliamentary and extra-parliamentary pressure from February 1861 onwards secured the establishment of the royal commission in 1862 which recommended the capitation grant although similar pressure between 1867 and 1870 failed to convince either Pakington or Cardwell that the grant should be increased. Renewed extra-parliamentary pressure orchestrated by Howard Vincent played a part in the establishment of the Bury departmental committee in 1878 but this also failed to achieve the desired increase and largely convinced Vincent of the desirability of greater parliamentary organisation. The first indication of the new determination and, indeed, of the benefits of an interest group now largely concentrated in one party, was Vincent's success – he was now MP for Sheffield Central – in reducing the government's majority to only 21 on a motion to increase the capitation grant by 10s 0d in 1886. Four years later, Stanhope's decision to require volunteers to provide items of equipment according to a War Office mobilisation schedule by a certain date upon pain of forfeiting the capitation grant resulted in the government's defeat by 31 votes and immediate concessions in terms of special equipment allowances. Then, in June 1895 it was the Liberals who suffered when the volunteers combined with other military members to defeat the government by seven votes on a motion to reduce the salary of the secretary of state, Campbell-Bannerman, in the so-called 'cordite vote' censuring him for the shortage of small arms ammunition due to the changeover to cordite as a propellant.

Unfortunately, the volunteers tended to confuse assimilation within one party with immunity which was to provoke bitter reaction to Conservative policies after the South African War, a conflict they assumed had won for them much of the recognition for which they had striven since 1859. In that regard at least they were not far wrong for South Africa was to provide the first real indication of their contribution to national defence. It also marked the way that the military values they had projected had assisted in the creation of a society which, if not overtly militaristic, was conditioned to an acceptance of militarism and the challenge of war.

Notes

1   G. Best, *Mid-Victorian Britain, 1851–75* (2nd edit., Panther, London, 1973), pp. 24–5; W. J. Reader, *Professional Men* (Weidenfeld & Nicolson, London, 1966), pp. 78–9.

2   Montefiore, *History of the Volunteer Force*, pp. 405–9.

3   Oxon RO, *Lieutenancy* L/M 1/v/3, Memorandum of 2nd Oxon A.B., 23 Apl 1860.

4   Beckett, *Riflemen Form*, pp. 31, 84–5.

5   M. J. Salevouris, 'Riflemen Form: The War Scare of 1859–60 in England', Unpub. Ph.D., Minnesota, 1971, pp. 292–3.

6   Beckett, *Riflemen Form*, pp. 48–9.

7   Patricia Morton, 'Another Victorian Paradox: Anti-militarism in a Jingoistic Society', *Historical Reflections* V, 2, 1981, pp. 169–89; Ibid., 'A Military Irony: The Victorian Volunteer Movement', *Journal of the Royal United Services Institute for Defence Studies* 131, 3, 1986, pp. 63–70.

8   Notes, *Journal of the Society for Army Historical Research* 37, 1959, p. 43.

9   Greater London RO (Middlesex), L/C/74, Salisbury to Shelley, 6 Nov 1860.

10   Beckett, *Riflemen Form*, pp. 55–7.

11   GLRO (M), *Cruikshank Mss*, Acc 534/1.

12   Mrs Patricia Morris, 'Leeds and the Amateur Military Tradition:

The Leeds Rifles and Their Antecedents, 1859–1918', Unpub. Ph.D., Leeds, 1983, p. 196.

13   Beckett, *Riflemen Form*, pp. 63–9.

14   Ibid., pp. 80–2.

15   R. W. Phipps, *Our Sham Army* (Exeter, 1868), p. 27.

16   H. Cunningham, *The Volunteer Force* (Croom Helm, London, 1975), pp. 121–2.

17   Morris, 'Leeds and the Amateur Military Tradition', p. 75.

18   J. O. Springhall, *Youth, Empire and Society* (Croom Helm, London, 1977), pp. 71–80; G. Anderson, *Victorian Clerks* (Manchester University Press, 1976), pp. 30–51, 74–86; R. Q. Gray, *The Labour Aristocracy in Victorian Edinburgh* (Oxford University Press, 1976), pp. 102–3, 130, 139–42; G. Crossick, 'The Labour Aristocracy and its Values', *Victorian Studies* XX, 1976, pp. 301–28.

19   *Volunteer Service Gazette* 15 Feb 1868, pp. 166–7.

20   J. K. Dunlop, *The Development of the British Army, 1899–1914* (Methuen, London, 1938), pp. 43–48.

21   S. D. Badsey, 'Fire and the Sword: The British Army and the Arme Blanche Controversy, 1871–1921', Unpub. Ph.D., Cambridge, 1982, p. 100.

22   F. H. Cripps, *Life's A Gamble* (Odhams, London, 1957), p. 64; I. F. W. Beckett, 'The Local Community and the Amateur Military Tradition: A Case Study of Victorian Buckinghamshire', *Journal of the Society for Army Historical Research* LIX, 238/9, 1981, pp. 95–110, 161–70.

23   National Army Museum, *Roberts Mss* 7101–23–221–10, DAG to Kelly-Kenny, 1 Jan 1904 quoted in Badsey, 'Fire and the Sword', p. 276; H. Le Roy Lewis, 'The Imperial Yeomanry in 1905', *Journal of the Royal United Service Institution* XLIX, 2, 1905, pp. 1023–49; 'The Scarcity of Horses in the British Empire', *Cavalry Journal* 6, 24, 1905 pp. 472–84. (I am grateful to Stephen Badsey and Gary Sheffield for bringing these references to my notice.)

24   Diana Henderson, *Highland Soldier* (John Donald, Edinburgh, 1989), pp. 219–20; H. Cunningham, 'The Language of Patriotism' in R. Samuel (ed), *Patriotism* (Routledge, London, 1989), pp. 57–89; P. Joyce, *Work, Society and Politics* (2nd edit., Methuen, London, 1982), pp. 29–41.

7

The challenge of reform (1899–1914)

By 1899 there was little doubt that British society was more militaristic than had been the case 40 years previously but this did not amount to an overt militarism. Indeed, the period between the South African War and the Great War was to be marked by the peculiarly British nature of the debate over the concept of a 'nation in arms' initiated by the perceived failure of British arms on the veldt. In the process, the auxiliary forces which most truly represented the 'nation in arms' in so far as it existed at all were to be transformed but in such a way as to have serious repercussions on their role during the Great War.

In terms of the growth of the military conditioning of British society generally, invasion panics, of which both the revived militia and also the volunteer movement had been products, had continued to excite the popular imagination, not least in generating a considerable popular literature such as George Chesney's celebrated invasion novel, *The Battle of Dorking*, published in January 1871 and narrated through the eyes of a volunteer. To some extent the existence of the volunteers contributed to a greater sense of security than during the 1840s or 1850s and volunteer numbers actually fell during the height of such fears in the late 1880s when War Office and Admiralty openly disputed on the probability or otherwise of invasion. None the less, invasion literature kept military matters in the public eye and increasing space was also devoted to military affairs in serious periodicals.

Another contributory factor was the ideal of the 'Christian hero' and the popularisation of its accompanying values. It owed more to the Crimean War and the Indian mutiny than to the militia or volunteers but Christian militarism was itself interwoven in the fabric of the volunteer movement. The harnessing of the patriotic and moral values of the volunteers to a primarily religious aim in the boys' brigades, which had some 35,000 members by 1899, similarly helped to undermine the traditional civilian values of non-conformism though there had also been a recognisable non-conformist militarism drawing strength from such international events as Garibaldi's struggle for the unification of Italy. In fact, before the rhetoric of patriotism became virtually the sole preserve of Conservatism in the 1870s, 'radical' patriotism was sufficiently commonplace in 1859 for many new volunteer corps to identify closely with Garibaldi's cause to the extent of adopting Garibaldian uniform and, in the case of many Scottish volunteers, of enlisting in Garibaldi's forces in defiance of the Foreign Enlistment Act.

The moral aspects of the volunteer movement and, indeed, of the revived militia also mirrored the cult of athleticism and of muscular Christianity developing both within the public schools and contemporary literature which, together with notions of social Darwinism disseminated by popular authors such as Benjamin Kidd, was to culminate after the South African War in the considerable concern with physical deterioration, fuelling such movements as the Boy Scouts in 1907 and contributing to the appeal of eugenics and the demand for 'efficiency'. The Boy Scouts may have appeared to adopt the rhetoric of citizenship rather than that of military training and to have distanced themselves from other more overtly militaristic organisations but the effect was still one of conditioning boys and girls – the Girl Guides had evolved by 1910 – for service to empire. Military drill had also become widely accepted as the most appropriate form of physical training in the majority of board schools where the regimented discipline and content of the syllabus was equally likely to instil military virtues. Indeed, pressure groups like the national service league, established in 1902, were to be active within both schools and youth organisations.

Beyond the classroom and adolescence, popular writers such as Henty and Haggard, the popular press, popular entertainment such as the music hall and, later, even the infant cinema all added to the evolution of militaristic values. But militia, yeomanry and volunteers were absolutely central to the process as a whole for no one could be unaware of their existence. While a relatively small proportion of the male population might be actively involved at any one time, the cumulative effect of participation through the second half of the nineteenth century was a crucial factor in extending familiarity with military values in the community. Indeed, it has been suggested that in 1903 over 8 per cent of British males aged between 15 and 49 had served in the volunteers alone at some time. Taking into account those who had also served in the other auxiliaries and the regular army or undertaken youth training of some kind, another calculation is that by 1898 no less than 22.42 per cent of the entire male population of the United Kingdom and Ireland aged between 17 and 40 had some current or previous military or quasi-military experience.[1]

When war broke out between Britain and the Boer republics in South Africa in October 1899 there was little expectation that such a potential reserve of military experience would need to be tapped in any way. Even though the government had consistently delayed reinforcing the existing garrison in South Africa and only ordered mobilisation of the reserve – including the militia reserve, of whom 13,598 were to serve with regular units – on 7 October, confidence was high. Indeed, offers made by volunteers to raise service companies or units were declined: Eustace Balfour commanding the London Scottish had made such an offer as early as July and Howard Vincent in August. Similarly, the proposal in October by the yeomanry's representative in the War Office, Lieutenant-Colonel A. G. Lucas of the Loyal Suffolk Hussars, to draw upon the yeomanry fell on deaf ears.

It was the case, of course, that legal difficulties prevented easy acceptance of such offers but it is also clear that most regulars did not believe that auxiliaries would be of any real utility. Indeed, when 38 militia battalions were embodied on 3 November, to be followed by three more on the following day and a further eight on 23 November, the initial intention was purely to release more regulars since the militia battalions were invited to volunteer for overseas garrison duty only. However, all was to be changed with the succession of British reverses in South Africa in December 1899.

The profound shock of 'black week' renewed the earlier agitation from the auxiliaries and the militia was now invited to go to South Africa itself with special legislation (61 & 62 Vict c 9) allowing for up to one year's service overseas. In all, 59 battalions totalling 45,566 officers and men were eventually to go to South Africa in addition to five battalions which served on Malta, three on St Helena and one in Egypt. Only four of the 72 battalions asked to volunteer for overseas duty failed to find the necessary 75 per cent majority in favour although it also appears the case that the normal age for overseas service of 19 years was waived or up to a third would not have been able to go. The remainder of the militia was also embodied, many doing garrison service in Ireland, the liability to serve anywhere in the United Kingdom, of course, having been laid down since 1859. Moreover, as well as those militia reservists who had been called up in 1899, a total of 74,217 militiamen enlisted in the regular army during the war.[2]

It would appear that the commander-in-chief, Wolseley, had considered the dispatch of volunteers to South Africa even before 'black week' and an offer by the lord mayor of London, Sir Alfred Newton, to raise the 1st City of London Imperial Volunteers based on a scheme by Colonel C. G. Boxall was made on 15 December. Rather as in 1859, the view of the secretary of state, Lord Lansdowne, was that it seemed impossible to refuse altogether and there was 'some advantage in affording an outlet to public feeling'.[3] Accordingly, Wolseley gave unofficial blessing to Newton's proposal on 16 December and the formal offer to raise 1,000 men in 21 days was officially accepted four days later. The raising of the City Imperial Volunteers (CIV) as the unit was soon renamed at Wolseley's suggestion proved a remarkable piece of improvisation with large sums donated by City institutions.

Recruited on the basis that they were fit, preferably unmarried and aged between 20 and 30, the CIV was enlisted for one year and comprised an infantry battalion, two mounted infantry companies and an artillery battery from the Honourable Artillery Company. Men from over 53 different volunteer units were enrolled and over 125 different occupations with the lower middle-class and artisan element equally contributing approximately 40 per cent of the total. Numerically, clerks formed the largest single occupational category – about 30 per cent of the overall total – but, while this is a greater ratio of clerks to artisans than the national average of the volunteer force, this may well be explained as much by the willingness of employers to release them as by a greater enthusiasm for the war among middle-class volunteers.

Given the apparent pressure applied to employees of legal and insurance firms to join the CIV and the fairly rigorous selection process, it is arguable that the unit was largely structured by and for the middle class but, in reality, class does not appear especially relevant to the response of the volunteer movement as a whole to the war. While the CIV was being organised – it was embarked for South Africa in three contingents on 13, 20 and 29 January 1900 and, with a draft in July 1900, eventually numbered 1,739 officers and men – the War Office had also taken steps to extend service opportunities to the men of ordinary volunteer units. On 2 January the authorities authorised the raising of 66 service companies and 66 'waiting' companies of 116 men each to be attached to regular battalions in South Africa. Again enlisted for one year and temporarily transferred to the army reserve these men were required to be between 20 and 35, physically fit, of good character, preferably unmarried or childless widowers, first-class shots and declared efficient for the last two years. A special grant of £9 was offered to corps to equip men volunteering and they would be permitted to continue to earn a capitation grant as supernumeraries.

On 13 January volunteer engineers were invited to enlist in sections – 38 were formed – and members of the medical staff corps were given the option of a year in South Africa or six months in a home hospital. The Elswick battery from the old Armstrong works at Newcastle also served in South Africa and a further call was made for service companies in January 1901 and, finally, in January 1902. By this time between 19,648 and 19,856 volunteers inclusive of the CIV had seen active service, representing roughly 8.5 per cent of the enrolled strength of the force. But it should also be noted that other volunteers who came forward – at least 6,861 in 1900 – were rejected on medical grounds or because they failed to satisfy the efficiency standards. The force itself also increased in strength with the net gain of 19,279 between 1 October 1899 and 1 March 1900 alone while some 7,000 volunteers joined the regular army.[4]

The response of the movement as a whole, therefore, was not unimpressive and not confined to middle-class volunteers. The same was equally true of another expedient of December 1899, the imperial yeomanry. Lucas had renewed his proposal to draw on the yeomanry on 14 November, only for the War Office to reply on 28 November that it had no intention of sending yeomen to South Africa. Buller's call after his defeat at Colenso for mounted infantry changed the situation and on 18 December lords Lonsdale and Chesham offered to raise 2,300 such mounted men from the yeomanry. Wolseley opposed the suggestion but the under-secretary of state for war, George Wyndham, himself a yeoman, then appears to have taken up the idea although he may have come to the decision earlier. He established an imperial yeomanry committee on 19 December consisting of Lucas, Viscount Valentia of the Oxfordshire yeomanry and Chesham who commanded the Royal Bucks Hussars. Announced on 24 December, the imperial yeomanry then received formal approval in a royal warrant of 2 January 1900.

Wyndham does not seem to have expected any more than the 2,300 men suggested by Chesham and Lonsdale but the response was far greater and, indeed, yeomen were to represent only a third of the force as a whole, which was to be organised on the basis of companies, squadrons and battalions. Wyndham had given the committee a free hand and a capitation grant of £25 (later £35) per man to provide clothing and equipment and £40 to provide a horse. In addition, however, large sums were contributed by individuals – over £10,000, for example, was subscribed in Northumberland and Durham in a single day and the Rand mining concern of Wernher-Beit provided £50,000. Some 10,242 men aged between 20 and 35 and of good character were enrolled in the first contingent, which went out to South Africa between January and April 1900 enlisted for a year or the duration of hostilities.

It had been anticipated that the war would not continue beyond a year and, with some restlessness becoming apparent, it was not felt desirable to hold the yeomen to serving beyond that period. Indeed, only 655 re-enlisted in 1901 and a separate second contingent of 16,597 'new yeomanry' was raised in January 1901 with the added incentive of daily pay of 5s 0d compared to the 1s 3d extended to the first contingent. The second contingent was not trained until it reached South Africa in April 1901 but this did not prove entirely satisfactory and a third contingent of 7,239 men raised in 1902 were concentrated for training at Aldershot, Edinburgh and the Curragh. In the event, the war ended before they could take any active part.

Initially, many men of the Imperial Yeomanry were drawn from the middle classes and traditional yeomanry sources. In the 37th and 38th Squadrons of the 10th Battalion, imperial yeomenry, for example, which was raised in the recruiting area of the Royal Bucks Hussars, 25 per cent were engaged in farming while of the 450 men raised by the Earl of Scarbrough from the area normally feeding the Yorkshire Dragoons, some 12.5 per cent were farmers. Similarly, of the 62 peers and MPs recorded as on active service in South Africa in April 1900 it can be noted that no fewer than 44 were serving with the imperial yeomanry. However, the middle-class content declined appreciably after January 1900 and especially in the second and third contingents, men of the 38th Squadron who re-enlisted referring to the newcomers in 1901 as 'yeomanry militia'.[5] Certainly, Chesham claimed that 75 per cent of the second contingent had never sat a horse before they reached South Africa and over 1,000 were actually sent home while militia and volunteer officers were pressed to fill the many commissioned vacancies that had arisen.

As the middle class departed so the working class took their place, not simply because the former declined but also due to an increase in domestic unemployment over the war period, one study of the Fifeshire coal field displaying a clear correlation between trade depression and local recruitment for the imperial yeomanry. Taking the force as a whole, some 58 per cent of the imperial yeomanry could be characterised as having working-class occupations although the largest single working-class group – labourers – representing 6 per cent of the total were only the fifth largest category overall behind commercial and clerical occupations (11.4 per cent), skilled artisans (8.9 per cent), grooms and servants (8.5 per cent) and farmers (8 per cent).[6]

By the time most auxiliaries reached the Cape the main Boer field army had surendered at Paardeburg. The CIV and many of the volunteer companies did participate in the advance on Pretoria, the CIV earning general praise for their efforts. However, by 1902 the majority of service companies were manning the blockhouses designed to impede the mobility of Boer commandos on the veldt. Nevertheless, presumably because they were actually attached to regular battalions, the volunteer service companies were held in higher esteem than the militia and imperial yeomanry. From the beginning the militia battalions were employed only on line of communications while the imperial yeomanry attracted so much criticism that St John Brodrick, who became secretary of state for war in October 1900, felt it necessary to produce a Cabinet paper defending the force in November 1901. Certainly, the imperial yeomanry lacked training, the attempt to train the second contingent in South Africa itself being the solution adopted by Chesham, who had become inspector-general of the force. But, as already related, the second contingent was something of a disappointment and the record of the imperial yeomanry generally was severely damaged by disasters such as that at Lindley on 31 May 1900 when the largely Irish 13th Battalion was surrounded and forced to capitulate, the 530 prisoners including no fewer than four peers.

Overall, the army suffered over 100,000 casualties in South Africa. Precise figures are not available for the militia and only for the first contingent of the imperial yeomanry, which suffered a relatively high 3,093 casualties (30.1 per cent) including 216 killed in action. Of the 1,739 men of the CIV, some 1,323 returned to England in October 1900, 122 having been killed or wounded, 155 invalided and 121 discharged or left in government employment in South Africa. Of the volunteer service companies, 361 were killed, wounded or died of disease with a further 1,309 men invalided and discharged and an additional wastage of 963 men for varying reasons, the whole amounting to an overall wastage rate of approximately 16 per cent.[7]

As a whole the effort required to wage the war was considerable and it is estimated that 14.2 per cent of the male population of the United Kingdom between the ages of 18 and 40 were in uniform at some stage between 1899 and 1902.[8] The regular commitment was such that at one stage only nine cavalry regiments, six infantry and three guards battalions remained in the United Kingdom and Wyndham acknowledged in the Commons on 12 February 1900 that the volunteer force was now the main defence against possible raids on the coast by hostile European powers. There was something of an invasion scare in the press and, as already noted, volunteer recruitment soared. The government responded to pressure from county councils such as those in Middlesex and Buckinghamshire to expand the force by authorising up to 1,000 men to be added to battalion establishments. Rifle clubs were also formed, largely as a result of a speech by the prime minister, Salisbury, to the Primrose League on 9 May 1900 although they were regarded with some suspicion by the volunteers as openly competing with the force and, equally, by those who saw them as an additional obstacle to the introduction of conscription. It would appear that many of the clubs were designed to appeal to working men but did not prove as popular as ambulance clubs in this regard.

In practice, however, the rifle clubs did not divert funding from the volunteers and in February 1900 Lansdowne and Wyndham announced a range of concessions including the re-equipping of volunteer artillery with modern guns, the offer of a limited number of regular commissions for volunteers, support for regimental transport and a reserve and additional allowances to enable the volunteers to go under canvas for emergency camps of exercise lasting for one month in the case of infantry and three months for artillery. More money was promised for ranges and a new Military Lands Act extended the provisions of earlier 1892 legislation for acquiring such ranges.

But there was a danger in increased commitment and many volunteers doubted the ability of men to go into camp for a month let alone three months. The government subsequently granted the allowances where at least 50 per cent of a corps was prepared to camp for 14 days, 179 out of 216 infantry battalions doing so while a few managed the full 28 days. More controversial still was the volunteer bill Lansdowne then introduced in May 1900 to enable volunteers to be called out in cases of imminent national danger or great emergency and to permit volunteers to enter into agreements to serve anywhere without the prior necessity of a royal proclamation. Lansdowne argued that the bill would allow the government to accept offers more readily in a crisis but it met some opposition in the Lords and from radicals in the Commons and, when it received the royal assent on 6 August 1900, it had been modified to the extent that volunteers could only undertake to do garrison service in specified places in Britain.

The public concessions to the volunteers were also further undermined by evidence of continuing hostility within the War Office, attempts continually being made to reduce the status of the auxiliary forces branch which had existed since 1860. Indeed, the inspector-general of auxiliary forces was bypassed in December 1901 when Brodrick followed the recommendations of a committee on volunteer training heavily influenced by the adjutant general's training branch and ordered compulsory annual camps of at least six day's duration with none allowed to miss camping in two consecutive years, additional drills in lieu of camping and an increased musketry standard. There was considerable opposition not least to the offensive way in which the 'Christmas card' order was actually worded and, after meeting various deputations, Brodrick established another committee and acted on its recommendation to grant exemption from the camps in special circumstances if additional drills were completed but still insisting that no corps would be exempted for two consecutive years.

There were further indications of regular hostility at the same time. In October 1901 the number of volunteer brigades was expanded from 34 to 51 but volunteers were allowed to command only eight while the limited field artillery provision granted in February 1900 was promptly abandoned in November 1901. It was true that Brodrick had also unfolded an army reform scheme in March 1901 for six army corps each comprising 40,000 men to which the volunteers would be invited to contribute 15 batteries and 25 battalions in the fourth, fifth and sixth corps designed for home defence. Similarly, six yeomanry regiments, 21 militia artillery batteries and 37 militia battalions were invited to join the three corps but the volunteer 'field army' battalions were required to fulfil special training liabilities including 13 days' annual camp exclusive of travelling. Thus, amid the prevailing uncertainty and the higher efficiency conditions, a force which had dramatically increased in strength in 1900 suffered the worst year of recruiting in its history just two years later with a net decline of nearly 20,000 men to leave it over 98,000 short of establishment by March 1903.

Brodrick's plans for increased volunteer efficiency were not strictly part of his larger six corps scheme and the scheme itself received little attention from volunteer MPs. However, Brodrick's attempt to answer the demand for reform after the perceived failings of the military system in South Africa was met with general scepticism and encountered particular opposition from a group of discontented young Conservatives led by Lord Hugh Cecil, some of whom including Winston Churchill and J. E. B. Seely subsequently crossed the floor to the Liberals on the issue of tariff reform.

It may be significant that at least four of the 'hughligans' were yeomanry officers since, with effect from a royal warrant on 15 April 1901, Brodrick had also decisively changed the nature of that force following the recommendations of a committee established in the previous autumn. Indeed, in many respects, as regulated by the subsequent Militia and Yeomanry Act (1 Edw VII c 14), which finally released the force from the provisions of the 1804 legislation, what was now renamed the imperial yeomanry resembled a mounted militia. It was now subject to some of the conditions of militia service, not least in the liability to be called out at the same time as the militia for national emergencies. Annual training would now be extended to 18 days, of which 14 were obligatory, and yeomen who joined after 17 August 1901 would also be enlisted for three years although they could purchase an earlier discharge. A uniform four squadron establishment was laid down, which would raise the strength of the force to 35,000. There was some concession in the return of regimental adjutants and there was a new forage allowance of 1s 6d a day on training and the £5 horse allowance referred to earlier in addition to the retention of the capitation grant. A yeomanry reserve was established in the same way that Brodrick also instituted a reserve for the militia in place of the former militia reserve, which had had the function of supplying the army rather than the militia.

However, the greatest change of all was the adoption of a mounted infantry role, hence the new title reflecting the experience in South Africa and the introduction of khaki uniforms and a machine gun section to be attached to each regiment. Unfortunately, a mounted infantry role was not welcome to many yeomanry officers. In 1903, for example, the regiments of Middlesex, Montgomeryshire and Gloucestershire all petitioned the King to be allowed to continue to carry swords on parade and, in the following year, all but one of 35 commanding officers petitioned the army council for its retention. Just as the regular cavalry succeeded in considerably modifying the efforts of the mounted infantry advocates so the yeomanry also saw the hated bayonet introduced in 1903 abandoned five years later and the sword restored for war mobilisation in 1913.

Notwithstanding the complaints of yeomen or volunteers, most attention was fixed on the regular recruiting difficulties presented by Brodrick's wider scheme and, subsequently, on the failure of his attempted reform of the organisation of the War Office to meet the criticisms advanced in the report of the Elgin commission on the conduct of the war in South Africa in July 1903. It is possible, therefore, that a number of auxiliaries were correct in seeing the appointment of a royal commission on militia and volunteers first proposed by Brodrick to the War Office council on 2 March 1903 as an attempt to deflect any additional agitation from their MPs. Certainly, it effectively muzzled discussion of volunteer grievances for 12 months.

The War Office resolved that the royal commission, which began work under the chairmanship of the Duke of Norfolk on 19 May 1903, would determine the minimum standard of efficiency required of volunteers, a minimum term of volunteer service and a definite military scheme for the auxiliary forces. It was intended to guide the commission by specifying the number of auxiliaries deemed necessary for imperial defence but the divergence of opinion between War Office and Admiralty on the likelihood of invasion led to the matter being deferred for discussion by the infant committee of imperial defence (CID). The CID itself declined to reveal either details of the existing mobilisation scheme or the results of its own deliberations on invasion to the commission and they were left to decide between approximate figures of 264,000 and 300,000 auxiliaries suggested by the director of military intelligence and the CID respectively only as a basis of discussion.

The whole thrust of regular military opinion submitted to the commission was that neither militia nor volunteers could be safely entrusted with the defence of the country unaided due to their deficiencies of officers and training and, indeed, the DMI's figure appears to have been calculated on the assumption that it would take two militiamen or three volunteers to equal one trained continental soldier. Even militia and volunteer witnesses were forced to the same conclusion and the commission reported on 20 May 1904 that neither force was fit to take the field. Detailed proposals were made for both forces but the majority of commissioners and, indeed, the majority of witnesses firmly believed in the possibility of invasion and that the only real solution was conscription. The commission therefore concluded that the only means of defeating an invasion without regular support would be a home defence army raised by conscription.

The unhappy Brodrick had been transferred to the India Office during the course of the commission's deliberations, the eventual choice of succession in October 1903 falling on H. O. Arnold-Forster. A distinctly junior minister within a Cabinet containing both his immediate predecessors, Arnold-Forster was also handicapped by his own difficult and tactless nature and frequent ill health. Influenced by the need to harness efficiency and economy, by the serious depletion in drafts for foreign service due to Brodrick's introduction of short service and his concurrence with the CID's decision to give priority to the defence of India, he proposed to create both long service and short service armies serving simultaneously. The militia, for which Arnold-Forster had no great regard, would in the final version of the scheme contribute 30 battalions to the short service army and have a further 34 battalions disbanded. But it would also retain 60 battalions separate from the scheme while the volunteers would be considerably reduced and divided into two classes of efficiency.

It might appear curious that that part of Arnold-Forster's scheme which met most resistance was the plan for the militia, which was currently 39,000 short of establishment with 42 per cent of its rank and file having less than two years' service and 73 per cent being under 20 years of age. Arnold-Forster was to complain of 'all those old women who look upon their regiments as a sort of honorary addition to their positions as County Magnates or as leading figures in some dull, ineffective society'. However, his real difficulty lay in the fact that two of the most powerful supporters of the militia were to be found in the Cabinet itself in the form of the Lord Privy Seal, Cranborne, and the First Lord of the Admiralty, Selborne. According to Arnold-Forster, prime minister Balfour supported them because they were 'good fellows and good Militiamen and naturally stick up for a force they have worked so hard to save from decay'.[9] Thus, Arnold-Forster's militia plans never reached the floor of the Commons and he was reduced to explaining his ideas there on 14 July 1904 merely as a personal view and even this statement was permitted only after the threat of a resignation the government could not afford. Moreover, a sub-committee of the CID established in January 1905 to examine Arnold-Forster's schemes endorsed an entirely different plan put forward by Balfour to retain the militia as the main home defence army.

In fact, the only part of the secretary of state's wider scheme that did reach the Commons was that for the reform of the volunteers but, whereas the militia had strength in the Cabinet and the Lords, the volunteers retained their strength in the lower house and there is a strong suspicion that Balfour recognised what fate might there befall the scheme. From the beginning Arnold-Forster took the view that more money could only be made available if overall numbers were reduced from an establishment of 364,000 to 200,000 with an anticipated field strength of 180,000 men, of whom 60,000 could be placed on higher efficiency conditions earning higher allowances. The fact that the CID had pronounced invasion improbable justified such a reduction and the amount saved could be ploughed back into the force to remedy deficiencies in such necessities as transport as well as further encouraging rifle clubs.

No decision was reached on how reductions might be accomplished and Arnold-Forster decided to await the report of the

Norfolk commission. However, its recommendation of conscription was at once rejected when it reported in May 1904, by which time Arnold-Forster had already clashed with the volunteers over his decision to reduce further the status of the auxiliary forces branch at the War Office. The issue only increased volunteer suspicion despite Arnold-Forster's attempts to explain what was undoutedly the most judicious part of his overall scheme but when parliamentary activity resumed in February 1905 the volunteers immediately obstructed the debate on the address. Arnold-Forster now claimed that he no longer intended to create two classes of volunteers but new proposals he had evolved during the winter would have much the same effect since it had been decided to effect reduction by a gradual raising of physical standards and the amalgamation or abolition of inefficient units. A reduction to 230,000 would now allow for better transport and an experimental divisional staff as well as enabling 60,000 men to camp for 14 days at a new allowance of 4s 0d per man per day with the existing capitation grant remaining at £1 15s 0d for campers but being reduced to £1 for non-campers.

Even these revised proposals came under attack when Arnold-Forster introduced the estimates on 28 March and he had some justification in his criticism of volunteers who appeared to 'take not the slightest interest or concern in the Army as a whole, and seem to regard the Regular Army rather as a necessary evil than as the principal land defence of the Empire'.[10] The crux of the volunteers' argument, principally led by Howard Vincent and the Scottish Liberal, Lieutenant-Colonel G. McCrae, rested on the assumption that a large volunteer force was still essential to home defence. When the volunteers disrupted the pay vote in early April, Balfour considerably annoyed Arnold-Forster by suggesting that, while the CID had indeed considered invasion unlikely under existing conditions, one such condition was the existence of the volunteers so that their necessity and the improbability of invasion were not mutually contradictory truths.

Arnold-Forster still claimed that most volunteers outside parliament actually supported him despite evidence to the contrary but any lingering good will at Westminster was certainly swept aside by the ambiguous wording of a circular issued on 20 June, which seemed to suggest that the government was introducing a severe medical examination to reduce the force. It had been decided in April that nothing could be achieved in the current year except obtaining

reports from GOCs on those units likely to be disbanded or amalgamated, to which was added an enquiry on the number of volunteers judged fit to serve abroad. No action was actually intended but
there was such a storm of protest at the implied medical standard
that the adjutant general and the director of auxiliary forces
immediately tried to dissociate themselves from the circular. While a
new one was issued on 11 July clearing any misunderstanding, a
special debate previously agreed by Balfour went ahead on 13 July in
which Arnold-Forster was subjected to bitter attack. In all, the
volunteers had taken up nine days allotted to supply and this was to
prove the last occasion on which any of Arnold-Forster's plans were
debated in the Commons.

Outside Westminster there was less criticism of the circulars and,
although some volunteers refused to be medically examined, by
November 1905 some 187,880 men had been examined of whom 84
per cent were declared fit. Arnold-Forster still hoped for some progress but faced with public speeches by Balfour in September and by
the King in October, both of which praised the force, and also aware
of the equal reluctance of his military advisers and the government
whips to risk reduction, he capitulated. In November 1905, therefore, it was agreed to alter the capitation grant to give 2 guineas to
those camping for 15 days, £1 18s 6d for 8 days and £1 for non-
campers; to reorganise volunteer brigades and to create an experimental division. The military members who had approved the
package, which added £170,000 to the estimates, then attempted to
cancel it because they did not wish the volunteers to be given
preference over the militia but they were too late. On 23 November
Arnold-Forster also secured reluctant agreement to a field artillery
experiment but on 11 December the new Liberal government took
office and in January 1906 the divisional and field artillery experiments were abandoned.

In 26 months of office Arnold-Forster had been no more successful
than Brodrick, volunteer MPs destroying his policies so effectively
that the CID's secretary, Sir George Clarke, and the influential Lord
Esher both believed they had become a grave public and political
danger. However, Arnold-Forster himself noted after meeting his
Liberal successor, R. B. Haldane, that whereas some volunteers were
already rejoicing at the prospect of wringing more money from
government, 'my impression is they may have a rude awakening'.[11]
He was most certainly correct even if, in his dealings with the

auxiliaries, as in his reforms generally, Haldane was forced to settle for a lowest denominator of practical political attainment rather than the grander design.

That original design as outlined by Haldane's second memorandum on army reform of 1 February 1906 was no less than the creation of a 'real national army, formed by the people',[12] the essential point of contact in welding a unity of army and society being depicted as a new territorial force replacing, absorbing and improving upon the existing auxiliaries. In practice this principally meant the volunteers since elements of the militia and yeomanry would be incorporated into the expeditionary force described in the first memorandum of 1 January 1906. The idea of educating the nation in its responsibilities for defence was then carried further in Haldane's fourth memorandum of 25 April, which suggested that as well as raising, supplying and administering the territorials, new county territorial associations might also promote military virtues in schools through encouraging drill, physical exercise, cadet units and rifle clubs. The composition of the associations would also forge links between army and society through a distinctive elective element provided by borough and county councils although they would also incorporate traditional county military elites with lords lieutenant, who would retain the right of nomination to first territorial commissions, normally becoming association presidents.

Few of Haldane's fellow Liberals appear to have been interested in this vision except in so far as it avoided the possibility of conscription and, indeed, their principal concern was a demand for economy which determined the secretary of state's freedom of action: it was demonstrated, for example, that the territorials would cost only £2.8 million per annum whereas the auxiliary estimates currently ran at £4.4 million annually. Haldane himself was clearly aware that the attachment to military virtues in the country as a whole did not necessarily run deep and his wider proposals were of a suitably long-term nature. It can also be noted that he believed his version of a nation in arms would actually negate militarism. Many individuals claimed to have inspired this aspect of his reforms. However, a number of contemporaries identified the guiding figure as Haldane's military secretary, Colonel Gerald Ellison, who had been working on plans for a new volunteer organisation while attached to the adjutant general's department in 1905 and had also earlier written a book in 1898 advocating a Swiss-style militia. Yet, Ellison himself gave the credit for the associations to Haldane and the territorials were more closely to resemble Germanic practice than Swiss for all that the Swiss model was highly influential in both Britain and the United States.

In some respects, too, the territorial scheme as it eventually evolved represented the fulfilment of older ideas as to the ultimate development of the volunteer force, albeit those of the 'advanced school' and of regulars. There would be a definite term of four years' enlistment terminable on three months' notice on penalty of a fine with the provision to re-engage for a further four years; the ability to enlist in the regulars at any time; between eight and 15 days' annual camp with pay; and the entire force permanently under military law with an obligation to be embodied for an additional year in addition to the term of engagement. Embodiment for service anywhere in the United Kingdom would be possible in the event of imminent national danger or grave emergency but there was to be no role in aid of the civil power for any territorials including yeomanry although those conditions applied to volunteers since 1867 allowing the possibility of individuals combining to use their military knowledge under common law and the use of arms in defence of armouries remained.

While relieving commanding officers of often crippling financial burdens, county associations would actually also encroach on their independence, which explains why Esher believed they might break volunteer 'trade unionism' by creating regional groups of conflicting interests and competing aims.[13] The War Office would also now be placed very firmly in control of training and command although it was hoped to place some territorials in command of divisions in due course and, by way of concession, all papers on the force would be referred to a new director-general of the territorial force before decision and the territorials would be represented on the army council by the parliamentary under-secretary of state.

The provision of full supporting services for the territorials including field artillery armed with 15 pounder field-guns and the redesignation of that portion of the imperial yeomanry – all but six regiments – not required for the expeditionary force as the mounted arm of the territorial force also accorded with old volunteer aims. Moreover, taking to heart the criticisms of the Norfolk commission regarding the inability of the auxiliaries to take the field against regulars and their inadequacy as a means of expanding the army upon mobilisation, Haldane originally intended that the territorials should both support and expand the army. As outlined in Haldane's seventh memorandum of 23 November 1906 they would garrison naval ports, replace regular garrisons and provide defence against the hostile raids which the CID invasion enquiry had pronounced possible. But, after six months' training upon mobilisation, the territorials would be ready for overseas service and Haldane hoped that between a sixth and a quarter of the territorials would volunteer for such overseas service in advance by taking what in 1910 became known as the imperial service obligation.

Unfortunately, the whole justification of both the obligation and the training period as a necessary preliminary to expanding the army was then made a nonsense by one of the crucial compromises Haldane made in response to supposed opposition. In this case, Haldane announced his proposals for the territorials' overseas role when presenting the estimates on 25 February 1907 but on the first reading of the territorial and reserve forces bill just eight days later switched the emphasis to home defence in order to forestall radical opposition in his own party. Similarly, radical and Labour opposition to the promotion of military values in schools was appeased by dropping financial assistance to cadets from county territorial associations. The Lords sought to reverse the concession and another compromise was effected to enable associations to support cadets from non-public funds only. Yet a further compromise had been made even before the bill reached Westminster for representatives of the volunteers and yeomanry had bitterly opposed the idea of the county associations. By September 1906 Haldane was contemplating removing all financial powers from the associations and abandoning the elective element, only to be persuaded by Esher and others in October to retain associations with financial powers although still disposing of the elective element.

In fact, parliamentary opposition to the bill was negligible. In their fears of the volunteers' parliamentary strength, for example, Esher and Clarke had appreciated no more than Haldane just how far the volunteer interest had been reduced by the Liberal electoral victory in January 1906 leaving just 157 Unionists in the house. Only 28 volunteers were elected – 13 for the first time – of whom 14 were Liberals and, in practice, the volunteer parliamentary opposition to Haldane came down to three old hands in Howard Vincent, Lord Balcarres and Sir Gilbert Parker and one new Unionist MP, W. W. Ashley. Vincent and the others were chiefly opposed to the six months' training liability upon mobilisation on the grounds of difficulties with employers and the transfer of authority to associations but his amendment to create a separate territorial forces department at the War Office went down by 295 to 113 votes on 3 June 1907. Earlier on 28 May amendments to exclude the militia and yeomanry from the bill had been lost by 260 to 80 and 291 to 89 respectively and, in the final vote on the Commons third reading on 19 June, Vincent, Ashley and Colonel W H Walker found themselves sharing the lobby with Sir Charles Dilke and assorted Labour and Irish members as the bill passed by 286 to 63 votes.

With the major exception of cadet finance the Lords left the bill substantially alone but, in reality, the support of its Unionist leadership had been bought by Haldane's concession in May 1907 to exclude the militia from the territorials. Haldane's second memorandum, of course, had envisaged incorporating a proportion of the militia in the expeditionary force amounting to 30,857 men drawn primarily from the supporting services and particularly from the militia's garrison artillery, which was no longer required for coastal defence. Moreover, the heavy casualties now expected in modern warfare following the experience of the Russo–Japanese war also required that some 56,000 militia infantry should be reserved as drafts for the expeditionary force with the remainder joining the territorial force. However, personified by the Duke of Bedford, the militia's colonels opposed absorption into either regulars or territorials.

In the summer and autumn of 1906 Haldane made three major attempts to reach agreement with the militia's representatives. All failed and, once more, Haldane had to be persuaded to stand by his scheme, resolving on 15 October that if the militia would not meet the responsibility of supplying drafts then another force must. Accordingly, and at the suggestion of the director of military operations, Spencer Ewart, he proposed to support the 74 pairs of linked regular battalions to which he had reduced the army with 74 special reserve battalions designed to attract those previously entering the militia and fulfilling the function of taking over regular depots upon mobilisation to train drafts and replace casualties. Thus, through its customary intransigence, the militia was finally condemned to extinction although, in theory, all but 23 of the militia's existing battalions would actually be converted into special reserve battalions. Those militiamen who chose not to transfer to the special reserve or territorials would be able to serve out their terms of enlistment and, in fact, as late as January 1913 there were still 636 militiamen and 64 militia reservists so doing.

Haldane had rejected a highly unrealistic proposal by the director of military training, Douglas Haig, to raise 900,000 territorials and had settled in his seventh memorandum on 42 brigades organised in 14 divisions with 14 mounted brigades and amounting to some 314,094 officers and men. But this set equally ambitious targets which could only be met if the those militiamen not incorporated into the expeditionary force or special reserve joined the territorials. Haldane's concession to exclude the militia from his bill effectively rendered his manpower targets unachieveable irrespective of how many volunteers or yeomen chose to transfer. Equally optimistic was Haldane's hope that his new officer training corps, which emerged as a recommendation of the Ward committee in February 1907 as a means of re-organising the university and public school cadet corps currently associated with the volunteers, could furnish at least 800 officers a year for the special reserve alone. Thus, just reaching establishment was to become a crucial test of the reforms once the Territorial and Reserve Forces Act (7 Edw VII c 9) received the royal assent on 2 August 1907 with a target starting date of 1 April 1908.

One element of Haldane's attempt to win auxiliaries' support for the reforms had been his energetic campaigning throughout the country at dinners and other gatherings. None the less, there had been considerable disquiet and by April the volunteers had declined to 224,217 men, representing the lowest strength for 17 years. Undaunted, Haldane continued his exhausting round of appearances and volunteers were offered the ability to enlist in the territorials up to 30 June 1908 for one year rather than four. However, the territorial force had reached a strength of only 144,620 officers and men by 1 June 1908 and, in fact, less than 40 per cent of the existing volunteers and yeomen were to transfer. Less than a third of those who did so enlisted for the full four years. While the permitted age range for enlistment was 17 to 35, Haldane had expressed a preference for those under 24, which automatically excluded many existing auxiliaries. Clearly, territorial service also implied greater commitment than that in volunteers or yeomanry and it has been argued that the pecuniary rewards now being offered may also have had the effect of deterring those previously serving in the auxiliaries as a 'labour of love'.[14]

Purely local factors could also be of considerable account in both the initial and subsequent recruitment and, just as in the past, the attitude of employers and local authorities could be significant. In Birmingham, for example, territorials were actively supported by large employers such as BSA, the Dunlop Rubber Company and Mitchell & Butler. The same was broadly true of Leeds while, in London, the Alliance Assurance Company and the Westminster Fire Office were to attract unwelcome publicity for insisting that their employees be territorials. By contrast, the corporations of Hull and Bradford and the North Eastern Railway Company were notably hostile to the force while smaller employers could rarely afford to be as generous as larger concerns in the matter of a second week of camp.

Accordingly, there was constant pressure from county territorial associations for further rewards for territorials and employers alike. In view of the continuing crucial role of women in supporting their menfolk's territorial aspirations, one demand was met by extending separation allowances to all married men and NCOs in 1912 if they attended the full 15 days' camp while, in the following year, men in camp were relieved of the necessity under the 1911 National Insurance Act of paying both their own and their employers' contributions. In February 1913 the national defence association, formed in 1906 and now something of a mouthpiece for territorial grievances, pressed the government to make new concessions, the county associations generally advocating such measures as higher separation allowances, jury exemption, income tax rebates for co-operative employers and, particularly supported by Scottish associations, an annual bounty. Following a major discussion in the council of county territorial associations in April 1913 the campaign culminated with a delegation to the prime minister, Asquith, in November 1913 at which most of the now familiar arguments were rehearsed. The government would go no further than announcing in March 1914 that it would now pay a £1 bounty to those attending the full 15 days at camp.

But it was not just the inadequate remuneration or the other frustrations of territorial service that affected recruiting, for territorials came under sustained assault from a number of different quarters. The failure of territorials to match Haldane's manpower targets increased criticism and, in turn, generated more disillusionment. Regulars had no more confidence in the territorials than the auxiliaries before them and the territorials were to have equally few friends in the military establishment. The likely efficiency of the new territorial field artillery provoked a major and essentially familiar controversy in 1908 in which Lord Roberts in particular played a prominent role in denigrating territorial achievements. Subsequently, standards of training, attendance at camp, the high annual wastage rate of 12.5 per cent and the attainment of musketry standards were all to come under close scrutiny and younger regulars often resisted being posted as territorial adjutants for fear that it would damage their careers. No proper mobilisation scheme existed for the territorials as late as 1912 and, in any case, priority was accorded to the expeditionary force since regulars questioned the validity of expending resources on formations that had no clear liability to overseas service. In 1914, therefore, territorial infantry still lacked the modern Lee Enfield rifle and the artillery was armed with 15 pounders and 5 in howitzers that were now obsolescent. Moreover, even before the force had been fully established, the doubts concerning its effectiveness partially prompted a second invasion enquiry by the CID, which recommended in October 1908 that two of the six regular divisions of the expeditionary force should be retained in Britain after mobilisation. The recommendation was reiterated in a third enquiry in April 1914 in view of continuing criticism of the lack of officers and NCOs and deficiencies in training and musketry.

Military criticism, however, rested upon more than narrow professional judgement for it was widely recognised that the territorials were, as Haldane himself had remarked, the 'practical test of the voluntary system'[15] and, as such, the last obstacle to the introduction of conscription. There was undoubted military support for some form of conscription and, in fact, the army council embraced it in April 1913. In the country generally the national service league claimed over 91,000 members by 1911 although its membership was noticeably more anglican than nonconformist and more Unionist than Liberal.[16] Moreover, despite the introduction of forms of universal training in Australia and New Zealand in 1909, conscription was never likely to prove popular even if disguised as universal training or national military service.

There was some indication of support for compulsion in the 1910 elections and at some subsequent by-elections but all five of the parliamentary bills introduced to implement universal training between 1908 and 1914, only one of which was sponsored by the league, failed. Initially, the league was not overtly critical of the territorials, many of whom were also its members, and the bill it sponsored in 1909 envisaged the use of the force as the organisational basis for compulsion while some of the others sought to apply a militia-style ballot to the territorials. However, Roberts, who had resigned from the CID to become president of the league in November 1905 and was also to resign from the national defence association when it championed the territorials, notably stepped up his attacks on the force immediately prior to introducing the league's bill. Thereafter, the league's growing frustration resulted in increasing attack on the territorials from November 1912 onwards to which a number of serving soldiers close to Roberts such as Henry Wilson willingly contributed. The campaign undoutedly damaged the territorials, the essential cynicism of Roberts and his circle being apparent during the escalating home rule crisis in early 1914 when the territorials were pressed into the political service of those who had spent so long denigrating the force by being openly encouraged to demonstrate support for the cause of Ulster. In fact, it would appear that a large proportion of the force would have refused in any case to assist in the coercion of Ulster by replacing in home garrisons regulars dispatched there.[17]

Even territorials themselves became sufficiently despondent to advocate conscription, ten associations – the first had been the East Riding in November 1912 – declaring for it by April 1913 and 17 backing a thinly veiled recommendation for compulsion first proposed by Essex in January 1913 although this was subsequently changed beyond recognition to form the basis for the proposals on territorial grievances put before Asquith at the end of the year. Territorial MPs, of whom there were 94 in 1912, also often criticised while one of the most damaging attacks in the columns of the conscriptionist *National Review* in September 1910 was penned by the chairman of the County of London association, Esher.

But there was also wider opposition to the territorial scheme. The trades union congress made clear its hostility in 1909 while Haldane also miscalculated in presenting a virtual ultimatum to uniformed youth organisations in 1910 to affiliate to county associations or risk forfeiting War Office assistance. The Church Lads Brigade, whose executive was dominated by conscriptionists, did affiliate but the Boy Scouts resisted similar influences and the Boys Brigades rejected affiliation by an overwhelming 87 per cent to 13 per cent in January 1911. More successful, however, was the augmentation after August 1909 of the new territorial force nursing service, by voluntary aid detachments organised locally by the Red Cross and which embraced some 26,000 women by 1912. In their own way the VADs, which became part of the territorial technical reserve but escaped actual territorial control, offered an alternative vision of participation to that of the suffragette movement. There was also the quasi-aristocratic first aid nursing yeomanry, formed in 1907 but with no connection to the actual yeomanry, while support for territorial recruiting had come from the British women's patriotic league.[18]

The VADs recruited best at the time of a renewed invasion scare in 1909 and this also boosted territorial numbers as Haldane sought to lend particular emphasis to the home defence role and to exploit the popularity of Guy du Maurier's topical invasion play, *An Englishman's Home*, which opened in January 1909. A recruiting booth was established in the theatre and, in all, 30,000 recruits were obtained in just seven weeks before the panic began to subside. Meeting criticism of the lord chamberlain, who had attempted to suppress satirical versions of du Maurier's play, Haldane defended what he regarded as 'modern methods of recruiting'.[19] As indicated earlier, he also sponsored Fortescue's *The County Lieutenancies and the Army*, which presented an unflattering image of the role of the auxiliaries during the Napoleonic wars in a way calculated to enhance his own reforms. The King was also pressed into service through the good offices of Esher, a meeting of lords lieutenant at Buckingham Palace in October 1907 seeing the culmination of a campaign to secure the co-operation of the lieutenancy: 115 peers had joined county associations by November 1909 although it must also be said that the Duke of Bedford resigned the Middlesex lieutenancy and at least 13 lords lieutenant were members of the national service league. In June 1909, too, there was a glittering ceremony at Windsor in which the King presented 108 territorial colours.

However, neither invasion scare nor royal support could achieve more than a temporary increase in territorial strength or offset the criticism directed at the force and it declined from 268,776 officers and men in June 1909 to 245,779 by September 1913 or some 64,778 short of establishment. Even more significantly, such large numbers had chosen not to re-engage on the expiry of their original term of service in 1912–13 that 80 per cent of the force had less than four years' service experience. The social composition of the force had become broader with the reward of pay – about 7 per cent joined the regular army each year – but the average age had also dropped and in 1913 some 40,000 were under the age of 19 at which service overseas became possible. A third of the force had failed the modest musketry requirement of firing off 23 rounds in 1910 and, in 1912, only 155,000 men had camped for a full 15 days while some 6,000 had totally absented themselves. Haldane's emphasis on home defence had also had its effect with only 1,090 officers and 17,788 men – barely 7 per cent – having taken the imperial service obligation by September 1913.[20]

Other aspects of the overall scheme had been similarly disappointing. Of the 18,000 young men who had already passed through the OTCs by March 1912, only 283 had joined the special reserve. The special reserve itself, which Haldane had regarded as fulfilling an additional purpose as a kind of unemployment relief during the winter months, had attracted about 60 per cent of the militia in 1908 but the momentum was not sustained and it continued between 16 and 18 per cent short of its 80,300 establishment and some 50 per cent short of subalterns. A territorial reserve was established in 1909 and, modelled upon the so-called Surrey veteran reserve, a national reserve was established in 1910 as part of the territorial reserve for those aged over 45 capable of filling territorial vacancies upon mobilisation or performing sedentary duties. The national reserve mustered 190,836 men by January 1913 and appears to have been rather more successful than the territorial reserve proper for those who had completed their term of service: in Buckinghamshire, for example, there were 1,724 officers and men in the national reserve by 1914 but only six officers and a single man in the county's territorial reserve.

By 1914, therefore, the territorial force had fallen a long way short of Haldane's optimistic manpower targets and it had been fatally weakened from the beginning by his political expediency. It did offer a better organisational framework than the previous auxiliaries and was far stronger in terms of its range of supporting services. Unfortunately, however, perceived weaknesses had undermined its status as a means of expanding the army and, when war broke out in August 1914, the pre-war record was to determine the employment of the territorial force to such an extent as to result in a long and deep-felt sense of grievance.

Notes

1 Cunningham, *Volunteer Force*, pp. 49–50; M. D. Blanch, 'British Society and the War' in P. Warwick and S. B. Spies (eds), *The South African War* (Longman, London, 1980), pp. 210–38; Ibid., 'Imperialism, Nationalism and Organised Youth' in J. Clarke, C. Critcher and R. Johnson (eds), *Working Class Culture* (Hutchinson, London, 1979), pp. 103–20.

2 Dunlop, *Development of the British Army*, pp. 89–93; Blanch, 'British Society and the War', pp. 210–38.

3 Salisbury Papers, Lansdowne to Salisbury, 15 Dec 1899.

4 Beckett, *Riflemen Form*, pp. 212–15.

5 Bucks RO, T/A 3/20(b); J. Brown, 'A Rough Sketch of the South African War as Experienced by the Undersigned in the 10th Regiment, Imperial Yeomanry from January 1900 to June 1901'.

6 R. Price, *An Imperial War and the British Working Class* (Routledge & Kegan Paul, London, 1972), pp. 200–1, 214–16.

7 Dunlop, *Development of the British Army*, p. 111; Beckett, *Riflemen Form*, p. 214.

8 Blanch, 'British Society and the War', p. 229.

9 British Library, H. O. Arnold Forster Mss, Add Mss 50339 Diary entry, 15 Jul 1904 and Add Mss 50338, Diary entry, 29 Jun 1904.

10 Ibid., Add Mss 50346, Diary entry, 14 Apl 1905.

11 Ibid., Add Mss 50353, Diary entry, 16 Dec 1905.

12 Quoted in E. M. Spiers, *Haldane: An Army Reformer* (Edinburgh University Press, 1980), p. 95.

13 M. V. Brett (ed), *The Journals and Letters of Reginald, Viscount Esher* (Ivor Nicolson & Watson, London, 1934), II, pp. 227–9.

14 M. D. Blanch, 'Nation, Empire and the Birmingham Working Class, 1899–1914', Unpub. Ph.D., Birmingham, 1975, p. 263; Morris, 'Leeds and the Amateur Military Tradition', pp. 227, 253–4.

15 PRO, Cab 3/2/4/55A quoted by J. Gooch, 'Haldane and the National Army' in I. F. W. Beckett and J. Gooch (eds), *Politicians and Defence* (Manchester University Press, 1981), p. 80.

16 M. Allison, 'The National Service Issue, 1899–1914', Unpub. Ph.D., London, 1975, p. 24. For the relationship generally between the territorials and the league, see Allison, pp. 86–126.

17 I. F. W. Beckett (ed), *The Army and the Curragh Incident, 1914* (The Bodley Head for the Army Records Society, London, 1986), pp. 6, 24.

18 Anne Summers, *Angels and Citizens: British Women as Military Nurses, 1854–1914* (Routledge & Kegan Paul, London, 1988), pp. 238–43, 250–70.

19 Spiers, *Haldane*, p. 171.

20 I. F. W. Beckett, 'The Territorial Force' in I. F. W. Beckett and K Simpson (eds), *A Nation in Arms: A Social Study of the British Army in the First World War* (Manchester University Press, 1985), p. 129; Spiers, *Haldane*, pp. 172, 182–6.

8

Wars and economies (1914–1940)

Your kind assistance is desired.

G. R.

County of Buckingham
Territorial Force Association.

RECRUITING FOR THE REGULAR ARMY
AND TERRITORIAL UNITS.

500 MEN ARE REQUIRED

From BUCKINGHAMSHIRE to complete the

8th Battalion of the
Oxfordshire and Buckinghamshire
Regiment.

Standard Height 5ft. 4ins.   Chest 34½in.
Age 19 to 38 years.

Recruits can be enlisted at any Recruiting Centre and sent to the Depôt at Oxford.

RECRUITS also Required, Riding Men, for the

Royal Bucks Hussars
Reserve Regiment,

Apply to their Headquarters at Buckingham, or their Depôt, Walton Street, Aylesbury.

THE

Bucks Reserve Battalion

Require RECRUITS. Apply to the Headquarters, Temple Square, Aylesbury.

GOD SAVE THE KING.

"Bucks Advertiser" Co., Ltd., Aylesbury.

Of all the peoples who found themselves at war in August 1914, the British had had least time to react, the preoccupation with Ireland resulting in most hardly becoming aware of the impending crisis in Europe until 29 July. Many territorials had only just returned from annual camp when units received mobilisation orders on the evening of 4 August, a common memory being the use of cinema screens to advertise mobilisation. But, whatever the expectations of the territorials at the outbreak of war, all were to be set aside by the appointment of Field Marshal Lord Kitchener as secretary of state for war on 5 August 1914.

On the morning he took over the War Office, Kitchener remarked that 'he could take no account of anything but regular soldiers'[1] and his decision to raise his 'New Armies' through the War Office rather than the county territorial associations remains one of the most controversial aspects of his tenure as secretary of state. In many respects, the raising of the new armies and especially the 115 'pals' battalions from industrial concerns and local communities mirrored the creation of the volunteers in the past but these men were recruited as temporary wartime regulars and thus served on a very different basis.

Undoubtedly, there was a measure of prejudice involved in Kitchener's decision. Contemporaries recorded Kitchener's distrust of amateur soldiers based upon his experience as a volunteer with Chanzy's army during the Franco–Prussian War and of irregulars in South Africa. He also referred to territorials as a 'town clerk's army',[2] implying a distrust of the measure of independence associations enjoyed and the opportunities for local nepotism in appointments although the new armies themselves proved no less subject to such nepotism. Indeed, in many respects, the decision appears an instinctive one for a regular who actually knew little of the home army.

Nevertheless, there was more to Kitchener's reasoning than simple prejudice, not least the dismal state of the territorial force in 1914 and the difficulties resulting from the pre-war compromises. There were no actual plans for expansion through associations and Kitchener appears to have believed that they would be swamped by rapid augmentation and could not recruit and train simultaneously. Similarly, it must be remembered that the territorials were not actually liable to go overseas unless they could be persuaded to take the imperial service obligation. Kitchener also seems to have been reluctant to put pressure on married men to volunteer to go abroad. The territorials were further handicapped by the removal of their regular adjutants and instructors to staff the new armies. But, most significant of all was Kitchener's preoccupation with invasion, against which territorials were the principal defence although, in line with the pre-war policy, two regular divisions were initially kept back from France and Flanders. Use of territorials to expand the expeditionary force would disorganise the force for its home defence role although Kitchener's scrapping of existing home defence plans did not materially contribute to organisation either.

Having taken his decision, Kitchener would not be swayed although he did indicate to Esher on 13 August that he would be prepared to use territorials who volunteered for overseas service and he did begin to send some overseas in September 1914. However, the majority of these were meant to release regulars from imperial garrisons rather than to afford the territorials opportunities, the 42nd (East Lancashire) Division sailing for Egypt on 10 September and the 43rd (Wessex) for India on 9 October to be followed by the 44th (Home Counties) and 45th (2nd Wessex) in December. Individual units also went to Gibraltar, Malta, Cyprus and Aden. Those divisions sent to imperial garrisons came to feel that they had been penalised for early readiness and those sent to India in particular were immensely dissatisfied with the conditions under which they were to serve until 1919 or even 1920 in apparent violation of Kitchener's categorical promise that they would be brought back to France within a year.

It would also appear that Kitchener was only reluctantly persuaded to allow territorials to 'fill the gap' on the Western Front in the winter of 1914–15 before his new armies were ready to take the field. The first two units to France – the 1/14th London (London Scottish) and the 1/1st Queen's Own Oxfordshire Hussars on 16 and 22 September respectively – were intended only as line of communications troops but, with additional pressure from Sir John French, seven yeomanry, three engineer, one medical and 22 infantry units had arrived by December. The total of infantry battalions rose to 48 in February 1915 with the first complete division – the 46th (North Midland) – arriving the same month and the first complete brigade – 149th Brigade of 50th (Northumbrian) Division going into action in April 1915.

In numerical terms, the territorials' eventual contribution to the war effort was considerable with 318 battalions and 23 infantry divisions serving overseas – 3 in India, 7 in the Mediterranean and Middle East (of which 4 later transferred to France), and 13 on the Western Front (of which one later transferred to Italy) – compared to 404 new army battalions and 30 new army divisions. By 1918, moreover, 692 territorial battalions had existed compared to 267 regular or reserve and 557 new army battalions. However, there was certainly duplication of effort and competition in recruiting and supply damaging to both territorials and new armies and the associations could have been used more constructively. Moreover, while it has been claimed that Kitchener 'was able to weld the force into the national army without dislocating it or totally destroying its original character',[3] in reality, the military authorities showed scant sympathy for the territorials' special legislative difficulties and consistently failed to address their grievances.

Admittedly, the expansion of the army from the 733,514 officers and men serving in the regulars, reserves and territorials in August 1914 to the situation reached by November 1918 when a further 4,907,902 men had been enlisted, was bound to present a monumental challenge in which much might need to be sacrificed to military necessity. It was understandable, therefore, if War Office and regulars found aspects of the existing territorial legislation irksome. A case in point was the question of the imperial service obligation.

Prior to the outbreak of war only five complete units had volunteered for overseas service. On 10 August an invitation was extended to the remainder with an announcement on 21 August that units where 80 per cent volunteered could complete to war establishment and others could combine to form service units. From 15 August associations were authorised to raise new units to replace those volunteeering, enabling the 'first line' units to complete from the 'second line' units and to return their own home service men to the second line as a nucleus: 'third line' units were raised in November 1914 as first line units went abroad and for all that had not yet done so in March 1915, a nomenclature of 1/1st, 2/1st and 3/1st for battalions in the respective lines being adopted from January 1915. In May 1915 the original 'territorial' designations of higher formations were also discontinued so that, for example, the East Lancashire Division became 42nd (East Lancashire) Division and its Lancashire Fusiliers, East Lancashire and Manchester Brigades became the 125th, 126th and 127th Brigades respectively. The original 14 territorial divisions were thus numbered 42nd to 44th and 46th to 56th with divisions formed from second line units being numbered 45th and 57th to 69th with a 74th Division later being formed in Egypt from dismounted yeomanry. Territorials also eventually formed five mounted divisions.

It was not uncommon to find units where 80 or 90 per cent did volunteer immediately but this was not always the case, hence the more realistic provision of 60 per cent as the percentage required to volunteer on 31 August. In some instances commanding officers made commitments on behalf of their men which proved wildly optimistic when men actually came to signify their assent personally on paper. In the 51st (Highland) Division the initial figure of a 75 per cent acceptance rate fell significantly, one entire brigade that had supposedly volunteered to a man subsequently opting for home service. There could be wide discrepancies even within a single unit as in the 1/4th Royal Scots where 90 per cent of an artisan company volunteered but only between 15 and 20 per cent of a bankers' company. Many pre-war territorials, of course, were older married men with more family responsibilities than new recruits while others were younger than the minimum age for overseas service set at 19 years. Fitness was also a factor with, for example, 15 per cent of the 1/1st Montgomeryshire Yeomanry and 20 per cent of the 1/6th West Yorkshire declared unfit for overseas service. The 1/6th Royal Welsh Fusiliers were passed only after multiple teeth extractions and the promise of dentures which actually failed to materialise for another year. Others took the view that the territorials were only for home defence and it can be noted that Lloyd George subscribed to this view in urging his son, serving in a Welsh territorial unit, not to be bullied into volunteering.

For whatever reason, therefore, numbers coming forward could be much reduced. Unfortunately, this could often lead to victimisation. In the case of the 1/1st Bucks Battalion, about 240 men declined to volunteer including many older NCOs and all 27 members of the band. They were deprived of their equipment, labelled 'Never Dies' by the commanding officer and compelled to camp apart from the battalion until returned to form the nucleus of the 2/1st Bucks. Similarly, those who refused to volunteer in C Squadron of the South Notts Yeomanry were put on fatigues and ultimately pelted with banana skins when they returned to Nottingham. However, in all, some 72 per cent of territorial rank and file had taken the imperial service obligation by 26 September 1914.

A second major problem facing territorials was the ability of individuals to continue to enlist for home service until March 1915. How far this was an important factor in territorial recruiting is unknown but it certainly remained relatively buoyant, notwithstanding successive War Office restrictions on particular categories of territorial recruiting such as the stop put on new artillery batteries in late 1914 and the cessation of yeomanry recruiting between June and September 1915. Territorials did have wider age limits and lower height requirements than the new armies but it was generally believed the latter would be more likely to go abroad first and the 'bringing money' for them was also higher. By 2 February 1915 the territorials had recruited 364,419 men but ultimately their recruiting declined and, when voluntary direct enlistment ceased in December 1915, the 725,842 territorials recruited represented only approximately half the number enlisted in the new armies during the same period.

There is some evidence to suggest that home service had been an attractive option, incomplete returns for Caernarfon between September and December 1914 suggesting that the ratio of home to foreign service enlistments ran four to one[4] and there were certainly enough home service territorials to form 68 provisional battalions in April 1915 whilst still leaving over 80,000 home servicemen on territorial returns four months later. Only the passing of the first of the Military Service Acts in January 1916 finally eradicated the home service option, those aged under 41 being obliged to take the imperial service obligation or resign and thus become liable to conscription. The same legislation also removed the ability of pre-war territorials to seek their discharge at the end of four years plus the automatic one year extension imposed by the war. Some 159,388 pre-war territorials would have been eligible for discharge between 1914–15 and 1916–17. It is impossible to say how many took advantage of this right rather than accept the alternative of a month's furlough and a bounty upon re-engagement for four years or the duration but there are examples of men doing so. In the 1/1st Bucks Battalion a total of 91 men went home time-expired between their arrival in France in March 1915 and the end of the concession: a further 33 men re-engaged while 26 were compulsorily retained in the service once the military service legislation was effected.

Clearly, the imperial service obligation and the term of engage-ment presented problems for the military authorities but an even greater difficulty was that of the integrity of territorial units for the 1907 legislation had made it illegal to transfer territorials between units, or to amalgamate or disband units. It was clearly stated on the standard form, E.624, which all territorials signed in accepting the overseas service obligation, that an individual would remain with his own unit. From the beginning some territorials feared that overseas service would lead to transfer and some of the reluctance to volun-teer was attributed to this. Then casualties began to exceed pre-war estimates and, with the new armies yet untrained and the limited resources of army and special reserve exhausted, only territorials were available.

As early as February 1915, therefore, consideration was given to amending legislation but opposition then led to the brief and unsuccessful attempt by the War Office between May and July 1915 to impose a new form, E.624A, by which those who had already volunteered as well as new recruits were required to agree to transfer. In fact, territorials could be attached under existing legislation but the idea of a new bill was revived in April 1916 before clauses were included in the second Military Service Act of May 1916 to enable transfers to take place.

Until the legislation was amended, there was still the problem of maintaining both regular and territorial units in the field. In March 1915, responsibility for supplying drafts to the first line had passed from the second to the third line units but sufficient numbers were simply not available and in both June and July second line battalions were raided for trained personnel. Constant losses damaged the efficiency of the second line and, whereas it had taken an average of just eight months to prepare first line units for service, the second line averaged 27 months. Even first line formations suffered as in the case of the 53rd (Welsh) and 54th (East Anglian) divisions whose poor performance at Suvla Bay on the Gallipoli peninsula in August 1915 was directly attributed to having previously lost so many trained men to units in France. Such expedients might have been accepted more readily if the drafting system in France and Flanders had not seemingly broken down completely at an early stage.

After December 1915 when direct recruiting into the territorial force was suspended for all but a handful of specialist units, drafting became even more haphazard and harmful to what territorials regarded as the 'character' of the force. There was occasionally an element of fiction in this supposed 'character' and cohesion born of close identification with a particular locality. Many units were indeed recruited from a restricted area such as the 1/6th Gordons, who had only 11 non-Scots among 867 officers and men in August 1914, but the 2/1st Denbighshire Yeomanry was only 27 per cent Welsh and the novelist Patrick MacGill claimed he and the commanding officer were the only genuine Irishmen in the 1/18th London (London Irish). In any case, there was likely to be a process of change as men went home time-expired or through acceptance for commissions or became sick. Clearly, however, it was the casualty rate that was most likely to determine a unit's survival as a recognised entity and in that regard disintegration was greatly accelerated with the heavy casualties on the Somme in the summer of 1916, which cost the territorials 83,696 casualties.

Drafts, of which the London Rifle Brigade received no less than 11 between July and October 1916 comprising 1,234 men, might fortuitously strengthen the territorial element as in the case of the 1/1st Bucks when it received a large draft from the 1/1st Hunts Cyclists to compensate for its 242 casualties around Ovillers and Pozieres on the Somme between 21 and 24 July 1916. But in the aftermath of another 291 casualties at St Julien on 16 August 1917 during the Passchendaele campaign the draft came from the Army Service Corps (Motor Transport) and resulted in a distinct increase in the battalion's crime rate, newcomers after July 1917 accounting for 33.8 per cent of all wartime crime. At one point during the Somme, the 1/16th London (Queen's Westminsters) were said to have men from 17 different regiments included kilted units serving in it and it is not surprising to find the distinguished historian, C. R. M. F. Cruttwell, reporting that, by the end of 1916, his battalion, the 1/4th Royal Berkshires, had 'lost its exclusive Berkshire character which at the beginning of the war had been its unique possession'.[5]

It was also the case that units increasingly faced the possibility of being amalgamated or disbanded. Temporary amalgamations followed heavy losses in early 1915 as in the case of the 1/1st, 2/1st and 3/1st Monmouthshire battalions. Amalgamations became more permanent in 1916 and in 1918 second line territorials in particular took the brunt of the reductions consequent upon the reorganisation of the expeditionary force. The 50th Division was reduced to cadre and then reconstituted without a single original unit and only one territorial battalion while the 53rd and 60th divisions serving in Palestine were completely reorganised by despatching all but one battalion of each brigade to France and replacing them with Indian battalions. The 59th and 66th divisions were also reduced and reconstituted in 1918, the 67th, 68th and 69th reconstituted – a fate that had earlier befallen the 64th – and the 65th broken up as the 63rd had been in 1916.

Difficulties with drafting and amalgamations affected regular and new army units equally and in most respects there was little to differentiate between territorials, regulars, new army volunteers or conscripts by 1918 for all that formations naturally varied greatly one from another. However, territorials felt additionally aggrieved by the patronising and frequently hostile attitude they encountered from regulars. This did not appear to exist at the level of the other ranks although there was a certain rivalry with new army formations but it did among officers. Haldane, of course, had promised that territorials would receive higher appointments but in 1914 none commanded a division and only three commanded brigades. In reply to increasing criticism, the under-secretary of state for war, Ian Macpherson, stated in February 1917 that 18 territorials had risen above the rank of lieutenant-colonel at the front and three at home and he also claimed that territorials and new army candidates were now filling over a third of all places on staff courses. In fact, this was hardly encouraging when the declining numnber of regular officers was taken into account and in January 1918 Lord Derby was forced to reiterate the War Office case by claiming that four territorials had now commanded divisions and 52 had commanded brigades while

61 below the rank of lieutenant in 1914 had risen to that of lieutenant-colonel. What Derby did not care to emphasise was that most of these appointments had been only temporary and at home and, in the following month, Macpherson was compelled to acknowledge that only ten territorials currently commanded brigades and that only three to date had become General Staff Officers grade 1.

Once more narrow professionalism had intruded on the relationship between amateur and regular. The situation was exacerbated by the pre-war convention that territorials ranked junior in precedence to regulars of the same rank, which left many older and experienced territorials theoretically subordinate to younger regulars or new army officers. They also got less pay and allowances. Consequently, there was friction and some accounts indicate that territorials were moved to cut the 'T's from their tunics as they felt it a badge of inferiority.

Few regulars appear to have expected much of the territorials although those, like French, who had been auxiliary forces' adjutants tended to be more sympathetic. French, indeed, was highly satisfied with their performance on the Western Front and contemplated using 50 territorial battalions in his projected Zeebrugge operation. Haig, too, favoured their early employment. Nevertheless, objective reports from France and India in December 1914 and April 1915 respectively concluded that territorials knew little of interior economy and, in France, had been slow to move. It was widely believed that they had fewer recuperative powers than regulars and the Kirke committee after the war was to conclude that they were better in static defence than attack. Yet, it must be borne in mind that territorials remained poorly equipped: the celebrated attack of the 1/14th London (London Scottish) at Messines in November 1914, resulting in 34 per cent casualties, was carried out with rifles incapable of rapid fire. Moreover, territorials were still arriving in France in 1915 armed with obsolete long Enfields, 15 pounders and 5 in howitzers.

A major cause of what one director-general of territorials called the 'craft unionism'[7] of regulars was the alleged lax discipline of territorial units. To a large extent, this was a failure to understand the traditional ethos of the amateur soldier, the recurrent imagery in so many wartime territorial accounts being the 'family' resting on a strong sense of self-discipline and the free intercourse of social equals. This was naturally more pronounced in the London 'class corps', which had passed from the volunteers to the territorials almost untouched, but even among the working-class units, which formed the overwhelming majority of the pre-war territorial force, life was generally more relaxed. Moreover, it appears to have had results, for territorial units were generally less affected by crime and it can be noted that of the 312 men executed under the provisions of the (British) Army Act between August 1914 and March 1920 only ten were territorials.[8] Similarly, it was somewhat ironic that territorials provided large numbers of candidates for wartime commissions. French asked the 1/28th London (Artists' Rifles) to provide 50 subalterns for immediate employment with the regular 7th Division in November 1914 and, subsequently, the Artists had 10,256 men commissioned. The Inns of Court OTC, also nominally a territorial unit, found over 11,000 officers for the army.

Faced with what appeared to be an intention on the part of the military authorities to destroy the character of the force, territorials and their representatives fought back. London units were particularly prominent in the criticism of the drafting system, which surfaced in the Commons as early as November 1914 and reached a climax in March and April 1916. In the spring of 1916 Scottish associations attempted to fight battlefield amalgamations but they received little support from those yet to experience the problem, encountering a near fatalism which bred insularity. Moreover, the ability of associations to exercise their statutory powers was itself being steadily eroded. Initially, as they attempted to equip their own formations, associations found themselves in direct competition with the War Office and those corporations, firms or individuals trying to secure equipment for the new armies. Expenditure in such circumstances was much greater than had been anticipated with Oxfordshire, for example, spending £48,972 1s 0d on mobilisation. East Lancashire was administering 49,000 men after seven months when its pre-war establishment had been 18,000 and there were also increasing amounts of separation allowances to pay dependants, with Worcestershire supporting 14,550 wives and children, East Lancashire some 60,000 and London over 78,000.

At first it had appeared that the associations would be required to help raise the new armies. Kitchener first requested co-operation on 7 August 1914 then, on 4 September, appointed a committee headed by Brodrick, now Lord Midleton, which immediately turned to the counties for help in housing and training recruits. But just seven days later the committee was dismissed and the invitations rescinded. Associations were yet again asked for help by the War Office in December and in fact Cambridgeshire and the Isle of Ely, Denbighshire and the East Riding raised 11 new army units between them but generally recruiting for territorials and new army was kept quite distinct and, of course, in December 1915 the end of territorial recruiting considerably reduced the role of associations. Responsibility for clothing their units was also taken away from associations, although they remained distributing agents, while in early 1916 control was lost over the territorial units of the Army Service Corps and the national reserve: the latter, which had formed supernumerary companies for local defence, was now incorporated in a Royal Defence Corps.

Alarmed by the implications, association representatives met Derby in January 1917. He denied that any further association powers would be curtailed without parliamentary sanction but in March 1917 the War Office centralised depots, closing many territorial ones, and later in the year closed territorial record offices. In September the council of county territorial associations met for the first time in three years to protest against the 'whittling away' of responsibilities and the 'gradual extinction' of the force in view of rumours that payment of separation allowances would now also be removed.[9] Another delegation met Derby in October, allowances were saved and remaining depots subsequently given a stay of execution but Derby's hint of a major role in demobilisation did not materialise and the only additional role assumed by associations during the war was the highly unpopular administration of a new manifestation of the volunteer spirit in the form of a revived volunteer force.

It has already been indicated that Kitchener was especially alarmed by the danger of invasion in August 1914. Although the two retained regular divisions were soon dispatched to France, the speed of the German advance towards the Channel ports and the fall of Antwerp in October heightened fears to such an extent that invasion was expected around 20 November 1914 when the tide and wind conditions on the east coast were favourable. Accordingly, 300,000 troops were deployed for a landing that never materialised while the CID, which had resolved on 7 October to begin secret preparations to remove livestock, vehicles and petrol supplies from the eastern counties, now decided that the work of the hastily organised local emergency committees be publicised. In so far as they had considered invasion at all, the German general staff had actually ruled it out as early as 1901. Moreover, the Admiralty had obtained a German appreciation which greatly exaggerated the strength of British defences but chose not to disclose it. Thus, fears were sustained, being fanned by the press and such cinematic epics as the *Daily-Express*-sponsored 'Wake Up' and Le Queux' and du Maurier's 'If England Were Invaded'. Nor were matters improved by the German naval bombardment of the east coast in December 1914 and the relative initial success of the allied landings at Gallipoli in April 1915. Indeed, by January 1916 it was believed that the Germans could land up to 160,000 troops before the navy could intervene and this amended scale of likely attack – the scale assumed throughout the pre-war invasion enquiries had been 70,000 – was not reduced until December 1917 when it was set at 30,000 before final adjustment to 5,000 in September 1918.

Originally, when contemplating the possibility of invasion in October 1914, the CID had envisaged only a passive role for ordinary citizens but, in reality, the public had already taken matters into its own hands. As early as 6 August, a prominent Liberal member of London County Council, Percy Harris, had suggested in *The Times* that a 'London volunteer defence force' be established. Harris claimed to represent a 'national patriotic association', which launched the scheme at a public meeting on 11 August and attracted considerable support, Lord Desborough becoming president of an interim committee. On 8 August both H. G. Wells and Sir Arthur Conan Doyle expressed support for new volunteer bodies, the latter reporting that volunteers were already drilling at Windlesham in Sussex. Within ten days 'town guards' had also appeared in Oxfordshire, Buckinghamshire, Lancashire and Surrey.

The government was understandably reluctant to countenance unofficial bodies of semi-trained volunteers when efforts were being made to expand the army and weapons were in short supply. Moreover, Harris's letter had also alluded to the somewhat unhappy example of the Ulster volunteer force and its nationalist equivalent. Official discouragement soon resulted in the national patriotic association dropping its support but Harris and Desborough persisted and a meeting with the under-secretary of state for war on 4 September resulted in Kitchener authorising the committee to instruct men not of military age in drill and musketry. By this time, so many requests for information were pouring in that the committee transformed itself into a central organisation of volunteer training corps on 27 September. With the invasion fear mounting and the Northcliffe press in particular urging the government to make its defence plans public, Kitchener then gave official recognition to what was now to be called a central association of volunteer training corps on 19 November 1914.

Recognition was conditional upon men of military age not being enlisted unless they had 'genuine' reasons for not joining the army, that no expense should fall on the state and that no conventional military ranks or uniform be adopted beyond an armlet. However, at the suggestion of the association's military adviser, Sir O'Moore Creagh, a lovat green uniform was recommended and a series of ranks ranging from volunteer to county commandant. It was also decided that attendance at 40 drills of an hour's duration and attainment of second-class musketry standard would qualify for an efficiency badge. Those not attending at least 12 drills in six months would be required to resign. There was still some confusion as to what constituted 'genuine' reasons for not enlisting and it is clear that some volunteers chose to leave, while at Preston a unit disbanded itself altogether rather than submit to the War Office and central association conditions.

The government had recognised the central association but not the volunteer training corps as such and throughout 1915 was content merely to advise units to affiliate to it. Thus, it was only through the initiative of Desborough and the Marquess of Lincolnshire that a short bill was introduced into the Lords in October 1915 to improve the status of the volunteers by enabling their services to be officially accepted in England and Wales and for the War Office to regulate the force under military law. Extended by amendment to include Scotland, the bill passed the Lords but ran out of parliamentary time, adding to the increasing concern over the legality of volunteers bearing arms without true recognition. MPs intervened in the debate on the address in February 1916 and, as a result, it was decided in May to apply the provisions of the Volunteer Act of 1863 which had not been removed from the statute book by the territorial legislation in 1907. In July 1916, therefore, the central association became one of 'volunteer regiments' rather than training corps and an advisory council to the director-general of the territorial force, whose staff

Desborough and Harris, now a Liberal MP, joined. Local administration devolved upon the territorial county associations in
September.

Application of the 1863 legislation had advantages in enabling
discipline to be imposed by fines recoverable under civil law and in
enabling officers to receive recognised commissions. Unfortunately,
it also created an anomaly in the context of the introduction of
conscription since, while the local government board decided in July
1916 that tribunals established to review claims for exemption could
make such exemption conditional upon serving in the volunteers, the
1863 act enabled an individual to resign on 14 days' notice. After a
conference of lords lieutenant and county commandants in October,
a new volunteer bill was introduced in the Lords in November 1916
to close the loophole. Receiving the royal assent on 22 December
1916, the new Volunteer Act required all volunteers to serve for the
duration and to undertake a statutory minimum of 14 (later ten)
drills per month and it enabled what was now officially the volunteer
force to undertake limited military duties at the request of GOCs.
Between January and May 1917 the new structure was completed by
introducing six distinct categories of volunteer: sections A, B and C
for men respectively above, of and under military age; section D –
abolished in 1918 – for those unfit for service in other sections; P for
those who were also special constables; and R for those such as
railway workers who would not be available in an emergency. From
January 1917, too, efficients in A and B received an annual
capitation grant of £2 to provide equipment. Subsequently, the War
Office agreed in May 1918 to clothe some classes of volunteers up to
a defined limit.

In theory the grant covered all expenses but rarely did so in
practice and volunteers were compelled to find alternative funding.
Government encouraged approaches to local authorities but this had
decidedly mixed results and, as already indicated, county territorial
associations were also reluctant to assist what they regarded as poor
substitutes for the erosion of their statutory powers and potential
rivals in promoting cadet corps. Indeed, the County of London
association was moved to protest in November 1917 at responsibilities afforded a force which had 'no history, no continuity, and
consists of those too old, or too young for active service, or of
exempted men who for the most part, at any rate, are not the keenest
fighting men'.[10]

The strictures of the London association on the military value of
the volunteers were widely shared, the Hampshire association
denouncing them as a 'colourable [sic] substitute' for territorials.[11]
Indeed, when the War Office had sought to induce volunteers under
the age of 40 to attest their willingness to enlist if required in May
and June 1915, many had resigned. In Portsmouth, for example,
numbers had declined from 1,200 to 520 and in Bournemouth from
900 to 500 while in Dulwich only half the 325 men of the local unit
had returned their forms and only 63 of those who did so agreed to
the commitment. The traditional ridicule of auxiliaries also
resurfaced with the GR on the volunteers' original armlets bringing
forth such epithets as 'George's Wrecks', 'Grandpapa's Regiment'
and 'Genuine Relics'.

In terms of volunteer military efficiency, equipment certainly
remained in short supply – as late as July 1917, for example, the 1st
Fife Volunteer Battalion had only 130 rifles between 1,900 men and
the 1st City of Aberdeen 190 between 1,007 men. But age was also a
drawback, a series of reports in the summer of 1917 constantly
calling attention to the dangers to which 40-year-olds would be
exposed in military activities such as bombing practice. The average
age of the 1,266 officers and men of the 3rd Buckinghamshire
Volunteer Battalion in 1916, for example, was just over 36 years and
that in the 2nd County of London Volunteer Battalion over 43
years.[12] Occupation, too, presented difficulties since those of military age were mostly in protected occupations. Some miners and
dockers were prohibited from enlistment and the board of trade
continued to attempt to gain total exemption for dock labour
throughout 1917 and 1918. In June 1918 War Office and ministry of
national service agreed a list of sixteen industrial occupations that
should be barred from participation in special service companies.
Agriculture was equally a key occupation in rural counties and, after
pressure from the national farmers' union, the War Office agreed in
1917 that those involved in harvesting need only attend half the
specified monthly drills between July and September. The status of
volunteers who were also wartime special constables responsible for
guarding key points and handling the evacuation of livestock and
refugees in the event of invasion was also a constant source of
friction with police authorities.

Yet further difficulties were encountered with the arrival of those
sent by tribunals after 1916, the 'tribunal men' concentrated in

section B being generally held to have changed the character of the force since they formed an increasingly large proportion of the total. By 1917 almost half of the 2nd Buckinghamshire Volunteer Battalion were such men and over half of the 3rd Battalion. In Leicestershire the same was true of 46 per cent of the 2nd Volunteer Battalion and of 50 per cent of the 3rd Battalion. In June 1917 102,000 out of 300,000 volunteers in the country as a whole had been directed into the force and it was further calculated that of the 198,000 men of military age only 83,000 could be compelled to become efficient. By November 1918 after conscription had been extended in the wake of the German spring offensives to sweep up men between 41 and 50, the proportion of tribunal men had increased to 44 per cent.[13]

Those who regarded themselves as genuine volunteers found many tribunal men unable or unwilling to complete drills and there were complaints in counties such as Oxfordshire, Buckinghamshire, Essex, Surrey, Gloucestershire and Lancashire that tribunals were often unhelpful in compelling them to do so. Many tribunals also resisted attempts by the volunteers to pursue defaulters through the courts and, following a dispute over a Dundee docker, immunity to prosecution was extended to all those directed by tribunals in November 1917. The general inconsistency was also displayed by tribunals often assuming that a volunteer before them was one who could be easily spared from his civilian occupation.

From the point of view of the War Office, the volunteers as a whole merely provided an escape route from military service, the adjutant-general, Lieutenant-General Sir Nevil Macready, considering by 1917 that 100,000 men had been lost to the army. In a series of conferences between July and December 1917, therefore, the director-general of the territorial force, the Earl of Scarbrough, was compelled to fight a rearguard action to save the volunteers for fear of the consequences of alienating the influential local interests that had raised units. In December it was agreed that 274 battalions with an establishment of 267,150 men should be retained with 38 reduced by amalgamation of weak units and dismissal of non-efficients.

Other suggestions such as compulsory seven-day camps were not implemented and in February 1918 the idea of special service companies was mooted with the aim of seeking 15,000 men capable of undertaking three months' duty on the coast. It was the lack of manpower in France that had prompted such an idea and the opening of the German spring offensive on 21 March gave additional urgency to the matter. Despite problems with employment and reservations on the part of the ministry of national service on the complications of exempted men undertaking such duty, a total of 13,224 men came forward by 25 June and served from 29 June to 28 September. Back in September 1915 the possibility of undertaking engineering work in France had been contemplated and in the critical months of 1918 there was now consideration of mobilising the force and even rumours of service in Ireland. In the event, neither proved necessary and the volunteer force's 16 wartime casualties all occurred in Dublin during the Easter Rising when a party of the 1st (Dublin) Battalion ran into insurgent fire on its way back from drill.

It was not the case, however, that special service companies were the only contribution the volunteers made to the war effort as a whole. Conceivably over a million men passed through the force during the war and, as the upper age limit for military service was progressively increased, so volunteers were enlisted or called up. The central association claimed over 2,000 had enlisted by the end of 1915 and 600 had attested under the Derby scheme. Had there been an invasion, volunteers would have performed a variety of tasks. Of the 312 battalions existing in September 1917, 84 were allocated to lines of communication, 71 to mobile defence, 70 to reserve, 45 to garrison and 42 to London. In practical terms, they released trained troops from guarding prisoners, bridges, factories and aerodromes including 16 installations of national importance such as Conway Bridge in Wales, Montrose airfield in Scotland and the Shanklin and Ventnor piers on the Isle of Wight. They brought in the harvest, worked in docks and munitions factories and between October 1915 and November 1917 devoted four to five million man hours to digging defences around London. Over 400 assisted the London Fire Brigade during air raids from May 1915 and some 5,000 manned anti-aircraft defences.

There was also a number of specialist corps such as a coastal artillery unit in the East Riding, three engineer units and 50 motor volunteer corps in 28 counties. A motor volunteer corps had briefly existed between 1903 and 1906 to convey general staff officers to manoeuvres before being absorbed into the army motor reserve. When the concept was revived in February 1915 it was initially intended merely to transport troops between London railway terminals in the expectation that this would prevent them becoming involved in immoral activities. In the same way volunteers also manned an army pay emergency office at Victoria in 1916 and are said to have officially welcomed over six million British, dominion and allied troops passing through London and other city terminals. No official recognition was received until January 1917 but, ironically, the 18,500 men and 10,000 vehicles of the motor corps were then retained in service until March 1921 through their potential usefulness in strike breaking.

As far as the remainder of the force was concerned, the War Office had turned its thoughts to the termination of volunteer service as early as January 1918. However, the Chief of Imperial General Staff, General Sir William Robertson, was wary of any premature decision and the matter was referred to Cabinet only to be effectively postponed by the crisis in France. Volunteers themselves exerted pressure through MPs and it was not until after the armistice that the Cabinet decided to suspend the provisions of the volunteer legislation. Both French, who had been appointed CinC, Home Forces in 1916, and Robertson, now GOC at Eastern Command, were unhappy with the effect of suspension on the volunteers and their inability in the absence of any formal disciplinary powers to continue temporary duties. The volunteers were then placed in suspended animation on 25 February 1919 and, eventually received a letter of thanks from the King – 'a lukewarm printed message of thanks signed in an unintelligible hand'[14] according to one recipient – in September together with the right to retain uniforms and for officers to retain honorary ranks.

The manner of the volunteers' demise was greatly resented but it was all a part with the opposition of the military authorities, indifference of government, ridicule of public and lack of adequate recognition or reward that was so often the traditional fate of auxiliary forces. And, of course, the territorial associations, who had themselves contributed to the volunteers' difficulties, had reason to believe that their own efforts were being equally ignored. Between 1914 and 1920 territorial units sustained 577,016 casualties in all theatres and territorial officers and men won 71 Victoria Crosses. There had been notable achievements such as the crossing of the St Quentin canal by the 46th (North Midland) Division in September 1918 and the surrender of Jerusalem to two NCOs of the 2/19th London on 8 September 1917 as well as that crucial role in 'filling the gap' in the first winter of the war on the Western Front. However, disembodiment, which began in December 1918, was marked by the army council resolving not to issue any special decoration to those who had taken the imperial service obligation in 1914.

Nor did the territorials fit easily into War Office perceptions of the post-war military situation. For all that the empire had been greatly expanded by the acquisition of former German colonies and parts of the Ottoman empire, that there were occupation duties to be performed, a campaign in Ireland to be waged and other nationalist stirrings with which to cope in India, Africa and the Middle East and all this amid the pressure for both economies and rapid demobilisation of wartime servicemen, the actual role of the territorials appeared superfluous.

There was now clearly little risk of invasion and part-time soldiers were unsuited to a garrison role in the empire. By adopting the ten-year rule in August 1919 the Cabinet assumed no major conflict in the immediate future and, of course, this basic tenet of inter-war policy was not finally abandoned until March 1932. But, in any case, the CID recognised in 1922 that only a comprehensive mobilisation of the state's resources would enable the country to survive the challenge of a major war and, in the following year, its defence manpower sub-committee established wartime conscription as a fundamental principle. That left a role for the territorials only in medium-scale conflict falling short of that for which conscription might be reintroduced. But that would require greater legislative flexibility on the key issues of obligation for general service and the integrity of units, which territorials were in no mood to concede after their wartime experiences. In turn, however, anything that rendered territorials virtually unusable could only result in the War Office regarding them as the most expendable part of the army at a time of considerable financial retrenchment.

In some respects, the battle lines over the precise conditions of post-war service were drawn as early as January 1918 when, in disbanding many second line units, the War Office declined to guarantee that such units would be reconstituted after the war. By early 1919 the War Office was under mounting pressure to declare its hand before trained wartime territorials lost interest in continuing their services but, understandably, the newly appointed secretary of state for war, Churchill, believed it better to establish wider military requirements before deciding on specific policies. However, it was clear that a general service obligation was essential on military grounds and, on 21 February 1919 the War Office issued an official defence of its wartime drafting policy, pointing out that military necessity had had to prevail over territorial integrity.

The problem lay in finding some form of obligation that was acceptable to the territorials yet sufficiently flexible for the War Office to be able to deploy them overseas. In March, therefore, a sub-committee on reconstitution chaired by the adjutant-general, Sir George Milne, recommended making territorials liable for general service once conscription had been introduced and, while allowing them to proceed overseas in their own units, declining to guarantee unit integrity thereafter. Better pay and allowances would compensate for loss of integrity and, in outlining the proposals to territorials on 1 April, Churchill indicated that brigade commands would be opened immediately to suitable territorials in an organisation corresponding to the pre-war structure of 14 infantry divisions and 14 mounted brigades.

Churchill also promised to meet territorial representatives again when the terms of service were finally agreed. However, when he did so in May 1919, nothing had been settled. It was not until January 1920 that the Cabinet finally debated the issue and then lack of agreement delayed a decision until 27 January. Three days later Churchill was able to announce that recruiting would begin on 1 February for a force recruited on a four-year term of engagement with provision for re-engagement for between one and four years to the age of 40 (50 for NCOs). All aged under 35 years would be liable to serve overseas but only after army reserves had been called out by proclamation of imminent danger or great emergency and after parliament had further legislated to authorise actual dispatch of territorials abroad. Moreover, Churchill also promised that territorial formations would retain their integrity in wartime. In what became known as 'the pledge', therefore, the general service obligation was so hedged with legislative qualification as to prevent the War Office either from using territorials in the very situation of medium-scale conflict which was regarded as their only likely employment or from drafting territorial manpower where it was most required. Nor, from the point of view of the War Office, did the new territorial force come cheap for Churchill also offered a £5 annual bounty for those completing a maximum of 50 drills, attending 15 days' camp and firing an annual musketry course: recruits would receive up to £4.

In Churchill's view, political necessity had demanded the reconstitution of what was now to be a territorial army well represented in both Commons and Lords. To some extent, military opposition was assuaged by the proposal to revive the 74 battalions of the special reserve, which would once more be renamed the militia, hence the title of the enabling legislation for the new organisation of Territorial Army and Militia Act (11/12 Geo V c 37) effected in 1921 and which repealed other surviving legislation such as that for local militia (1812), volunteers (1863) and imperial yeomanry (1901). In the event, no effort was made to recruit the revived militia and its function was absorbed by the supplementary reserve. The latter was established in August 1924 to provide technical support in times of emergency on such favourable conditions in terms of peacetime commitment and pecuniary reward that it would seriously dent recruiting for similar territorial specialist units.

In fact, the terms offered the territorials were not as generous as the War Office suspected since immediate post-war wages were relatively high while the commitment to 50 drills appeared excessive. There was also the considerable disadvantage of lingering distrust of the War Office with recruiting proving especially difficult in those counties whose formations had been sent to India in 1914. It was reported that the delay in announcing the government's proposals had had a detrimental effect in many cases and, in any case, it was by no means guaranteed that wartime servicemen would wish to find themselves back in uniform so soon – almost half the recruits enlisted in the first eight months after reconstitution had not seen war service – and it was for just this reason that a large number of associations chose not to go to camp in 1920. In some areas, too, there was resentment at Churchill's other decision in January 1920 to reorganise the 56 yeomanry regiments in view of their declining utility for modern warfare. Over the period 1920–1, 16 were disbanded (one voluntarily) while 26 converted to other roles such as armoured car companies – the first cavalry units to be mechanised in the army as a whole – or artillery batteries. Only 14 were retained in a mounted role, six with regular brigades and but eight allocated to the territorial army. Some 20 infantry battalions were also converted and 20 disbanded or amalgamated.

Churchill also failed to deliver on the recommendation by Milne's committee – endorsed by many associations – that employers be legally obliged to grant privileges to territorials such as allowing them to attend camp. In fact, of course, this would have created considerable difficulties for smaller employers in particular and it was never implemented, not least because it would also have created friction with other non-privileged employees and trade unions. Similarly, periodic calls for a 'King's roll' of co-operative employers to be favoured with preferential government contracts were impracticable and associations had to find other ways of encouraging support from the business community, especially once rising unemployment increasingly deterred men from risking their jobs by joining the territorials or encouraged absenteeism from camp. More often than not, associations established liaison committees but, just as before 1914, some firms co-operated and others did not. The response from local authorities was equally varied with Labour-controlled councils in particular proving hostile even as late as 1937 or 1938, by which time growing recognition of impending national danger had resulted in generally improved support for territorials.

To some degree socialist hostility – Labour governments cut territorial funding support for cadets in both 1924 and 1930 – reflected a wider anti-militarism in the inter-war years and there was undeniably an image problem for the 'Saturday night soldiers' until the late 1930s. There were still other problems although Lord Raglan was only partly correct when he remarked in July 1925 that the real enemies of the territorial army were 'women, trade unions and motor bicycles'.[15] Above all, there was the growing financial pressure on the territorial army, which increasingly threatened its one great attraction to those who chose to enlist, namely recreational facilities. Although many larger employers rivalled the territorials in providing for sport and other social activities, the annual camp was an enormous draw, especially if arranged at a seaside location, and it was noticeable that recruitment always picked up immediately prior to such a camp. Men frequently arranged for their families to holiday nearby and it was also often the only opportunity for them to enjoy an annual break. Thus, there was considerable disquiet when the War Office appeared to counsel cancellation of the camps in 1921 on the grounds of transport difficulties and widespread opposition led by Staffordshire when some camps were cancelled on similar grounds in 1926. The cancellation of all camps in 1932 was accepted with greater equanimity in view of the serious economic position but, as will be seen, in subsequent negotiations over the pledge that autumn, associations made it clear that any agreement was conditional upon restoration of camps.

Attending camp was not necessarily without cost to individuals despite the regular army rates of pay granted in 1920. It was not until March 1936, for example, that married men under the age of 26 received separation allowances while in camp despite associations pointing out in 1924 that extension of the allowance would involve only 6,690 men and cost only £8,395 even if every one so eligible attended the full 15 days. Until the situation was corrected, however, there was the unfortunate spectacle of some territorials' wives having to seek parish relief and being turned down by local authorities on the grounds that it was a government responsibility. Similarly, unemployed men were refused benefits in camp until May 1936 while their annual bounty or proficiency grant had only been exempted from means testing in 1934. Indeed, the War Office generally had little sympathy for the increasing numbers of unemployed enlisted in the territorials, choosing in May 1934 to decline a request by 16 county associations for free issue of shirts and socks at camp in the belief that any man could be expected to provide his own. However, recruitment among this sector held up with the military correspondent of *The Times*, Basil Liddell Hart, calculating over half the territorials in many northern, Welsh and Scottish units as unemployed after touring camps in 1935 and 1937.[16]

Out of the camping season, units had to rely on other ways of attracting recruits. The provision of public spectacle and its coverage in the local press was still a routine part of recruiting as was the pull of friendship often encouraged by the reward of 'bringing in' money. Unfortunately, however, territorial premises were frequently in poor repair until new accommodation standards were finally agreed in 1937 and compared unfavourably with civilian clubs or the increasing lure of the cinema. Financial reductions also continued to bite at territorial grants, activities and equipment with the treasury and War Office alike consistently taking a cue from the territorials' perceived lack of purpose. In March 1922, for example, as a result of the Geddes committee's demand for reductions, the abolition of some territorial divisions was among options considered although, in the end, territorial establishments were cut at all levels, the bounty reduced to £3 for trained men and to £2 10s 0d for recruits and a range of officers' allowances also reduced with the effect of finding some £1,175,000 of the total savings required from the army.

Overall, the Geddes cuts had done such damage to the army that the Cabinet accepted that no more reductions could be contemplated for some time but in February 1926 a further round of economies proved necessary. On this occasion, the territorials agreed to save £160,000 by trimming training, building and clothing grants and by yielding five per cent of the surpluses which War Office block grants had enabled some associations to acquire. Indeed, the issue of surpluses was an unfortunate one for the territorials since the determination of associations to husband such resources could be readily attacked by the treasury, accumulated surpluses amounting to £360,000 in 1926.

As already indicated, in May 1926 the War Office then went on to cancel some camps and, following lengthy internal discussions, demanded another £231,000 savings in February 1927 which it was suggested could only be achieved by reducing establishments, amalgamating the two London divisions, reducing travel grants and abolishing the bounty for all new recruits and those re-engaging after 1 March. Associations were outraged, not least by the lack of prior consultation, and the War Office compromised by dropping the cuts in establishment and compensating for the loss of bounty with a so-called proficiency grant of £1 10s 0d. The reaction appeared to spare territorials from more cuts for a time but in 1930 another £236,000 was trimmed from territorial grants, officers' allowances further cut in 1931 and in September 1931 a saving of up to £1 million announced by limiting recruitment and cancelling all camps for the following year.

Under such constant pressure from differing quarters, the territorial army fell consistently well short of its establishment. In 1922 when the establishment had been 216,041 officers and men, the territorials had numbered only 136,600 although they did attain a strength of 148,742 in 1926 at a time when the establishment had been trimmed to 184,161. Thereafter, however, numbers declined steadily to a reach a low of 128,757 officers and men in October 1932. Although Liddell Hart was to claim that territorials and members of associations were social climbers,[17] in reality, recruitment of officers whose allowances were so often reduced was especially difficult with a deficiency of 1,055 in 1933 although 350 of these were admittedly chaplains or doctors.

Clearly, the territorials had reached a particularly low point by 1932 and there was a growing recognition on the part of associations that a fundamental revision of the restrictions of the pledge was necessary if they were to justify their continued existence. In 1921 the Geddes committee had recommended a role in anti-aircraft defence and, in fact, the War Office had already resolved to create two territorial anti-aircraft divisions. Lack of funding meant that only low priority was afforded anti-aircraft defence and only air defence brigades were established. This new fear had all but supplanted the traditional fear of invasion. Indeed, the CID's recently established chiefs of staff sub-committee resolved to reduce coastal defence to the minimum commensurate with security in December 1923 and by 1929 had reduced the expected scale of invasion to but 2,000 men. The role of coastal defence, too, was handed over to the territorials in 1932 but answered no more than did air defence the problem of what to do with the large number of territorials not required for either role.

Yet another role – that of aid to the civil power – had been contemplated at least by Churchill when reconstituting the force but this had proved too controversial to sustain not least because it was recognised that what had been another of Haldane's concessions to the labour movement sensibly recognised the damage that might be done to recruiting by outright trade union opposition. Indeed, recruiting for the supplementary reserve was affected by its potential liability for use in strike breaking and the military authorities generally were extremely reluctant to have any military personnel become involved in industrial disturbances. During the October 1919 rail strike, therefore, the army proposed raising a 'citizen guard' in preference even to the Home Office suggestion of a permanent special constabulary. Fortuitously, the strike ended before the citizen or civil guard could be raised. As the army's demobilisation gathered pace, Churchill was still reluctant to give any firm new guarantee that territorials would not be used and in June 1920 the War Office would only respond to the concern expressed by the Dundee association by claiming that existing safeguards were adequate.

A feared triple alliance of rail, transport and miners' unions had not materialised in 1919 but became a possibility once more with the begining of the miners' strike and lock out in April 1921. Little had been done since 1919 and the general opinion of those GOCs consulted by the War Office was that use of territorials should not be contemplated. As a result, on 8 April it was announced that the government intended to call out army reserves and to raise an armed defence force for 90 days' service in support of the police but under army command. However, territorials were specially invited to enlist and the defence force would be based on territorial premises and organised by territorial staff and officers. Moreover, while territorials were obliged to resign in order to join the defence force, it was made clear that they would be immediately readmitted after the expiry of the 90-day period with defence force service counted towards territorial obligation.

There was some restlessness among reservists, who were demo-bilised on 24 May, but the response to the defence force was such that some 40,000 men had been enrolled by 13 April and possibly as many as 80,000 by the time the force was stood down. It is not clear how many territorials did enlist since many in regular employment simply could not serve for three months but in East Lancashire, Derbyshire and Leicestershire between 20 and 30 per cent of territorials joined the defence force with territorials representing between 41 and 50 per cent of the total enlistments.[18] Given the territorials' own dependence upon the unemployed, therefore, it would appear that many in the defence force were also probably unemployed and it can be noted that there was some apprenhension in Birmingham, Nottingham and south Wales that strikers them-selves might be enlisting. Certainly, many associations came to regret accepting non-territorial recruits once the defence force was discharged and there was a considerable increase in the weeding-out rate for 'undesirables'.

While there was no apparent effect on the acceptability or other-wise of the territorials to the labour movement, the War Office was convinced that it had not been appropriate and that the influx of defence force personnel into the territorial army had been damaging. It therefore fully supported legislation in 1923 making permanent the arrangements adopted in 1914 whereby special constabulary could be sworn for 'any immediately apprehended disturbance'[19] and strongly advised against raising another defence force. There was thus War Office approval for the arrangements made during the general strike in May 1926 of calling for volunteers to undertake such duties as driving lorries, raising some 226,000 special con-stables and for the decision on 7 May to raise a 300,000 strong civil constabulary reserve under Home Office control. Once more Churchill, now chancellor of the excchequeur, had wanted to bring out the territorials but this was resisted although, like the defence force, the civil constabulary reserve was again based upon territorial organisation and buildings. This time, however, if the territorials were subsequently embodied, non-territorials would be transferred to the special constabulary to spare associations from an influx of undesirables. Recruiting began on 10 May but was suspended two days later and the strike collapsed on 15 May, by which time possibly only 18,000 men had been enlisted.

In its short existence it would seem that the civil constabulary reserve had drawn the hostility of strikers in London but the War Office was well satisfied with its escape from responsibility for aid to the civil power and attempted to persuade the Home Office to make the civil constabulary reserve permanent. The matter was eventually thrashed out in the autumn of 1932 but never implemented since the territorials, who would have been expected to form the backbone of the civil constabulary reserve, were increasingly required for other purposes and it was agreed in May 1939 that territorials could not be enrolled. Effectively put in abeyance by that decision, the idea of a civil constabulary reserve was finally abandoned in November 1945.

But if aid to the civil power was another role denied the territorials, at the moment that arrangements for the civil constabulary reserve were being reviewed in 1932, the debate on the pledge was gathering momentum. Although effectively re-iterated in 1928, a committee recommended in May 1931 that the pledge be abolished in order to enable the territorials to provide and maintain an immediate reinforcement of eight infantry divisions and a cavalry brigade for any expeditionary force outside Europe. As a former secretary of state for war and long-time president of the West Lancashire association, Lord Derby offered some support when discreetly canvassed but opposition was led in the council of county territorial associations in May 1932 by Scarbrough, the former director-general and equally long serving chairman of the West Riding association. The moment was hardly auspicious in view of the cancellation of camps that summer and it became increasingly clear that no agreement could be reached unless camps were restored for the following year. The War Office could give no such guarantee when financial decisions were not theirs to make and abandoned the attempt.

When improved financial conditions enabled a decision on restoration to be made, the War Office tried again in February 1933 with the suggestion that the pledge would be withdrawn only from new recruits and that the rights of those already serving or subsequently re-engaging would not be affected. Recognising that they could never play a full role unless they abandoned the restrictions on territorial service, associations found this more acceptable and all but five voted for abolition for all territorials on 24 May 1933 although it would appear that many commanding officers were unhappy. However, the War Office decided only to withdraw it from new recruits with effect from 1 May 1934 but then foolishly communicated with an association not represented on the council and gave an assurance that it would honour territorial integrity in that men would only proceed overseas in their own units. Consequently, it had to honour the same guarantee for all and rather than again submit to complicated negotiations settled for a general service obligation and dropped the matter of integrity for another five years.

Nevertheless, a difficult issue had been effectively resolved to the satisfaction of both War Office and territorials and, in many respects, the territorials had turned the corner of military acceptability. This was something of a necessity given the deteriorating security situation. The ten-year rule was abandoned in March 1932 and in November 1933 the Cabinet agreed that a specially constituted defence requirements sub-committee of the CID would evaluate and make recommendations on deficiencies. Regarding the defence of the Low Countries as central to the defence of Britain, the first DRC report in February 1934 therefore recommended the creation of an expeditionary force. This could only be reinforced by territorials and the committee proposed to spend £250,000 per annum for five years on modernising the territorial army. Its third report in November 1935 called for the expenditure of £26 million to enable the territorials to reinforce the expeditionary force in four division contingents at intervals of four, six and eight months after mobilisation.

However, the committee's proposals were not acceptable to the treasury and the chancellor, Neville Chamberlain, was to prove a formidable obstacle to territorial rearmament although he was prepared to see the anti-aircraft role enhanced. Cabinet consideration of the first DRC report, therefore, resulted in just £50,000 per annum being allocated to the territorials and there were only minor adjustments to grants such as the extension of the separation allowances. Even less survived from the third report with agreement in

February 1936 to spend only £250,000 per annum and to re-assess the situation within three years. Duff Cooper, who became secretary of state for war in November 1935, did his best to improve matters, restoring the level of the 1920 bounty in March 1936 by increasing proficiency grant to £3 and adding allowances of 10s 0d and £1 10s 0d for weapons training and extra drills respectively.

In postponing consideration of the preparation of the territorials to reinforce the expeditionary force, the Cabinet had not actually ruled out that role and it was implied that it would be undertaken once the regular army had been suitably re-equipped. In fact, the director-general of munitions production, Sir Harold Brown, seemed to question the assumption that enough reserve industrial capacity did not exist to re-equip the territorials and, accordingly, Duff Cooper pressed for modernisation to begin in December 1936. As a compromise the minister for co-ordination of defence, Sir Thomas Inskip, suggested spreading sufficient equipment across the territorial army to be pooled to equip one or two divisions in an emergency but the matter was not fully resolved when Chamberlain, who opposed the provision of training equipment and would only accept modernisation of four territorial divisions by April 1941, became prime minister in May 1937. Duff Cooper was promptly removed from the War Office and the flamboyant and controversial Leslie Hore-Belisha was installed to enforce the prime minister's belief in a strictly limited continental role for army and territorials alike.

Initially, Hore-Belisha suggested equipping four territorial divisions to reinforce the expeditionary force but this was rejected by the Treasury and priority was given instead to anti-aircraft defence, the two divisions originally proposed in 1921 having now been created from the 47th (2nd London) and 46th (North Midland) divisions. In the major review of policy undertaken by Hore-Belisha and Inskip between December 1937 and February 1938 it was proposed to convert three more divisions into anti-aircraft formations and to use others to maintain public order in the aftermath of air attack. The remainder of the territorial army, which it became clear during 1938 would now also contain three motorised divisions (50th, 55th and 56th) and a new territorial armoured division, would be available to reinforce an expeditionary force designated for employment only in an 'eastern theatre'. But it was the role in home defence that was now the main priority and Hore-Belisha moved to signify the new importance of the territorials by bringing their director-general on to the army council in October 1937 and appointing the Northampton architect and former commanding officer of 162nd (East Midlands) Infantry Brigade, Colonel Sir John Brown, deputy director-general with the rank of major-general.

Churchill, of course, had promised that territorials would achieve higher commands but as late as 1936 only eight out of 50 territorial brigades were commanded by territorials and the old excessive professionalism survived as indicated by the way regulars serving as territorial adjutants received less pay than their counterparts in regular units and also found it difficult to gain entrance to staff college. Under Hore-Belisha, however, some changes were effected with the number of territorial brigade commanders rising to ten by mid 1938 with the assumption that 14 would be appointed by the end of the year. Moreover, in October 1937 he also announced the appointment of Colonel Claude Liardet, a Lloyds insurance broker, as the first territorial divisional commander although the considerable military opposition meant that Liardet did not take over 56th Division until early 1938. The staff college was also opened to territorial candidates as the imperial defence college had been in 1937.

In fact, the more limited army role envisaged by Hore-Belisha and Inskip was determined as much by financial considerations as strategy and this was not materially changed by the increasing pace of events in Europe. None the less, events such as the Anschluss in March 1938 had triggered a new interest in home defence and the territorials generally. In particular, anti-aircraft units drew more and more recruits in 1937 and 1938 with a distinct echo of the old volunteer movement in the way firms, sporting clubs and old boys' associations formed new batteries. Yet, new recruits not only demanded better facilities and equipment but also better instruction, the resulting friction between older and newer territorials being marked by circulation by the War Office in June 1938 of a memorandum submitted by new recruits in a London anti-aircraft battery critical of instructional standards.

At the same time, the new rush of recruits, which was to see total strength reach 200,190 by December 1938, was potentially disruptive of manpower planning and some 12,000 territorials were to be returned to industry in the first three months of the Second World War. It was not until January 1939, however, that the government acted – somewhat unsuccessfully – to give some direction to patriotically minded citizens with the so-called national service appeal, by which time the territorials were clearly competing with the deluge of recruits for the air raid protection service.

The Munich crisis of September 1938 not only further stimulated recruitment of territorials when the treasury agreed to allow units to recruit between 10 and 30 per cent over establishment but also proved their first significant challenge since the end of the Great War. On 26 September the first of some 58,000 territorial anti-aircraft personnel were mobilised and coast defences were also manned, territorials being stood down on 14 October. However, the lack of modern equipment was acute and it transpired that the territorial 1st AA Division covering London had been able to deploy only 126 guns when its establishment was 216 guns. The territorials had also taken between 12 and 48 hours to become operational. Hore-Belisha was compelled to find two regular anti-aircraft regiments to give London immediate protection in the event of hostilities and pressed to explain the deficiencies in equipment. The latter was doubly difficult for, earlier in 1938, the dubious nature of some of Hore-Belisha's claims concerning the modernisation of territorial anti-aircraft equipment had been exposed by Churchill's son-in-law, Duncan Sandys, who was not only an MP but a second lieutenant in one of the London anti-aircraft batteries.

In fact, Munich generally exposed the difficulties under which the territorials were still labouring. In October 1938 no territorial division had full equipment and none could be expected to take the field for at least eight months after mobilisation. The territorial army possessed no tanks, no mortars, no proper mechanised transport and no gas masks. With the French now pressing strongly for a greater commitment to an expeditionary force, limited liability was effectively abandoned and Hore-Belisha proposed in December 1938 that four territorial divisions be prepared to reinforce such an expeditionary force between four and six months after mobilisation and the remainder properly equipped for training purposes. The new policy was accepted by the Cabinet in February 1939 but, by the time Hore-Belisha presented his annual estimates to the Commons on 8 March, he not only announced that the number of territorial anti-aircraft divisions would be raised from five to seven but also that territorials would eventually contribute nine infantry divisions, a motorised division, an armoured division and two cavalry brigades to the planned field force.

On 15 March 1939 German troops occupied what was left of Czechoslovakia to set off a further surge of volunteers, more demands from the French and a growing press campaign for the reintroduction of conscription. With the latter still anathema to the labour and union movement, Chamberlain was desperate for some gesture and with a meeting of the Conservative backbench 1922 committee scheduled for the evening of 28 March, the prime minister met Hore-Belisha that afternoon. Hore-Belisha recommended conscription but, when Chamberlain rejected it, suggested on the spur of the moment that the territorial army be doubled. Hore-Belisha was immediately aware of the practical difficulties but Chamberlain eagerly took up the idea and on the following day it was announced that the peacetime establishment of 130,000 would be made up to wartime establishment of 170,000 then doubled. Two days later came another gesture in the form of a guarantee of support to Poland.

There had been no consultation whatsoever with the government's military advisers over the doubling of the territorials but the crisis did enable the War Office to close the matter of the pledge. In fact, association representatives had agreed on total abolition in June 1938 if surviving pre-1933 territorials were allowed to re-engage on the new terms and if the War Office promised not to use territorials merely as drafts unless absolutely unavoidable. But there had been some confusion over whether abolition could be achieved without a full consultation process extending to individuals affected by the pledge's withdrawal. Now, however, the War Office was prepared to allow a discharge to those not accepting general service terms and on 29 March a specially convened meeting of the council of county territorial associations finally swept away the pledge. It also agreed that all territorials be asked to sign their assent to an agreement already put to the anti-aircraft and coast defence units to come out in an emergency before the territorial army was formally embodied.

The agreement reached with the anti-aircraft units had been regarded as particularly important in case the Germans launched a sudden offensive against the west. However, Chamberlain's belief that territorials could continue their civil employment by day and man anti-aircraft batteries by night for anything up to six months was clearly unrealistic. Ultimately, he was forced to accept a limited measure of conscription so that territorials and reservists could be relieved of the burden as conscripts became trained. Accordingly, on 26 April 1939, conscription was re-introduced with a Reserve and Auxiliary Forces Act (2 & 3 Geo VI c 24) enabling the government to call out territorials and reservists without declaring a state of emergency and a Military Training Act (2 & 3 Geo VI c 25) to call up 250,000 'militiamen' annually from among the nation's 20-year-olds for six months' training to be followed by a three-year territorial liability. Of these, some 80,000 would be prepared to take over anti-aircraft defences, the first batch of approximately 35,000 militiamen being due to arrive at units on 15 July.

Doubling the territorial army alone presented enormous difficulties but these were greatly compounded by the return of conscription and the inevitable competition that ensued for equipment and instructors. Indeed, since government and War Office alike felt it necessary to conciliate public opinion after so suddenly reversing accepted policy by introducing compulsion in peacetime, it was the militia rather than the territorials who were given priority. Indeed, there was not even any precise guidance on how the territorial army should be expanded and individual units followed their own whim. However, although the territorials had yet again failed to become the sole means of expanding the army, there was not the resentment of 1914 due to the fact that militiamen would pass on into the territorials and because the territorials themselves were attracting plenty of recruits, some conceivably motivated by the exemption from the new militia. Some 80,000 recruits had already come in by the end of April 1939 and there was also a rush of older men who were directed towards the national defence corps, which had been formed in 1936 to utilise men between the ages of 45 and 55 to provide guards for vulnerable points.

Before any of the problems had been resolved, of course, war broke out, anti-aircraft and coastal units being called out on 21 August, the national defence corps on the 25 and 26 August, reservists on 31 August and the remainder of the territorials on 1 September 1939. It could be argued that within weeks the territorial army had effectively ceased to exist as a separate entity. The Armed Forces (Conditions of Service) Act (2 & 3 Geo VI c 68) created a single national army with territorial status suspended for the duration and removed any remaining restrictions on liability to general service and to transfer between units while the Military and Air Forces Act (2 & 3 Geo VI c 91) extended all terms of service for the duration.

Following on from the new legislation came an order for territorial officers to remove the 'T's from their uniforms, a move resented by many but, in an echo of the Great War, equally regarded by others as dispensing with a mark of inferiority. There was also much cross-posting to even out strengths with some 'first line' formations posting back younger men to the 'second line' in the manner of August 1914 although there was no official authority to do so. Units were also interchanged, with most territorial divisions receiving one regular battalion per brigade and regular divisions receiving between one and three territorial battalions in return.

Thereafter, territorials had as much or as little training as the rest of the army but, of course, often beginning from a weaker position in terms of equipment, yet being expected to be ready for overseas service in advance of any pre-war calculations. Indeed, three territorial divisions – the 48th (South Midland), 50th (Northumbrian) and 51st (Highland) – arrived in France in January 1940. But, despite the manifold disadvantages, territorial performance in the battles of May to June 1940 was certainly the equal of regular units. The 1st Buckinghamshire Battalion, for example, had undertaken only company and platoon exercises in England with only one battalion, one brigade and one divisional exercise. Once in France with 48th Division, they were mostly employed in digging defences and repairing roads and had to absorb a large draft in April 1940 with only six months' training. There was little practice ammunition available and both officers and men were inexperienced. Yet, their doomed defence of Hazebrouck between 26 and 28 May was described by a German broadcast as 'truly worthy of the highest traditions of the British army'.[20]

Similarly, the Queen Victoria's Rifles had received a large draft of militiamen in place of many pre-war trained territorials when they were detached from 56th Division and landed at Calais. Although a motor cycle battalion, they landed without any transportation and a third were only armed with revolvers with which they had had no practice. There were no bombs for their 2 in mortars and only five rounds for each Boys anti-tank rifle, which few had actually fired. Riflemen had fired only a maximum of 50 rounds in practice and the battalion as a whole had had only once fired a bren gun course. The territorial 1st and 2nd Searchlight Batteries, also involved in the defence of Calais between 22 and 26 May had no infantry training, had never fired an anti-tank rifle and only rarely fired a bren gun.[21]

Yet, these territorials, too, performed valiantly as did elements of 50th Division in the Arras counter-attack on 20–1 May and the 51st Division in its attempt to hold St Valery between 10 and 12 July.

One of the more remarkable performances was that of the 12th, 23rd and 46th divisions landed in April 1940 purely as lines of communication and labour troops. Without equipment or training, these divisions were all second line territorial formations mostly comprising those recruited at the time of doubling or early militiamen. Without artillery, maps, air support or any means of communication other than dispatch riders and with limited ammunition and rations, they were committed to the support of the French on 20 May well south of the perimeter forming around Dunkirk. Although virtually destroyed, in marked contrast to the French troops involved, they were given full credit by German war diaries for their efforts. And, in a report on the battle of France as a whole, the German IV Corps concluded that, while they were less well trained, territorials had proved the equal of British regulars in morale.[22]

After the 1940 campaign there was almost constant change within the army as formations were broken up or reconstituted and innumerable specialists such as infantry support units, paratroops and commandos were also created. Of the 22 territorial divisions existing during the war, nine were broken up: the 12th, 23rd and 66th in June 1940, the 42nd in 1941, the 44th in 1943 and the 38th, 45th, 47th and 59th in 1944. Nevertheless, territorial formations survived and it is interesting to note that territorial loyalties were a major contributory factor in the one large-scale mutiny of British troops during the war at Salerno in Italy on 20 September 1943 when 191 men from the 50th and 51st divisions declined to be used as a reinforcing draft for 46th Division. And, of course, territorials fought in every theatre of war with nine divisions serving in the 1940 campaign, one in Norway, four in North Africa, two in Sicily, one in Burma, eight in north-west Europe and one – the 18th – was lost at Singapore. Territorials won 17 Victoria Crosses.

Indeed, there was nothing logically to determine that a territorial should not be as good a soldier as a regular after an appropriate period of training; territorials were likely to be better trained than the majority of new recruits and better motivated in that they had made a conscious decision in peacetime to commit themselves in advance of their fellow citizens. It was unfortunate, therefore, that regulars so often misunderstood the limitations placed upon territorials by the nature of their civilian employment and gave far too little forethought and consideration to territorial susceptibilities. In turn, territorials failed to recognise that jealously preserved safeguards of integrity were a luxury in face of the enormous demands for manpower in modern total war and that, even in peacetime, an exceptionally difficult financial position compelling the War Office to give priority to the needs of the regular army, might equally legitimately imperil such safeguards.

Notes

1   Sir Charles Harris, 'Kitchener and the Territorials: First Hours at the War Office', *The Times* 28 Aug 1928, p. 13.

2   Viscount Grey of Falloden, *Twenty Five Years* (Hodder & Stoughton, London, 1925), II, p. 68.

3   Peter Simkins, *Kitchener's Army* (Manchester University Press, 1988), p. 46.

4   Clive Hughes, 'Army Recruitment in Gwynedd, 1914–16', Unpub. M.A., Wales, 1983, p. 166.

5   C. R. M. F. Cruttwell, *The War Service of the 1/4th Royal Berkshires (TF)* (Basil Blackwell, Oxford, 1922), p. 99.

6   Beckett, 'Territorial Force' in Beckett and Simpson (eds), *Nation in Arms*, p. 141.

7   General Sir Edward Bethune, 11 Oct 1922, *Journal of the Royal United Services Institution* LXVII, 1922, p. 735.

8   J. Putkowski and J. Sykes, *Shot at Dawn* (Wharncliffe Publishing, Barnsley, 1989), p. 19.

9   Duke of York's Headquarters, Council of County Territorial Association Papers, Minutes of CCTA, 17 Sep 1917.

10   Guildhall Library, Ms 12613,2, Minutes of County of London Territorial Association, 15 Nov 1917.

11   Hampshire RO, 37M69/3, Minutes of Hampshire County Territorial Association, 19 Mar 1915 and 21 May 1915.

12   PRO, WO 161/111; Bucks RO, TAC 7/13, Muster Roll of 3rd Bucks VB, 1916; Guildhall Library, Ms 14521, Muster Roll of 2nd City of London VB, 1916–18.

13   Ministry of Defence Library, Returns of Strength of the Volunteer Force, 1917–18.

14   Imperial War Museum, DS/MISC/17, Yearsley Mss, pp. 99–101.

15   P. Dennis, *The Territorial Army, 1907–1940* (Boydell Press for Royal Historical Society, Woodbridge, 1987), p. 147.

16   Ibid., p. 160.

17   P. Dennis, 'The County Associations and the Territorial Army', *Army Quarterly and Defence Journal* 109, 2, 1979, pp. 210–19.

18   Dennis, *Territorial Army*, p. 74.

19   K. Jeffery & P. Hennessy, *States of Emergency* (Routledge & Kegan Paul, London, 1983), p. 75.

20   J. E. H. Neville (ed), *The Oxford and Buckinghamshire Light Infantry War Chronicle* (Gale & Polden, Aldershot, 1949), I, p. 149.

21   A. Neave, *The Flames of Calais* (Hodder & Stoughton, London, 1972).

22   D. Edgar, *The Day of Reckoning* (John Clare Books, London, 1983); B. Karslake, *1940: The Last Act* (Leo Cooper, London, 1979).

9

Last flourish (1940–1945)

The integration of existing auxiliary forces into a single national army in September 1939 for the first time since the establishment of the militia in the mid sixteenth century left the county territorial associations with no real function beyond welfare. Yet, within a relatively short time, a new threat of invasion was to result in the associations having to administer a new auxiliary force – the local defence volunteers or, as they were soon renamed, the home guard. Much fixes the home guard in a particular time and place but, of course, it was just one more manifestation of the amateur military tradition. And, though much has changed since the end of the Second World War, that tradition still endures.

In February 1937 it had been concluded that full-scale invasion was an unlikely possibility although raids were still conceivable. For all its emphasis on home defence Chamberlain's policy of limited liability had not changed this assessment and it also appeared to be borne out by the first months of war. Thus, although a former director-general of the territorial army, General Sir Walter Kirke, had been appointed CinC of home forces on 3 September 1939, his function was to train the new army and facilitate its dispatch to reinforce the expeditionary force in France. Churchill, who had been recalled to the Admiralty, voiced some fears in October and, despite the belief of the chiefs of staff that even raids were unlikely, a reluctant Kirke was directed to prepare a defence scheme. The so-called 'Julius Caesar' plan of November 1939 assumed up to 4,000 German paratroops and 15,000 glider or air transported troops might be employed in support of an amphibious operation of between 15,000 and 30,000 men aimed at Harwich or the Humber.

Many of those troops available to Kirke were either poorly

equipped or under-trained and even those, mainly first line, territorial divisions judged to be fit for the field were already earmarked for France. None the less, it was estimated that only seven divisions would be required and there were currently 14 in Britain in various stages of readiness. It later transpired that November was the very month in which the German navy initiated some preliminary studies of invasion but disagreements between the German armed forces surfaced almost immediately and the studies were shelved in January 1940.

The possibility of mounting an invasion was not revived within German planning circles until 21 May and it was not until 16 July 1940 that Hitler's directive No. 16 effectively established the preconditions necessary for attempting what was now to be known as Operation Sealion, not least the elimination of the Royal Air Force. As is obvious, the preconditions were never to be achieved and the initial decision to attempt the invasion on 15 September was first postponed to 21 September and then finally postponed until 1941 on 12 October. Some preparations were again ordered in the spring of 1941 to cover those for the German invasion of Russia and there is some evidence that a Sealion II was contemplated in July 1941 but that September the required planning notice was set at eight months and on 2 March 1942 at 12 months.

With the benefit of hindsight, the deliberations within the German high command on whether an invasion should be launched on a 'broad' or a 'narrow' front may appear academic, the final version envisaging the landing of some 50,000 men in a first assault by nine divisions between Folkestone and Brighton. Nevertheless, it must be recognised that, while all had depended upon Hitler's intentions, there was a capability of launching the attempt on ten days' notice in late September albeit at reduced strength and at great hazard. Yet faced with that possibility of invasion, which first became apparent when the Germans compounded pre-war theories concerning the effectiveness of air and naval power for interdiction by successfully invading Norway on 9 April 1940, British military planners were still initially complacent. Thus, on 10 May 1940, the chiefs of staff concluded that, although raids might now be more likely, invasion was still not 'a practicable operation of war and would not be attempted'.[1] It was the same day, of course, that the German offensive opened in the west with further extensive use of the paratroops who had proved so effective in Norway and it was that specific threat which led to the creation of the new auxiliaries.

Rather as in the case of the rifle volunteers, there were many who claimed credit for the establishment of the local defence volunteers and, in fact, just as in 1914, various proposals were forwarded to the authorities for the creation of new auxiliary military bodies prior to summer of 1940. Indeed, when raising the matter of invasion Churchill himself had suggested on 7 October 1939 a 500,000 strong 'home guard' of men over the age of 40. It would also appear that some preliminary planning based on the example of the volunteer training corps was begun in the adjutant-general's department of the War Office in the following month after an approach to the under-secretary of state by the lord lieutenant of Essex, who had had representations from the legion of frontiersmen. At least one unofficial quasi-military group, Lady Helena Gleichen's 'Much Marcle Watchers' near Ross on Wye, was active by March 1940. Nevertheless, the immediate impetus came from the concern voiced by the air ministry on 10 May at the effectiveness of paratroops in Norway and the discussion of the most appropriate means of finding additional manpower for searchlight detachments.

Over the next three days agreement was reached within the War Office on the creation of the local defence volunteers. It was arranged that Kirke, who had advocated using auxiliaries to undertake static guard duties and free regulars, would broadcast to the nation on the evening of 14 May. In the event, it was the new secretary of state for war in the Churchill coalition, Anthony Eden, who went on the air following the BBC 9 p.m. news. As outlined by Eden, any man aged between 17 and 65 with a knowledge of firearms and 'capable of free movement' could register with the police for the LDV, the very name of which 'describes its duties in three words'.[2] The response, of course, was considerable with many men hastening to their local police station even before Eden had finished speaking. It is claimed that there were 1,000 registrations in Chelmsford that same evening but there were certainly at least 1,000 in Kent by 17 May and 3,584 in Buckinghamshire by 29 May. In all, there may well have been approaching 400,000 LDV in the country as a whole by the end of May and Kirke's successor, General Sir Edmund Ironside, gave the figure of 471,000 men on 10 June 1940.

It is generally accepted that the strength of the home guard, a title introduced by Churchill against the opposition of Eden and announced officially on 23 July, had reached approximately

1,750,000 by March 1941. The progressive call-up of younger men into the army led to a drop in home guard strength to 1,394,546 by February 1942. However, the introduction of compulsion for the home guard itself then materially revived the force and a new ceiling was set at 1,810,000 men in June 1942. Peak strength in March 1943 was 1,793,000 and in September 1944 the home guard was still 1,727,095 strong.

The initial role as outlined by the War Office on 22 May was a purely limited and static one in the event of parachute assault with an emphasis upon observation, hence the early epithet of 'look, duck and vanish', but also entailing the blocking of roads and the guarding of perceived vulnerable points. Kirke, whose 'Julius Caesar' plan had been much disrupted by the subsequent dispatch of units to France, had always envisaged a mobile role for regulars at his disposal but Ironside abandoned this on 25 June in favour of a coastal 'crust' of mostly second line territorial divisions backed by what became known as a 'GHQ Line' of some 2,500 pillboxes. Many of the latter were to be manned by the LDV whom Ironside believed capable of a more active role in denying mobility to an invader but there was considerable doubt as to the wisdom of placing mobile reserves well to the rear of the GHQ Line and he was replaced by General Sir Alan Brooke on 20 July 1940.

Brooke, who also came to believe that the home guard was capable of a wider role, placed the emphasis on holding the coast in greater strength with mobile reserves much closer to the beaches in anticipation of a likely invasion force of upwards of 200,000 men. The return of the expeditionary force from Dunkirk by 2 June and of other forces sent to France by 22 June had materially improved the manpower situation, of course, and even excluding the LDV and allied contingents some 1.3 million men were theoretically available. In reality, only approximately half were sufficiently trained to act as a field army and the losses of equipment in France had been considerable, necessitating the breaking up of territorial and other divisions in June and July. Not surprisingly, only 94,000 rifles had been made available for the LDV by 1 June and units were left to improvise. On 28 May 1940, for example, the 286 men of what was to become C Company of the 1st Battalion, Buckinghamshire Home Guard possessed 27 .303 in rifles, seven 2.2 in rifles and 50 shotguns while what was to become D Company of the same battalion managed to acquire the manufacturer's last 23 cartridges for a 500 bore elephant gun. In June the entire battalion received just 75 rifles, of which 30 were allocated to the town of Aylesbury and three to each of 15 villages.

None the less, the equipment situation steadily improved. To use the example of A Company of the 4th Battalion in Buckinghamshire, 200 rifles were received in August 1940 to be followed by four Browning automatic rifles in September, two Lewis guns in February 1941, 17 Thompson sub-machine guns and two Northover projectors in August 1941, sten guns in July 1942 and a Blacker Bombard in February 1943. Similarly, eight denim suits arrived in May 1940 and battledress in January 1941 although enough was not issued for all recruits until 1944. So-called pikes were issued to the home guard in the autumn of 1941 but were received with such antipathy that few appear to have been actually distributed, echoing the reception of pikes by volunteers in 1803.

Undoubtedly the greatest period of risk was that in which the LDV and home guard were least well equipped and organised but there was a commendable if occasionally over-enthusiastic response to the notorious invasion scare of 7 September 1940 when, as a result of the lack of any intermediate stage of alert, the codeword 'Cromwell' was issued erroneously in many areas and church bells rung to summon defenders. Brooke immediately instituted new procedures and, although the new interim stage of 'Stand To' was in force on 22–3 September this did not involve the home guard. Such a high alert stage never again proved necessary, winter stand down being authorised on 27 October 1940.

Hitler's subsequent invasion of Russia made an attempt on Britain far less likely and by November 1941 it was generally accepted that more advanced aerial reconnaissance would provide sufficient warning of any renewed German interest. Various 'anti-tank islands' and 'centres of resistance' were still identified in many local defence plans until the possibility of armoured attack was ruled out in May 1942. Parachute attack on airfields, vulnerable points and communications remained a possibility but by November 1943 home guard operational instructions envisaged only armed sabotage. With the approach of 'D Day', plans were updated against the possibility of suicidal spoiling raids with night guards on vulnerable points and inlying battle platoons at instant readiness but the successful allied advance from the Normandy bridgehead finally eradicated all risk. Many of the invasion committees, which like the local emergency committees of the Great War had prepared plans to safeguard essential supplies, had ceased to function by June 1943. The home guard itself was stood down on 31 December 1944.

Presumably because it has been the most recent of the wartime auxiliary forces, the home guard has attracted continuing popular attention. One such current image is that summed up by the title of the BBC television series, 'Dad's Army', first broadcast in 1969. To a certain extent, of course, 'Dad's Army' has some validity in terms of the age and previous military experience of many of those who enlisted in the local defence volunteers in May 1940 since the specified upper age limit of 65 was widely ignored but it is clear that there were many variations. George Orwell, for example, recorded in his diary for 21 June 1940 that only three or four out of the 60 men in his platoon in St John's Wood were not ex-servicemen while John Brophy's supporting text to illustrations by Eric Kennington in *Britain's Home Guard* published in 1945 claimed that up to 75 per cent of the original force were ex-servicemen.[3]

However, a history of the 20th (Sevenoaks) Battalion in Kent gives a figure of 45 per cent ex-servicemen while figures available for some Buckinghamshire units reveal an even smaller percentage. The Stoke Mandeville platoon of D Company, 1st Battalion reported only 23 per cent ex-servicemen on 25 May 1940 although a further 70 per cent had some knowledge of firearms. Similarly, D Company of the 4th Battalion centred on Marlow had 142 ex-servicemen and 59 with some knowledge of firearms but 57 with no knowledge at all. A random sample of 900 men who enlisted in Buckinghamhire in 1940 and 1941 yields only 35.8 per cent with previous military experience and an average age of 35 years.[4] Thus, while it can be accepted that there were many older veterans in the home guard – the oldest is generally recorded as an 80-year-old in Perthshire who had seen service in Egypt in 1884 – it should not be supposed that they necessarily represented the majority.

As early as August 1941 Orwell noted the steady disappearance of the under-40s called up into the army. Indeed, of 180,000 men who departed from the home guard in the course of that year, 60 per cent were conscripted into the regular forces. But this did not increase the preponderance of older veterans for the loss of men of serviceable age was compensated for by an influx of boys of 17. Moreover, under the terms of the National Service (no. 2) Act of November 1941, not only was compulsion introduced to the home guard but also a firm age restriction with effect from 16 February 1942, although a handful of prominent individuals were allowed to continue to serve beyond the retirement age. In fact, all existing personnel were given the opportunity of resigning by the latter date rather than accepting the new conditions even if those under 51 might find themselves redirected into the home guard. In practice, however, it would appear that resignations were restricted to those over 65.

Compulsory directions into and compulsory duties for the home guard were not suspended until 16 September 1944 and from April 1943 there was also provision for directing so-called 'nominated women' between the ages of 18 and 65 into supporting clerical, driving and catering roles. In a sense this only regulated an unofficial practice that had continued since 1940, Dr Edith Summerskill having subsequently sponsored 'women's home defence' in May 1941, and nominated women were actually volunteers whose service did not exempt them from direction into other full or part-time occupations. It had been hoped to attract up to 80,000 women into these roles but by 1944 there were only approximately 32,000 serving. Nevertheless, women's support for or opposition to the force's demands on men was as crucial to efficiency as it had been for other auxiliaries in the past.

An effective age limit of 40 was also introduced for those serving in 3.7 in and 4.5 in anti-aircraft batteries, the manning of which by home guard had begun in April 1942. The net result was a progressive erosion of older personnel with previous military experience. A second sample of 600 Bucks Home Guard enlisted from 1942 to 1944 indicates only 15 per cent with previous military experience and an average age of 32.6 years. In Kent by 1943 just 7 per cent had previous military experience, reflecting the national average calculated for the home guard as a whole at the same time that the average age had reached under 30.[5]

Further to the 'Dad's Army' image it is certainly also the case that the more absurd aspects of the local defence volunteers and home guard were reflected in the contemporary treatment of the force by those whom one 1945 account characterised as the 'cartoonists, humourists and iconoclasts of to-day'.[6] 'Look, duck and vanish' and similar epithets such as 'last desperate venture' and 'long dentured veterans' were supplemented by the pages of *Punch* and the monologues of Robb Wilton. There is some evidence that such ridicule was resented but it was no more and no less than that endured by other auxiliaries in the past. Moreover, many of the relentlessly anecdotal unit histories published immediately after the war also consciously highlighted the more farcical aspects of home guard service. But if, in some respects, as has been suggested, the home guard was a wartime substitute for cricket, golf and amateur dramatics,[7] it should not be forgotten that in the summer of 1940 there seemed every prospect that it might have to fight in earnest.

Yet there was another contemporary image of the LDV and home guard – that of a 'people's militia'. This is most readily associated with literary figures of radical persuasion and similarly called to mind by the involvement of Spanish civil war veterans in home guard training. However, it was also consciously reflected in official policy and publications and had some wider currency among many home guardsmen. One such literary figure was J. B. Priestley and it is significant that it was in the context of his first duties with the local defence volunteers that he introduced in the third of his radio 'postscripts', broadcast on 16 June 1940, the concept of a 'sense of community' that was to provide an underlying theme for the series as a whole. Another literary recruit, of course, was George Orwell, who believed that, by branding the home guard as a fascist body, many on the political left had failed to recognise the opportunity presented by its 'democratic' nature. While he did not deny the element of 'blimpocracy' that existed among the home guard's officers and the political naivety among many of its working-class rank and file, Orwell still detected a covert politicised struggle over such issues as organisation, discipline and tactics and he anticipated that a 'million British working men' would not lightly surrender the rifles now placed in their possession.[8]

Even more radical attitudes were held by other former veterans or war correspondents who had been intimately connected with republican forces in Spain and who now offered their services to the home guard. Based at his training school at Burwash in Sussex John Langdon-Davies wrote a weekly home guard column for the *Sunday Pictorial* and lectured to over a hundred different units in the course of 1940, preaching class equality and future social reconstruction and viewing the home guard as playing a major role in 'building up a new idea of social life'.[9] An even better known home guard training school was that established at Osterley Park, Middlesex by Tom Wintringham in July 1940 with the financial backing of the radically

minded proprietor of *Picture Post*, Edward Hulton. A former com-
mander of the British battalion of the International Brigade,
Wintringham was joined at Osterley by another civil war veteran,
Hugh Slater, who had acted as chief of staff to the republican XV
Brigade.

The idea for the school had stemmed from the response to
Wintringham's articles on guerrilla warfare, which appeared in
Picture Post and the *Daily Mail* in May and June 1940. Running
through all Wintringham's wartime writings was the theme of
'people's war' as the only appropriate counter to 'totalitarian war'. It
was Wintringham above all who saw the home guard as a 'people's
army' and, in much the same way that Ranelagh had advocated a
separate volunteer army in the 1860s, he foresaw a four million
strong citizen army governed by its own separate council. As in
Langdon-Davies's work, there was the same constant allusion to the
example of the Spanish republican militias and it is not perhaps
surprising that what amounted to a semi-official history of the home
guard, Charles Graves's *The Home Guard of Britain* published in
1943, should refer to Wintringham and Hulton as seeming 'inclined
to make a political issue of their admirable enterprise'.[10] Certainly,
there was some tension before the War Office officially took over
Osterley Park in September 1940. However, the lectures delivered by
Wintringham and his staff were officially published in August 1940
and books by Wintringham, Langdon-Davies and Slater, while
unofficial, were all allowable against expenditure from training
grants.

But such hopes of a political awakening could not have been
realistically entertained by radicals had it not been for the fact that it
was also seemingly endorsed by the authorities. Although partly
dictated both by reason of economy and by the haste with which the
force had been organised in the first place, early official policy tended
to encourage an overtly democratic character even if volunteers
initially required the endorsement of two householders or a magistrate in order to be accepted for registration by the police. Army
council instruction 924 of 15 August 1940, which replaced ACI 653
establishing the force under the order-in-council of 17 May 1940
and amounted to the charter of the home guard, specifically stated
that it was 'a citizen force organised on the principles of equality of
service and status. There is, accordingly no system of ranks, though
there are appointments suitably graded for the commanders of

various formations.'[11] The titles given to the ranks thus ranged from volunteer to zone commander though no home guard appointment was actually regarded as carrying a military status above that of army private.

Nor did home guard appointments confer any disciplinary powers other than the right to discharge a man who, in any case, had the ability to resign on 14 days' notice under the 'housemaids clause', reflecting a standard auxiliary forces' right since the 1804 legislation. Churchill was concerned about home guard status, not least in the light of German threats to regard such amateurs as mere *francs tireurs* unprotected by the laws of war, and instituted a War Office study in September 1940. However, it is significant that even when the under-secretary of state for war, Sir Edward Grigg, announced on 6 November 1940 that the King's commission would be extended to the officers of the home guard – they were eventually commissioned retrospectively on 12 February 1941 – he was careful to stress that there would still be no power of summary punishment since informality 'breathes the spirit of the old trained bands, and we do not wish to impair that democratic and very British spirit in any way'.

Thirteen days later, in discussing the appointment of selection boards, Grigg remarked that the introduction of commissioned ranks would not destroy the character of the home guard since no 'political, business nor social affiliations are to be regarded as conducing in themselves to fitness for command'.[12] Moreover, commissions were only notified in command orders and did not appear in the *London Gazette* and all home guard officers had to revert to the rank of private before quitting the force. Later, those attaining the age of 65 were able to retire in their commissioned rank but were still not allowed to carry it into civil life. The lowest rank of volunteer was not retitled private until February 1942.

Similarly, when addressing the demand from some quarters for first class rail travel for home guard officers in September 1941 – the point had been made that battalion commanders might find themselves travelling third class to an exercise while regular adjutants, who were appointed from September 1940, went first class – Grigg again stressed the democratic character of the force and argued that, since commissions were only granted to 'fix responsibility' for command, no financial privileges should be given any group. While this decision smacked of a somewhat cynical financial expediency, there is no doubt that many other official pronouncements also played consciously or unconsciously on the supposed democratic nature of the force. Ironside, for example, in a rather patronising address to LDV commanders on 5 June 1940 had urged them to avoid 'what I shall call, County Council rows' in the interests of national defence. The director-general of the home guard appointed in September 1940, Lieutenant-General T. R. Eastwood, similarly told two visiting representatives from the Massachusetts committee of public safety in March 1941 that the force had resulted in 'an extraordinary getting together of all classes creating a sympathetic understanding of how the other fellow lives and the realisation of the good there is in each other regardless of class'.[13]

The positive democratic image was also reflected in film, two home guard 'members' portrayed by Percy Walsh and Bernard Miles being made the mouthpiece for a discussion on post-war reconstruction in one of the most memorable of the wartime shorts by the ministry of information, the Boulting brothers' 1941 production, 'The Dawn Guard'. Only the fourth such short officially classified under the 'government and citizenship' heading, the film had Miles's character concluding with a rousing vision of a future of full employment and social harmony arising from a war in which 'we found out . . . as how we were all neighbours, and we ain't going to forget it when it's all over'.[14]

The ideal of the home guard as an instrument of democracy and social reconstruction runs in similar vein through wartime publications of an official or semi-official nature. Brophy's *Britain's Home Guard*, for example, was provided with a foreword by the secretary of state for war, Sir James Grigg, dated 6 November 1944, which referred to the home guard as 'an outward and visible sign of an inward unity and brotherhood without distinction of class or calling . . . to be carried forward into the future . . .'. Brophy himself penned somewhat purple passages on regeneration and social harmony while both the illustrated ministry of information pamphlet, *The Home Guard of Britain* published in September 1943, and A. G. Street's *From Dusk till Dawn*, published in 1943 and mixing autobiographical fact with semi-fictional descriptions of the LDV and home guard in the Wiltshire village of 'Sedgebury Wallop', had underlying themes of social unity.[15]

There is also evidence from battalion histories and personal accounts that many ordinary members of the home guard took just such a view of the character of the force as did a Priestley, Wintringham or Brophy. Both the historians of the 5th (Bideford) and 10th (Torbay) Battalions in Devon chose to emphasise the democratic nature of the home guard while the history of the 44th (London Transport) Battalion carefully listed the civil occupations of all its wartime officers including six drivers and four conductors to demonstrate that there had been no favouritism according to status for the battalion 'prided itself on being thoroughly democratic and, in fact, was so'. The battalion's officers had been elected and there are similar examples at Hailsham in Sussex and at Hauxton in Cambridgeshire, where there was also a democratic vote in 1940 on whether or not to man night observation posts on a shift basis. The 11th Denbighshire Battalion raised from ministry of food personnel evacuated to Colwyn Bay apparently contained a significant faction who wanted the unit to resemble the 'Red Army in 1917' and its historian certainly personally compared the home guard with the republican 'people's army', regretting the passing of a force that had also broken barriers between different generations.[16]

But while there were such examples of a democratic spirit flowing through the home guard, it must be noted that there was also Orwell's 'blimpocracy'. Indeed, Orwell remarked that it was a people's army officered by blimps, the lack of financial assistance – ACI 653 had specified a miserly officers' travelling allowance of between 2*d* and 3*d* a mile depending upon vehicle – ensuring that only the wealthy could sustain the expense of becoming officers. Not surprisingly, Langdon-Davies also subscribed to such views but Basil Liddell Hart and A G Street equally regarded the process of officer selection as near feudal.

Initially, area commanders were nominated by lords lieutenant and although appointments were subject to ratification, they had considerable latitude. Lady Gleichen's unit had more than a hint of a bygone age and Sir Adrian Baillie MP formed a unit from his tenants at Leeds Castle in Kent. There was at least one case of a man in Devon complaining that he had been excluded on social grounds and a Labour MP claimed in November 1940 that there had been instances of men excluded for belonging to 'unpopular political parties'.[17] Another persistent complaint was that, while many former regulars of rank and eminence were ready to serve in the ranks as volunteers, some persisted in doing so while wearing their old uniforms. There is little doubt that this caused particular resentment until the denim suits originally promised by the War Office on 15 May 1940 gradually found their way to units.

It was also the case that former high ranking officers might take exception to the democratic spirit being fostered. General Sir Hubert Gough, for example, who became a zone commander in Chelsea at the age of 70 and was publicly criticised by Wintringham, had little time for notions of equality. Perhaps an even wider anti-democratic trait commonly experienced in the first few months was the officiousness with which many men undertook road block duties and, there were a number of fatalities caused by trigger-happy local defence volunteers. None the less, there is little doubt that the force could not have been organised so quickly without the assistance of the traditional leaders of the community, who gave generously of their money and their privately owned weapons. It was also the case, as Gough maintained, that most men welcomed traditional drill and discipline since they wished above all to be treated as real soldiers. Certainly, the inevitable result of the growth of organisation was attendant bureaucracy and regulation, one commanding officer judging the absurd lengths the latter reached by his receipt of a special instruction in April 1942 concerning the burial of 'mohammedan' personnel.

It had not been the original intention of the War Office to revive the functions of the county territorial associations but these were pressed into service to assist the administration of the force on 30 May 1940 under the direction of Major-General Sir John Brown. From 24 June 1940 associations were permitted to authorise the appointment of administrative assistants for battalion strength formations with a grant of £300 per annum for such purposes while the same instruction also provided for a capitation grant to the associations of £1 per man per annum. Home guard units were affiliated to county regiments on 3 August 1940 and, of course, Eastwood was then appointed as director-general and later inspector-general. The clearest change in the character of the home guard, however, was the introduction of compulsion in February 1942 for this inevitably militated against the democratic image.

There were many who believed that the special 'character' of the home guard would be destroyed by compulsion. Indeed, Eastwood's successor, Major-General the Viscount Bridgeman, and Sir Edward Grigg, both opposed any extension of compulsion to the home guard and, initially, it was intended to apply it only in those areas where manpower deficiencies were greatest. A number of command districts did not believe it necessary and the lack of equipment also suggested that wholesale compulsion was impracticable but the general opposition to a partial application of compulsion among the home guard led to the army council concluding on 26 March 1942 that it must be introduced uniformly.

Rather as had happened when 'tribunal men ' had arrived in the volunteer training corps in 1916, various difficulties and anomalies arose from the appearance of the 'directed men' in the home guard. One source of dispute was that not all local appeals boards chose to exercise powers of direction. In Cornwall the boards were accused of excessive leniency towards anyone claiming to be a farmer and it has been calculated that, of the 946,000 directions between January 1942 and September 1944, only about 50 per cent may actually have been enforced.[18] However, the process was not all one way since an official circular issued in January 1943 reminded commanding officers that home guard duties were only undertaken in a man's spare time and that they should respect the difficulties of those working long hours: in November another circular defined the latter as being 60 hours a week inclusive of overtime but exclusive of meal breaks and travelling. Yet another circular in May 1943 noted that commanding officers were also using their right to refuse directed men to a much greater extent than had been envisaged when the authority was granted.

Nevertheless, there was justified criticism of the application of direction to anti-aircraft batteries since the ministry of labour and national service persisted in allocating shift workers who had a ready excuse of night work for 'dodging the column'. The situation was hardly improved when the deficiencies in manpower available for anti-aircraft batteries of all kinds, which amounted to 20,941 men in August 1943, led to ordinary general service battalions being required to fill quotas for anti-aircraft service. Battalions often responded by sending their worst men while others complained bitterly that any loss of manpower had a detrimental effect upon their efficiency. The solution was to establish from January 1944 local home guard manpower boards to adjudicate on conflicting demands.

Again as had happened with the volunteer training corps, compulsion also introduced the possibility of prosecution for those unwilling to fulfil their duties. Originally, the War Office had laid down a suggested duty of ten hours per week in May 1940 and, in practice, many men had done far more. With compulsion those unwilling to undertake a maximum of 48 hours' duty in a four-week period faced a £10 fine or a month's imprisonment. There had been pressure to demand 60 hours' duty but this was rejected since 48 hours was the standard for the civil defence services and firewatching. Although the reduced requirement was not excessive, battalions inevitably had to face the prospect of mounting prosecutions but, even though only the most persistent offenders could be treated in this way, there was a steady stream of such cases.

There were often complaints that agricultural workers were not fulfilling their duties in the home guard and there were undeniable problems in any case with widely scattered units such as the 4th Warwickshire Battalion, 10th Westmorland (Appleby) Battalion or Rutland generally, where one battalion covered 47 separate towns and villages spread over 287 square miles. However, it is perhaps symptomatic that the general impression was that the problem was essentially that of industrial workers for yet another popular image of the home guard was that it was very much a force of the countryside. Thus, many contemporary accounts were redolent with a rustic imagery of oak, elm, cow-byres and village cricket grounds that paid only lip service to the realities of a force largely urban and industrial in its social composition. The pastoral symbolism even extended to the radicals, Priestley's 'postcript' broadcast on 16 June conjuring up a vision of 'one of those rich chapters of Thomas Hardy's fiction in which his rustics meet in the gathering darkness on some Wessex hillside' and one in which there was a continuity with those who had previously kept 'watch and ward over the sleeping English hills and fields and homesteads'.[19]

It was true that the initial priority was to organise and arm rural units because the danger from parachute assault was greatest in those areas where the population was most dispersed. However, from the very beginning industrial concerns made a considerable contribution to the growth of a voluntary movement, just as they had done in the 1790s or the 1860s. Some 1,800 employees of the Liverpool Corporation passenger transport services had enlisted within seven days in May 1940 while 4,000 employees from 36 different industrial firms in East and West Ham quickly formed a company of the 13th City of London Battalion. ICI enlisted 5,000 of their employees within days. Composite industrial battalions included the 6th Birmingham (Factories) Battalion and 9th and 10th Birmingham (Public Utilities) Battalions while those recruited from individual enterprises included the 3rd Surrey (Southern Railway) Battalion, 40th County of London (Gas, Light and Coke Company) Battalion, 10th Surrey (Vickers Armstrong) Battalion and 19th City of London (South Suburban Gas Company) Battalion. Elsewhere companies in battalions were frequently found from a particular firm such as Daimler at Coventry, Lockheed at Leamington, A. V. Roe at Manchester, Singer on Clydebank, Vosper at Cosham and Marconi at Chelmsford.

In reality, then, there was considerable dependence upon industry and urban areas within the home guard and, as noted by Orwell in 1941, the working class predominated among the rank and file. The introduction of compulsion could only enhance the process. Occupations were not required to be stated on home guard enlistment forms until 1942 and, therefore, there is no ready comparison that can be made but 50.6 per cent of the sample of 600 Buckinghamshire home guard personnel between 1942 and 1944 referred to earlier were skilled industrial manual workers. Unskilled industrial workers comprised 14.5 per cent of the sample and were the next largest category followed by professional men (9.4 per cent) and unskilled agricultural workers (7.7 per cent).

The reliance upon industry did bring difficulties even if urban units invariably had greater access to convenient premises and were able to organise more social entertainments. One problem was that many of the original factory units were not incorporated into local battalions initially but allowed to remain separate with the result that large numbers of men were not fully utilised in local defence plans: their only concern was the defence of their own premises. Similarly, the public utility battalions clearly faced something of a conflict of interests in the event of an emergency and were generally organised on a regional basis unsuited to any active participation in local defence. It was not long before most factory units were integrated into local defence schemes but those factories and airfields coming under the management of the ministry of aircraft production not only remained exempt but were also allowed separate light anti-aircraft batteries in 1942.

In addition, there were always potential problems in accommodating home guard duties and essential war production and so-called 'whole-timers' were most likely to be the unemployed. ACI 924 of 15

August 1940 authorised a subsistence allowance of 1s 6d for five hours' continuous duty and 3s 0d for ten hours' continuous duty: in 1942 it was amended with 3s 0d now paid for eight hours' duty and 4s 6d for over 15 hours' duty. Initially, the allowance was only to be paid in exceptional circumstances where a man could not normally provide his own food but it appears to have been first introduced in Thanet in order to entice those unemployed through the collapse of the seasonal holiday trade to remain in the area and undertake home guard duties in an area where numbers were deemed essential. In anti-aircraft batteries official practice was to arrange shifts in such a way that a man did duty on only one night in eight.

Yet, despite all the potential problems, what has been described as the 'only truly spontaneous grouping of the people' during the Second World War[20] achieved much. Initially confined to a limited and static role, the home guard did become an increasingly important component of the forces available for home defence and, in the run up to the allied invasion of Normandy in June 1944, not only mounted guard against last ditch German raids on vulnerable points as already described but also secured routes to embarkation ports. Like the volunteer training corps, home guard general service companies also took on full-time duties in coastal counties on a rota basis from the autumn of 1943 onwards. Initially deploying horsed patrols in some areas, the home guard formed motor transport companies from May 1941 and manned specialist units, 145,000 men serving in varying kinds of anti-aircraft batteries and 7,000 in coastal artillery batteries. An additional 7,000 men in bomb disposal squads were incorporated in the home guard in September 1942 while the force as a whole did invaluable service in assisting civil defence services during both the 'blitz' and the later V weapon offensives.

The home guard also provided cover for the 'auxiliary units' established in July 1940 to organise guerrilla warfare against the Germans in the event of a successful invasion. That invasion never came, of course, but the home guard did differ from some earlier auxiliary forces in sustaining casualties from enemy action, 1,206 being killed or dying from injuries received whilst on duty with a further 557 injured. While some casualties were the result of accidents on ranges, the great majority resulted from enemy aerial attack and the home guard received 137 gallantry awards including two George Crosses. It was also home guard officers from the 3rd Renfrew Battalion who arrested Rudolf Hess in May 1941.

Much has already been said to indicate that the home guard fell fully into the amateur military tradition and, in fact, this was not lost on contemporary writers such as Priestley, Wintringham and Brophy although their historical analogies were invariably inappropriate. The home guard did have some unique characteristics but it was not as unique as contemporaries apparently believed. Nevertheless, it is the last example of the ad hoc wartime manifestations of the amateur military tradition to date. The post-1945 development of the territorial army with its constant changes and amalgamations of units extinguishing many links with the past must await its own historian but it is appropriate to outline it briefly here.

Reconstituted in March 1947, the territorials essentially remained within the single army concept of 1939 since, in view of the army's need for manpower to meet both occupation commitments and the growing threat of insurgency in colonial and dependent territories, conscription was retained in the form of national service into which territorials were fully integrated. Under the National Service Act of 1947 national servicemen initially served 18 months with the colours and four years in the territorials, this being changed in 1950 to two years with the colours and three years in the territorials. In effect, however, the territorials were deprived of the 17–20 age group while national servicemen were only liable to 60 days' training in their three years inclusive of the 15-day annual camp. True volunteers were liable to 30 hours a year in addition to camp with a bounty offered for an additional 30 hours' training. Moreover, post-war conditions were very different from those of the inter-war years since employment was fuller and most families could afford a summer holiday, the acquiesence of women in territorial commitments remaining important. As a result, the territorials became dependent upon the national servicemen to maintain strength, conscripts representing over 60 per cent of the territorials by 1960.

National service was phased out from 1960 with the last conscript leaving the army in May 1963 and the territorials in 1966. But by this time manpower was less in demand as technology improved and the territorial role appeared inappropriate to the short war scenarios of a missile age. After 1955 only two of the territorials' ten infantry divisions were actually earmarked as reinforcements for NATO in defence of western Europe while territorial anti-aircraft units were disbanded in 1955 and coastal artillery units in 1956. One curious anomaly was the revival of the home guard during the Korean War under the provisions of the Home Guard Act of April 1951 (15 Geo VI c 8). It was intended to raise 170,000 men in approximately 1,000 cadre units on the basis of a two-year term of enlistment and a liability of 15 hours' training every three months. However, only 300 cadres of 100 men each were raised in November 1952 and these were first reduced in 1955 and then disbanded in August 1957.

The lowest point of post-war territorial fortunes was reached between 1965 and 1968. Civil defence was placed on a care and maintenance basis and county territorial associations just survived extinction, a total of 14 larger regional groupings only being retained. Following the controversial review of the territorial role by General Sir John Hackett and Major-General (later Field Marshal Lord) Carver and under the provisions of the Reserve Forces Act of 1966, the territorial army became absorbed into the new territorial army and volunteer reserve on 1 April 1967. The new organisation was divided into four categories – TAVR I consisted of former territorial emergency reservists or 'ever readies', formed in April 1962 to be immediately available for overseas service without recourse to special proclamation – some were dispatched to Aden in 1965 – and other specialists; TAVR II of those units with a NATO role; TAVR III of the bulk of the former territorial army reduced to cadres with a home defence role; and TAVR IV of miscellaneous units such as officer training corps. In January 1968 TAVR III was axed and in November 1968 the first three categories were all effectively merged with regional affiliations substituted for county loyalties in widespread amalgamations. Not surprisingly, overall numbers fell from 116,500 in December 1964 to 54,800 by March 1968 and to 47,589 by March 1970.

The territorials were revived somewhat by the return of a Conservative administration between 1970 and 1974 and far more so by the next Conservative administration coming to office in 1979. In 1980 a new Reserve Forces Act replaced surviving legislation from 1921 and the various reserve forces measures of the 1950s and 1960s. The title of territorial army was revived on 7 April 1982 and an expansion programme announced to reach 91,000 by 1990. In addition, amid calls in some quarters both for the revival of a kind of home guard or for conscription for territorial service, a home service force was created for the defence of vulnerable points with the intention of reaching a strength of 4,500 by 1990.

Constituting some 28 per cent of the army's mobilised strength and some 50 per cent of those forces available for home defence, the territorial army averaged 88.9 per cent of its establishment between 1979 and 1989. An average of 76.9 per cent were trained at any one time during the same period, the liability for the non-specialist or 'independent' units being an annual camp of 15 days and 12 days of week night or weekend training in order to qualify for the bounty. However, despite the 'one army concept' outlined by Carver in 1972, it is clear from the most recent scholarly study of the contemporary territorial army[21] that many of the old attitudes remain in terms of the relationship between regulars and auxiliaries. The incentives and disincentives of territorial service also appear consistent with the past, the annual turnover running at between 25 and 30 per cent. Moreover, while there is now a national employers' liaison committee, many of the old difficulties with employers prevail and public awareness of the territorials remains low. Indeed, in 1989–90 the 72,823 serving territorials represented just 0.12 per cent of the British population as a whole and only 0.65 per cent of males aged 17 to 30.

At the close of 1990, too, there are yet further echoes of the past. On the one hand, a lack of territorial volunteers for overseas duties resulted in the compulsory call-up of some specialist personnel for service in the Gulf under the provisions of the 1980 legislation. On the other, it was rumoured that the large-scale economies in military expenditure being contemplated as a result of the dramatic changes in Europe would include a reduction of the territorial army's strength to 60,000 as soon as the Gulf crisis permitted.[22] An historian of the amateur military tradition may be permitted a knowing smile.

Notes

1   PRO, Cab 80/10 quoted in D. J. Newbold, 'British Planning and Preparations to Resist Invasion on Land, September 1939 to September 1940', Unpub. Ph.D., London, 1988, p. 84.

2   The full text of Eden's broadcast is reproduced in a number of unit histories including H. L. Wilson, *Four Years: The Story of 5th Battalion,*

Caernarvonshire Home Guard (Privately printed, Conway, 1945), pp. 16–17 and D. C. Crombie, *A History of 5th (Bideford) Battalion, Devon Home Guard* (Burleigh Press, Bristol, 1946), pp. 9–10.

3   S. Orwell & I. Angus (eds), *The Collected Essays, Journalism and Letters of George Orwell* (Secker & Warburg, London, 1968), II, p. 353; J. Brophy, *Britain's Home Guard: A Character Study* (Harrap, London, 1945), p. 19.

4   *A Short History of the 20th (Sevenoaks) Battalion, Kent Home Guard* (Privately printed, Maidstone, 1945), p. 5; Ministry of Defence, Home Guard Enlistment Papers, sample from Boxes 1252–1311.

5   Ministry of Defence, Home Guard Enlistment Papers, Boxes 1252–1311; Graves, *Home Guard of Britain*, p. 168.

6   J. Radnor, *It All Happened Before* (Harrap, London, 1945), p. 11.

7   Calder, *People's War*, p. 397.

8   J. B. Priestley, *Postscripts* (Heinemann, London, 1940), pp. 9–13; Orwell & Angus (eds), *Collected Essays*, pp. 116–17, 149–54.

9   J. Langdon-Davies, *Home Guard Warfare* (Routledge, London, 1941), pp. 54, 64, 83–4, 127–34.

10   T. Wintringham, *New Ways of Warfare* (Penguin, Harmonsworth, 1940), pp. 73–91, 122–3; Graves, *Home Guard of Britain*, p. 79.

11   Ministry of Defence Library, *Defence (LDV) Regulations* of 17 May 1940 and *Army Council Instructions* Numbers 653 of 24 Jun 1940 and 924 of 15 Aug 1940.

12   Graves, *Home Guard of Britain*, pp. 13, 109–20.

13   Ibid., pp. 70–5, 136–7; Ministry of Defence Library, *Notes of a Meeting Between CinC, Home Forces and the Leaders of the LDV held on Wednesday 5 June 1940* (War Office pamphlet G.144); PRO, Cab 106/1189 'Summary Report: British Home Guard' by J. K. Howard and H. W. Endicott for the Massachusetts Committee of Public Safety and the US War Department, 6 Aug 1941.

14   PRO, INF 6/442 Production file for 'The Dawn Guard'.

15   Brophy, *Britain's Home Guard*, pp. 5, 24–7, 47–8; *The Home Guard of Britain* (Ministry of Information, London, 1943), p. 2; A. G. Street, *From Dusk Till Dawn* (Harrap, London, 1943), pp. 12–13, 24, 73.

16   Crombie, *5th (Bideford) Battalion*, p. 58; G. H. Lidstone, *On Guard: A History of the 10th (Torbay) Battalion, Devon Home Guard* (Torquay Times, Torquay, 1946), p. 11; *A History of 44th (London Transport) Battalion, Home Guard* (Privately printed, 1946), pp. 12–13; H. Smith, *Bureaucrats in Battledress: A History of the Ministry of Food Home Guard* (Privately printed, Conway, 1945), pp. 11, 145, 204–5.

17   Graves, *Home Guard of Britain*, p. 113.

18   Longmate, *Real Dad's Army*, p. 60.

19   Priestley, *Postscripts*, pp. 9–13.

20   E. R. Chamberlain, *Life in Wartime Britain* (Batsford, London, 1972), p. 36.

21   W. E. Walker, *Reserve Forces and the British Territorial Army: A Case Study for NATO in the 1990s* (Tri-service Press, London, 1990). Statistics in this paragraph are taken from Walker, pp. 89 and 101.

22   *The Sunday Times*, 23 Dec 1990.

Conclusion

As has been already remarked, in contemplating the home guard during the Second World War, contemporary popular writers did have a sense of the continuities of the amateur military tradition just as authors of Victorian and Edwardian militia regimental histories also perceived a link with the distant past. Even ignoring perhaps tenuous connections in mediaeval legislation, the continuities from 1558 to 1945 are clear. But, as this book has attempted to demonstrate, the amateur military tradition rests on more than a legislative inheritance.

First, of course, there were the purposes for which auxiliaries have been raised. The constant threat of invasion, whether real or merely perceived, found a frequent response in the development of auxiliaries. However, auxiliaries were equally regarded as fulfilling a constabulary role and, while social control is not necessarily an easy concept to define, it is clear that auxiliaries were often also regarded as providing a measure of social control. Auxiliaries also existed both as alternative to and supplement to the standing army, the perception of the militia in particular being that of a counterweight to the army. This had less meaning after the seventeenth century but there were occasional echoes of the old arguments even in the nineteenth century. But, even as the militia's role as constitutional safeguard declined, there was increasingly the question of how far auxiliaries could genuinely supplement the army, regulars tending to interpret this as meaning that the militia in particular could be used simply as a manpower quarry. In most periods, regulars adopted a narrow professional view which gave scant encouragement to auxiliaries but it must be acknowledged that local patriotism frequently had a decidely local flavour and that auxiliary forces were often poor substitutes for trained military manpower. Nevertheless, auxiliaries could be employed overseas although this invariably implied special enabling legislation and overcoming inbuilt resistance at least until the creation of a single national army in 1939.

That single national army was forged through the application of universal conscription, one of the ironies being that the existence of auxiliaries had long effectively prevented its introduction. On the one hand, they had done so by the militia itself being subject to compulsion between 1757 and 1831, the sustained opposition increasing the realisation that compulsion for overseas service was not practical when that for home defence was so detested. But the very existence of auxiliaries in such large numbers was also an additional argument against the necessity for conscription, those favouring compulsion recognising the auxiliaries as an insurmountable barrier until the demands of mass modern warfare finally made it unavoidable.

But it was not just in preserving the voluntary system that the auxiliary forces performed a major role for the best part of four centuries. On occasions, auxiliary forces were a major issue in national politics as in the 1640s and, at other times, large numbers of auxiliaries sat as members of parliament where they often proved sufficiently powerful to frustrate government policy. Certainly, the relative independence of the auxiliary forces at different times was of frequent concern to the state and governments invariably employed financial means to assert control.

Inevitably, however, although their existence had consequences for state and society as a whole, it was at the local level that the presence of auxiliaries was most felt. They were far more visible to British society as a whole than regulars, their administration alone proving a constant burden to the gentry and to local county and parochial officials. It was in their nature, too, to operate in the full glare of publicity. Vast crowds frequently attended auxiliary spectacle and, in all their activities, auxiliaries clearly projected military values. In the late nineteenth and early twentieth century at least, that contributed to the recognised growth of militarism. Moreover, the auxiliaries were projecting those values in a way that the regular army could not, for the auxiliaries were far more representative of society as a whole even if they often fell short of a particular government's ideal of respectability.

Nevertheless, whatever the general impression of a largely

working-class pursuit over the period as a whole, auxiliaries were unlikely to be those who would readily have joined the army or those who would otherwise have taken part in military affairs. They thus embraced a far broader cross-section of society either by choice or by coercion than the army ever did. Ironically, however, in transmitting certain values to themselves and to those who merely watched them – values which would not have been transmitted but for their existence – the auxiliaries also bore the brunt of popular anti-militarism. This might take the form either of physical confrontation or, more often, of popular ridicule which, in being reflected in popular literature, itself indicated the cultural impact of the amateur military tradition.

Yet, in certain circumstances, the prestige of a community could become linked to its local auxiliary forces and, in reality, there was a close inter-dependence between auxiliaries and society embracing such aspects as trade and, especially, employment, for auxiliaries were civilians first and soldiers second. In particular, their ability to fulfil military commitments depended upon the co-operation of employers who often opposed the military demands made upon their employees.

It might well be wondered why men chose to serve in the auxiliary forces in such numbers in the face of frequent opposition and criticism. However, it is clear that auxiliaries provided opportunity. This might be the opportunity of experiencing something different or of enjoying recreational facilities or comradeship, which might not otherwise have been enjoyed. It might be a conscious commitment to the status quo or a demonstration of loyalty to community, landlord or employer. For many officers service in the auxiliaries was clearly a route to social assimilation although advancement was by no means assured if the rank and file had particular ideas as to the kind of officer they wanted and, of course, elections were hardly unknown. Equally, newcomers of wealth and property found a ready route into county society through service in the auxiliaries, notably the yeomanry. At the same time, however, auxiliaries often provided the traditional elite with an outlet for leadership as some other avenues were increasingly closed to them through the nineteenth and twentieth centuries. Indeed, the role of the auxiliaries in offering opportunities for local political or other patronage should not be ignored.

In short, the purpose fulfilled by the auxiliary forces was

many-faceted and is a ready guide to the paradoxes of British attitudes towards the military. Indeed, auxiliary forces have been the real point of contact between army and society in Britain. None the less, it should never be overlooked that their most enduring *raison d'être* was the threat to stability posed by foreign invasion, internal disorder or both. Effectively, for all that some served overseas (not least in two world wars), the auxiliary forces were never tested against an invading army and this fact has perhaps obscured their wider significance for too long. Even in merely existing at times of crisis, auxiliaries were providing a focus and outlet for many who wished only to demonstrate their commitment to their country and, in doing so, to enjoy, in the words of John Brophy, 'the incommunicable satisfaction of a job whose value lies beyond questioning'.[1]

Notes

1 Brophy, *Britain's Home Guard*, pp. 26–7.

Appendix: Ireland

Some reference has been made to the inter-relationship between the auxiliary forces in Ireland and those in Great Britain but, while there were often similarities, the invariably more troubled state of Ireland and the actual occasional landing of foreign forces made for rather more differences.

A semi-feudal system of raising manpower appears to have survived in Ireland until the mid seventeenth century although a militia of sorts seemingly existed in Ulster from the early part of the same century. A militia was finally established in 1666 in response to the Dutch threat but its reliability was suspect and it was disarmed in 1685. Re-established in 1690, the militia remained subject to the royal prerogative and there was no actual militia legislation until 1715 (2 Geo I c 9). Even then, the militia was only occasionally arrayed as in 1745 and 1756 when over 148,000 men supposedly saw duty although it would appear more likely that this was the number eligible rather than those called. Indeed, militia service was restricted to Protestants between the ages of 16 and 60 although Catholics were taxed double for its upkeep.

The militia provisions effectively lapsed in 1766 and, despite the relative success of the militia in opposing Thurot's landing at Carrickfergus in February 1760, bills to renew them failed until the dispatch of many regular troops to the American war in 1778 brought new legislation (17 & 18 Geo III c 13). However, raising the militia was thought to be too expensive and the legislation was never utilised except in the form of authorising independent companies of volunteer militia. But, in any case, the entry of Spain into the war against Britain in June 1779 stimulated the growth of a volunteer movement, whose origin tends to be dated from the resolutions passed by the Belfast volunteer company on 17 March 1778. In fact, one volunteer corps had been formed in Wexford as early as 1766 and there were at least 13 such corps in existence before 1778 although the picture is somewhat confused by the parallel existence of other volunteer militia companies in the 1770s.

What was significant about the Belfast and other similar resolutions passed thereafter was the ringing declaration of total independence from government, heralding a much wider politicisation of volunteering than was to be the case in mainland Britain. There was some consideration given to suppressing the movement but, in the absence of a militia, necessity required the issue of government arms in July 1779 which, in turn, stimulated further growth to some 40,000 men by December 1779. It is clear that many of the volunteers were raised solely for local defence and in aid of the civil power and there is certainly a continuity between their officers, those formerly in the militia and those later to be in the yeomanry. Although some Catholic corps were to be raised and wealthier Catholics admitted to others by 1784, the volunteers were overwhelmingly Protestant and of the 100,000 or so in existence by February 1782 the largest proportion – over 34,000 – were to be found in Ulster.

Nevertheless, in Belfast, Dublin and some other larger centres the volunteers tended to be Presbyterian professionals and tradesmen rather than the traditional Episcopalian landed elite. Moreover, there is no doubt that the volunteers not only represented a challenge to that elite but also gave coherence to a growing national political consciousness as expressed in resolutions for free trade and legislative independence passed by volunteer delegates at Dungannon in February 1782. Yet, the achievement of both aims cannot be divorced either from the course of English domestic politics or the machinations of factions within the Irish parliament, with which the volunteer movement enjoyed a somewhat fragile alliance. It is also clear that there was by no means universal volunteer support for the wider political reforms demanded by the so-called national convention of volunteer delegates at Dublin in November 1783 and subsequently decisively rejected by the Irish parliament.

But whether essentially conservative or otherwise, and the movement certainly split on the issue of Catholic emancipation, armed men pursuing a political platform were unacceptable to the authorities and it was fortunate both that the immediate threat of invasion terminated with the war's end and that internal divisions also weakened the movement. In 1782 and 1783, moreover, many were induced to enlist in new fencible regiments and in February 1785 the Irish parliament declared itself in favour of reviving the militia. In fact, it did not do so and surviving volunteer corps, which had declined to fewer than 20,000 men, were employed in suppressing 'whiteboy' and 'rightboy' disturbances in 1786 although Dublin police legislation in the same year represented an alternative solution to the problem of order. With the outbreak of the French war in December 1792 there was some indication of volunteers attempting to recruit but it was resolved to revive the militia instead, a proclamation outlawing the volunteers on 11 March 1793.

The new legislation (33 Geo III c 22), which received the royal assent on 9 April 1793, was modelled on that in England in 1786 and, significantly, did not exclude Catholics. Indeed, it was the imposition of the new burden of militia service on a Catholic population at the very same time that the Catholic Relief Act removed other penalties that appears to have resulted in the widespread and violent anti-militia riots which affected all but four counties and resulted in the loss of possibly over 250 lives. However, some 13,366 men had been raised by February 1795 and there was then a voluntary augmentation which increased establishment to 21,660. Thereafter the ballot proved largely unnecessary and it was only revived on any scale in 1807. As in the case of the militia in Britain, the role increasingly became one of supplying drafts to the army and conceivably some 88,400 Irish militiamen enlisted in the line between 1806, when legislation made permanent provision for it, and 1813. From 1799 Irish militia regiments were also dispatched to the Channel Isles and to the mainland in 1804 although there was no formal interchanging of Irish and British militia regiments until 1811, the continuing service of some Irish regiments in Britain delaying final disembodiment until March 1816.

Despite some indiscipline and some subversion of militiamen by the United Irishmen prior to the outbreak of rebellion in Ireland in May 1798, the Irish militia proved generally reliable notwithstanding the fact that the majority of its rank and file remained solidly Catholic. Nevertheless, its potential unreliability was a factor in legislation authorising the establishment of 'county cavalry and infantry' (37 Geo III c 2) in September 1796. Generally known as yeomanry whether mounted or otherwise, the forces raised amounted to 24,000 men by January 1797 and possibly 40,000 by June 1798 and were overwhelmingly Protestant in composition. They were also formally under government control in a way that the volunteers had not been although, ironically, the yeomanry developed a reputation for undisciplined brutality.

All were called out for permanent duty in May 1798 and although yeomanry and militia were among those put to flight by Humbert's French invading force at Castlebar in August they performed creditably on other occasions and it would seem took a substantial proportion of the 1,600 or more government casualties that summer and autumn. After the rebellion, the yeomanry continued to increase in size and may have attained a strength of 78,000 in 1804 before being trimmed to 20,000 at the end of the Napoleonic wars. With the disembodiment of the militia, however, it had a major role in aid to the civil power with substantial numbers out on duty in both 1821 and 1822. Unfortunately, such service was not only costly but frequently bloody and it speeded the establishment of constabularies in all Irish counties by 1824. The beginning of the so-called tithe war in 1830 saw the yeomanry revived only for new excesses, such as the death of 14 or more persons at Newtownabbey in June 1831, to result in its effective dismantling with permanent staffs abolished in March 1834 and progressive disarming from July 1834.

In 1859 the British government determined that too many risks would be run by permitting the raising of new volunteer corps in Ireland and, despite frequent interventions by Irish MPs and attempted bills in 1860, 1879 and 1880, the Victorian volunteer movement was never extended there. The militia did still exist and its development paralleled that of Britain. Special reserve units were raised in 1908 but not territorials. In 1913, of course, the two communities raised their own paramilitary volunteers, the Protestant and loyalist Ulster volunteer force (UVF) formed in January 1913 numbering some 90,000 by February 1914 and the rival nationalist Irish national volunteers, formed in November 1913, perhaps 10,000 men. Most of the UVF was incorporated into the 36th (Ulster) Division of Kitchener's new armies in 1914. Volunteer training corps were formed in 1914 and that in Dublin took casualties during the Easter Rising of 1916 but all were suspended in November 1916.

With the division of Ireland in 1921, Ulster still lacked territorials until a heavy artillery battery and an engineer squadron were established in Antrim in 1937 together with an Antrim county association. By 1939 three anti-aircraft units and an army service corps unit had been added but there was no further expansion of the territorial presence until 1947 and, in the absence of associations, home guard units were affiliated to the special constabulary, receiving the title of home guard only in 1942: they amounted to 30,000 men by March 1944. While containing both full and part-time members, the present Ulster defence regiment is not part of the territorial army but of the regular army and territorials in Ulster have no role in aid of the civil power.

Bibliography

Unpublished primary sources

Army Museums Ogilby Trust: OTP.30 (Acc 553); Order Book, West Somerset Yeomanry, 1794–1819; *Benson Freeman*; Muster Book of Westminster Volunteer Cavalry; Mins of Liverpool Rifle Corps, 1803; Orders of 1st Loyal London Vols

Bedfordshire Record Office: M10/2/81, 82

Berkshire Record Office: *Radnor* D/ERa 07, 08/1, 025

Bodleian Library: MS Top Oxon e 241; MS Top Oxon c 223

British Library: Add Mss 5552; *Dropmore* Add Mss 59291; *Stowe* 805, 806; *Upcott* Add Mss 32558; *Arnold–Forster* Add Mss 50338, 50339, 50346, 50353

Buckinghamshire Record Office: AR78/77/7; *Howard–Vyse* D/HV/15/25; *Lieutenancy* L/Y 2/7, 5/11, L/P 15, 16, L/Md 5/7; PR 198/3/2; D 86/31/55; D/W 88/9; T/A 3/20(b), 5/1, 7/13; *Morgan–Grenville* D55 AR40/63(L); *Carrington* 28/A/1,2, 28/B/11; Q/FBM/1–3

Cheshire Record Office: DJW 1/113

Clywd Record Office: D/HA/1262

Devon Record Office: *Seymour of Berry Pomeroy* 1392 M/Box 8, 18/12

Dorset Record Office: *Featherstone–Frampton* D29/X10

Duke of York's Headquarters, Chelsea: Papers of the Council of County Territorial Associations

Essex Record Office: Q/SBb 393/76; D/P 129/17/5; L/U 3/2

Gloucestershire Record Office: D 149 X19

C. C. Goodwyn Esq: Log Book of Sgt Major Goodwyn, Tetbury Loyal Vols

Greater London Record Office (Middlesex): L/C/74; *Cruikshank* Acc 534/1

Guildhall Library: Ms 12613,2; 14521

Hampshire Record Office: Q30/L.L. 26, 27, 28; 37M69/3

Hatfield House: *Salisbury Mss*

Hereford and Worcestershire Record Office: *Coventry* 705:73 Acc 2868/4, 3261/3

Hertfordshire Record Office: D/EHa.Z5

Humberside Record Office: *Lieutenancy* LT 9/52

Huntington Library: *Stowe* STG 1 (7); 2 (4, 5); 3 (3); 4 (1)

Imperial War Museum: *Yearsley* DS/MISC/17
Lancashire Record Office: *Lieutenancy* LM 1/1
Manchester Central Library: L1/40/4/1; *Leigh–Philips* M84/1/1/12
Ministry of Defence: Home Guard Enlistment Papers
Ministry of Defence Library: Returns of the Strength of the Volunteer Force, 1917–18
National Army Museum: *Roberts* 7101–23–221–10
Northumberland Record Office: QSB 90/3/30
Nottingham University Library: *Drury–Lowe* Dr.N 2/6, 4/3.
Oxfordshire Record Office: *Lieutenancy* L/M I/v/3, II/iii/1, VI/i/1, XI/iii/1
Public Record Office: Cab 3, 80, 106; HO 41, 42, 50, 52; INF 6; WO 43, 161
Somerset Record Office: DD/DR 53
Southampton University Library: *Wellington* 4/1/3/2/57
Staffordshire Record Office: D 1460
Wiltshire Record Office: WRO 361/4

Published primary sources

Ashcroft, M.Y.(ed), *To Escape the Monster's Clutches* (North Yorkshire County Record Office Publication No. 15, 1977).

Beckett, I.F.W.(ed), *The Buckinghamshire Posse Comitatus, 1798* (Buckinghamshire Record Society, 1985).

Bloomfield, P.(ed), *Kent and the Napoleonic Wars* (Alan Sutton for the Kent Archives Office, Gloucester, 1987).

Chibnall, A.C.(ed), *The Certificate of Musters for Buckinghamshire, 1522* (HMSO, London, 1973).

Cozens–Hardy, B.(ed), *Norfolk Lieutenancy Journal, 1676–1701* (Norfolk Record Society, 1961).

Douch, H.L.(ed), *Cornwall Muster Rolls, 1569* (Privately published, Almondsbury, 1984).

Dunn, R.M.(ed), *Norfolk Lieutenancy Journal, 1660–1676* (Norfolk Record Society, 1977).

Emsley, C.(ed), *North Riding Naval Recruits: The Quota Acts and the Quota Men* (North Yorkshire County Record Office Publication No. 18, 1978).

Faraday, M.A.(ed), *Herefordshire Militia Assessments of 1663* (Royal Historical Society, London, 1972).

Farrow, M.A. and Bradfer-Lawrence, H.L.(eds), *The Musters Returns for Norfolk, 1569, 1572, 1574 and 1577* (Norfolk Record Society) Vol VI (1935) and Vol VII (1936).

Goring, J. and Wake, J.(eds), *Northamptonshire Lieutenancy Papers, 1580–1614* (Northamptonshire Record Society, 1974).

Green, E.(ed), *The Preparations in Somerset against the Spanish Armada, 1558–1588* (Somerset Record Society, 1888).

Harland, J.(ed), *The Lancashire Lieutenancy under the Tudors and Stuarts* (Manchester, 1859).

Hatley, V.A. (ed), *Northamptonshire Militia Lists, 1777* (Northamptonshire Record Society, 1973).

Historical Manuscripts Commission, *Manuscripts of J. B. Fortescue Esq preserved at Dropmore* (HMC, London, 1892–1927) 10 vols.

Hoskins, W.G.(ed), *The Exeter Militia List, 1803* (Phillimore, Chichester, 1972).

Howard, A.J. and Stoate, T.L.(eds), *The Devon Muster Roll for 1569* (Privately published, Almondsbury, 1984).

Jarvis, R.C.(ed), *Collected Papers on the Jacobite Risings* (Manchester University Press, 1971) 2 vols.

Kussmaul, A. (ed)., *The Autobiography of Joseph Mayett of Quainton, 1783–1839* (Buckinghamshire Record Society, 1986).

Murphy, W.P.D.(ed), *The Earl of Hertford's Lieutenancy Papers, 1603–1612* (Wiltshire Record Society, 1965).

Pound, J.(ed), *The Military Survey of 1522 for the Babergh Hundred* (Suffolk Record Society) XXVIII (1986).

Rye, W.(ed), *State Papers relating to Musters, Beacons, Ship Money, etc in Norfolk* (Norfolk and Norwich Archaeological Society, 1907).

Scott Thomson, G. (ed), *The Twysden Lieutenancy Papers, 1583–1668* (Kent Archaeological Record Society, 1926).

Stoate, T.L.(ed), *Dorset Tudor Muster Rolls* (Privately published, Almondsbury, 1978).

Tibbutt, H.G.(ed), *The Letter Book of Sir Samuel Luke, 1644–45* (HMSO, London, 1963).

Wake, J.(ed), *Musters, Beacons and Subsidies* (Northamptonshire Record Society, 1926).

Wake, J.(ed), *The Montagu Musters Book, 1602–1623* (Northamptonshire Record Society, 1935).

Wicks, A.(ed), *Bellum Civile* (Partizan Press, Leigh on Sea, 1988).

Wood, R.G.E.(ed), *Essex and the French Wars, 1793–1815* (Essex County Record Office SEAX Publication No. 70, 1977).

Note: Two invaluable guides to both primary sources and published primary sources are Gibson, J. and Medlycott, M. (eds), *Militia Lists and Musters, 1757–1876* (Federation of Family History Societies, Birmingham, 1989) and Gibson, J. and Dell, A. (eds), *Tudor and Stuart Muster Rolls* (Federation of Family History Societies, Birmingham, 1989).

Theses and dissertations

Allison, M., 'The National Service Issue, 1899–1914', Unpub. Ph.D., London, 1975.

Anderson, D., 'The English Militia in the mid-Nineteenth Century: A Study of its Military, Social and Political Significance', Unpub. D.Phil., Oxford, 1982.

Badsey, S.D., 'Fire and Sword: The British Army and the Arme Blanche Controversy, 1871–1921', Unpub. Ph.D., Cambridge, 1982.

Beckett, I.F.W., 'The English Rifle Volunteer Movement, 1859–1908',

Unpub. Ph.D., London, 1974.

Bennett, M., 'The Royalist War Effort in the North Midlands, 1642–46', Unpub. Ph.D., Loughborough, 1986.

Bertie, J., 'H. O. Arnold-Forster at the War Office, 1903–1905', Unpub. Ph.D., Liverpool, 1974.

Blanch, M.D., 'Nation, Empire and the Birmingham Working Class, 1899 1914', Unpub. Ph.D., Birmingham, 1975.

Bohstedt, J.H., 'Riots in England, 1790–1810 with special reference to Devon', Unpub. Ph.D., Harvard, 1972.

Bonavita, R.V., 'The English Militia, 1558–1580: A Study in the Relations between the Crown and the Commissioners of Musters', Unpub. M.A., Manchester, 1972.

Booth, A., 'Reform, Repression and Revolution: Radicalism and Loyalism in the North West of England, 1789–1803', Unpub. Ph.D., Lancaster, 1979.

Carter, D.P., 'The Lancashire Lieutenancy, 1625–40', Unpub. M.A., Manchester, 1973.

Carter, D.P., 'The Lancashire Lieutenancy, 1660–1688', Unpub. M.Litt., Oxford, 1982.

Farrar-Hockley, A.H., 'National Service and British Society', Unpub. Defence Fellowship dissertation, Oxford, 1974.

Ferguson, K.P., 'The Army in Ireland from the Restoration to the Act of Union', Unpub. Ph.D., Dublin, 1981.

Goring, J., 'The Military Obligations of the English People, 1511–1558', Unpub. Ph.D., London, 1955.

Hall, C.D., 'Factors Influencing British Strategic Planning and Execution during the Napoleonic War, 1803–1814', Unpub. Ph.D., Exeter, 1984.

Hughes, C., 'Army Recruitment in Gwynedd, 1914–16', Unpub. M.A., Wales, 1983.

Huitson, J.A., 'Defence and Public Order in Northumberland, 1793–1815', Unpub. M.Litt., Durham, 1966.

Ive, J.G.A., 'The Local Dimensions of Defence: The Standing Army and the Militia in Norfolk, Suffolk and Essex, 1649–1660', Unpub. Ph.D., Cambridge, 1986.

Johnson, A.M., 'Buckinghamshire, 1640–60', Unpub. M.A., Wales, 1963.

Johnson, R.A., 'The Warwickshire Volunteers: A Social History, 1859–1900' Unpub. B.A. Dissertation, University of Warwick, 1989.

Lodge, M. M., 'The Militia Issue: The Case of the Buccleuch Fencibles, 1778–1783', Unpub. M.Litt., Edinburgh, 1985.

McGurk, J.J.N., 'The Recruitment and Transportation of Elizabethan Troops and their Service in Ireland, 1594–1603', Unpub. Ph.D., Liverpool, 1982.

Moon, H., 'The Invasion of the United Kingdom: Public Controversy and Official Planning, 1888–1918', Unpub. Ph.D., London, 1968. 2 vols.

Morris, P., 'Leeds and the Amateur Military Tradition: The Leeds Rifles and Their Antecedents, 1859–1918', Unpub. Ph.D., Leeds, 1983. 2 vols.

Morton, P. M., 'The Volunteer Rifle Movement in England, 1859–1863', Unpub. Ph.D., Toronto, 1976.

Nagel, L.C., 'The Militia of London, 1641–49', Unpub. Ph.D., London, 1982.

Newbold, D.J.,' British Planning and Preparations to Resist Invasion on Land, September 1939 to September 1940', Unpub. Ph.D., London, 1988.

Newman, P.R., 'The Royalist Army in Northern England, 1642–45', Unpub. D.Phil., York, 1978.

Peters, H., 'The Volunteer Force, 1914–1920', Unpub. typescript, 1968 (Copy in Ministry of Defence Central Library).

Pimlott, J.L., 'The Administration of the British Army, 1783–1793', Unpub. Ph.D., Leicester, 1975.

Reese, H.M., 'The Military Presence in England, 1649–60', Unpub. D.Phil., Oxford, 1981.

Renn, E.M., 'British Civil and Military Preparations against Napoleon's Planned Invasion, 1803–1805', Unpub. Ph.D., Florida State, 1974.

Roy, I., 'The Royalist Army in the First Civil War', Unpub. D.Phil., Oxford, 1963.

Salevouris, M.J., 'Riflemen Form: The War Scare of 1859–60 in England', Unpub. Ph.D., Minnesota, 1971.

Smith, S.C., 'Loyalty and Opposition in the Napoleonic Wars: The Impact of the Local Militia, 1807–1815', Unpub. D.Phil., Oxford, 1984.

Smyth, D.H., 'The Volunteer Movement in Ulster: Background and Development, 1745–1785', Unpub. Ph.D., Belfast, 1974.

Wanklyn, M.D.G., 'The King's Armies in the West of England, 1642–46', Unpub. M.A., Manchester, 1966.

Wilson, J.B., 'The Morale and Discipline of the British Expeditionary Force, 1914–18', Unpub. M.A., New Brunswick, 1978.

Secondary sources

(a) Books

Abels, R., *Lordship and Military Obligation in Anglo-Saxon England* (University of California Press, Berkeley, 1988).

Adams, R.J.Q. and Poirier, R., *The Conscription Controversy in Great Britain, 1900–1918* (Macmillan, London, 1987).

Addison, P., *The Road to 1945* (Cape, London, 1975).

Ahrenfeldt, R.H., *Psychiatry in the British Army in the Second World War* (Routledge & Kegan Paul, London, 1958).

Alderman, G., *The Railway Interest* (Leicester University Press, 1973).

Amey, G., *City under Fire* (Lutterworth Press, Guildford, 1979).

Anderson, G., *Victorian Clerks* (Manchester University Press, 1976).

Anderson, M.S., *War and Society in Europe of the Old Regime, 1618–1789* (Fontana, London, 1988).

Anderson, Olive, *A Liberal State at War* (Macmillan, London, 1967).

Angel, W., *Hitler Confronts England* (Duke University Press, Durham, N.C., 1960).

Anglesey, Marquess of, *A History of the British Cavalry, 1816–1919* (Leo Cooper, London, 1973–86). 4 vols.

Ashton, R., *The English Civil War: Conservatism and Revolution,*

1603–1649 (Weidenfeld & Nicolson, London, 1978).

Aubrey, P., *The Defeat of James Stuart's Armada, 1692* (Leicester University Press, 1979).

Bailey, P., *Leisure and Class in Victorian England* (Routledge & Kegan Paul, London, 1978).

Bailey, V. (ed), *Policing and Punishment in Nineteenth Century Britain* (Croom Helm, London, 1981).

Baker, H., *The Territorial Force: A Manual of its Law, Organisation and Administration* (Murray, London, 1909).

Barnes, T.G., *Somerset, 1625–40: A County's Government during the Personal Rule* (Oxford University Press, 1961).

Bartlett, T. and Hayton, D.W. (eds)., *Penal Era and Golden Age: Essays in Irish History, 1690–1850* (Ulster Historical Foundation, Belfast, 1979).

Baxter, J.P., *The Introduction of the Ironclad Warship* (Harvard University Press, Cambridge, Mass., 1933).

Bayley, C.C., *Mercenaries in the Crimea* (McGill–Queens University Press, Montreal, 1977).

Beckett, I.F.W., *Riflemen Form: A Study of the Rifle Volunteer Movement, 1859–1908* (Ogilby Trusts, Aldershot, 1982).

Beckett, I.F.W., *Call to Arms: Buckinghamshire's Citizen Soldiers* (Barracuda, Buckingham, 1985).

Beckett, I.F.W., *The Army and the Curragh Incident, 1914* (Bodley Head for the Army Records Society, London, 1986).

Beckett, I.F.W. & Gooch, J. (eds), *Politicians and Defence: Studies in the Formulation of British Defence Policy, 1845–1970* (Manchester University Press, 1981).

Beckett, I.F.W. & Simpson, K.(eds), *A Nation in Arms: A Social Study of the British Army in the First World War* (Manchester University Press, 1985).

Beloff, M., *Public Order and Popular Disturbances, 1660–1714* (Oxford University Press, 1938).

Bennett, B., *A Handbook of Kent's Defences* (Kent Defence Research Group, Privately published, 1977).

Bennett, B. T., *British War Poetry in the Age of Romanticism, 1793–1815* (Garland, New York, 1976).

Berry, R. Potter., *A History of the Formation and Development of Volunteer Infantry* (Simpkin, Marshall, Hamilton, Kent & Co, London and Broadbent & Co, Huddersfield, 1903).

Best, G., *Mid Victorian Britain, 1851–75* (2nd edit., Panther, London, 1973).

Bohstedt, J.H., *Riots and Community Politics in England and Wales, 1790–1810* (Harvard University Press, Cambridge, Mass., 1983).

Bond, B., *The Victorian Army and the Staff College* (Eyre Methuen, London, 1972).

Bond, B., *British Military Policy between the Two World Wars* (Oxford University Press, 1980).

Bond, B. and Roy, I. (eds), *War and Society: A Yearbook of Military History* (Croom Helm, London, 1976).

Bond, G.C., *The Grand Expedition: The British Invasion of Holland in*

1809 (University of Georgia Press, Athens, Ga., 1979).

Bordau, D.J. (ed), *The Police: Six Sociological Essays* (Wiley, New York, 1967).

Bourne, K., *Palmerston: The Early Years, 1784–1841* (Allen Lane, London, 1982).

Boyd, L.G., *The Role of the Military in Civil Disorders in England and Wales* (University of Tennessee Press, Knoxville, 1977).

Boynton, L., *The Elizabethan Militia, 1558–1638* (2nd edit., David & Charles, Newton Abbot, 1971).

Brock, M., *The Great Reform Act* (Hutchinson, London, 1973).

Brophy, J., *The Home Guard Handbook* (Hodder & Stoughton, London, 1940).

Brophy, J., *Britain's Home Guard: A Character Study* (Harrap, London, 1945).

Brown, K.D. (ed), *Essays in Anti-Labour History* (Macmillan, London, 1974).

Brown, R. Allen (ed), *Anglo-Norman Studies* Vols I, IV and VII (Boydell Press, Woodbridge, 1979, 1982 and 1985).

Bruce, A.P., *The Purchase System in the British Army, 1660–1871* (Boydell Press for Royal Historical Society, Woodbridge, 1980).

Butt, J. and Clarke, I.F. (eds), *The Victorians and Social Protest* (David and Charles, Newton Abbot, 1973).

Calder, A., *The People's War* (2nd edit, Panther, London, 1971).

Cassar, G., *Kitchener: Architect of Victory* (William Kimber, London, 1977).

Central Association of Volunteer Regiments, *The Volunteer Force and the Volunteer Training Corps during the Great War* (London, 1920).

Chaloner, W.H. & Henderson, W.O., *Engels as Military Critic* (Manchester University Press, 1959).

Chandler, D.G., *Sedgemoor, 1685* (Anthony Mott, London, 1985).

Childs, J., *The Army of Charles II* (Routledge & Kegan Paul, London, 1976).

Childs, J., *The Army, James II and the Glorious Revolution* (Manchester University Press, 1980).

Childs, J., *Armies and Warfare in Europe, 1648–1789* (Manchester University Press, 1982).

Childs, J., *The British Army of William III, 1688–1702* (Manchester University Press, 1987).

Chorley, K.C., *Armies and the Art of Revolution* (Faber, London, 1943).

Christie, I.R., *Stress and Stability in Late Eighteenth Century Britain* (Oxford University Press, 1984).

Clark, P. et al. (eds), *The English Commonwealth: Essays presented to Joel Hurstfield* (Leicester University Press, 1979).

Clarke, I.F., *Voices Prophesying War, 1763–1984* (Oxford University Press, 1966).

Clarke, J., Critcher, C. and Johnson, R.(eds), *Working Class Culture* (Hutchinson, London, 1979).

Clemoes, P. and Hughes, K. (eds), *England before the Conquest* (Cambridge

University Press, 1971).

Cliffe, J.T., *The Yorkshire Gentry from the Reformation to the Civil War* (Athlone Press, London, 1969).

Clifton, R., *The Last Popular Rising* (Temple Smith, London, 1984).

Coate, M., *Cornwall in the Great Civil War and Interregnum, 1642–1660* (Oxford University Press, 1933).

Codrington, G.R., *The Territorial Army* (Sifton Praed, London, 1938).

Coleby, A.M., *Central Government and the Localities: Hampshire, 1649–1689* (Cambridge University Press, 1987).

Collier, B., *The Defence of the United Kingdom* (HMSO, London, 1957).

Colls, R. and Dodd, P. (eds), *Englishness: Politics and Culture, 1880–1920* (Croom Helm, London, 1986).

Cope, E., *Politics without Parliament* (Allen & Unwin, London, 1987).

Cookson, J.E., *Lord Liverpool's Administration* (Scottish Academic Press, Edinburgh, 1975).

Cornwall, J., *The Revolt of the Peasantry, 1549* (Routledge & Kegan Paul, London, 1977).

Corvisier, A., *Armies and Societies in Europe, 1494–1789* (Indiana University Press, Bloomington, 1979).

Cousins, G., *The Defenders* (Muller, London, 1968).

Cox, R., *Operation Sea Lion* (Thornton Cox, London, 1974).

Cress, L.D., *Citizens in Arms: The Army and Militia in American Society to the War of 1812* (University of North Carolina Press, Chapel Hill, 1982).

Critchley, T.A., *A History of the Police in England and Wales* (Constable, London, 1967).

Cruickshank, C.G., *Elizabeth's Army* (2nd edit., Oxford University Press, 1966).

Cruickshank, C.G., *Army Royal: Henry VIII's Invasion of France, 1513* (Oxford University Press, 1969).

Cunliffe, M., *Soldiers and Civilians: The Martial Spirit in America, 1775–1865* (Eyre & Spottiswoode, London, 1969).

Cunningham, H., *The Volunteer Force* (Croom Helm, London, 1975).

Dallas, G. and Gill, D., *The Unknown Army* (Verso, London, 1985).

Darvall, F.O., *Popular Disturbances and Public Order in Regency England* (Oxford University Press, 1934).

Dennis, P., *Decision by Default* (Routledge & Kegan Paul, London, 1972).

Dennis, P., *The Territorial Army, 1907–40* (Boydell Press for Royal Historical Society, Woodbridge, 1987).

Derthick, M., *The National Guard in Politics* (Harvard University Press, Cambridge, Mass., 1965).

Desbrieres, E., *Projets et Tentatives de Debarquement aux Iles Britanniques* (Paris, 1900–2). 4 vols.

Dewar, M., *Defence of the Nation* (Arms & Armour Press, London, 1989).

Dickinson, H.T.(ed)., *Britain and the French Revolution* (Macmillan, London, 1989).

Donajgrodzki, A.P.(ed)., *Social Control in Nineteenth Century Britain* (Croom Helm, London, 1971).

Douglas Brown, R., *East Anglia, 1940* (Terence Dalton, Lavenham, 1981).

Douglas-Home, C., *Britain's Reserve Forces* (RUSI, London, 1969).

Dozier, R.R., *For King, Constitution and Country* (University of Kentucky Press, Lexington, 1983).

Dunbabin, J.P.D.(ed), *Rural Discontent in Nineteenth Century Britain* (Faber & Faber, London, 1974).

Dunham, W.H., *Lord Hastings' Indentured Retainers, 1461–1483* (Yale University Press, New Haven, 1955).

Dunlop, J.K., *The Problems and Responsibilities of the Territorial Army* (Hugh Rees, London, 1935).

Dunlop, J.K., *The Development of the British Army, 1899–1914* (Methuen, London, 1938).

Edgar, D., *The Day of Reckoning* (John Clare Books, London, 1983).

Edsall, N.C., *The Anti-Poor Law Movement, 1834–1844* (Manchester University Press, 1971).

Emsley, C., *British Society and the French Wars, 1793–1815* (Longman, London, 1979).

Emsley, C., *Policing and its Context, 1750–1870* (Macmillan, London, 1983).

Emsley, C. and Walvin, J.(eds)., *Artisans, Peasants and Proletarians, 1760–1860* (Croom Helm, London, 1985).

Emsley, C., *Crime and Society in England, 1750–1900* (Longman, London, 1987).

Evans, E.J., *The Contentious Tithe* (Routledge & Kegan Paul, London, 1976).

Everitt, A., *The Local Community and the English Civil War* (Historical Association, London, 1969).

Fissel, M.C.(ed), *War and Government in Britain, 1598–1650* (Manchester University Press, forthcoming).

Fleming, P., *Invasion 1940* (Hart-Davis, London, 1957).

Fletcher, A., *A County Community in Peace and War: Sussex, 1600–1660* (Longman, London, 1976).

Fletcher, A., *The Outbreak of the English Civil War* (Edward Arnold, London, 1981).

Fletcher, A., *Reform in the Provinces: The Government of Stuart England* (Yale University Press, New Haven, 1986).

Foot, M.R.D.(ed), *War and Society* (Paul Elek, London, 1973).

Fortescue, The Hon. J.W., *The County Lieutenancies and the Army, 1803–1814* (Macmillan, London, 1909).

Fortescue, Sir J.W., *History of the British Army* (Macmillan, London, 1899–1930). 13 vols.

Fowler, K.(ed), *The Hundred Years War* (Macmillan, London, 1971).

Fox, K.O., *Making Life Possible* (Privately printed, Kineton, 1982).

Fraser, D., *And We Shall Shock Them* (Hodder & Stoughton, London, 1983).

French, D.W., *British Economic and Strategic Planning, 1905–15* (Allen & Unwin, London, 1982).

Gash, N., *Lord Liverpool* (Weidenfeld & Nicolson, London, 1984).

Gash, N.(ed)., *Wellington* (Manchester University Press, 1990).

Gates, D., *The British Light Infantry Arm, c.1790–1815* (Batsford, London, 1987).

Gibbs, N.H., *Grand Strategy* (HMSO, London, 1976). Vol I.

Gillingham, J., *The Wars of the Roses: Peace and Conflict in Fifteenth Century England* (Weidenfeld & Nicolson, London, 1981).

Gillingham, J. and Holt, J.C.(eds), *War and Government in the Middle Ages* (Boydell Press, Woodbridge, 1984).

Glover, C.W., *Civil Defence* (Chapman & Hall, London, 1941).

Glover, R., *Peninsular Preparation: The Reform of the British Army, 1795–1809* (Cambridge University Press, 1963).

Glover, R., *Britain at Bay: Defence against Bonaparte, 1803–1814* (Allen & Unwin, London, 1973).

Gooch, J., *The Plans of War* (Routledge & Kegan Paul, London, 1974).

Gooch, J., *Armies in Europe* (Routledge & Kegan Paul, London, 1980).

Gooch, J., *The Prospect of War: Studies in British Defence Policy, 1847–1942* (Frank Cass, London, 1981).

Goodman, A., *The Wars of the Roses: Military Activity and English Society, 1452–1497* (Routledge & Kegan Paul, London, 1981).

Goold-Walker, G., *The Honourable Artillery Company, 1537–1926* (The Bodley Head, London, 1926).

Gough, H. and Dickson, D.(eds), *Ireland and the French Revolution* (Irish Academic Press, Dublin, 1989).

Gray, R.Q., *The Labour Aristocracy in Victorian Edinburgh* (Oxford University Press, 1976).

Graves, C., *The Home Guard of Britain* (Hutchinson, London, 1943).

Green, W.E., *The Territorial in the Next War* (Geoffrey Bles, London, 1939).

Grierson, J.M., *Records of the Scottish Volunteer Force, 1859–1908* (Blackwood & Sons, Edinburgh, 1909).

Grieves, K.R., *The Politics of Manpower, 1914–18* (Manchester University Press, 1988).

Gulvin, K.R., *The Kent Home Guard: A History* (North Kent Books, Rochester, 1980).

Guy, A.J.(ed), *The Road to Waterloo: The British Army and the Struggle against Revolutionary and Napoleonic France, 1793–1815* (National Army Museum, London, 1990).

Hale, J.R., *Renaissance War Studies* (Hambledon Press, London, 1983).

Hale, J.R., *War and Society in Renaissance Europe, 1450–1620* (Fontana, London, 1985).

Hamburger, J., *James Mill and the Art of Revolution* (Yale University Press, New Haven, 1963).

Hamer, W.S., *The British Army: Civil–Military Relations, 1885–1905* (Oxford University Press, 1970).

Harries-Jenkins, G., *The Army in Victorian Society* (Routledge & Kegan Paul, London, 1977).

Harvey, A.D., *English Literature and the Great War with France* (Nold Johnson, London, 1981).

Hay, G.J., *An Epitomised History of the Militia* (United Service Gazette,

London, 1905).

Hay, D. and Snyder, F.(eds), *Policing and Prosecution in Britain, 1750–1850* (Oxford University Press, 1989).

Hayes, D., *Conscription Conflict* (Sheppard Press, London, 1948).

Hayter, A.J., *The Army and the Crowd in Mid-Georgian England* (Macmillan, London, 1978).

Henderson, D., *Highland Soldier* (John Donald, Edinburgh, 1989).

Hewitt, H.J., *The Organisation of War under Edward III, 1338–1362* (Manchester University Press, 1966).

Higham, R.(ed), *Security and Defence in South-west England before 1800* (University of Exeter Studies in History No. 19, 1987).

Hill-Norton, Admiral of the Fleet Lord, Sowery, Sir F. and Wills, Sir D., *Defence Begins at Home* (Sherwood Press, London, 1982).

Hirst, F.W., *The Six Panics and Other Essays* (Methuen, London, 1913).

Hobsbawm, E. and Ranger, T.(eds), *The Invention of Tradition* (Cambridge University Press, 1983).

Hobsbawm, E. and Rudé, G., *Captain Swing* (2nd edit., Penguin, Harmonsworth, 1973).

Hollister, C.W., *Anglo–Saxon Military Institutions* (Oxford University Press, 1962).

Hollister, C.W., *The Military Organisation of Norman England* (Oxford University Press, 1965).

Holmes, C., *The Eastern Association in the English Civil War* (Cambridge University Press, 1974).

Horn, P., *Labouring Life in the Victorian Countryside* (Gill & Macmillan, Dublin, 1976).

Horn, P., *The Rural World, 1780–1850* (Hutchinson, London, 1980).

Houlding, J.A., *Fit for Service: The Training of the British Army, 1715–1795* (Oxford University Press, 1981).

Howard, M., *Studies in War and Peace* (Temple Smith, London, 1970).

Hudson, D., *Martin Tupper: His Rise and Fall* (Constable, London, 1949).

Hussey, F., *Suffolk Invasion: The Dutch Attempt on Landguard Fort, 1667* (Terence Dalton, Lavenham, 1983).

Hutton, R., *The Royalist War Effort, 1642–46* (Longman, London, 1982).

Hutton, R., *The Restoration* (Oxford University Press, 1985).

Huxley, G., *Victorian Duke* (Oxford University Press, 1967).

Hynes, S., *The Edwardian Turn of Mind* (Princeton University Press, 1968).

Jeffery, K., *The British Army and the Crisis of Empire, 1918–1922* (Manchester University Press, 1984).

Jeffery, K. and Hennessy, P., *States of Emergency* (Routledge & Kegan Paul, London, 1983).

John, E., *Land Tenure in Early England* (Leicester University Press, 1960).

John, E., *Orbis Britanniae* (Leicester University Press, 1966).

Johns, J.T., *Ideology, Reason and the Limitations of War: Religious and Secular Concepts, 1200–1700* (Princeton University Press, 1975).

Jones, C.(ed)., *Britain and Revolutionary France* (University of Exeter Studies in History, No. 5, 1983).

Jones, D., *Before Rebecca* (Allen Lane, London, 1973).

Jones, D., *Crime, Protest, Community and Police in Nineteenth Century Britain* (Routledge & Kegan Paul, London, 1982).

Jones, D.J.V., *The Last Rising* (Oxford University Press, 1985).

Jones, D.J.V., *Rebecca's Children* (Oxford University Press, 1989).

Jones, E.H.S., *The Last Invasion of Britain* (University of Wales Press, Cardiff, 1950).

Joyce, P., *Work, Society and Politics* (Harvester, Hassocks, 1980).

Kaeper, R.W., *War, Justice and Public Order* (Oxford University Press, 1988).

Karslake, B., *1940: The Last Act* (Leo Cooper, London, 1979).

Keith-Lucas, B., *The Unreformed Local Government System* (Croom Helm, London, 1980).

Kenyon, J.P., *The Civil Wars of England* (Weidenfeld, London, 1988).

Kinross, J., *Fishguard Fiasco* (Knowling Mead, Tenby, 1974).

Kishlansky, M.A., *The Rise of the New Model Army* (Cambridge University Press, 1979).

Kitchen, F., *Fire over England: The Armada Beacons* (Privately published, Brighton, 1988).

Klee, K., *Das Unternehman Seelöwe* (Musterschmidt–Verlag, Göttingen, 1958). 2 vols.

Knight, D., *Harvest of Messerschmidts* (Frederick Warne, London, 1981).

Lambert, A., *Battleships in Transition: The Creation of the Steam Battlefleet, 1815–1860* (Conway Maritime, London, 1984).

Lamont, W., *Volunteer Memories* (Mckeline & Sons, Greenock, 1911).

Lampe, D., *The Last Ditch* (Cassell, London, 1968).

Langdon-Davies, J., *Home Guard Warfare* (Routledge, London, 1941).

Lichfield, N, *The Militia Artillery, 1852–1909* (Sherwood Press, Nottingham, 1987).

Lichfield, N. and Westlake, R., *The Volunteer Artillery, 1859–1908* (Sherwood Press, Nottingham, 1982).

Lloyd, H.A., *The Rouen Campaign, 1590–1592* (Oxford University Press, 1973).

Logue, K., *Popular Disturbances in Scotland, 1780–1815* (John Donald, Edinburgh, 1979).

Longmate, N., *The Real Dad's Army* (Arrow, London, 1974).

Longmate, N., *Defending the Island* (Grafton Books, London, 1990).

Luvaas, J., *The Military Legacy of the Civil War* (University of Chicago Press, 1959).

Lyon, H.R., *The Governance of Anglo–Saxon England, 500–1087* (Edward Arnold, London, 1984).

McAnally, Sir Henry, *The Irish Militia, 1793–1816* (Clonmore & Reynolds, Dublin and Eyre & Spottiswoode, London, 1949).

Macdonald, J.H.A., *Fifty Years of It: The Experiences and Struggles of a Volunteer of 1859* (Blackwood & Sons, Edinburgh and London, 1909).

Mackesy, P., *The Strategy of Overthrow* (Longman, London, 1974).

Mackesy, P., *War without Victory* (Oxford University Press, 1984).

Macksey, K.J., *Invasion: The German Invasion of England, July 1940* (Arms & Armour Press, London, 1980).

McLynn, F.J., *The Jacobite Army in England, 1745* (John Donald, Edinburgh, 1983).

McLynn, F.J., *Invasion* (Routledge, London, 1987).

Mahon, J.K., *History of the Militia and the National Guard* (Macmillan, New York, 1983).

Malcolm, J.L., *Caesar's Due: Loyalty to King Charles in 1642–45* (Boydell Press for Royal Historical Society, Woodbridge, 1983).

Manning Foster, A.E., *The National Guard in the Great War, 1914–18* (Cape & Fenwick, London, 1920).

Marlow, J., *The Peterloo Massacre* (Rapp & Whiting, London, 1969).

Martin, G. and Parker, G.(eds), *The Spanish Armada* (Hamish Hamilton, London, 1988).

Marwick, A., *The Home Front* (Thames & Hudson, London, 1976).

Mather, F.C., *Public Order in the Age of the Chartists* (Manchester University Press, 1959).

Middleton, R., *The Bells of Victory* (Cambridge University Press, 1985).

Millar, G.J., *Tudor Mercenaries and Auxiliaries, 1485–1547* (University Press of Virginia, Charlottesville, 1980).

Mingay, G.E.(ed), *The Victorian Countryside* (Routledge & Kegan Paul, London, 1981). 2 vols.

Montefiore, C. Sebag, *A History of the Volunteer Force: From the Earliest Times to 1860* (Archibald Constable & Co, London, 1908).

Morrill, J.S., *Cheshire, 1630–1660* (Oxford University Press, 1974).

Morrill, J.S., *The Revolt of the Provinces: Conservatives and Radicals in the English Civil War, 1630–50* (2nd edit., Longman, London, 1980).

Morris, A.J.A., *The Scaremongers* (Routledge & Kegan Paul, London, 1984).

Morris, J.E., *The Welsh Wars of Edward I* (Oxford University Press, 1901).

Morton, D., *A Military History of Canada* (Hurtig, Edmonton, 1985).

Neave, A., *The Flames of Calais* (Hodder & Stoughton, London, 1972).

Newsome, D., *Godliness and Good Learning* (John Murray, London, 1961).

Nicholson, R., *Edward III and the Scots: The Formative Years of a Military Career, 1327–1335* (Oxford University Press, 1965).

Norfolk, R.W.S., *Militia, Yeomanry and Volunteer Forces of the East Riding, 1689–1908* (East Yorks. Local History Society, Hull, 1965).

O'Brien, G., *Anglo–Irish Politics in the Age of Grattan and Pitt* (Irish Academic Press, Dublin, 1987).

O'Brien, T.H., *Civil Defence* (HMSO, London, 1955).

O'Connell, M.R., *Irish Politics and Social Conflict in the Age of the American Revolution* (Pennsylvania University Press, Philadelphia, 1965).

O'Day, A.(ed), *The Edwardian Age: Conflict and Stability, 1900–1914* (Macmillan, London, 1979).

Osborne, J.M., *The Voluntary Recruiting Movement in Britain, 1914–16* (Garland, New York, 1982).

Owen, B., *The History of the Welsh Militia and Volunteer Corps: Anglesey and Caernarfonshire* (Palace Books, Caernarfon, 1989).

Owen, B., *The History of the Welsh Militia and Volunteer Corps: The Glamorgan Regiments of Militia* (Palace Books, Caernarfon, 1990).

Pakenham, T., *The Year of Liberty* (Hodder & Stoughton, London, 1969).

Pakenham, T., *The Boer War* (Weidenfeld & Nicolson, London, 1979).

Packett, C.N., *H. M.'s Commission of Lieutenancy for the City of London* (Privately printed, Bradford, 1987).

Palmer, S.H., *Police and Protest in England and Ireland, 1780–1850* (Oxford University Press, 1988).

Partridge, M.S., *Military Planning for the Defence of the United Kingdom, 1814–1870* (Greenwood Press, Westview, 1989).

Patterson, A. Temple, *The Other Armada* (Manchester University Press, 1960).

Peacock, A.J., *Bread or Blood* (Gollancz, London, 1965).

Peden, G.C., *British Rearmament and the Treasury, 1932–39* (Scottish Academic Press, Edinburgh, 1979).

Peedle, B., *Encyclopaedia of the Modern Territorial Army* (Patrick Stephens, London, 1990).

Perry, F.W., *The Commonwealth Armies: Manpower and Organisation in Two World Wars* (Manchester University Press, 1988).

Philips, D., *Crime and Authority in Victorian England* (Croom Helm, London, 1977).

Playne, C.E., *The Pre-war Mind in Britain* (Allen & Unwin, London, 1928).

Powicke, M., *Military Obligation in Mediaeval England* (Oxford University Press, 1962).

Prebble, J., *Mutiny* (Secker & Warburg, London, 1975).

Preston, A. and Dennis, P.(eds), *Swords and Covenants* (Croom Helm, London, 1976).

Prestwich, M., *The Three Edwards: War and State in England, 1272–1377* (Weidenfeld & Nicolson, London, 1980).

Prestwich, M., *War, Politics and Finance under Edward I* (Faber, London, 1972).

Price, R., *An Imperial War and the British Working Class* (Routledge & Kegan Paul, London, 1972).

Putkowski, J. and Sykes, J., *Shot at Dawn* (Wharncliffe Publishing, Barnsley, 1989).

Quinault, R. and Stevenson, J.(eds), *Popular Protest and Public Order* (Allen & Unwin, London, 1974).

Radnor, J., *It All Happened Before* (Harrap, London, 1945).

Radzinowicz, L., *A History of the English Criminal Law IV: Grappling for Control* (Stevens & Sons, London, 1968).

Read, D., *Peterloo* (Manchester University Press, 1958).

Reader, W.J., *Professional Men* (Weidenfeld & Nicolson, London, 1966).

Reaney, B., *The Class Struggle in Nineteenth Century Oxfordshire: The Social and Communal Background to the Otmoor Disturbances of 1830–1835* (History Workshop Pamphlet No. 3, Oxford, 1970).

Richards, W., *His Majesty's Territorial Army* (Virtue & Co, London, n.d.). 4 vols.

Richmond, Sir Herbert, *The Invasion of Britain* (Methuen, London, 1941).

Richter, D., *Riotous Victorians* (Ohio University Press, Athens, Ohio, 1981).

Riker, W., *Soldiers of the States* (Public Affairs Press, Washington, 1957).

Robertson, J., *The Scottish Enlightenment and the Militia Issue* (John Donald, Edinburgh, 1985).

Rodriguez-Salgado, M.J. (ed), *Armada, 1588–1988* (National Maritime Museum and Penguin, Harmondsworth, 1988).

Rogers, P., *Battle in Bossenden Wood* (Oxford University Press, 1961).

Rootes, A., *Front Line County* (Robert Hale, London, 1980).

Rose, J. Holland and Broadley, A.M., *Dumouriez and the Defence of England against Napoleon* (London, 1909).

Rudé, G., *The Crowd in History* (Wiley & Son, New York, 1964).

Russell, C., *Parliaments and English Politics, 1621–29* (Oxford University Press, 1979).

Sainsbury, J.D., *Hertfordshire Soldiers* (Herts Local History Council, Hitchin, 1969).

Sainsbury, J.D., *Hazardous Work* (Hart Books, Welwyn, 1985).

Sainty, J.C., *Lieutenants of Counties, 1585–1642* (Institute of Historical Research Special Supplement No 8, 1970).

Samuel, R.(ed), *Patriotism: I History and Politics* (Routledge, London, 1989).

Sanders, I.J., *Feudal Military Service in England* (Oxford University Press, 1956).

Saville, J., *1848* (Cambridge University Press, 1987).

Schenk, P., *Invasion of England 1940: The Planning of Operation Sealion* (Conway Maritime Press, London, 1990).

Schlight, J., *Monarchs and Mercenaries: A Reappraisal of the Importance of Knight Service in Norman and Early Angevin England* (University of Brideport Press, Brideport, 1968).

Schwoerer, L.G., *No Standing Armies: The Anti-army Ideology in Seventeenth Century England* (Johns Hopkins University Press, Baltimore, 1974).

Scott Thomson, G., *The Origin and Growth of the Office of Deputy Lieutenant* (Longmans, London, 1922).

Scott Thomson, G., *Lords Lieutenant in the Sixteenth Century: A Study in Tudor Local Administration* (Longmans, London, 1923).

Searle, G., *The Quest for National Efficiency* (Basil Blackwell, Oxford, 1971).

Searle, G., *Eugenics and Politics in Britain, 1900–1914* (Sijthoff, The Hague, 1976).

Sellwood. A.V., *The Saturday Night Soldiers* (Wolfe Publishing, London, 1966).

Sherwood, R.E., *Civil Strife in the Midlands, 1642–1651* (Phillimore, Chichester, 1974).

Simkins, P., *Kitchener's Army: The Raising of the New Armies, 1914–16* (Manchester University Press, 1988).

Simon, B. and Bradley, I.(eds), *The Victorian Public School* (Gill & Macmillan, Dublin, 1975).

Speck, W.A., *The Butcher: The Duke of Cumberland and the Suppression of the '45* (Oxford University Press, 1981).

Spencer, W.F. and Parker, L.S. (eds), *Proceedings of the Consortium on Revolutionary Europe, 1750–1850* (University of Georgia, Athens, Ga., 1989). 2 vols.

Spiers, E.M., *The Army and Society, 1815–1914* (Longman, London, 1980).

Spiers, E.M., *Haldane: An Army Reformer* (Edinburgh University Press, 1980).

Spiers, E.M., *Radical General: Sir George de Lacy Evans, 1787–1870* (Manchester University Press, 1983).

Springhall, J.O., *Youth, Empire and Society* (Croom Helm, London, 1977).

Stacey, C.P., *Canada and the British Army, 1846–1871* (2nd edit., University of Toronto Press, 1963).

Steedman, C, *Policing the Victorian Community* (Routledge & Kegan Paul, London, 1984).

Steiner, Z., *Britain and the Origins of the First World War* (Macmillan, London, 1977).

Stevenson, J., *Popular Disturbances in England, 1700–1870* (Longman, London, 1974).

Stevenson, J. (ed), *London in the Age of Reform* (Blackwells, Oxford, 1977).

Stone, J.C. and Schmidl, E.A., *The Boer War and Military Reforms* (University Presses of America, Lanham, 1988).

Storch, R.D. (ed)., *Popular Culture and Custom in Nineteenth Century England* (Croom Helm, London, 1982).

Strachan, H., *The History of the Cambridge University OTC* (Midas, Tunbridge Wells, 1976).

Strachan, H., *Wellington's Legacy: The Reform of the British Army, 1830–1854* (Manchester University Press, 1984).

Street, A.G., *From Dusk Till Dawn* (Harrap, London, 1943).

Summers, A., *Angels and Citizens: British Women as Military Nurses, 1854–1914* (Routledge & Kegan Paul, London, 1988).

Sutcliffe, S., *Martello Towers* (David & Charles, Newton Abbot, 1972).

Sweetman, J., *War and Administration* (Scottish Academic Press, Edinburgh, 1984).

Thomas, J.A., *The House of Commons, 1832–1901* (University of Wales Press, Cardiff, 1939).

Thomis, M.I., *The Luddites* (David & Charles, Newton Abbot, 1970).

Thomis, M.I. and Holt, P. (eds)., *Threats of Revolution in Britain, 1789–1848* (Macmillan, London, 1977).

Thompson, D., *The Chartists* (Temple Smith, London, 1984).

Thompson, E.P., *The Making of the English Working Class* (Gollancz, London, 1965).

Thompson, G.N. and Nevill, T., *The Territorial Army* (Ian Allen, London, 1987).

Tibbie, J.W. and A. (eds), *The Prose of John Clare* (Routledge & Kegan Paul, London, 1951).

Travers, T.H.E., *The Killing Ground* (Unwin Hyman, London, 1987).

Underdown, D., *Somerset in the Civil War and Interregnum* (David & Charles, Newton Abbot, 1973).

Vincent, D., *Bread, Knowledge and Freedom: A Study of Nineteenth Century Working Class Autobiography* (Europa, London, 1981).

Vincent, J., *The Formation of the British Liberal Party, 1857–68* (2nd edit., Pelican, Harmonsworth, 1972).

Vine, P.A.L., *The Royal Military Canal* (David & Charles, Newton Abbot, 1972).

Walker, W.E., *Reserve Forces and the British Territorial Army* (Tri-service Press, London, 1990).

Walmsley, R., *Peterloo: The Case Reopened* (Manchester University Press, 1960).

Walter, J., *The Volunteer Force: History and Manual* (Clowes & Sons, London, 1881).

War Office, *The Territorial Army and National Service* (HMSO, London, 1951).

Warner, P., *Invasion Road* (Cassell, London, 1980).

Warwick, P. and Spies, S.B.(eds), *The South African War: The Anglo–Boer War, 1899–1902* (Longman, London, 1980).

Webb, H.J., *Elizabethan Military Science* (University of Wisconsin Press, Madison, 1965).

Webb, S.S., *The Governors-General: The English Army and the Definition of Empire, 1569–1681* (University of North Carolina Press, Chapel Hill, 1979).

Wells, R.A.E., *Dearth and Distress in Yorkshire, 1793–1802* (Borthwick Papers No. 52, York, 1977).

Wells, R.A.E., *Insurrection: The British Experience, 1795–1803* (Alan Sutton, Gloucester, 1983).

Wernham, R.B., *After the Armada* (Oxford University Press, 1984).

Western, J.R., *The English Militia in the Eighteenth Century: The Story of a Political Issue, 1660–1802* (Routledge & Kegan Paul, London, 1965).

Western, J.R., *Monarchy and Revolution: The English State in the 1680s* (Blandford, London, 1972).

Westlake, R., *The Rifle Volunteers* (Picton Publishing, Chippenham, 1982).

Westlake, R., *The Territorial Battalions* (Spellmount, Tunbridge Wells, 1986).

Wheatley, D., *Operation Sealion* (Oxford University Press, 1958).

Wheeler, H.F.B. and Broadley, A.M., *Napoleon and the Invasion of England* (John Lane, London, 1908). 2 vols.

Whittaker, L., *Stand Down* (Westlake Military Books, Newport, 1990).

Williams, D., *The Rebecca Riots* (University of Wales Press, Cardiff, 1955).

Williams, G.A., *The Merthyr Rising* (Croom Helm, London, 1978).

Wills, H., *Pillboxes* (Leo Cooper, London, 1985).

Winter, J.M., *The Great War and the British People* (Macmillan, London, 1986).

Wintringham, T., *New Ways of Warfare* (Penguin, Harmonsworth, 1940).

Wood, D. and Dempster, D., *The Narrow Margin* (Hutchinson, London, 1969).

Wood, E. et al., *The Citizen Soldier* (Hutchinson, London, 1939).

Woodburne, G.B.L., *The Story of Our Volunteers* (Newman & Co, London, 1881).

Woolrych, A., *Soldiers and Statesmen* (Oxford University Press, 1987).

Zagorin, P., *The Court and the Country* (Routledge & Kegan Paul, London, 1969).

(b) Articles

Abels, R., 'Bookland and Fyrd Service in Late Saxon England' in Brown, R.Allen (ed), *Anglo–Norman Studies VII* (Boydell Press, Woodbridge, 1985), pp. 1–25.

Allen, D., 'The Role of the London Trained Bands in the Exclusion Crisis, 1678–1681', *English Historical Review* 87, 1972, pp. 287–303.

Anderson, O., 'Early Experiences of Manpower Problems in an Industrial Society at War: Great Britain, 1854–1856', *Political Science Quarterly* LXXXII, 4, 1967, pp. 526–45.

Anderson, O., 'The Growth of Christian Militarism in Mid-Victorian Britain', *English Historical Review* 86, 338, 1971, pp. 46–72.

Arch, N., 'Thomas Lloyd and the Leeds Volunteers', *Journal of the Society for Army Historical Research* LIX, 1981, pp. 201–6.

Bagwell, P.S., 'The Railway Interest: Its Organisation and Influence, 1839–1914', *Journal of Transport History* VII, 1965–6, pp. 65–86.

Baldwin, S.S., 'The Story of the Territorial Army', *The Territorial Army Magazine* 53, 4, 1988, pp. 4–19.

Barnes, T.G., 'Deputies not Principals, Lieutenants not Captains: The Institutional Failure of Lieutenancy in the 1620s' in Fissel, M. C.(ed), *War and Government in Britain, 1598–1650* (Manchester University Press, forthcoming).

Bartlett, T., 'An End to Moral Economy: The Irish Militia Disturbances of 1793', *Past and Present* 99, 1983, pp. 41–64.

Bartlett, T., 'Indiscipline and Disaffection in the French and Irish Armies during the Revolutionary Period' in Gough, H. and Dickson, D.(eds), *Ireland and the French Revolution* (Irish Academic Press, Dublin, 1988), pp. 179–201.

Beckett, I.F.W., 'Buckinghamshire Militia Lists for 1759: A Social Analysis', *Records of Buckinghamshire* 20, 3, 1977, pp. 461–9.

Beckett, I.F.W., 'The RUSI and the Volunteers', *Journal of the Royal United Services Institute for Defence Studies* 122, 1, 1977, pp. 58–63.

Beckett, I.F.W., 'The Problems of Military Discipline in the Volunteer Force, 1859–1899', *Journal of the Society for Army Historical Research* LVI, 226, 1978, pp. 66–78.

Beckett, I.F.W., 'The Local Community and the Great War: Aspects of Military Participation', *Records of Buckinghamshire* XX, 4, 1978, pp. 503–15.

Beckett, I.F.W., 'The Amateur Military Tradition: New Tasks for the Local Historian', *The Local Historian* XIII, 8, 1979, pp. 475–81.

Beckett, I.F.W., 'The Local Community and the Amateur Military Tradition: A Case Study of Victorian Buckinghamshire', *Journal of the Society for Army Historical Research* LIX, 238/9, 1981, pp. 95–110, 161–70.

Beckett, I.F.W., 'Arnold-Forster and the Volunteers' in Beckett, I.F.W. and Gooch, J. (eds), *Politicians and Defence* (Manchester University Press, 1981), pp. 47–68.

Beckett, I.F.W., 'Wilkes and the Militia, 1759–1763', *Army Quarterly and Defence Journal* 112, 2, 1982, pp. 173–7.

Beckett, I.F.W., 'Edward Stanhope at the War Office, 1887–1892', *Journal of Strategic Studies* V, 2, 1982, pp. 278–307.

Beckett, I.F.W., 'The Evolution and Decline of the Restoration Militia in Buckinghamshire, 1660–1745', *Records of Buckinghamshire* 26, 1984, pp. 28–43.

Beckett, I.F.W., 'The Stanhope Memorandum of 1888: A Re-interpretation', *Bulletin of the Institute of Historical Research* LVII, 136, 1984, pp. 240–7.

Beckett, I.F.W., 'The Nation in Arms, 1914–18' in Beckett, I.F.W. & Simpson, K. (eds), *A Nation in Arms* (Manchester University Press, 1985), pp. 1–36.

Beckett, I.F.W., 'The Territorial Force' in Beckett, I.F.W. & Simpson, K. (eds), *A Nation in Arms* (Manchester University Press, 1985), pp. 127–64.

Beckett, I.F.W., 'The Territorial Force in the Great War' in Liddle, P.(ed), *Home Fires and Foreign Fields* (Brasseys, London, 1985), pp. 21–38.

Beckett, I.F.W., 'Aspects of a Nation in Arms: Britain's Volunteer Training Corps in the Great War', *Revue Internationale d'Histoire Militaire* 63, 1985, pp. 27–39.

Beckett, I.F.W., 'The Amateur Military Tradition in Britain', *War and Society* 4, 2, 1986, pp. 1–16.

Beckett, I.F.W., 'The British Army, 1914–18: The Illusion of Change' in Turner, J.(ed), *Britain and the First World War* (Unwin Hyman, London, 1988), pp. 99–116.

Beckett, I.F.W., 'The Real Unknown Army: British Conscripts, 1916–1919' in Becker, J.-J. and Audoin-Rouzeau, S.(eds), *Les Sociétés Européennes et la Guerre de 1914–1918* (Centre d'Histoire de la France Contemporaine, Université de Paris X-Nanterre, 1990), pp. 339–56.

Beckett, I.F.W., 'The Militia and the King's Enemies, 1793–1815' in A. J. Guy (ed), *The Road to Waterloo* (National Army Museum, London, 1990), pp. 32–9.

Benest, D., 'Roberts Reconsidered: Compulsory TA Service', *Journal of the Royal United Services Institute for Defence Studies* 133, 4, 1988, pp. 73–8.

Berrington, H., 'Partisanship and Dissidence in the Nineteenth Century House of Commons', *Parliamentary Affairs* XXI, 1967–8, pp. 338–74.

Best, G., 'Militarism and the Victorian Public School' in Simon, B. and Bradley, I.(eds), *The Victorian Public School* (Gill & Macmillan, Dublin, 1975), pp. 129–46.

Blanch, M.D., 'Imperialism, Nationalism and Organised Youth' in Clarke, J., Critcher, C. and Johnson, R.(eds), *Working Class Culture* (Hutchinson, London, 1979), pp. 103–20.

Blanch, M.D., 'British Society and the War' in Warwick, P. and Spies, S.B.(eds), *The South African War* (Longman, London, 1980), pp. 210–38.

Bond, B., 'The Effect of the Cardwell Reforms, 1874–1904', *Journal of the Royal United Services Institute for Defence Studies* CV, 1960, pp. 515–24.

Bond, B., 'The Prelude to the Cardwell Reforms', *Journal of the Royal United Services Institute for Defence Studies* CVI, 1961, pp. 229–36.

Bond, B., 'Recruiting the Victorian Army, 1870–1892', *Victorian Studies* V, 1962, pp. 331–8.

Bond, B., 'R. B. Haldane at the War Office, 1905–12', *Army Quarterly* 86, 1963, pp. 33–43.

Bond, B., 'The Territorial Army in Peace and War', *History Today* XVI, 3, 1966, pp. 157–66.

Bond, B., 'Leslie Hore-Belisha at the War Office' in Beckett, I. F. W. and Gooch, J.(eds), *Politicians and Defence* (Manchester University Press, 1981), pp. 110–31.

Booth, A., 'Food Riots in the North West of England, 1790–1801', *Past and Present* 77, 1977, pp. 84–107.

Booth, A., 'Popular Loyalism and Public Violence in the North West of England, 1790–1803', *Social History*, 8, 1983, pp. 295–313.

Bourne. K., 'British Preparations for War with the North, 1861–62', *English Historical Review* LXXVI, 1961, pp. 600–32.

Boyden, P., 'Fire Beacons, Volunteers and Local Militia in Napoleonic Essex, 1803–1811', *Essex Archaeology and History* 15, 1983, pp. 113–18.

Boyden, P., 'A System of Communication through each County: Fire Beacons and their role in the Defence of the Realm, 1803–1811', *National Army Museum Annual Report*, 1978–9, pp. 9–13. Revised and reprinted in Guy, A. J.(ed), *The Road to Waterloo* (National Army Museum, London, 1990), pp. 126–31.

Boynton, L., 'Billeting: The Example of the Isle of Wight', *English Historical Review* LXXIV, 1959, pp. 23–40.

Boynton, L, 'The Tudor Provost-Marshal', *English Historical Review* LXXVII, 1962, pp. 437–55.

Boynton, L., 'Martial Law and the Petition of Right', *English Historical Review* LXXIX, 1964, pp. 255–84

Breen, T.H., 'English Origins and New World Development: The Case of the Covenanted Militia in Seventeenth Century Massachusetts', *Past and Present* 57, 1972, pp. 74–96.

Brooks, N., 'The Development of Military Duty in Eighth and Ninth Century England' in Clemoes, P. and Hughes, K.(eds), *England before the Conquest* (Cambridge University Press, 1971), pp. 69–84.

Brooks, N., 'England in the Ninth Century: The Crucible of Defeat', *Transactions of the Royal Historical Society* 29, 1979, pp. 1–20.

Brundage, A., 'Ministers, Magistrates and Reformers: The Genesis of the Rural Constabulary Act of 1839', *Parliamentary History* 5, 1986, pp. 55–64.

Busby, J.H., 'Local Military Forces in Hertfordshire, 1793–1814', *Journal of the Society for Army Historical Research* XXXI, 1953, pp. 15–24.

Carter, D.P., 'The Exact Militia in Lancashire, 1625–40', *Northern History*

11, 1975, pp. 87–106.

Carter, D.P., 'The Lancashire Militia, 1660–1688' in Kermode, J.L. and Phillips, C.B.(eds), *Seventeenth Century Lancashire: Essays presented to J. J. Bagley* (Transactions of the Historical Society of Lancashire and Cheshire, LXXXII, 1982), pp. 155–81.

Childs, J., '1688', *History* 73, 239, 1988, pp. 398–424.

Coleby, A.M., 'Military–civilian Relations on the Solent, 1651–89', *Historical Journal* 29, 1986, pp. 949–61.

Colley, L., 'Whose Nation? Class and National Consciousness in Britain, 1750–1830', *Past and Present* 113, 1986, pp. 97–117.

Cookson, J.E., 'Political Arithmetic and War in Britain, 1793–1815', *War and Society* 2, 1983, pp. 37–60.

Cookson, J.E., 'The English Volunteer Movement of the French Wars, 1793–1815: Some Contexts', *Historical Journal* 32, 4, 1989, pp. 867–91.

Cookson, J.E., 'The Rise and Fall of the Sutton Volunteers, 1803–4', *Bulletin of the Institute of Historical Research* 64, 153, 1991, pp. 46–53.

Cope, E.S., 'Politics without Parliament: The Dispute about Muster-Master's Fees in Shropshire in the 1630s', *Huntington Library Quarterly* XLV, 1982, pp. 271–4.

Cornford, J., 'The Transformation of Conservatism in the Late Nineteenth Century', *Victorian Studies* VII, 1963–4, pp. 36–8.

Crapster, B.L., 'A. B. Richards, 1820–76: Journalist in Defence of Britain', *Journal of the Society for Army Historical Research* XLI, 166, 1963, pp. 94–7.

Crossick, G., 'The Labour Aristocracy and Its Values: A Study of Mid-Victorian Kentish Town', *Victorian Studies* XX, 1976, pp. 301–28.

Cunningham, H., 'Jingoism and the Working Classes, 1877–78', *Bulletin of the Society for the Study of Labour History* 19, 1969, pp. 6–9.

Cunningham, H., 'Jingoism in 1877–78', *Victorian Studies* XIV, 1971, pp. 429–54.

Cunningham, H., 'The Language of Patriotism' in Samuel, R.(ed), *Patriotism* (Routledge, London, 1989), pp. 57–89.

Dennis, P., 'The Reconstitution of the Territorial Force, 1918–20' in Preston, A. and Dennis, P.(eds), *Swords and Covenants* (Croom Helm, London, 1976), pp. 190–215.

Dennis, P., 'The County Associations and the Territorial Army', *Army Quarterly and Defence Journal* 109, 2, 1979, pp. 210–19.

Dennis, P., 'The Territorial Army in Aid of the Civil Power in Britain, 1919–26', *Journal of Contemporary History* 16, 1981, pp. 705–24.

Dewey, P., 'Military Recruiting and the British Labour Force during the First World War', *Historical Journal* 27, 1, 1984, pp. 199–224.

Dickinson, H.T., 'Popular Conservatism and Militant Loyalism, 1789–1815' in Dickinson, H. T. (ed), *Britain and the French Revolution* (Macmillan, London, 1989), pp. 103–25.

Douglas, R., 'Voluntary Enlistment in the First World War and the Work of the Parliamentary Recruiting Committee', *Journal of Modern History* 42, 1970, pp. 564–85.

Duffin, A., 'The Defence of Cornwall in the Early Seventeenth Century' in

Higham, R. (ed), *Security and Defence in South-west England before 1800* (University of Exeter Studies in History, No. 19, 1987), pp. 69–77.

Dunlop, J.K., 'The Territorials in the Early Years', *Army Quarterly* XCIV, 1967, pp. 53–5.

Emsley, C., 'Political Disaffection and the British Army in 1792', *Bulletin of the Institute of Historical Research* XLVIII, 1975, pp. 230–45.

Emsley, C., 'The Military and Popular Disorder in England, 1790–1801', *Journal of the Society for Army Historical Research* LXI, 245/6, 1983, pp. 10–21, 96–112.

Emsley, C., 'The Thump of Wood on a Swede Turnip: Police Violence in Nineteenth century England', *Criminal Justice History* VI, 1985, pp. 125–49.

Emsley, C., 'The Social Impact of the French Wars' in Dickinson, H. T. (ed), *Britain and the French Revolution* (Macmillan, London, 1989), pp. 212–27.

Emsley, C., 'The Volunteer Movement' in Guy, A. J. (ed), *The Road to Waterloo* (National Army Museum, London, 1990), pp. 40–7.

Englander, D. and Osborne, J., 'Jack, Tommy and Henry Dubb: The Armed Forces and the Working Class', *Historical Journal* 21, 3, 1978, pp. 593–621.

Ferguson, K.P., 'The Volunteer Movement and the Government, 1778–1793', *The Irish Sword* 13, 52, 1978/9, pp. 208–216.

Ferguson, K.P., 'The Army and the Irish Rebellion of 1798' in Guy, A. J. (ed), *The Road to Waterloo* (National Army Museum, London, 1990), pp. 88–100.

Fissel, M.C., 'Scottish War and English Money: The Short Parliament of 1640' in Fissel, M. C. (ed), *War and Government in Britain, 1598–1650* (Manchester University Press, forthcoming).

Flower-Smith, M.A., 'The Able and the Willynge: The Preparations of the English Land Forces to Meet the Armada', *British Army Review* 95, August 1990, pp. 54–61.

Forde, F., 'The Liverpool Irish Volunteers', *Irish Sword* X, 1971, pp. 106–23.

Forster, G.C.F., 'Government in Provincial England under the Later Stuarts', *Transactions of the Royal Historical Society* 33, 1983, pp. 29–48.

Foster, R., 'Wellington and Local Government' in Gash, N.(ed), *Wellington* (Manchester University Press, 1990), pp. 214–37.

Fraser, P., 'The Growth of Ministerial Control in the Nineteenth Century House of Commons', *English Historical Review* LXXV, 1960, pp. 444–663.

Fyfe, J., 'Scottish Volunteers with Garibaldi', *Scottish Historical Review* 57, 1978, pp. 168–81.

Gentles, I., 'Arrears of Pay and Ideology in the Army Revolt of 1647' in Bond, B.J. and Roy, I.(eds), *War and Society: A Yearbook of Military History* (Croom Helm, London, 1976), pp. 44–66.

Gilley, S., 'The Garibaldi Riots of 1862', *Historical Journal* XVI, 4, 1973, pp. 697–732.

Gillingham, J., 'The Introduction of Knight Service into England' in Brown, R. Allen (ed), *Anglo–Norman Studies IV* (Boydell Press, Woodbridge, 1982), pp. 53–64.

Ginter, D.E., 'The Loyalist Association Movement of 1792–3 and British Public Opinion', *Historical Journal* IX, 2, 1966, pp. 179–90.

Gooch, J., 'Attitudes to War in Late Victorian and Edwardian England' in Bond, B. and Roy, I. (eds), *War and Society: A Yearbook of Military History* (Croom Helm, London, 1976), pp. 88–102.

Gooch, J., 'The Bolt from the Blue' in Gooch, J.(ed), *The Prospect of War* (Frank Cass, London, 1981), pp. 1–34.

Gooch, J., 'Mr Haldane's Army', in Gooch, J.(ed), *The Prospect of War* (Frank Cass, London, 1981), pp. 92–115.

Gooch, J., 'Haldane and the National Army' in Beckett, I.F.W. and Gooch., J.(eds), *Politicians and Defence* (Manchester University Press, 1981), pp. 69–86.

Goring, J., 'The General Proscription of 1522', *English Historical Review* CCCXLI, 1971, pp. 681–705.

Goring, J., 'Social Change and Military Decline in Mid-Tudor England' *History* 60, 1975, pp. 185–97.

Grieves, K.R., 'Military Tribunal Papers: The Case of Leek Local Tribunal in the First World War', *Archives* XVI, 70, 1983, pp. 145–50.

Grieves, K.R., 'Total War: The Quest for a British Manpower Policy, 1917–18', *Journal of Strategic Studies* 9, 1, 1986, pp. 79–95.

Hall, C.D., 'Addington at War: Unspectacular but not Unsuccessful', *Bulletin of the Institute of Historical Research* 61, 146, 1988, pp. 306–15.

Hamilton, C.I., 'The Diplomatic and Naval Effects of the Prince de Joinville's Note Sur L'Etat des Forces Navales de la France of 1844', *Historical Journal* 22, 3, 1989, pp. 675–87.

Hanham, H., 'Religion and Nationality in the Mid-Victorian Army' in Foot, M.R.D. (ed), *War and Society* (Paul Elek, London, 1973), pp. 159–82.

Hargrave, E., 'The Leeds Volunteers, 1820', *Miscellanea 7 of the Thoresby Society* 24, 1919, pp. 451–68.

Harris, J.P., 'The British General Staff and the Coming of War, 1933–39', *Bulletin of the Institute of Historical Research* LIX, 140, 1986, pp. 196–211.

Harris, J.P., 'Two War Ministers: A Reassesment of Duff Cooper and Hore-Belisha', *War and Society* 6, 1, 1988, pp. 65–78.

Harris, J.P., 'The Sandys Storm: The Politics of British Air Defence in 1938', *Bulletin of the Institute of Historical Research* 62, 149, 1989, pp. 318–36.

Hassell-Smith, A., 'Militia Rates and Militia Statutes, 1558–1663' in Clark, P. et al. (eds), *The English Commonwealth: Essays presented to Joel Hurstfield* (Leicester University Press, 1979), pp. 93–110.

Haythornthwaite, P.J., 'The Volunteer Force, 1803–1804', *Journal of the Society for Army Historical Research* LXIV, 260, 1986, pp. 193–204.

Hewitt, H.J., 'The Organisation of War' in Fowler, K.(ed), *The Hundred Years War* (Macmillan, London, 1971), pp. 75–95.

Higgins, G.P., 'The Militia in Early Stuart Cheshire', *Chester Archaeological Society* 61, 1977, pp. 39–49.

Hooper, N., 'Anglo–Saxon Warfare on the Eve of the Conquest: A Brief Survey' in Brown, R. Allen (ed), *Anglo–Norman Studies I* (Boydell Press, Woodbridge, 1979), pp. 84–93.

Horn, P., 'The Mutiny of the Oxfordshire Militia in 1795', *Cake and Cockhorse* VII, 8, 1979, pp. 232–41.

Howard, M., 'Lord Haldane and the Territorial Army' in Howard, M., *Studies in War and Peace* (Temple Smith, London, 1970), pp. 86–98.

Howard, M., 'Empire, Race and War', *History Today* 31, 12, 1981, pp. 4–11.

Jeffery, K., 'The British Army and Internal Security, 1919–39', *Historical Journal* 24, 2, 1981, pp. 377–97.

Jeffery, K., 'The Post-war Army' in Beckett, I. F. W. and Simpson, K. (eds), *A Nation in Arms* (Manchester University Press, 1985), pp. 211–34.

John, E., 'War and Society in the Tenth Century', *Transactions of the Royal Historical Society* 27, 1977, pp. 173–195.

Kauffman, C.J., 'Lord Elcho, Trade Unionism and Democracy' in Brown, K.D.(ed), *Essays in Anti-Labour History* (Macmillan, London, 1974), pp. 183–207.

Kiernan, V.G., 'Conscription and Society in Europe before the War of 1914–18' in Foot, M.R.D.(ed), *War and Society* (Paul Elek, London, 1973), pp. 143–58.

King, S., 'The Middlesex and Westminster Royal Volunteers, 1779–1780', *Bulletin of the Middlesex Local History Council* XVI, 1963, pp. 3–5.

Large, D., 'London in the Year of Revolution, 1848' in Stevenson, J.(ed), *London in the Age of Reform* (Blackwells, Oxford, 1977), pp. 177–211.

Lawson, P., 'Reassessing Peterloo', *History Today* 38, 3, 1988, pp. 24–9.

Leventhal, F.M., 'Why a Massacre? The Responsibility for Peterloo', *Journal of Interdisciplinary History* 2, 1971, pp. 109–18.

Lindley, K.J., 'Riot Prevention and Control in Early Stuart London', *Transactions of the Royal Historical Society* 33, 1983, pp. 109–26.

Lomas, M.J., 'Militia and Volunteer Wind Bands in Southern England in the late Eighteenth and early Nineteenth Centuries', *Journal of the Society for Army Historical Research* LXVII, 271, 1989, pp. 154–66.

Lowell, A.L., 'The Influence of Party Upon Legislation in England and America', *Annual Report of the American Historical Association* (Washington 1902), I, pp. 319–542.

McAnally, Sir Henry, 'The Militia Array of 1756 in Ireland', *The Irish Sword* 1, 1949–51, pp. 94–104.

McGuffie, T.H., 'The Lord Bradford Militia Documents in the Shirehall, Shrewsbury', *Journal of the Society for Army Historical Research* XLIV, 1966, pp. 135–46.

McGurk, J.J.N., 'A Letter Book relating to the Lieutenancy of Kent, 1604–1628', *Archaeologia Cantiana* LXXXII, 1967, pp. 124–42.

McGurk, J.J.N., 'Armada Preparations in Kent and Arrangements made after the Defeat', *Archaeologia Cantiana* LXXXV, 1970, pp. 71–93.

McGurk, J.J.N., 'Levies from Kent to the Elizabethan Wars, 1589–1603', *Archaeologia Cantiana* LXXXVIII, 1973, pp. 57–72.

McGurk, J.J.N., 'The Clergy and the Militia, 1580–1610', *History* 60,

1975, pp. 198–210.

Main, T.F., 'General Matters in the Salerno Mutiny', 9 Jan 1945 (Copy in Staff College Library, Camberley).

Malcolm, J., 'A King in Search of Soldiers: Charles I in 1642', *Historical Journal* 21, 2, 1978, pp. 251–74.

Mather, F.C., 'Army Pensioners and the Maintenance of Civil Order in Early Nineteenth Century England', *Journal of the Society for Army Historical Research* XXXVI, 1958, pp. 110–24.

Mayhew, G.J., 'Rye and the Defence of the Narrow Seas: A Sixteenth Century Town at War', *Sussex Archaeological Collections* 122, 1984, pp. 107–26.

Medlycott, Sir Mervyn, 'Some Georgian Censuses: The Militia Lists and Defence Lists', *Genealogists Magazine* 23, 2, 1989, pp. 55–9.

Mileham, P.J.R., 'The Stirlingshire Yeomanry Cavalry and the Scottish Radical Disturbances of April 1820', *Journal of the Society for Army Historical Research* LXIII, 253/4, 1985, pp. 20–30, 104–12.

Miller, E.A., 'Some Arguments used by English Pamphleteers, 1697–1700 concerning a Standing Army', *Journal of Modern History* 18, 1946, pp. 306–13.

Miller, J., 'The Militia and the Army in the Reign of James II', *Historical Journal* XVI, 4, 1973, pp. 659–79.

Mitchell, A., 'The Association Movement of 1792–3', *Historical Journal* IV, 1966, pp. 56–77.

Mitchell, G.B., 'The Frampton Volunteers, 1798–1802', *Journal of the Society for Army Historical Research* VII, 1928, pp. 219–21.

Mitchinson, K.W., 'The Reconstitution of 169 Brigade, July–October 1916', *Stand To* 29, August 1990, pp. 8–11.

Morrill, J.S., 'Mutiny and Discontent in English Provincial Armies, 1645–47', *Past and Present* 56, 1972, pp. 49–74.

Morris, A.J.A., 'Haldane's Army Reforms, 1906–1908: The Deception of the Radicals', *History* 56, 181, 1971, pp. 17–34.

Morris, R.J., 'Voluntary Societies and British Urban Elites, 1780–1850: An Analysis', *Historical Journal* XXVI, 1, 1983, pp. 95–118.

Morton, P., 'Another Victorian paradox: Anti-militarism in a Jingoistic Society', *Historical Reflections* V, 2, 1981, pp. 169–89.

Morton, P., 'A Military Irony: The Victorian Volunteer Movement', *Journal of the Royal United Services Institute for Defence Studies* 131, 3, 1986, pp. 63–70.

Morton, R.G., 'The Rise of the Yeomanry', *Irish Sword* 8, 1967, pp. 58–64.

Navias, M., 'Terminating Conscription: The British National Service Controversy, 1955–56', *Journal of Contemporary History* 24, 1989, pp. 195–208.

Neave, D., 'Anti-militia Riots in Lincolnshire, 1757 and 1796', *Lincolnshire History and Archaeology* XI, 1976, pp. 21–6.

Neilson, K., 'Kitchener: A Reputation Refurbished', *Canadian Journal of History* 15, 2, 1980, pp. 207–27.

Newman, P.R., 'The Royalist Officer Corps, 1642–60', *Historical Journal* 26, 4, 1983, pp. 945–58.

Norrey, P.J., 'The Restoration Regime in Action: The Relationship between Central and Local Government in Dorset, Somerset and Wiltshire, 1660–1678', *Historical Journal* 31, 4, 1988, pp. 789–812.

Osborne, J.M., 'Defining their Own Patriotism: British Volunteer Training Corps in the First World War', *Journal of Contemporary History* 23, 1, 1988, pp. 59–75.

O'Snodaigh, P., 'Some Police and Military Aspects of the Irish Volunteers', *Irish Sword* 13, 52, 1978–9, pp. 217–29.

O'Snodaigh, P., 'The Volunteers of '82: A Citizen Army or Armed Citizens – A Bicentennial Retrospect', *Irish Sword* 15, 60, 1983, pp. 177–88.

O'Snodaigh, P., 'Class and the Irish Volunteers', *Irish Sword* 16, 64, 1986, pp. 165–84.

Otley, C.B., 'The Social Origins of British Army Officers', *Sociological Review* 18, 2, 1970, pp. 213–40.

Otley, C.B., 'The Educational Background of British Army Officers', *Sociology* 7, 2, 1973, pp. 191–209.

Palmer, S.H., 'Calling out the Troops: The Military, the Law and Public Order in England, 1650–1850', *Journal of the Society for Army Historical Research* 56, 1978, pp. 198–214.

Palmer, S.H., 'Power, Coercion and Authority: Protest and Repression in 1848 in England and Ireland', in Spencer, W. F. and Parker, L. S. (eds), *Proceedings of the Consortium on Revolutionary Europe, 1750–1850* (University of Georgia, Athens, 1989), II, pp. 274–89.

Parker, G., 'If the Armada had landed', *History* 61, 1976, pp. 358–68.

Partridge, M., 'The Defence of the Channel Isles, 1814–1870', *Journal of the Society for Army Historical Research* LXIV, 257, 1986, pp. 34–42.

Partridge, M., 'The Russell Cabinet and National Defence, 1846–1852', *History* 72, 235, 1987, pp. 231–50.

Partridge, M., 'Wellington and the Defence of the Realm, 1819–1852' in Gash, N.(ed)., *Wellington* (Manchester University Press, 1990), pp. 238–62.

Patient, A., 'Mutiny at Salerno', *The Listener*, 25 Feb 1982.

Perkin, H., 'Land Reform and Class Conflict in Victorian Britain' in Butt, J. and Clarke, I.F.(eds), *The Victorians and Social Protest* (David & Charles, Newton Abbot, 1973), pp. 177–217.

Prestwich, J., 'The Military Household of the Norman Kings', *English Historical Review* 96, 1981, pp. 1–35.

Razzell, P.E., 'The Social Origins of Officers in the Indian and British Home Armies, 1758–1962', *British Journal of Sociology* 14, 3, 1963, pp. 248–61.

Richardson, J., 'Tennyson: Most English of Englishmen', *History Today* XXIII, 11, 1973, pp. 776–84.

Richmond, C., 'The Nobility and the Wars of the Roses, 1459–1461', *Nottingham Mediaeval Studies* 21, 1977, pp. 72–84.

Rizzi, R., 'The British Army and Riot Control in Early Nineteenth Century England', *Army Quarterly* 109, 1979, pp. 74–85.

Rogers, N., 'Popular Disaffection in London during the 45', *London Journal* 1, 1, 1975, pp. 5–26.

Rogers, N., 'Popular Protest in Early Hanoverian London', *Past and Present* 79, 1978, pp. 70–100.

Ropp, T., 'Conscription in Great Britain, 1900–1914: A Failure in Civil–military Communication?', *Military Affairs* 20, 1956, pp. 71–6.

Rose, R.B., 'Liverpool Volunteers of 1859', *Liverpool Bulletin* VI, 1954, pp. 47–66.

Rose, R.B., 'The Volunteers of 1859', *Journal of the Society for Army Historical Research* XXXVII, 1959, pp. 97–110.

Roy, I., 'The English Civil War and English Society' in Bond, B.J. and Roy, I.(eds), *War and Society: A Yearbook of Military History* (Croom Helm, London, 1976), pp. 24–43.

Roy, I., 'England turned Germany?: The Aftermath of the Civil War in its European Context', *Transactions of the Royal Historical Society* 28, 1978, pp. 127–44.

Sager, E.W., 'The Social Origins of Victorian Pacifism', *Victorian Studies* 23, 2, 1980, pp. 211–36.

St George, B., 'General Sir William Kirke: Champion of the Territorial Army, 1933–40', *Army Quarterly and Defence Journal*, 1986, pp. 191–203.

Satre, L.J., 'St John Brodrick and Army Reform, 1901–1903', *Journal of British Studies* 15, 2, 1976, pp. 117–39.

Schwoerer, L.G., 'The Literature of the Standing Army Controversy, 1697–99', *Huntington Library Quarterly* 18, 1965, pp. 187–212.

Schwoerer, L.G., 'The Fittest Subject for a King's Quarrel: An Essay on the Militia Controversy, 1642', *Journal of British Studies* II, 1971, pp. 45–76.

Searle, E. and Burghart, R., 'The Defence of England and the Peasants' Revolt', *Viator* 3, 1972, pp. 365–88.

Searle, G., 'Critics of Edwardian Society: The Case of the Radical Right' in O'Day, A.(ed), *The Edwardian Age* (Macmillan, London, 1979), pp. 79–96.

Silver, A., 'The Demand for Order in Civil Society: A Review of Some Themes in the History of Urban Crime, Police and Riot' in Bordau, D. J.(ed), *The Police: Six Sociological Essays* (Wiley, New York, 1967), pp. 1–24.

Silver, A., 'Social and Ideological Bases of British Elite Reactions to Domestic Crisis in 1829–32', *Politics and Society* 2, 1971, pp. 179–201.

Simkins, P., 'Kitchener and the Expansion of the Army' in Beckett, I.F.W. and Gooch, J.(eds), *Politicians and Defence* (Manchester University Press, 1981), pp. 87–109.

Smyth, P.D.H., 'Our Cloud–Cap't Grenadiers: The Volunteers as a Military Force', *Irish Sword* 13, 52, 1978–79, pp. 185–207.

Smyth, P.D.H., 'The Volunteers and Parliament, 1779–84' in Bartlett, T. and Hayton, D.W.(eds), *Penal Era and Golden Age: Essays in Irish History, 1690–1850* (Ulster Historical Foundation, Belfast, 1979), pp. 113–36.

Soldon, N., 'Laissez Faire as Dogma: The Liberty and Property Defence League' in Brown, K.D.(ed), *Essays in Anti-Labour History* (Macmillan, London, 1974), pp. 208–33.

Spence, R.T., 'The Pacification of the Cumberland Borders, 1593–1628', *Northern History* XIII, 1977, pp. 60–160.

Springhall, J.O., 'Lord Meath, Youth and Empire', *Journal of Contemporary History* 5, 4, 1970, pp. 97–111.

Springhall, J.O., 'The Boy Scouts, Class and Militarism in Relation to British Youth Movements, 1908–1930', *International Review of Social History* 16, 2, 1971, pp. 125–58.

Springhall, J.O., 'Baden Powell and the Scout Movement before 1920: Citizen Training or Soldiers of the Future?', *English Historical Review* CII, 405, 1987, pp. 934–42.

Stater, V.I., 'The Lord Lieutenancy on the Eve of the Civil Wars: The Impressment of George Plowright', *Historical Journal* 29, 2, 1986, pp. 279–96.

Stater, V.I., 'War and the Structure of Politics: Lieutenancy and the Campaign of 1628' in Fissell, M. C. (ed), *War and Government in Britain, 1598–1650* (Manchester University Press, forthcoming).

Stearns, S., 'Conscription and English Society in the 1620's', *Journal of British Studies* XI, 3, 1972, pp. 1–24.

Stevenson, J., 'Food Riots in England,1792–1818' in Quinault, R. and Stevenson, J.(eds), *Popular Protest and Public Order* (Allen & Unwin, London, 1974), pp. 33–74.

Stevenson, J., 'Social Control and the Prevention of Riots in England, 1789–1829' in Donajgrodzki, A.P.(ed), *Social Control in Nineteenth Century Britain* (Croom Helm, London, 1977), pp. 27–49.

Stewart, R.W., 'Arms Accountability in the Early Stuart Militia', *Bulletin of the Institute of Historical Research* 57, 1984, pp. 113–17.

Storch, R.D., 'The Plague of Blue Locusts: Police reform and Popular Resistance in Northern England, 1840–1857', *International Review of Social History* XX, 1975, pp. 61–90.

Storch, R.D., 'The Policeman as Domestic Missionary: Urban Discipline and Popular Culture in Northern England, 1850–1880', *Journal of Social History* 4, 1976, pp. 481–509.

Storch, R.D., 'Policing Rural Southern England before the Police: Opinion and Practise, 1830–56' in Hay, D. and Snyder, F.(eds), *Policing and Prosecution in Britain, 1750–1850* (Oxford University Press, 1989), pp. 211–66.

Strachan, H. 'The Early Victorian Army and the Nineteenth Century Revolution in Government', *English Historical Review* CXV, October 1980, pp. 782–809.

Strachan, H., 'Lord Grey and Imperial Defence' in Beckett, I.F.W. and Gooch, J.(eds), *Politicians and Defence* (Manchester University Press, 1981), pp. 1–23.

Summers, A., 'Militarism in Britain before the Great War', *History Workshop* 2, 1976, pp. 104–23.

Summers, A., 'Scouts, Guides and VADs: A Note In Reply to Allen Warren', *English Historical Review* CII, 405, 1987, pp. 943–7.

Summers, A., 'Edwardian Militarism' in Samuel, R.(ed), *Patriotism* (Routledge, London, 1989), I, pp. 236–58.

Taylor, R.I., 'Manning the Royal Navy, 1852–1862', *Mariner's Mirror* XLIV, 1958, pp. 302–13; XLV, 1959, pp. 46–58.

Teichman, O., 'The Yeomanry as an Aid to the Civil Power, 1795–1867', *Journal of the Society for Army Historical Research* XIX, 1940, pp. 75–91, 129–46.

Thompson, F.M.L., 'Social Control in Victorian Britain', *Economic History Review* 34, 1981, pp. 189–208.

Thomson, C., 'The Cornish Volunteers', *Devon and Cornwall Notes and Queries* XXVII, 1956–8, pp. 229–36, 326–31; XXVIII, 1959–61, pp. 10–16.

Travers, T.H.E., 'The Hidden Structural Problems in the British Officer Corps, 1900–1918', *Journal of Contemporary History* 17, 1982, pp. 523–44.

Tucker, A.V., 'Army and Society in England, 1870–1900: A Re-assessment of the Cardwell Reforms', *Journal of British Studies* II, 1963, pp. 110–41.

Tucker, A.V., 'The Issue of Army Reform in the Unionist Government, 1903–1905', *Historical Journal* IX, 1, 1966, pp. 90–100.

Wanklyn, M.G.D. and Young, P., 'A King in Search of Soldiers: A Rejoinder', *Historical Journal* 24, 1, 1981, pp. 147–54.

Warren, A., 'Sir Robert Baden Powell, the Scout Movement and Citizen Training in Great Britain, 1900–1920', *English Historical Review* CI, 399, 1986, pp. 376–98.

Warren, A., 'Baden Powell: A Final Comment', *English Historical Review* CII, 405, 1987, pp. 948–50.

Wells, R.A.E., 'The Revolt of the South West,1800–1801', *Social History* 6, 1977, pp. 713–44.

Wells, R.A.E., 'Rural Rebels in Southern England in the 1830s' in Emsley, C. and Walvin, J.(eds), *Artisans, Peasants and Proletarians, 1760–1860* (Croom Helm, London, 1985), pp. 124–65.

Western, J.R., 'The Formation of the Scottish Militia in 1797', *Scottish Historical Review* XXXIV, 1955, pp. 1–18.

Western, J.R., 'The Volunteer Movement as an Anti-revolutionary Force, 1793–1801', *English Historical Review* LXXI, 1956, pp. 603–14.

Western, J.R., 'The County Fencibles and the Militia Augmentation of 1794', *Journal of the Society for Army Historical Research* XXXIV, 1956, pp. 3–11.

Whiting, J.R.S., 'The Frampton Volunteers', *Journal of the Society for Army Historical Research* XLVIII, 1970, pp. 14–28.

Wilkinson, P., 'English Youth Movements, 1908–30', *Journal of Contemporary History* 4, 2, 1969, pp. 3–24.

Williams, J.R., 'The Dudley Loyal Association, 1792–1802', *The Blackcountryman* 10, 4, 1977, pp. 56–65.

Winter, J.M., 'Britain's Lost Generation of the First World War', *Population Studies* 31, 3, 1977, pp. 449–66.

Winter, J.M., 'Some Aspects of the Demographic Consequences of the First World War in Britain', *Population Studies* 30, 3, 1976, pp. 539–52.

Winter, J.M., 'Military Fitness and Civilian Health in Britain during the First World War', *Journal of Contemporary History* 15, 1980, pp. 211–44.

Woolrych, A., 'The Cromwellian Protectorate: A Military Dictatorship?', *History* 75, 244, 1990, pp. 207–31.

Wright, A.C., 'Essex and the Volunteers', *Essex Journal* 6–7, 1972, pp. 3–5, 77–81.

Youings, J., 'Bowmen, Billmen and Hackbutters: The Elizabethan Militia in the South-west' in Higham, R. (ed), *Security and Defence in South-west England before 1800* (University of Exeter Studies in History, No. 19, 1987), pp. 51–68.

Index